Teaching Psychological Skills

Models for Giving Psychology Away

Teaching Psychological Skills

Models for Giving Psychology Away

Edited by **Dale Larson**
The University of Santa Clara

 Brooks/Cole Publishing Company
Monterey, California

Brooks/Cole Publishing Company
A Division of Wadsworth, Inc.

Printed in the United States of America

10 9 8 7 6 5 4 3 2 1

Library of Congress Cataloging in Publication Data

Main entry under title:
Teaching psychological skills.

   Bibliography: p.
   Includes index.
   1. Helping behavior—Study and teaching.   2. Adjustment (Psychology)—Study and
teaching.   I. Larson, Dale, 1949–
BF637.H4T43   1983   158′.3   83-3839
ISBN 0-534-02897-7

Subject Editor: *Claire Verduin*
Production Editor: *Fiorella Ljunggren*
Manuscript Editor: *Rephah Berg*
Permissions Editor: *Mary Kay Hancharick*
Interior and Cover Design: *Vernon T. Boes*
Illustrations: *Tim Keenan*
Typesetting: *Instant Type, Monterey, California*

PREFACE

I can imagine nothing we could do that would be more relevant to human welfare, and nothing that could pose a greater challenge to the next generation of psychologists, than to discover how best to give psychology away.

George A. Miller
1969 Presidential Address,
American Psychological Association

Today a growing number of psychologists are developing better strategies for sharing the psychological skills and knowledge of their profession, and a new model of mental health training and delivery is emerging from these efforts to improve the quality of human life. Throughout the mental health field, psychological principles and knowledge are being converted into teachable skills and disseminated by means of systematic methods and programs. This book presents pioneering people, ideas, and programs forming the vanguard of this movement to give psychology away through the teaching of skills for effective helping and living.

I first became involved with the people and innovative programs in this book while teaching counseling skills to student therapists and health professionals. Finding traditional clinical training models not sufficient for the tasks at hand, I sought more effective strategies for giving therapeutic skills to others. The programs I discovered at that time—Microcounseling, Interpersonal Process Recall, the Human Resources Development Model, and Focusing—all presented a new outlook on mental health training and delivery. They offered strategies so different from traditional approaches that they could even be considered elements of a new paradigm in the mental health field.

As I continued to explore other skills training programs, I became aware of the emerging identity of a new field. Noting the many features, themes, and goals that skills programs had in common, I was inspired to assemble this first anthology for those in the mental health and other human services who are also seeking more pragmatic and accessible models for training and helping. Some of the skills programs presented here have been developed primarily for training helpers, both professional and nonprofessional; others teach coping skills directly to clients. The prototypic programs in this volume are the most widely used and extensively researched efforts in this new field.

H. L. Mencken wrote: "There's always an easy solution to every human problem—neat, plausible, and wrong." The skills training movement is not a panacea; it will not inevitably lead to solutions for the pressing mental health needs we face today. Still, I feel a sense of excitement for what seems to promise a significant step forward in the mental health field. The authors in this volume have seen that skills training works—it can and does make a real difference in the lives of the people exposed to it—and these encouraging results support our faith that if we continue the innovative work described here, we can maximize psychology's contribution to human welfare.

v

Acknowledgments

I feel extremely fortunate that so many extraordinary individuals have shared their ideas and lives with me. These people have made invaluable contributions to my development as a person and as a psychologist. "In order of appearance," they are Philip Holzman, Donald Fiske, Sheldon Korchin, Charles Garfield, Margaret Singer, Oren Harari, Keith McConnell, Joel Crohn, Allen Ivey, Gerald Goodman, and Gerard Egan. I am especially grateful to my parents, Donald and Dorothy Larson, who have encouraged me to make the most of my life, and to my sister, Leanne, for being a true friend. Most of all, I want to thank Deborah Kennedy for her keen ideas and unflagging patience; with her I have learned to dance.

I am indebted to the National Institute of Mental Health (Grant #MH16067) for partially supporting my work on this anthology and for backing my own efforts to give psychology away to people caring for critically ill and dying patients. The University of Santa Clara has provided a supportive and stimulating context to work in.

Many persons have assisted me in this project. Claire Verduin at Brooks/Cole has been a tremendously competent and compassionate guide throughout this project. Working with Fiorella Ljunggren, who coordinated the production of the book, and Rephah Berg, who edited the manuscript, has been a pleasure for myself and the contributing authors. The comments of the reviewers whom Brooks/Cole consulted have enhanced the overall quality of the book. They are James R. Barclay of the University of Kentucky, Donald Blocher of the State University of New York at Albany, Arthur Bohart of California State University at Dominguez Hills, and Fred H. Borgen of Iowa State University. Paula Zerkle assisted in the preparation of the manuscript. Allen Ivey, Sheldon Korchin, Gerard Egan, Enrico Jones, and Susan Sands reviewed my chapter and gave me encouragement and challenging feedback.

I want to express my deepest gratitude to the contributing authors. They made this book possible not only through their written contributions but also through their generous and thoughtful suggestions and support at each step along the way. In my interactions with these visionary pragmatists, I have learned more than methods for giving psychology away: I have deepened my commitment to the responsible sharing of psychological skills for a more healthful and helpful society.

Dale Larson

CONTENTS

CHAPTER SEVEN
Skilled Helping: A Problem-Management Framework for Helping and Helper Training   133
by Gerard Egan

CHAPTER EIGHT
Three Decades of Democratizing Relationships through Training   151
by Thomas Gordon

CHAPTER NINE
Relationship Enhancement Therapy and Training   171
by Bernard G. Guerney, Jr.

CHAPTER TEN
Microcounseling:
A Metamodel for Counseling, Therapy,
Business, and Medical Interviews   207
by Allen E. Ivey and Maryanne Galvin

CHAPTER ELEVEN
Interpersonal Process Recall:
Basic Methods and Recent Research   229
by Norman Kagan

CHAPTER TWELVE
The Human Resources
Development Model   245
by Robert W. Cash

Teaching Psychological Skills

Models for Giving Psychology Away

CHAPTER ONE

Giving Psychology Away: The Skills Training Paradigm

Dale Larson

Dale Larson received his B.A. degree from the University of Chicago and his Ph.D. in clinical psychology from the University of California at Berkeley. He is currently an assistant professor of counseling psychology in the Graduate Division of Counseling Psychology and Education at the University of Santa Clara. Larson's work in the psychological skills training area has focused in the health care field. As codirector of the Berkeley Hospice Training Project (under the auspices of a three-year NIMH grant), he developed and conducted a national mental health skills training program for health professionals working in hospice settings; he now conducts workshops on this topic for diverse health-professional groups nationwide. He has organized a major national conference on interpersonal skills in health care and is director of the Health Psychology program at the University of Santa Clara.

"Give a man a fish, he has one meal; teach him to fish, he can eat for the rest of his life." This ancient Chinese proverb captures the central goal and promise of the skills training approach: giving people psychological skills for managing their own lives and/or for helping others more effectively.

Skills training is a reflection of a more fundamental shift occurring at the interface of the human services and the larger society. We are witnessing the public's growing interest in and desire for psychological and other human services and a corresponding recognition by professionals that psychological knowledge can be shared with greater and greater numbers of people. It has also become increasingly clear that we cannot share psychological knowledge without adopting new kinds of services and new models for delivering these services. Almost 20 years ago, Hobbs (1964) hailed "mental health's third revolution," pointing to shifts from clinical to public health and educational models, from exclusively professional to nontraditional helper populations, and from remedial to preventive strategies of intervention. Miller (1969) later urged that the principles and skills of psychology be "given away" to the public to maximize the contribution of psychology to human welfare.

Giving psychology away is now possible in the form of psychological skills training. Psychological skills are being taught both to clients as a form of direct treatment and prevention and to therapists and other helpers as a means of enhancing their effectiveness. The leading thinkers of the skills training movement have wide-ranging theoretical orientations, from the behavioral to the humanistic; the programs vary from simple, self-contained audio-cassette training presentations to complex packages of videotapes, manuals, and instruction; and the skills they teach range from the straightforward skill of eye contact to the more subtle processes of empathy and problem solving. All those involved in the skills training movement do, however, share a common goal: giving psychology away by converting psychological principles into teachable skills and disseminating these skills by means of systematic methods and programs.

A new model for mental health training and delivery is emerging from these efforts, and this model is rapidly gaining influence and recognition. A substantial research base has developed. Skills training has been the subject of issues of *The Counseling Psychologist,* of the *Canadian Counsellor,* of the *Personnel and Guidance Journal,* of recent training texts (Carkhuff, 1977; Carkhuff & Anthony, 1979; Cormier & Cormier, 1979; Egan, 1982; Hammond, Hepworth, & Smith, 1977; Hosford & deVisser, 1974; Ivey, 1980; Kanfer & Goldstein, 1975; Okun, 1976; Schulman, 1974), and of major books and reviews (Authier, 1977; Authier, Gustafson, Guerney, & Kasdorf, 1975; Bellack & Hersen, 1979; Brammer & Allmon, 1977; Burstein, 1980; Carkhuff, 1969a, 1969b, 1971; Carkhuff & Berenson, 1976; Egan & Cowan, 1979; Ford, 1979; Goldstein, 1981; Hurst, 1977; Ivey & Authier, 1978; Mosher & Sprinthall, 1971).

Despite the growing interest in skills training, the identity of the emerging skills training field remains fragmented; its defining features and themes have not been identified, and leading programs and authors have not been brought together in one volume to illustrate the common methods and goals that unify these seemingly disparate efforts. This book is a response to the need for an integrative presentation of these innovative developments in the mental health field.

IMPETUS FOR THE SKILLS TRAINING MOVEMENT

The psychological skills training movement is the product of numerous historical forces, both in the society at large and in the mental health field. Two major forces have been a receptive social climate and the new demands being made on the mental health field.

Social Climate

The public's psychological sophistication—its "psychological IQ," if you will—is rising rapidly. A growing portion of the public is being introduced to the concepts and practices of mental health—through the media, the self-help or bibliotherapy literature, the educational system, and formal mental health education efforts. People's views of themselves and of what they can achieve are changing. Many are actively seeking solutions to the demoralization (Frank, 1974) and alienation that characterize our times. We are witnessing what Rogers (1977) calls a "quiet revolution" in which people are, more and more, taking control of their psychological and physical destinies. We are a people who have grown weary of professional mystification, and whether it is the art of medical care or psychological healing, Americans have an almost insatiable desire to "do it themselves"—to learn skills they can use to enhance the quality of their lives and to solve their own problems.

When a panel of 32 experts in the psychotherapy field was asked to predict future trends in psychotherapy (Prochaska & Norcross, in press), its forecasts reflected these same themes. These experts predicted "a revival of self-reliance in psychotherapy" over the next decade, which would be expressed in a growing popularity of self-change approaches, self-help groups, and self-control procedures. Other therapeutic interventions expected to increase were problem-solving techniques, homework assignments, communication skills training, videotaping, imagery and fantasy techniques, behavior modification, behavioral contracting, biofeedback, and relaxation techniques. In addition to client self-reliance, a second theme is readily discernible from this list: the therapist as a teacher of psychological skills. These twin themes—the client as a responsible, active learner of specific psychological skills and the therapist as a teacher of these skills—are central elements of the skills training approach.

Demands on the Mental Health Field

It is clear that traditional mental health strategies are not meeting, and perhaps cannot meet, our nation's growing needs for psychological help. According to the National Institute of Mental Health (Regier, Goldberg, & Taube, 1978), an estimated 15% (32 million) of our population suffers from serious mental disorders; yet only 3% (6.5 million) are helped by mental health specialists. Kiesler (1980) underlines the failure of current practices:

> If the nation used the whole 65 million hours of service delivery potentially available to it through licensed psychologists and psychiatrists, a total pool of approximately three hours per person needing treatment per year would be involved, for the *most optimistic estimates* of need. This would vary downward to 40 minutes per person per year at the most pessimistic estimate [p. 1070].

Narrowing the gap between need and supply must be a central goal of any future mental health effort. Recent budget cuts for the human services will intensify the need for effective strategies to achieve this goal.

To help resolve the crisis of need, Kiesler urges that the mental health field shift its emphasis toward "(a) prevention, (b) paraprofessionals or techniques of devising different levels of professional help, (c) indigenous support resources, (d) self-help, (e) mental health training for other professionals so as to screen and refer competently and reduce the frequency of inappropriate care, and (f) greater development of professional human resources" (p. 1070). These are radical shifts, but they are in fact occurring. Prevention is a growing force in mental health services (Miller, Mazade, Muller, & Andrulis, 1978). Paraprofessionals now make up the largest single category of workers in mental health and human services (Alley, Blanton, & Feldman, 1978). Self-help groups are rapidly expanding in both number and scope (Gartner & Riessman, 1977). Increasingly, interpersonal and mental health skills are being taught to health professionals and other workers in the human services (Kahn, Cohen, & Jason, 1979).

Psychological skills training programs have also developed in response to the need for large-scale dissemination of psychological skills. The brevity, accessibility, portability, efficiency, and replicability of skills training procedures make them ideal vehicles for reaching expanded populations of both traditional and nontraditional clients and helpers.

THE EMERGING SKILLS TRAINING PARADIGM

As the mental health field struggles to respond to the crisis of need, we can see the signs of what Kuhn (1962) would call the "blurring" of a paradigm: "pronounced professional insecurity," "turbulence," experimentation, and the emergence of new ideas. According to Kuhn, a crisis occurs as the inadequacy of the dominant paradigm is recognized, indicating that an "occasion for retooling has arrived" (p. 76).

Such a crisis is occurring in the mental health field today. We have an "occasion for retooling" and, with the psychological skills movement, one set of tools for meeting the new mental health demands. These new skills training tools—both conceptual and technological—point toward a new paradigm for mental health training and delivery.

The skills training movement marks a coalescence of more general philosophical trends (psychoeducation, demystification of professional knowledge, and prevention) and innovations in teaching method (from psychology's social-learning theory and from education's pedagogic principles) that will be discussed shortly. The skills training movement is integrative, transcending the bounds of discipline or school. As such, it reflects a more general trend toward eclecticism and conceptual flexibility among contemporary psychotherapists (for example, Garfield, 1980; Garfield & Kurtz, 1974, 1976; Goldfried, 1980) and can be expected to help reduce the "dogma-eat-dogma" existence of contemporary psychotherapy (Larson, 1980).

The defining elements of the skills training paradigm, to be discussed in the following sections, are (1) basic ingredients—skills, methods, and programs, (2) a psychoeducational model, (3) expanded target populations of helpers and clients, and (4) the goal of prevention.

Basic Ingredients: Skills, Methods, Programs

Three elements are common to all efforts within the skills training movement: (1) identification of specific *skills*, or competencies; (2) use of systematic *methods* for teaching these skills; and (3) development of *programs* for skill dissemination using these methods.

Skills

The word *skills* suffers from some rather ignoble associations. In our culture, skills are something you learn in the army, and training is something you do with your dog. For purposes of this book, therefore, it will be useful to provide a definition of skills. Skills are "the competencies that are necessary for effective living" (Egan & Cowan, 1979, p. 8). They are behaviors that are "operational, repeatable, trainable, and predictable within a delimited range of effects" (Carkhuff & Berenson, 1976, p. 189). They arise from talent, training, or practice (*Random House Dictionary*, 1969). Kaye (1979) extends the boundary of the skill concept into the personality realm:

> To some extent we learn many differentiated skills for dealing with the different individuals and the different social situations in our lives. At the same time, there are continuities and similarities in the behavior of an individual person across a variety of situations and in

interaction with many different people. "Personality" can be viewed as nothing other than this sort of transfer of skills out of the social dyads, families or other interaction systems in which they are originally developed, into new social situations [p. 52].

Learning a new skill—whether it is active listening, dancing, cooking, playing the violin, managing money, assertiveness, or "experiential focusing"—involves learning subskills, which are then hierarchically organized in the execution of the skill. With time and practice the components require less and less conscious attention, allowing the person to devote increasing attention to higher-level strategies for the achievement of the sought-after goal. In all these instances of skill acquisition, there is a period during which the subskills are not integrated and the learner is self-conscious and awkward. This phenomenon is described by nearly all skills trainers as a generic characteristic of skill acquisition. Egan and Cowan (1979) comment: "In the beginning, skills and models use the trainee, but with sufficient time for practice and application . . . the trainee begins to use the skills and models" (p. 62). The golf swing of Jack Nicklaus, the dancing of Fred Astaire, and the therapeutic responses of Carl Rogers are skillful performances involving the integration of many internal cues with complex behaviors.

It is useful to distinguish between those psychological skills that are predominantly taught to clients (psychosocial *coping* skills) and those that are predominantly taught to therapists and other helpers (interpersonal *helping* skills). The programs of Part One in this book teach mainly the former, while those of Part Two teach the latter. However, there is considerable overlap between helping and coping skills, since all the helping skills programs of Part Two have also been used in a training-as-treatment context.

Psychosocial coping skills.   One large group of programs has focused on helping clients develop a repertoire of psychosocial coping skills (called "life skills" by Egan, Adkins, and Gazda in this volume) that facilitate adaptation and performance in a variety of situations. The teaching of these skills constitutes a direct form of treatment, either preventive or remedial. To teach coping skills, the skills trainer must develop a "working knowledge" (Egan & Cowan, 1979, p. 8) of the competencies people need to master specific life challenges. Every problem, whether it involves mastering a developmental task, resolving a life crisis, or deepening a human relationship, is conceptualized as involving specific skills that can be taught. Thus, assessment of skill deficits and intervention (that is, skills training) are closely linked in the skills training paradigm.

A vast array of psychosocial coping skills are taught by the programs of the current volume, including skills for managing money, active listening, planning, conversation, assertiveness, "experiential focusing," relaxation, job finding, and problem solving, for example. Most of these skills can be viewed as problem-solving skills—that is, as skills for coping with the predictable problems of development in the modern world.

Interpersonal helping skills.   A second large group of programs teaches interpersonal helping and communication skills to therapists and other helpers as a means of enhancing their effectiveness in helping others. These programs are indirect in their treatment effects, although the helper/trainee populations may themselves benefit directly from acquisition of these skillful behaviors. In her review of 20 interpersonal helping skills training programs, Burstein (1980) identifies 78 communication skills taught by these programs, including, for example, acknowledgment, advisement, affective response, interpretations, questions, self-disclosure, silence, and warmth.

Many of the helping skills in the current volume will be recognized as so-called effective ingredients of psychotherapy identified by psychotherapy researchers over the past three decades. It was Rogers who first insisted on demystifying the helping process by opening it to public and research scrutiny. In his classic work *Counseling and Psychotherapy* (1942), Rogers published the first full-length transcript of a whole course of therapy. His use of audiotapes and verbatim transcripts as training and research tools created a bridge between the classroom and the real-life therapeutic encounter. By being willing to study closely the therapeutic encounter, identify the "active ingredients," and teach these to others, Rogers pioneered the demystification and subsequent giving away of therapeutic skills.

The demystification and identification of coping and helping skills involve a shift in perspective: the art of living/coping and the art of helping become teachable, though complex, sets of skills or competencies. Having identified these specific skills, the next step for the skills trainer is the development of methods for teaching them to large numbers of trainees.

Skills training methods

The teaching/learning methods of the skills training movement derive both from education and from psychology. From the field of education come programmed texts, structured discussion, simulation, and gaming. The field of psychology has provided the principles of social-learning theory—in particular, transfer of training, observational learning techniques such as modeling and self-confrontation, behavioral rehearsal, and feedback (cueing or reinforcement). Manuals, oral instructions, and audio and video technologies are also used.

A number of themes run through these teaching/learning methods:

1. They all involve the active participation of clients and trainees in the learning process.
2. There is a focus on specific behaviors (internal and external) and the mastery and maintenance of these behaviors.
3. The programs are based on established learning principles of modeling, observing, discriminating, reinforcing, and generalizing.
4. Each program includes both didactic and experiential emphases.
5. The programs are highly structured.
6. Goals are clear.
7. Progress is monitored.
8. Mystification is minimized.

Programs for delivery

Once specific skills are identified and methods for teaching them developed, these must then be integrated into a program or package so they can be systematically acquired. The programs in the current volume have been singled out because they are among the most well-developed, well-researched, well-packaged, and influential in the skills training field.[1] They are prototypes for skills training programs of the future.

While sharing a philosophy of demystifying psychology through skills dissemination, the programs in this book vary greatly on the following dimensions: skills taught, learning methods used, number of participants, trainer populations, time frame for training, and degree of dependence on instructor. In addition, these programs are aimed at a variety of client and helper populations, including disadvantaged adolescents and adults (Life Skills Education, Chapter 3), hospital patients and adolescents (Structured Learning Therapy, Chapter 4), inpatient and outpatient psychiatric populations and normal populations of all ages (Multiple Impact Training, Chapter 5, and the social skills training programs of Chapter 6), parents and marital partners (Effectiveness Training, Chapter 8, and Relationship Enhancement Therapy and Training, Chapter 9), professional and paraprofessional workers in the human services (Microcounseling, Chapter 10, Interpersonal Process Recall, Chapter 11, and Human Resources Development, Chapter 12), and self-help groups and the general public (SASHAtapes, Chapter 13, Focusing, Chapter 14, and Changes, Chapter 15).

Psychoeducational Model

The psychoeducational model, as it has evolved over the past two decades, rests on three basic assumptions: the helper is viewed as a teacher rather than as a physician; clients' problems are thought of as learning deficits or maladaptive overlays, rather than as symptoms; and clients are seen as capable of directing their own learning rather than as passively receiving treatment.

The first assumption reflects a shift in roles for the psychological practitioner and the person seeking help. The physician has become a teacher; the patient has become a student. Of course, for many years psychologists have viewed psychotherapy as a learning process—particularly those of behavioral persuasions. It has recently been argued, for example, that many forms of learning—emotional learning, cognitive learning, operant conditioning, identification, modeling, and decision making—are processes common to all forms of psychotherapy (Korchin & Sands, 1982). But most thinkers who have identified therapy as learning have failed to acknowledge the corollary—that the therapist is a teacher (Guerney, 1977;

---

[1]The programs in the current volume are, of course, only a small sample of the skills training programs currently available. Following are references for programs not already cited, taken from Goldstein's (1981) review of psychosocial coping skills programs and Burstein's (1980) review of interpersonal helping skills programs: Arbes and Hubbell, 1973; Argyle, Trower, and Bryant, 1974; Bash and Camp, 1980; Berzon and Reisel, 1976; Burka, Hubbell, Preble, Spinelli, and Winter, 1972; Cox and Gunn, 1980; Curran, 1977; Danish and Hauer, 1973; Elardo and Cooper, 1977; Galassi and Galassi, 1977; Gottman, Motarius, Gonso, and Markham, 1977; Hackney and Nye, 1973; Hanson, 1971; Hare, 1976; Hawley and Hawley, 1975; Heiman, 1973; Hersen and Eisler, 1976; Johnson, Foyle, and Kazmar, n.d.; Johnson, 1978; Liberman, King, DeRisi, and McCann, 1975; Lyle and Nyer, 1976; McBain, 1975; McFall, 1976; Miller, Nunnally, and Wachman, 1975; Patterson, Hops, and Weiss, 1975; Rhode, Rasmussen, and Heaps, 1971; Robin, 1980; Rosenberg, 1972; Rotheram, 1980; Stephens, 1976; Terkelson, 1976; Thiel, 1977; Varenhorst and Hamburg, n.d.; and Wehman and Schleien, 1980.

Guerney, Stollak, & Guerney, 1970, 1971; Rioch, 1970). In skills training approaches, the teaching function of the psychotherapist has been made explicit.

Under the second assumption of the psychoeducational model, clients' problems are viewed as skills or competency deficits rather than as abnormalities or illnesses or thwarted potentials. In the education/training-as-helping approach, the sequence "abnormality (or illness) → diagnosis → prescription → therapy → cure" becomes "client dissatisfaction (or ambition) → goal setting → skills teaching → satisfaction or goal achievement" (Authier et al., 1975, p. 31). According to Guerney et al. (1971), the practicing psychologist following an educational model is one whose work derives "directly or indirectly from a concern not with 'curing' neurosis and not with eliminating symptoms (or 'complaints'), and not with intellectual growth per se, but rather with the teaching of personal and interpersonal attitudes and skills" (p. 277). This view of clients' problems as skills deficits, Goldstein (1981, p. 1) observes, is a significant departure from the prevailing belief systems of therapists from the three major therapeutic orientations—psychoanalytic/psychodynamic, humanistic, and behavioral:

> Though each differs from the others in several major respects, one of their significant commonalities was the shared assumption that the patient had somewhere within himself, as yet unexpressed, the effective, satisfying, or healthy behaviors whose expression was among the goals of the therapy. Such latent potentials, in all three approaches, would be realized by the patient if the therapist were sufficiently skilled in reducing or removing obstacles to such realization.
>
> In the early 1970s, an important new intervention approach began to emerge— psychological skills training, an approach resting upon rather different assumptions. Viewing the helpee more in educational, pedagogic terms rather than as a patient in need of therapy, the psychological skills trainer assumed he was dealing with an individual lacking, deficient, or at best weak in the skills necessary for effective and satisfying daily living. The task of the skills trainer became, therefore, not interpretation, reflection, or reinforcement but the active and deliberate *teaching* of desirable behaviors. Rather than an intervention called psychotherapy between a patient and psychotherapist, what emerged was training, between a trainee and a psychological skills trainer.[2]

In short, what is being challenged by skills trainers is the assumption that clients already have what they need—if obstacles were only removed—to live more successfully. Skills training thinkers argue that clients are actually lacking something— something that must be "added to" the client through training.

The third assumption of the psychoeducational model is that by labeling problems as competency deficiencies rather than as diseases, one enlists the active participation of clients in solving their own problems. Labeling clients' problems as mental illnesses, according to Danish and Smyer (1981), makes them "feel less able to master the problem themselves and therefore less able to help themselves" (p. 19). By framing clients' problems as skill deficits and giving them the tools to correct these deficits, the psychoeducator encourages them to take charge of their own treatment and, by extension, their own lives. For example, a client who is taught problem-solving skills is in a better position to solve many different problems in diverse situations than the client who solves one problem with one therapist. According to Authier et al. (1975), "The willingness to respect and encourage clients

[2]Reprinted with permission from *Psychological Skills Training: The Structured Learning Technique*, by A. P. Goldstein. Copyright 1981, Pergamon Press.

to choose their own goals knowledgeably and a high degree of respect for the clients' own ability to reach them, given the appropriate environmental circumstances, is a keystone of the 'therapist-as-teacher-movement'" (p. 35). Returning to my introductory metaphor: to treat is to give a person a fish, to train is to teach that person how to fish.

Expanded Populations of Helpers and Clients

The replicability, accessibility, portability, brevity, and efficiency of skills training approaches make them ideal vehicles for extending training in helping skills beyond the circumscribed traditional populations of mental health workers. Four populations —paraprofessionals, health care workers, self-help-group members, and "significant others"—illustrate the potential delivery power of the skills training approach.

Paraprofessionals. The idea of training expanded populations of helpers in interpersonal helping skills and of reaching expanded populations of clients grew directly from the community mental health movement, which began in the early 1960s. Staffing the new community centers around the country required the hiring and training of unprecedented numbers of noncredentialed counselors, and the paraprofessional movement was born (Guerney, 1969; Sobey, 1970). To meet the growing need for paraprofessionals, community psychologists were compelled to develop effective short-term training programs with wide applicability. Helping skills training programs (some of which can be found in this book) were the result. Major among these were the Human Resources Development Model of Robert Carkhuff (Chapter 12) and the Microcounseling program of Allen Ivey (Chapter 10).

Today, paraprofessionals make up the largest single category of workers in mental health and human services. Evidence that paraprofessionals perform as well as or better than highly credentialed mental health practitioners (Durlak, 1979) recommends the continued development and training of paraprofessional populations as a future mental health strategy. In my opinion, the mental health skills curriculum of the paraprofessional can most profitably be drawn from the skills training paradigm.

Health care workers. For our second population, health professionals, the teaching of interpersonal skills has become a major area of activity in recent years. One reason is the rising incidence of chronic illness, which has necessitated greater involvement of patients in the physical and psychological management of their own illnesses. Health care providers, in helping patients cope with the emotional concomitants of chronic illness, must act as educators and counselors. It has been estimated that 50% of medical visits are primarily psychological in nature, suggesting a staggering frequency of "inappropriate care," given the lack of formal mental health training for health professionals (Kiesler, 1980). Finally, there is a substantial literature showing that the interpersonal skills of the health professional are an integral part of the treatment process itself and not just elements of a congenial bedside manner (DiMatteo, 1979).

The parallels between the changing emphases in health care and those in psychology and the mental health field are not coincidental. Both fields are responding to the larger paradigm shift discussed earlier. The more progressive members of the medical profession—as of the psychological profession—are educating their patients about their own illnesses or disorders, training them in specific therapeutic techniques, and urging them to participate directly in the treatment, management, and prevention of their own conditions.

In a survey of nearly 500 medical schools and programs in health care education, Kahn et al. (1979) found that 93% of the schools offered one or more courses in interpersonal skills. Among the skills taught were empathy, listening, self-awareness, and team membership. Nearly a third of the schools responding used the Interpersonal Process Recall method (Chapter 11) in their training programs. However, when we look more closely at the mental health curricula in these schools, their lack of breadth and emphasis suggests that this is a particularly important arena for skills training.

A program recently developed at Harvard illustrates the use of skills training approaches in the medical field. Sobel and Worden (1982) have developed a problem-solving intervention program for cancer patients. This portable, self-contained program consists of a manual, problem-solving cards, and four audio-tapes and provides cancer caregivers with a practical method for helping patients deal more effectively with typical psychosocial concerns. Sobel and Worden state that they chose a problem-solving, cognitive-behavioral orientation because of its "short-term structure, here-and-now focus, emphasis on psychotherapy as a learning or psychoeducational experience, and an attitude which promotes the value of patient self-control, collaboration with the clinician, and responsibility for health" (p. 6).

Another application of skills training in the health care field is the Mental Health Skills for Hospice Workers program developed by Larson and Garfield. A national survey of mental health training in the hospice community (Garfield, Larson, & Schuldberg, 1982) had indicated a pressing need for systematic training geared to the specific challenges of hospice work. A program designed to meet this need, incorporating elements from the Interpersonal Process Recall method, Focusing, and the Human Resources Development Model, as well as didactic presentations addressing psychosocial aspects of terminal care, has now been conducted with hospice workers from 91 hospice organizations in 28 states.

Self-help groups. Another promising arena for skills training is the self-help or mutual-support group. The self-help movement, with its antiprofessional and activist ethos, does not lend itself to traditional mental health intervention. Self-help groups typically develop their own change and support processes, and they seem to be highly effective in doing so. In fact, psychologists have begun to study self-help groups to better understand the mechanisms of their success. Self-help groups empower their members by helping them learn skills (although they may not identify them as such) and solve problems on their own. Egan and Cowan (1979) point out that "the growing self-help movement is not waiting for the institutions of society to develop technologies to give the arts and sciences of the professions away. Rather, these groups are seizing what they see as rightfully theirs" (p. 14).

Human service professionals might well ask what, if anything, they have to offer these fiercely autonomous groups. One answer is skills training. For example, as the

Changes program (Chapter 15) illustrates, the specific psychological skills of experiential focusing and listening can be taught in a self-help-group context. Because many skills training programs are self-contained, portable, and not dependent on the presence of a professional trainer, self-help groups can easily incorporate them into their own helping methods. Goodman's SASHAtapes program (Chapter 13), for example, requires no professional trainer. The tapes and an accompanying manual are all that a group needs to use the program.

In my opinion, more packaged skills training programs designed specifically for self-help groups could be and should be developed. Videotapes, audiotapes, and manuals teaching facilitative interpersonal skills and relevant coping skills could become a major contribution of the mental health field to the self-help movement. Professionals might also serve as consultants in the development of training programs by the self-help groups themselves.

Parents, teachers, and other lay helpers.   Once demystified, skills of helping can be acquired not only by identified helpers but by any persons who perform helping functions. Foremost among the informal helpers who have been conceptualized as change agents and who have received skills training are parents and teachers (Guerney, 1969).

The most popular parent training program is Thomas Gordon's Parent Effectiveness Training, which teaches listening and problem-solving skills (see Chapter 8). More than one-half million people have graduated from P.E.T. courses. For Gordon (1978), the transition from child counselor to parent trainer was a natural one:

> From the earliest beginning of P.E.T. my objective was to teach parents all that I knew from my own professional training about being an effective counselor or helping agent. I wanted to "give away" to parents the very skills I employed as a professional counselor and therapist. They had worked for me—that I knew [p. 44].

Other pioneering programs include Guerney's "filial therapy," which teaches parents child-centered (Rogerian) play-therapy techniques (see Chapter 9), and the efforts of Patterson, McNeal, Hawkins, and Phelps (1967) to train parents in behavior modification techniques. Freud himself, in his treatment of Little Hans, used the parent as a therapeutic agent. It is ironic, therefore, that psychoanalysis has evolved into the system of therapy most dependent on the direct involvement of a highly trained professional (Korchin, 1976).

Teachers have also been a focus of skills training efforts. Gordon's Teacher Effectiveness Training program and Carkhuff's Human Resources Development Model have made major contributions in this area. A substantial research literature demonstrates that training in interpersonal communication skills enhances the teaching effectiveness of educators (Gazda, Asbury, Balzer, Childers, & Walters, 1977). The therapeutic function of the teacher, like the educational function of the therapist, is slowly being acknowledged and can be maximized through direct training.

The demystification and widespread dissemination of interpersonal helping and life skills are closely linked to a change in the definition of who can be a helper and who can be helped. In the skills training paradigm, anyone (professional or not) who has been taught helping skills can be a helper, and anyone who is in need of life skills can be helped. Matarazzo (1978), referring to behavior therapy, writes: "A therapist is anyone who uses systematic methods of modifying the behavior of the targeted individual" (p. 954). In Brammer's (1977) "deprofessional view,"

> Those persons with special expertise should spend their time teaching others the skills and attitudes of helping. In other words, they should "give their helping skills away" to parents, teachers, managers, political leaders, police and others in direct influential contacts with people. This is directly counter to the trend of professional groups to mystify helping functions with rituals, jargon, and legal restriction [p. 306].

While Brammer mentions five possible helper populations, Burstein (1980, pp. 20–21), in a review of 20 helping skills training programs, lists an impressive 62. Indeed, there is probably no occupation or role in society involving face-to-face contact between people in which interpersonal skills are not a critical element.

Traditional mental health training practices cannot reach, nor would they be appropriate to, the diverse "helpers" we are considering here. But these are precisely the people the skills training movement has effectively engaged. When Kiesler (1980) recommended that the mental health field shift its attention toward the use of paraprofessionals, self-help and indigenous support resources, and the teaching of mental health skills to other human service workers, he might have been addressing a congress of skills trainers, so relevant were his suggestions to the goals and potentials of that audience, whether he intended it or not.

Expanded client populations.   Reaching expanded populations of clients is another goal of the skills training movement that reflects the spirit of the community mental health movement. Many skills programs have been developed to meet the mental health needs of patients that traditional approaches have failed to address effectively. For example, the Structured Learning Therapy of Goldstein and associates (Chapter 4) was created to meet the special needs of the half-million lower-social-class and skill-deficient chronic patients released from America's public mental hospitals in the 1960s and 1970s. Similarly, Adkins developed his Life Skills Education program (Chapter 3) to address the needs of disadvantaged/undereducated adults for training in specific coping skills. His Life Skills/Employability program now has more than 350,000 graduates. However, the potential impact of Adkins's training model extends even further. In seeking "multiplier effect" and improved learning effectiveness for psychosocial competencies, Adkins has over the past 18 years pioneered a technology of program development that has extensive implications for cable TV, videodiscs, and microcomputers. According to Adkins, the cultural mechanisms for teaching the life skills necessary for living in a rapidly changing society are inadequately preparing large numbers of people. A comprehensive life skills curriculum and a new kind of program development capability are Adkins's response to this pressing need.

It should also be pointed out that many of the programs originally designed for helper training have subsequently been used in a training-as-treatment approach with a variety of clients. For example, the Human Resources Development Model (Chapter 12) and Microcounseling (Chapter 10) have been adapted to teach communication and relationship skills to diverse patient groups.

Indeed, once systematic skills training programs have been developed, the range of "trainees" for whom these programs are appropriate often expands at a phenomenal rate. In a major review of social skills training. Hersen (1979) notes that whereas early efforts (primarily assertion training) were directed largely to out-patient neurotic populations, today the range of applicability has been extended to elderly institutionalized patients, explosive patients, drug addicts, alcoholics, schizophrenics, and other patient groups. (See also Gambrill's discussion of social skills training, Chapter 6.)

Prevention and a Psychosufficient Society

Skills training is thus a vehicle for more effectively disseminating mental health skills to both traditional and nontraditional helpers. By teaching helping skills to other human service workers, to paraprofessionals, to self-help-group members, and to parents and teachers and others, a much larger helper base can be developed. In the same manner, the skills training approach is a vehicle for reaching more clients, teaching them a wide array of life/coping skills. This capacity for dissemination has enormous implications for the prevention of psychological distress.

Whether it be teaching active listening to parents so that they can provide a better psychological environment for their children, teaching problem-solving skills to students who are not succeeding in school, or teaching listening skills to members of self-help groups, prevention through skills training emphasizes empowering people with the competencies necessary for successfully negotiating life's challenges. If we can anticipate and prevent mental health problems or address them early on, human suffering and the need for extensive psychological "treatment" can be substantially reduced.

There is a story (also recounted by Egan in Chapter 2) of a man who is walking beside a river and notices that someone is drowning. He jumps in, pulls the person to shore, and revives him. Then another drowning person calls for help, and again the man successfully rescues him. As the man is about to walk away, a passer-by shouts "Hey, there's another person drowning out there. Where are you going?" The man replies "I'm going upstream to see who's throwing all these people in." The story illustrates two possible kinds of intervention available to mental health workers: upstream, preventive interventions and downstream, remedial efforts. Although recent funding cutbacks have had a drastic impact on the mental health system, in 1978 Miller et al. reported significant "upstream" movement in mental health services. Their survey of 178 mental health programs in the eastern United States showed "a clear trend toward decreasing traditional 'clinical' services which require extended, expensive, one-to-one involvement between a mental health professional and a client.... .The growth trend is toward prevention rather than remediation and is characterized by programs in which participants may not necessarily be consid-ered 'patients'" (p. 198). Prevention must become a major thrust of future mental health efforts, and the teaching of psychosocial coping and interpersonal helping skills can make a significant contribution to this end (Albee, 1982).

The large-scale giving away of psychological skills can have a transforming impact on our society. Clack (1975) writes: "This approach leads to a strengthening and broadening of individual self-reliance and interpersonal support. If people can be assisted in the use of cultural and societal resources, in making autonomous decisions, and to rely on themselves, we will be moving toward a psycho-sufficient society" (p. 2). When psychological skills and knowledge are in the hands of the public, our collective psychological IQs will be raised to the point that individuals need not struggle in isolation to solve problems that are universally experienced. No longer will they need to "reinvent the wheel" each time they face life crises: they will be able to draw on the collective problem-solving wisdom of an entire culture.

There is no guarantee that a psychosufficient society will become a reality for our generation or those that follow. The skills training approach does, however, open up new directions for achieving this goal. The exciting work of the new paradigm has begun.

REFERENCES

Albee, G. W. Preventing psychopathology and promoting human potential. *American Psychologist,* 1982, *37*(9), 1043–1050.

Alley, S., Blanton, J., & Feldman, R. *Paraprofessionals in mental health: Theory and practice.* New York: Human Sciences Press, 1978.

Arbes, B. H., & Hubbell, R. N. Packaged impact: A structured communications skills workshop. *Journal of Counseling Psychology,* 1973, *20*(4), 332–337.

Argyle, M., Trower, P., & Bryant, B. Explorations in the treatment of personality disorders and neuroses by social skill training. *British Journal of Medical Psychology,* 1974, *47,* 63–72.

Authier, J. The psychoeducation model: Definition, contemporary roots and content. *Canadian Counsellor,* 1977, *12,* 15–22.

Authier, J., Gustafson, K., Guerney, B., Jr., & Kasdorf, J. The psychological practitioner as a teacher: A theoretical-historical and practical review. *Counseling Psychologist,* 1975, *5,* 31–50.

Bash, M. S., & Camp, B. W. Teacher training in the Think Aloud Classroom Program. In G. Cartledge & J. F. Milburn (Eds.), *Teaching social skills to children.* New York: Pergamon Press, 1980.

Bellack, A. S., & Hersen, M. *Research and practice in social skills training.* New York: Plenum, 1979.

Berzon, B., & Reisel, J. *Effective interpersonal relationships* (formerly titled *Encountertapes for personal growth).* La Jolla, Calif.: University Associates, 1976.

Brammer, L. M. Who can be a helper? *Personnel and Guidance Journal,* 1977, *55,* 303–308.

Brammer, L. M., & Allmon, D. Training packages. *Personnel and Guidance Journal,* 1977, *55,* 612–618.

Burka, J., Hubbell, R., Preble, M., Spinelli, R., & Winter, N. *Communication skills workshop manual.* Fort Collins: University of Colorado Counseling Center, 1972.

Burstein, B. *Basic tools for more effective service delivery: Self-contained instructional programs for training paraprofessionals in interviewing skills and face-to-face helping competencies—a review.* San Rafael, Calif.: Social Action Research Center, 1980.

Carkhuff, R. R. *Helping and human relations.* Vol. 1: *Selection and training.* New York: Holt, Rinehart & Winston, 1969. (a)

Carkhuff, R. R. *Helping and human relations.* Vol. 2: *Practice and research.* New York: Holt, Rinehart & Winston, 1969. (b)

Carkhuff, R. R. Training as a preferred mode of treatment. *Journal of Counseling Psychology,* 1971, *18,* 123–131.

Carkhuff, R. R. *The art of helping III.* Amherst, Mass.: Human Resource Development Press, 1977.

Carkhuff, R. R., & Anthony, W. A. *The skills of helping: An introduction to counseling skills.* Amherst, Mass.: Human Resource Development Press, 1979.

Carkhuff, R. R., & Berenson, B. G. *Teaching as treatment.* Amherst, Mass.: Human Resource Development Press, 1976.

Clack, J. Report of the Midwest Subcommittee on Prevention. Unpublished paper, Counseling Center, Illinois State University, Bloomington/Normal, 1975.

Cormier, W. H., & Cormier, L. S. *Interviewing strategies for helpers: A guide to assessment, treatment, and evaluation.* Monterey, Calif.: Brooks/Cole, 1979.

Cox, R. D., & Gunn, W. B. Interpersonal skills in the schools: Assessment and curriculum development. In D. P. Rathjen & J. P. Foreyt (Eds.), *Social competence: Interventions for children and adults.* New York: Pergamon Press, 1980.

Curran, J. P. Skills training as an approach to the treatment of heterosexual-social anxiety: A review. *Psychological Bulletin,* 1977, *84,* 140–157.

Danish, S. J., & Hauer, A. L. *Helping skills: A basic training program.* New York: Behavioral Publications, 1973.

Danish, S. J., & Smyer, M. A. Unintended consequences of requiring a license to help. *American Psychologist,* 1981, *36,* 13–21.

DiMatteo, M. R. A social-psychological analysis of physician-patient rapport: Toward a science of the art of medicine. *Journal of Social Issues,* 1979, *35*(1), 12–33.

Durlak, J. A. Comparative effectiveness of paraprofessional and professional helpers. *Psychological Bulletin,* 1979, *86,* 80–92.

Egan, G. *The skilled helper: A model for systematic helping and interpersonal relating* (2nd ed.). Monterey, Calif.: Brooks/Cole, 1982.

Egan, G., & Cowan, M. A. *People in systems: A model for development in the human-service professions and education.* Monterey, Calif.: Brooks/Cole, 1979.

Elardo, P., & Cooper, M. *AWARE: Activities for social development.* Reading, Mass.: Addison-Wesley, 1977.

Ford, J. D. Research on training counselors and clinicians. *Review of Educational Research,* 1979, *49,* 87–130.

Frank, J. D. Psychotherapy: The restoration of morale. *American Journal of Psychiatry,* 1974, *131*(3), 271–274.

Galassi, M. D., & Galassi, J. P. *Assert yourself!* New York: Human Sciences Press, 1977.

Garfield, C. A., Larson, D. G., & Schuldberg, D. Mental health training and the hospice community: A national survey. *Death Education,* 1982, *6,* 189–204.

Garfield, S. L. *Psychotherapy: An eclectic approach.* New York: Wiley, 1980.

Garfield, S. L., & Kurtz, R. A survey of clinical psychologists: Characteristics, activities, and orientations. *Clinical Psychologist,* 1974, *28,* 7–10.

Garfield, S. L., & Kurtz, R. Clinical psychologists in the 1970's. *American Psychologist,* 1976, *31,* 1–9.

Gartner, A., & Riessman, F. *Self-help in the human services.* San Francisco: Jossey-Bass, 1977.

Gazda, G. M., Asbury, F. R., Balzer, F. J., Childers, W. C., & Walters, R. P. *Human relations development: A manual for educators* (2nd ed.). Boston: Allyn & Bacon, 1977.

Goldfried, M. R. Toward the delineation of therapeutic change principles. *American Psychologist,* 1980, *35,* 991–999.

Goldstein, A. P. *Psychological skill training: The structured learning technique.* New York: Pergamon Press, 1981.

Gordon, T. *P.E.T. in action.* New York: Bantam, 1978.

Gottman, J., Motarius, C., Gonso, J., & Markham, H. *A couple's guide to communication.* Champaign, Ill.: Research Press, 1977.

Guerney, B. G., Jr. (Ed.). *Psychotherapeutic agents: New roles for nonprofessionals, parents, and teachers.* New York: Holt, Rinehart & Winston, 1969.

Guerney, B. G., Jr. *Relationship enhancement.* San Francisco: Jossey-Bass, 1977.

Guerney, B. G., Jr., Stollak, G. E., & Guerney, L. A format for a new mode of psychological practice; or, how to escape a zombie. *Counseling Psychologist,* 1970, *2*(2), 97–104.

Guerney, B. G., Jr., Stollak, G. E., & Guerney, L. The practicing psychologist as educator—an alternative to the medical practitioner model. *Professional Psychology,* 1971, *2*(3), 276–282.

Hackney, H. L., & Nye, S. *Counseling strategies and objectives.* Englewood Cliffs, N.J.: Prentice-Hall, 1973.

Hammond, D. C., Hepworth, D. H., & Smith, V. G. *Improving therapeutic communication.* San Francisco: Jossey-Bass, 1977.

Hanson, R. W. Assertion training program. Unpublished manuscript, Veterans Administration Hospital, Palo Alto, Calif., 1971.

Hare, M. A. Teaching conflict resolution simulations. Paper presented at meeting of Eastern Community Association, Philadelphia, March 1976.

Hargie, O. *Social skills training: Selected microteaching papers from Ulster Polytechnique.* Jordanstown, Northern Ireland, June 1979.

Hawley, R. C., & Hawley, I. L. *Developing human potential: A handbook of activities for personal and social growth.* Amherst, Mass.: Education Research Association, 1975.

Heiman, H. Teaching interpersonal communications. *North Dakota Speech & Theatre Association Bulletin,* 1973, *2,* 7–29.

Hersen, M. Skill deficits in psychiatric patients. In A. S. Bellack & M. Hersen (Eds.), *Research and practice in social skills training.* New York: Plenum, 1979.

Hersen, M., & Eisler, R. M. Social skills training. In W. E. Craighead, A. E. Kazdin, & M. J. Mahoney (Eds.), *Behavior modification: Principles, issues and applications.* Boston: Houghton Mifflin, 1976.

Hobbs, N. Mental health's third revolution. *American Journal of Orthopsychiatry,* 1964, *34*(5), 822–833.

Hosford, R., & deVisser, L. *Behavioral approaches to counseling: An introduction.* Washington, D.C.: American Personnel and Guidance Press, 1974.

Hurst, J. C. The role of skills dissemination in counseling psychology. *Counseling Psychologist,* 1977, *7*(2), 61–64.

Ivey, A. E. *Counseling and psychotherapy: Skills, theories, and practice.* Englewood Cliffs, N.J.: Prentice-Hall, 1980.

Ivey, A. E., & Authier, J. *Microcounseling: Innovations in interviewing, counseling, psychotherapy, and psychoeducation* (2nd ed.). Springfield, Ill.: Charles C Thomas, 1978.

Johnson, D. G., Foyle, T. T., & Kazmar, B. *Relating is . . .* n.d. (Available from Interpersonal Communications, Inc., P.O. Box 1667, Orange, Tex. 77630.)

Johnson, D. W. *Human relations and your career: A guide to interpersonal skills.* Englewood Cliffs, N.J.: Prentice-Hall, 1978.

Kahn, G. S., Cohen, B., & Jason, H. The teaching of interpersonal skills in U.S. medical schools. *Journal of Medical Education,* 1979, *54,* 29–35.

Kanfer, F. H., & Goldstein, A. P. (Eds.). *Helping people change.* New York: Pergamon, 1975.

Kaye, K. The development of skills. In G. J. Whitehurst & B. J. Zimmerman (Eds.), *The functions of language and cognition.* New York: Academic Press, 1979.

Kiesler, C. A. Mental health policy as a field of inquiry for psychology. *American Psychologist,* 1980, *35,* 1066–1080.

Korchin, S. J. *Modern clinical psychology.* New York: Basic Books, 1976.

Korchin, S. J., & Sands, S. H. Principles common to all psychotherapies. In C. E. Walker (Ed.), *Handbook of clinical psychology.* Homewood, Ill.: Dow Jones–Irwin, 1982.

Kuhn, T. S. *The structure of scientific revolutions.* Chicago: University of Chicago Press, 1962.

Larson, D. Therapeutic schools, styles, and schoolism: A national survey. *Journal of Humanistic Psychology,* 1980, *20,* 3–20.

Liberman, R. P., King, L. W., DeRisi, W. J., & McCann, M. *Personal effectiveness.* Champaign, Ill.: Research Press, 1975.

Lyle, B. R., & Nyer, L. *Communication.* CETA Counselor Training Project, University of Texas at Austin, 1976. (Available from Adult Performance Level Project, Education Annex S21, Austin, Tex. 78712.)

Matarazzo, R. Research on the teaching and learning of psychotherapeutic skills. In S. L. Garfield & A. E. Bergin (Eds.), *Handbook of psychotherapy and behavior change* (2nd ed.). New York: Wiley, 1978.

McBain, S. L. *Competency-based education for guidance to counseling personnel: A catalog of programs and competencies.* American Institute for Research, 1975. (Available from The American Institute for Research, P.O. Box 113, Palo Alto, Calif. 94302.)

McFall, R. M. *Behavioral training: A skill acquisition approach to clinical problems.* Chicago: General Learning Press, 1976.

Miller, F. T., Mazade, N. A., Muller, S., & Andrulis, D. Trends in community mental health programming. *American Journal of Community Psychology,* 1978, *6,* 191–198.

Miller, G. Psychology as a means of promoting human welfare. *American Psychologist,* 1969, *24,* 1063–1075.

Miller, S., Nunnally, E. W., & Wachman, D. B. *Alive and aware: Improving communication in relationships.* Minneapolis: Interpersonal Communication Programs, 1975.

Mosher, R., & Sprinthall, N. Psychological education: A means to promoting personal development during adolescence. *Counseling Psychologist,* 1971, *2*(4), 3–82.

Okun, B. F. *Effective helping: Interviewing and counseling techniques.* North Scituate, Mass.: Duxbury Press, 1976.

Patterson, G. R., Hops, H., & Weiss, R. L. Interpersonal skills training for couples in early stages of conflict. *Journal of Marriage and the Family,* 1975, *37,* 295–301.

Patterson, G. R., McNeal, S., Hawkins, N., & Phelps, R. Reprogramming the social environment. *Journal of Child Psychology and Psychiatry,* 1967, *8,* 180–195.

Prochaska, J. O., & Norcross, J. C. The future of psychotherapy: A Delphi poll. *Professional Psychology,* in press.

Regier, D. A., Goldberg, I. D., & Taube, C. A. The de facto U.S. mental health services system: A public health perspective. *Archives of General Psychiatry,* 1978, *35,* 685–693.

Rhode, N., Rasmussen, D., & Heaps, R. A. Let's communicate: A program designed for effective communication. Paper presented at meeting of American Personnel and Guidance Association, Atlantic City, April 1971.

Rioch, M. J. Should psychotherapists do therapy? *Professional Psychology,* 1970, *1*(2), 139–142.

Robin, A. Parent-adolescent conflict: A skill-training approach. In D. P. Rathjen & J. P. Foreyt (Eds.), *Social competence: Interventions for children and adults.* New York: Pergamon Press, 1980.

Rogers, C. R. *Counseling and psychotherapy.* Boston: Houghton Mifflin, 1942.

Rogers, C. R. *Carl Rogers on personal power.* New York: Dell, 1977.

Rosenberg, J. *Breakfast: Two jars of paste—a training manual for workers in the human services* (2nd ed.). Cleveland, Ohio: The Press of Case Western Reserve University, 1972.

Rotheram, M. J. Social skills training programs in elementary and high school classrooms. In D. P. Rathjen & J. P. Foreyt (Eds.), *Social competence: Interventions for children and adults.* New York: Pergamon Press, 1980.

Schulman, E. D. *Intervention in human services.* St. Louis: Mosby, 1974.

Sobel, H. J., & Worden, J. W. *Practitioner's manual: Helping cancer patients cope.* New York: Guilford, 1982.

Sobey, F. *The non-professional revolution in mental health.* New York: Columbia University Press, 1970.

Stephens, T. M. *Social skills in the classroom.* Columbus, Ohio: Cedars Press, 1976.

Terkelson, C. Making contact: Parent-child communication skill program. *Elementary School Guidance and Counseling,* 1976, *11,* 89–99.

Thiel, S. A. (Ed.). *Inventory of habilitation programs for mentally handicapped adults.* Portland, Ore.: Portland Rehabilitation Center, 1977.

Varenhorst, B., & Hamburg, B. *Curriculum for the peer counseling students.* Palo Alto, Calif.: Palo Alto Unified School District, n.d.

Wehman, P., & Schleien, S. Social skills development through leisure skills programming. In G. Cartledge & J. F. Milburn (Eds.), *Teaching social skills to children.* New York: Pergamon Press, 1980.

PART ONE

TEACHING COPING SKILLS

CHAPTER TWO

People in Systems: A Comprehensive Model for Psychosocial Education and Training

Gerard Egan

Gerard Egan is professor of psychology at Loyola University of Chicago. He is program coordinator for the Program in Community and Organizational Development at Loyola and is a member of the editorial review board of *Group and Organization Studies.* He is the author of *The Skilled Helper, Interpersonal Living,* and (with Michael Cowan) *People in Systems* and *Moving into Adulthood.* Forthcoming books are *Systematic Helping* and *Change Agent Skills.*

Gerard Egan's leadoff chapter is both a hortatory call to action and a comprehensive framework for guiding that action. His people-in-systems model requires that helpers develop a "working knowledge" of developmental processes across the life span, of human systems, and of the "life skills" that people need to pursue developmental tasks. Unique is Egan's emphasis on the need for helpers to understand the social settings in which clients are embedded—that is, the need to develop "systems sensitivity." Egan argues that helpers in all fields are in a particularly strategic position to give psychology and other social sciences away and that they should receive formal training in how to do so through skills training.

THE DEMORALIZATION OF HELPERS AND CLIENTS

It goes without saying that people who seek out helpers of one kind or another often come to them demoralized. They are agitated or dejected or both because they feel incapable of managing their lives in some way. It may be that their personal concerns and struggles stem from or are aggravated by social events such as war, the denial of human rights, intractable poverty, corruption in government, repressive social settings, and the like. These are by no means new in human experience, but perhaps the ways they affect individuals are being seen more clearly and therefore

This chapter is based on *People in Systems: A Model for Development in the Human-Service Professions and Education* by Gerard Egan and Michael A. Cowan (Monterey, Calif.: Brooks/Cole, 1979).

being felt more intensely. Mische and Mische (1977) spell out concretely the sense of powerlessness that pervades the lives of many people:

> The types of phrases that would complete the sentence "As a citizen of _____ I have power to _____" are declining rapidly in people's estimation of their own individual capacities as citizens. The type of phrases that would complete the negative phrasing of that sentence, "As a citizen of _____ I am not able to _____," are increasing:
>
> "Not able to ensure adequate food and housing."
> "Not able to ensure quality education for my children."
> "Not able to ensure clean air and water."
> "Not able to ensure a healthy environment."
> "Not able to ensure adequate medical care."
> "Not able to walk the streets safely."
> "Not able to get a good job."
> "Not able to trust our elected officials."
> "Not able to influence governmental policy."
> "Not able to control technology and technological processes" [p. 9].

The cumulative effect on some people can be described as a type of social demoralization (Frank, 1973; Mische & Mische, 1977, Chapter 1); that is, some people give up trying to cope with some events in their world because they no longer expect to be able to cope effectively.

Sociologist Robert Nisbet (1969) suggested that alienation is rooted in this kind of social demoralization:

> By alienation I mean the state of mind that can find a social order remote, incomprehensible, or fraudulent; beyond real hope or desire; inviting apathy, boredom, or even hostility. The individual does not feel a part of the social order; he has lost interest in being a part of it. For a constantly enlarging number of persons . . . this state of alienation has become profoundly influential in both behavior and thought. . . . For millions of persons such institutions as state, political party, business, church, labor union, and even family have become remote and increasingly difficult to give any part of one's self to [p. ix].

Alienation and feelings of powerlessness are not new problems in the history of the human race, but the growing complexity of the contemporary world makes them more complicated, if not more intractable, and people's relative psychological sophistication, combined with the explosion of news media that has made the world a "global village" (McLuhan, 1964), makes many of us more intensely aware of them.

Not only clients but also helpers—that is, those who are committed by their profession to the development of human beings—are vulnerable in a special way to the social-demoralization syndrome. Anyone who has worked in the helping professions for even a short time has probably witnessed the "burned-out helper" phenomenon (Edelwich, 1980; Moore, 1977; Warnath & Shelton, 1977), in which an intense desire to help gives way to an exhausted day-to-day coping with persons in difficulty. Most people in the helping professions would probably acknowledge such feelings from time to time, even though they do not become full-fledged "burned-out cases."

The phenomenon of demoralized helpers has its roots in at least two factors. First, helpers spend a great deal of time in direct contact with the tragedies that signal failed human development. Newman and Newman (1979) describe what happens.

In daily work interactions, human service professionals often encounter situations that are emotionally arousing, frustrating, and perhaps personally threatening. In response to these intense experiences some people begin to take a very cynical, derogatory view of the people they are hired to help. They become callous, claiming that the clients deserve their fate. They begin to experience physical symptoms, increased use of drugs, marital conflict, and needs for solitude or detachment from all social contacts. They come to see themselves as bad people and their clients as deserving of bad treatment. In this and other examples of stagnation, the person loses sight of the potential for nurturing, educating, or guiding others and becomes trapped in the struggle to protect or maintain the self [p. 430].

Edelwich (1980) suggests four stages in the genesis of this kind of disillusionment—enthusiasm, stagnation, frustration, and apathy—and suggests that remedies must focus on both individual helpers *and* institutions.

Second, helpers typically work "downstream," treating the casualties of ill-functioning human systems such as the family or the neighborhood or the school system and then sending them back to the same settings. Although it is hardly surprising that "successfully" treated cases often return from these settings in six months, a year, or two years with the same or even more severe problems, it is certainly frustrating and discouraging. Let us take a closer look at the notion of "downstream" helping.

THE LIMITS OF DOWNSTREAM HELPING

There is a contemporary fable that goes something like this. A person walking beside a river sees someone drowning. This person jumps in, pulls the victim out, and begins artificial respiration. Then another drowning person calls for help. The rescuer jumps into the water again and pulls the second victim out. This process repeats itself several times until finally, much to the amazement of the bystanders who have gathered to watch this drama, the rescuer, even though the screams of yet another victim can be clearly heard from the river, gets up from administering artificial respiration and begins to walk upstream. One of the bystanders calls out: "Where are you going? Can't you hear the cries of the latest victim?" The rescuer replies: "You take care of him. I'm going upstream to find out who's pushing all these people in and see whether I can stop it." He might have added: "I'm also going to find out why all these people can't swim and see whether I can teach them how." In this fable the helper is optimistic, determined to strike at the social conditions that spawn individual casualties and to teach those who suffer from oppressive social settings how to cope.

Helpers are working "downstream" if they are working with clients who are involved in malfunctioning systems (family, school, economic system, or whatever) without being able to do anything about the system or systems that are contributing to their clients' problems and if they are not equipped to help their clients cope with these systems more effectively.

The demoralization of helpers raises a key question: How did the helping professions arrive at downstream (remedial) approaches as the preferred mode of responding to people in trouble? It seems that two ways of thinking about helping have fostered these approaches.

First, as Szasz (1961) has noted, the assumptions of the *medical model,* which has traditionally defined many problems in social living as types of illness, lead to the conclusion that clients need treatment. Therefore, a person with problems in living becomes a patient. But, as Schofield (1964) noted, "the total case load of those who are mentally and emotionally diseased is composed primarily of persons who are neither in need of, nor responsive to, specific medication, surgery, hospitalization, or other physical regimens" (p. 1). A patient, in the root sense of the word, is one who is helped by having things done for him or her. Indeed, once identified as patients, many people hand themselves over to mental health professionals to be cured. Patienthood often means a loss of agency or assertiveness. In dealing with people who seek help for a wide variety of problems in living, there has been a steady movement away from the medical model of helping (Ellis, 1967; Hoffman, 1979; Morrison, 1979; Szasz, 1961, 1970a, 1970b, 1974a, 1974b, 1979). Since helping exists for the benefit of the client, not for the benefit of either the individual helper or any particular guild of helpers, it seems that models of helping should be open to contributions from any source, including, of course, the field of medicine.

A second and related source of current approaches to helping is to be found, as Sarason (1974) has observed, in psychiatric and psychological theories and research on personality. Almost the entire focus of North American psychology has been on the *individual.* Sociocultural systems, which have such a profound effect on the development of individuals, have, with few exceptions, been neglected in favor of a focus on individual behavior. A theoretical view giving primacy to the individual's thoughts, feelings, values, and behaviors while disregarding the sociocultural settings in which these emerge has led to highly individual-centered approaches to helping. In programs that prepare people for the helping professions, the emphasis is on the study of individuals rather than on the study of individuals in the context of the human systems in which they live out their lives.

In the estimate of some, this overemphasis has led us to blame people for problems that originate primarily with society (Caplan & Nelson, 1973; Ryan, 1971). Insensitivity to the *context* of human development has resulted in the failure of the helping professions to reflect in practice the distinction between "troubles" and "issues" suggested by Mills (1959). Troubles are the personal difficulties of particular individuals; issues are difficulties resulting from the social structures in which people live. A case of depression, for example, is a trouble that may, however, be related to some issue (for instance, unemployment) that is due to economic conditions. Chronic demoralization within a social group, such as working-class families (see Rubin, 1976), is an issue that can contribute to a wide variety of troubles. What Ryan (1971) calls "blaming the victim" prevents us from seeing the real cause of certain social problems and from developing ways of helping clients cope with the negative effects of social systems.

PEOPLE IN SYSTEMS: A WORKING MODEL FOR GIVING THE SOCIAL SCIENCES AWAY

It would seem that helpers of all sorts—counselors, clinical psychologists, social workers, ministers, nurses, doctors, lawyers, teachers, and the like; that is, all those who help people manage the problem situations of life—are in a prime position to "give away" not only psychology but all the relevant social sciences. But it also seems that they will be inclined to do so only if learning how to "give away" is part of their formal training. It is not uncommon for helpers to be trained in models of psychopathology or social-emotional disorders (American Psychiatric Association, 1980), but it *is* uncommon for them to be trained in what Heath (1980a, 1980b) calls "a comprehensive and valid model of human development and psychological maturity." He urges the members of the helping professions to develop and use such a model. This chapter outlines such a model or framework.

A model can be defined as a visual portrayal of how things actually work or how they should work under ideal conditions. A working model is one that enables the user to achieve behavioral goals effectively. It is a framework or cognitive map with "delivery" potential. There are two criteria for such models: they must be complex enough to account for the reality they attempt to portray, and they must be simple enough to use. A model that meets only the first criterion is likely to be of interest solely to theoreticians and researchers, whereas a model that meets only the second criterion will tend to be simplistic rather than simple and will therefore be useless as a working model. Lippitt (1973) suggests that models with applied utility need to be two-dimensional, linear, and basically nonmathematical. Three-dimensional, non-linear, and highly mathematical models are usually too complicated for most practitioners to use.

The people-in-systems model is based on the familiar Lewinian equation

$$B = f(P \times E)$$

That is, behavior *(B)* is a function of *(f)* the interaction between ($\times$) the person *(P)* and the person's environment *(E)*. This equation can be expanded to read:

$$HD = f\,[(P \times S) \times (S \times S)]$$

That is, human development *(HD)* is a function of *(f)* the interaction between ($\times$) people *(P)* and the human systems *(S)* in which they are involved, and this interactional system *(P × S)* is in turn affected by ($\times$) other systems in the environment *(S × S)*.

The Three Elements of the Model

The three basic elements of the equation are the three basic elements of the model: people *(P)*, human systems *(S)*, and the kinds of interaction ($\times$) between people and the systems of their lives and between these systems themselves.

People (P).   This refers to individual human beings moving through the developmental stages of life, undertaking lifelong and stage-specific developmental tasks, and coping with lifelong and stage-specific developmental crises.

Human systems (S).   This refers to the groups to which individuals belong, by which their lives are affected for better or worse, and in the context of which they move through life stages, undertake developmental tasks, and cope with developmental crises. This model represents the world as hierarchical, with smaller human systems nested in more complex ones. The family, for example, is nested in and greatly affected by community, economic, and governmental systems of various types.

Interactions (x). These interactions go in both directions. For instance, the mother *(P)* of a family not only affects the system called the family *(S)* but is also affected by the other interactions that take place there. In turn, this family *(S)* not only is affected by the school *(S)* that the children attend but also affects the school in some ways. Groups, organizations, institutions, and communities affect individuals; individuals affect them; and systems affect one another. These interactions can lead to the growth and development or the stagnation and debilitation of both individuals and systems. This interactional picture can become quite complex. A student *(P)* interacting with a high school *(S)* might experience intellectual growth, physical stagnation, and social-emotional debilitation. In the meantime, the school itself is being affected by its interactions with families, the local school board, state accrediting agencies, the neighborhood in which it is located, and a variety of government agencies.

At any given moment individuals bring both resources and deficits to their interactions with any given human setting. For instance, a student who has learned practically no discipline at home can have a debilitating effect on a classroom, whereas a student who has learned self-management skills and developed intellectual curiosity at home can have a positive impact. In the same way, a system, such as a high school, or a subsystem, such as the counseling and guidance service of a high school, can bring both positive and negative forces to bear on individual students. A teacher, for example, unaware of a natural "kicking against systems" that many students show in the process of identity formation, or a teacher lacking the ability to deal positively with such adolescent rebelliousness, might emphasize discipline or punishment to such an extent that potentially growthful oppositional tendencies and conflicts are suppressed.

Working Knowledge and Life Skills

The xs in the people-in-systems equation represent interactions that can be analyzed from the standpoint of *quality.* These interactions may be, on the part of the people involved, unenlightened and unskilled and may therefore lead to negative results. However, if the interactions between individuals and systems are reasonably enlightened and skilled, the results have a higher probability of being positive.

Working knowledge refers to information or understandings concerning self and the world that enable individuals to face both self and the world resourcefully. Working knowledge facilitates behavior in some direct way. If someone were to give you an engaging lecture on the history of safes and a fascinating overview of the metallurgy involved, this would not provide you with any working knowledge with respect to opening a particular safe. However, if someone told you the combination of the safe, then you would have information that enabled you to *do* something. Working knowledge enables people to apply basic skills or abilities. It is not suggested here that merely understanding something enables people to act; however, understanding a problem situation increases the probability of coping with it.

Skills, in the sense used here, refers to competencies that are necessary for effective living in such areas as self-management, interpersonal communication, and effective participation in communities and organizations. Working knowledge informs and enhances skills, and skills translate working knowledge into action. Individuals need both in order to become positively involved in the social settings of their lives. Those who design, manage, and preside over human systems (parents, teachers, supervisors, managers, and the like) also need particular kinds of working knowledge and skills to help fashion settings where both system goals are accomplished and the human development of members is fostered.

As a framework for counselor training, the people-in-systems model suggests that helpers develop—

- a working knowledge of developmental processes across the life span,
- a working knowledge of the ways human systems work and how they affect human development,
- the kinds of life skills that people need to effectively pursue developmental tasks in the context of the social systems of their lives.

Helpers should first be able to apply these kinds of working knowledge and skills to their own lives and then develop the ability to help others do the same. A word, now, about each area of the model—developmental processes, human systems, and life skills.

Developmental Stages, Tasks, and Crises

Helpers often do not have enough knowledge about the normal developmental stages, tasks, and crises of their clients. They are currently being urged to develop practical expertise in the area of developmental psychology so that they can put this expertise at the service of their clients (Blocher, 1980; Cooney & Selman, 1980; Elkind, 1980; Havighurst, 1980; White, 1980). Even when training programs do provide helpers with some sort of training in developmental psychology, it is often not the kind of practical training that results in *working* knowledge on the part of the practitioner. "Despite the lip service paid to developmental principles, there is such divergence in practice that common ideological ancestry is all but unrecognizable. A concurrent problem is that a developmental approach does not automatically translate into a practical system of educational and therapeutic interventions" (Gazda & Brooks, 1980, p. 120).

The people-in-systems model provides a framework that enables helpers to see the importance of developmental realities and to incorporate them into their approaches to helping. Furthermore, through this model *all* individuals, including clients insofar as this is possible, are encouraged to develop a working knowledge of the stage of human development they are in, the tasks related to that stage, and the normative crises associated with it (Egan & Cowan, 1980; Levinson, Darrow, Klein, Levinson, & McKee, 1978; Newman & Newman, 1979).

Life stages.   Different theoreticians and researchers divide life into different stages, or periods. For instance, Levinson and his associates (1978), in studying the developmental patterns of adult men, divide life into three "eras," each introduced by a period of "transition," as shown in the following chart.

Age	Definition of Life Stage
17–22	A transitional period of life. The person is moving from adolescence to early adulthood.
22–40	The first adulthood "era," the era of early adulthood.

40–45	The next transitional period, a time when men ordinarily experience the "midlife crisis."
45–60	The second adulthood era, the era of middle adulthood.
60–65	The third transitional period, a time of preparation for late adulthood and old age.
65–death	The final adulthood era, which includes early, middle, and late old age.

Levinson outlines the characteristics of each of these stages, or periods, indicates the tasks the person faces at each stage of life, and describes the characteristic or normal "crises" that individuals must face at each period. He shows that each era can be broken down into further relatively well-defined periods. For instance, the era of early adulthood includes a period of "entering the adult world" (22–28), the "age-30 transition" (28–33), and a "settling down" period (33–40). Each of these subperiods has its own characteristics and tasks.

A working knowledge of a client's developmental stage enables helpers to listen to, understand, and orient themselves toward clients in a more informed way. For instance, Norm, a 20-year-old college student, is in a transitional stage that has certain characteristics:

1. *Boundary zone.* A transitional period is a boundary zone between two more or less well-defined or structured periods of life (in Norm's case adolescence and early adulthood). Boundary zones are often times of uncertainty and turbulence. Norm may at times feel suspended between the past and the future. His roles are not as certain as they used to be; boy-or-man feelings may arise in him as he struggles to find out who he really is. For some young people these feelings are quite intense; for others they are mild enough most of the time to seem almost nonexistent.

2. *A time of termination or modification.* In this transitional period Norm is most likely terminating or modifying his relationships with important people such as his parents and with important institutions such as school or church. Even though transitions lead to growth and development, they are also times of uprooting, separation, and loss. Norm is moving away from his parents and becoming more his own man. But his feelings are ambivalent—sometimes home seems like a very comforting place; at other times there are fights. He also misses the comfort and security of high school. He was a bigger fish in that smaller pond.

3. *A time of questioning.* People in transitional periods often question the world around them and their place in it. They question their values and the ways they put them into practice. For example, Norm has begun to question what he now sees as the dogmatic imposition of values by his church. He questions what has been told him about sexuality and sexual behavior. He wants to create his own values.

4. *A time of experimentation.* Questioning leads naturally to experimenting with new behaviors or different ways of doing things. Norm, who up to now had been shy around girls, becomes much more assertive in his relationships with women. He wants to experiment with sexual behavior. Doing things differently is a way of breaking out of the old mold and giving oneself a wider experience on which to base decisions about the future. As Levinson and associates (1978) note, during a transitional period, neglected parts of the self more urgently seek expression. This leads to experimentation.

5. *Initiation of new patterns.* As transitional periods move along, new patterns of commitment begin to emerge. After testing some preliminary choices related to adult living, Norm is ready to say something like this: "At least for now, I will settle for this." For instance, he says "At least for now, I'll stick with my major in

business" or "At least for now, I will develop a close relationship with a woman without immediately choosing to marry." Because of these initial choices and commitments, a new life structure begins to emerge. Norm begins to picture himself more and more as a member of the world of young adults.

6. *The temporary nature of transitional periods.* When the tasks of questioning, exploring, and experimenting begin to lose their urgency and new commitments are being made, the transitional period is coming to an end. Sometimes people get bogged down in transitional periods. They feel they cannot or do not want to move on. Norm is enjoying the "moratorium" that society provides for him in his college years—he is not yet obliged to go out and earn a living. And now, toward the end of the moving-into-adulthood period, he finds himself reluctant to give up the comforts of the moratorium. He wants to keep postponing decisions about work and marriage. For him experimenting has not yet lost its urgency.

Helpers who understand the general characteristics of the life stages of their clients have a developmental map that helps them in the assessment process. A counselor with a good working knowledge of developmental stages would be able to see Norm and his problems in living against the background of the moving-into-adulthood transitional period. The counselor would see that the kind of turbulence that goes with questioning, exploring, and experimenting is normal during these years. Of course, the amount and kind of turbulence will differ from person to person. If Norm is having a rough time, then the counselor can explore with him the developmental realities he is facing and help him find ways of coping with the storm. This does not make Norm an abnormal person. However, if he were to come back at 27 with the same kinds of problems, then he could well be suffering from some kind of serious developmental lag.

Developmental tasks.   A developmental task is an expectation or demand placed on a person to develop certain skills and competencies. The demand may come from the fact that the person is maturing physically or intellectually, from the social settings of which he or she is a member, or from the culture and subcultures in which the social systems of his or her life are immersed. For instance, in our society there is an expectation that a child will begin to learn cooperative social relations sometime between ages 8 and 12. Newman and Newman (1979) explain developmental tasks as follows:

> Developmental tasks (Havighurst, 1953) consist of a set of skills and competencies that are acquired as the person gains increased mastery over the environment. The tasks may reflect gains in motor skills, intellectual skills, social skills, and emotional skills. Mastery of the tasks of later stages of development often depends on the acquisition of earlier and simpler skills. One of the critical developmental tasks of infancy, for example, is the development of a social relationship with the caregiver. This task presents itself early in the person's development and must be mastered at this time of life. The person's ability to develop warm and rewarding friendship and marriage relationships depends, to some extent, on having been able to develop an initial sense of attachment to a mother figure [pp. 18–19].

Developmentally speaking, a person can limp into any given psychosocial stage of life because he or she, for whatever reasons, has not adequately handled one or more of the tasks of some previous stage.

Norm is beginning to grapple with tasks that he will have to face, though in different ways at different stages, throughout the rest of his life:

- *Competence:* developing physical, mental, and social-emotional competence.
- *Autonomy:* working toward reasonable independence and interdependence.
- *Values:* fashioning a coherent set of values that are now his own, whatever their source.
- *Identity:* developing an abiding sense of who he is and a feeling for how that sense is confirmed by those around him.
- *Sexuality:* coming to grips with his sexual identity, orientation, preferences, and behavior and relating them to the values he is developing.
- *Friendship and intimacy:* establishing and developing friendships of varying degrees of intimacy and patterns of socializing.
- *Marriage:* thinking about and developing the competencies needed for love, marriage, and establishing a family.
- *Work:* thinking about the place of work, occupation, or career in his life and preparing himself for the occupation of his choice.
- *Community and society:* thinking about his relationship to society and the possible roles he would like to play in his community and society.
- *Leisure:* learning to use the time he has free from work and other obligations in ways that provide him rest, relaxation, and self-enhancement.

As noted, some of these tasks are seen by Norm as more urgent than others, but these are ten basic areas of development that will be important throughout the rest of his life. A helper with a working knowledge of these task areas can help Norm assess his ability to cope with these tasks. A further hypothesis is that if Norm himself develops a practical understanding of the developmental tasks that are specific to his stage of life, he will be better able to marshal his resources and direct his behavior toward a rewarding execution of these tasks.

Normative developmental crises.   Developmental crises represent the process of developmental change as it is experienced by the individual. The word *crisis* (Erikson, 1963) is appropriate in this connection for two reasons. The Greek origin of the word *crisis* is *krino,* "I divide." Developmental crises represent significant "dividing points" at which the individual's life is deeply affected. The second reason for the use of the word *crisis* is that these critical dividing points tend to be experienced as times of excitement, turmoil, and anxiety. Let's consider Norm and the task of identity formation.

Identity formation is considered by some (for instance, Erikson, 1963, 1968; Marcia, 1966, 1975; Marcia & Friedman, 1970) to be the central task of later adolescence. One definition of identity is "a stable sense of who you are that is confirmed by the people in your life who are important to you." Identity is, therefore, a *psychosocial* construct that is based on both self-appraisal and the reflected appraisals of others. Identity questions a person in Norm's age group might ask are: Who am I? Where am I going in life? Are my values really me? Can I honestly be the person "they" want me to be? Why do I sometimes feel like a stranger when I go home for a visit? A person who has achieved a sense of identity knows who he or she is, and this is reflected in actual integration of and commitment to a set of family, work, political, and religious values. Identity is an integrating concept. It has much to do with how Norm sees himself as a unique, separate person, but still a person with past identifications and future possibilities that are significantly related to important people in his life and to the organizations, institutions, and cultural dictates of society.

Marcia (1966, 1975), through his research, has elaborated a framework that is useful for the practitioner who is trying to help people like Norm sort out their feelings about themselves and set goals in life. The current identity status of any given person might be one of the following:

· *Foreclosed identity.* People in this category have not experienced the often turbulent work of challenging the commitments they grew up with. They demonstrate strong occupational and value commitments that society (for instance, parents) has "given" them. They have not questioned traditional values and reformulated a set that makes sense to them. According to Marcia, they often respect strong leadership and value obedience to authority. Such an approach to identity formation has its obvious disadvantages and has been called "brittle and vulnerable" (Newman & Newman, 1979, p. 332).

· *Psychosocial moratorium.* People in this category are still in the process of questioning, exploring, and experimenting with life before committing themselves to a coherent set of choices. Although this process is normal and useful during the transitional years, it can become self-defeating if it gets too turbulent or goes on too long. Norm at age 20 is still in the middle of a psychosocial moratorium. He is beginning to see some commitments he would like to make, but he has not yet made them.

· *Diffused identity.* People in this category have difficulty making any kind of solid commitment. They have given up many of the commitments they grew up with but have failed to find viable alternatives. They may not even be searching for viable alternatives. According to Marcia, they have a cavalier attitude toward life, and their "playboy" or "playgirl" attitudes allow them to cope with the college environment. Marcia also suggests that the most serious cases of identity diffusion are probably not in college at all because they would be unable to cope with its demands.

· *Achieved identity.* People in this category have come to a stable sense of who they are, which is manifested in their ability to make commitments to themselves and to others. They can get on with such tasks as choosing a marriage partner and investing themselves in an occupation or career. Achieved identity is part of what Heath (1980a, 1980b) calls maturity.

We know a great deal about how people develop from the vast amount of research that has been conducted by developmental psychologists. However, much of this research has lain dormant, as it were, waiting for people to "translate" it into useful working knowledge for the practitioner (Cooney & Selman, 1980) and for individuals themselves. There is emerging a relatively new specialty—the "clinical developmental psychologist"—that is, the developmental psychologist practitioner as opposed to the developmental psychologist who restricts his or her work to formulating theory, conducting research, and teaching (Bibace & Walsh, 1979). However, the hypothesis here is that not enough is being done by either helpers or educators to "give away" working knowledge of human development to ordinary people.

The Social Settings of Life

The people-in-systems model also urges helpers to develop an understanding of how individuals and the developmental tasks they are pursuing are being affected by the various social settings and systems of life and to translate this understanding into practical helping strategies. They can also help clients to do the same for themselves. The four "levels" of social settings or human systems are:

· *Level I: Personal systems—The immediate settings of life.* The way people develop is constantly being affected by the immediate settings of their lives such as family, friends, school settings, workplace, church groups, and the like. Depending on what happens to people in these settings and how they react, development is for better or for worse.

The family is a prime example of such a setting, and there is a vast literature on the family and its relation to individual human development. During the past 10 or 15 years *family therapy* as a specialty has come into its own (Goldenberg & Goldenberg, 1980; Okun & Rappaport, 1980; Haley, 1976); the family as a unit is the object of helping, not just the member who happens to be pushed forward as the "identified patient" or helpee. Andrews (1974), in Figure 2-1, provides us with an excellent illustration of the family as a system.

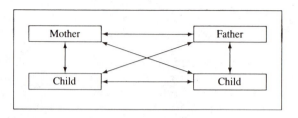

Figure 2-1.   The family as a system.

In a family of four . . . there exist six dyadic, reciprocal relationship possibilities. These tie each member of the family to every other member directly and indirectly through another person to whom he is directly related. One might construct a physical model of this diagram [Figure 2-1] by using paper clips to represent each family member and connecting rubber bands to represent the relationship vectors in the diagram. If the paper clips are each fastened down and the rubber bands drawn taut, the model will assume a stability that can be altered at any time. Plucking any of the rubber bands will reverberate the entire model. Similarly, any action or reaction pattern between any two family members will resonate throughout the entire family. Marital difficulties between parents will often manifest themselves in symptomatic behavior in one of the children. This "family resonance" phenomenon is the perpetuating mechanism of characteristic behavior within a family. Reinforcement of certain kinds of behavior is not unilateral or even bilateral but multilateral [p. 8].

Similar models could be drawn for other kinds of personal systems, such as a person's workplace or friendship group.

· *Level II: The network of personal settings.* People act as "linking pins" between the various personal systems of life. One setting affects another through individual members, and a network of mutual influence is established. For instance, Norm leaves the house after an argument with his parents, and this affects how he involves himself at school; that is, his interactions at home affect his interactions in the various social settings at school. Because he is a linking pin, the family and the school, through him, affect each other in a variety of ways.

City neighborhoods are networks of social systems in themselves, affecting both personal systems, such as families and schools, and individuals.

Nelson, a 19-year-old unemployed youth, sat at a table opposite a probation officer. As she looked at him, she was reviewing some of the background factors of his case. He had just been arrested for peddling drugs near a school and was already on probation for breaking and entering. The ghetto area in which he lived was a school for antisocial behavior. He and his two brothers and three sisters came from a one-parent family. His mother worked both a full- and a part-time job and consequently provided practically no supervision at home. He had hated school, played the truant as often as he could, and quit as soon as he was allowed. He belonged to a gang that fought with other gangs to protect its turf. Recently he had met an older man who introduced him to the world of drug sales. Nelson had no interest in drugs himself, but selling them seemed to be a quick way out of the depressing conditions in which he lived.

The probation officer, because of her understanding of the effects of social systems on the development of individuals, does not fall into the trap of "blaming the victim." However, she realizes that she is still dealing directly and immediately with Nelson, not with the social settings in which he has developed his current life-style. She still sees him as a person with a degree of responsibility for his behavior. She also sees him as a person who has not been able to cope with the devastating effects of the systems in which he has developed. She knows that others have faced the same kinds of social conditions without turning to antisocial solutions.

· *Level III: The larger organizations and institutions of society.* The larger organizations and institutions of life affect Norm's development both directly and indirectly. For instance, since Norm is a male between ages 18 and 22, what Congress does about registering people for possible military service affects him directly. If Norm is looking for a part-time job and can't find one because of a recession, then he is experiencing the effects of the system called the economy. The larger organizations and institutions of life affect individuals, the smaller systems of life, and one another. While it is obvious that individuals can do little to control these larger systems directly, they can learn, at least to a degree, how they are being affected by them and hope to cope with these effects. The people-in-systems model encourages helpers to see clients in the perspective of the social settings of their lives and encourages individuals to develop their own "working sociology" as a way of coping with the larger organizations and institutions of life.

What is being suggested here is that helpers are more effective if they can put clients and their problems in living in as wide a perspective as possible. This does not make them agents of social change, but it does increase their ability to be empathic, to become realistic about the social constraints imposed on their clients, and to help their clients face these constraints realistically. It is not enough to understand the "inner workings" of clients and how they go about creating patterns of self-defeating behavior for themselves, as if they lived separate from the forces that mold people within society.

Jordan is a part-time counselor in a halfway house. Men who have been in prison for some time come here voluntarily in order to ease themselves back into society. Jordan has studied the penal system in the United States and has a fairly good understanding of it as an institution. He knows how it works, and he knows its shortcomings. He has also visited prisons often enough and talked to enough prisoners to have a good idea of what day-to-day prison life is like. The ex-prisoners appreciate their sessions with him because they quickly see that he knows what he's talking about. They don't try to "con" him, and he talks straight with them.

In order to get by in prison, these men had to learn quickly how the particular institution to which they were committed worked. Knowing the larger picture—that is, how the penal system "works" and the impact it usually has on inmates—makes Jordan a more sensitive and realistic helper. He doesn't say stupid things that alienate his clients.

• *Level IV: Culture in its systematic effects.* Culture has been called the largest, the most pervasive, and the most influential of the social systems of life. It may seem odd to call culture a system, but it does have systematic effects on individuals and on every other level of systems. Novak (1979) defines culture as "the system of symbols, values, ideas, rituals, practices, and institutions that define the attitudes and daily operations of our people, and that give substance and meaning to their political and economic activities" (p. 40).

All the systems of life are "carriers" of social "blueprints" that set norms for and limitations on human behavior. For instance, behavior that is allowed in a suburban school may not be allowed in an inner-city school, and behavior that is allowed in a secondary school in the United States may not be allowed in a secondary school in Japan. People are often unaware of the ways in which these unwritten cultural blueprints affect their lives. However, at least to a degree, it is possible for helpers to develop a "working anthropology"—that is, a working knowledge of the principal cultural and subcultural blueprints that are affecting the development of their clients. Further, they can help clients themselves become aware of the ways they are running afoul of cultural and subcultural blueprints and of the potential resources embedded in the cultural systems of their lives.

Culture helps us see reality in certain specified ways: "One of the functions of culture is to provide a highly selective screen between man and the outside world. In its many forms, culture therefore designates what we pay attention to and what we ignore. This screening function provides structure for the world" (Hall, 1977, p. 85). This limiting of vision can work at times for people and at other times against them. For instance, if a family moves from Mexico to the United States, the "filtering" that proved useful in Mexico might prove self-defeating in the United States.

Helpers sensitive to the pervasiveness of culture can help clients see their presenting problems in the light of relevant cultural blueprints.

Nell, a college freshman from a small Midwestern farm community who is a friend of Norm, begins to experience fainting spells and other "hysterical" symptoms during her second semester at the main campus of the state university, located some 300 miles from her home. A thorough physical examination shows nothing wrong. She begins seeing Eunice, one of the counselors in the Center for Student Development. Eunice sees Nell's presenting problems, at least in part, in terms of the kinds of cultural adaptation she has been undergoing. The blueprints for living at the university are quite different from those at home. To make things more complicated, Nell arrived eager to get involved in drama, her favorite subject and extracurricular activity in high school. Consequently, she has to adapt not only to the university culture but also to the subculture represented by the people in the drama department. Eunice helps Nell sort things out in terms of the cultural expectations she has been experiencing and relates this process to the developmental task of examining and reformulating values. Nell has been exposed to cultural "overload" and has tried to handle it by getting more and more involved in schoolwork and in drama. She finally collapsed.

Perhaps one of the most useful things that helpers can do with clients experiencing difficulty in some social setting is to help them explore how they are being affected by the cultural blueprints of that setting and their characteristic ways of reacting to them. In the example just cited, Nell, who was ordinarily outgoing and lively, responded to what she saw as drastically new social blueprints by alternating between social isolation and throwing herself into schoolwork and drama. These strategies were not helping her come to grips with the problem situation.

Very often people are in need of special help when they become involved for the first time in a social system that is unfamiliar to them. For instance, people who are admitted to the hospital, go to jail, become involved with lawyers, or are introduced to the court system for the first time often become disoriented because they do not know how these systems work and they encounter them when they are already in distress. Special "systems" sensitivity is needed on the part of helpers in such situations.

Development of Life Skills

We live in a society where acquiring certain kinds of "life skills" is left to chance or is, at best, a rather haphazard process. This seems strange in a society that prides itself on its pragmatism. However, it is also a society that, even though it puts men on the moon, does not handle its social problems very well. It seems that "life skills *acquired, practiced, and used*" is not one of the valued accomplishments of education, either formal or informal. The assumption is made that the kinds of skills to be discussed here are best picked up through experience, and there is some truth in this. Most people pick up enough skills to "get by," but herein lies the problem. "Getting by" is another term for Maslow's (1968) "psychopathology of the average." Therefore, when helpers see people failing to cope with even normal, "garden variety" developmental problems in living, they need not immediately assume that such things as deep intrapsychic conflicts, lack of the courage to be, ill will, or an unhealthy childhood are to blame. It may be that the person simply does not have the kinds of physical, intellectual, and social-emotional skills and competencies needed to handle problem situations. The answer then is not to help clients probe their psyches but to see to it that they acquire the skills and other resources needed to face life. What follows is a brief description of seven "packages" of life skills.

Skills related to physical development.   The purpose of this set of skills is not merely to keep the body intact and free from disease but also to make it a source of energy and to use it artfully. Included in this package are such skills as those related to physical fitness, personal hygiene, nutrition, personal health care, athletics, the esthetic use of the body, and grooming. That is, this first set of skills deals with physical competence in the broadest sense. If Barb complains to a helper of "low energy," it may not mean that her problem is social-emotional in nature. It may mean that she is not eating properly or exercising enough—that is, that she is not doing whatever is necessary to make her body a source of energy. She might need the relevant working knowledge and skills to handle her problem.

There is no suggestion here that helpers become junior physicians (unless they are already physicians), diagnosing physical complaints and ministering to them. Rather, they help clients assess their body-related skills and resources so that deficits in this area that are contributing to current problems of living can be tended to.

Learning-how-to-learn skills. If people are to continue to develop across the entire life span, they need to become lifelong learners. Learning is one of those basics of life that are engaged in constantly but reflected on very little. For instance, people can spend from 10 to 20 years in formal educational systems without ever being given any kind of formal instruction in how to learn. Since people are to be lifelong learners in both formal and informal ways, it seems odd, if not criminal, that learning how to learn is not a principal educational goal. For some, formal learning proves to be such a distasteful experience that once they are no longer required to attend school, they quit, leaving behind not only school but any desire to make even informal learning a value. As they move through the various stages of life, they do learn because they are forced to, but they may never become efficient or happy learners.

Sallyann Johnson complained to her doctor of "low energy." An examination indicated that there was no physical cause for her condition. The doctor discovered that she was in a job that was well below her talents. Her problem of low energy was related to her frustration and boredom. When her husband died suddenly, she found herself 40 and needing a job. Friends, realizing that she had a number of talents, suggested that she return to school or some training program in order to turn raw talent into useful skills. Some suggested that she seek out jobs that would provide on-the-job education and training—for instance, managerial trainee programs. Sallyann, remembering how she had hated school and formal learning, utterly refused to explore any job that demanded education and training. As a result, she ended up as a clerk in a large department store. She hated the dead-end nature of her work, but she felt trapped.

Learning-how-to-learn skills go beyond acquiring the basic instruments of learning, such as the ability to read and write; they include such skills as the ability to formulate realistic and personally rewarding learning objectives, the ability to identify important or core ideas in what one reads or experiences, and the ability to translate ideas and principles into useful programs.

Skills related to value clarification and reformulation. As we have seen, the moving-into-adulthood years are a time when individuals question the values that have been handed down to them by people in the various social settings of life and begin to construct a personal set of values to which they feel they can commit themselves. This begins a process that continues over the life span, for, directly or indirectly, values need to be reviewed and reformulated from time to time. It therefore seems to make sense to teach people how to go about clarifying and reformulating values. People would benefit from at least four skills:

- The ability to identify the values that are currently operative in their lives.
- The ability to identify the values that other significant people in their lives are pursuing and assess the ways these people are influencing them to conform to those values.
- The ability to identify the values "pushed" by the various social systems in which they participate and which influence their behavior.
- The ability to direct the process of value reformulation in their lives without turning a natural reformulation process into an artificial one.

Curran (1968) has suggested that many people experience social-emotional crises in their lives because, without realizing it, they are trying to live out conflicting values.

Jeanne, a 20-year-old college student, saw one of the school counselors because of feelings of guilt and anxiety over conflicts at home. Exploration indicated that she still valued obedience to legitimate authority but at the same time valued the development of her own autonomy. Once she was able to identify the ways in which these values conflicted in the course of a normal developmental struggle, she was ready to set some reasonable goals and develop programs to implement them.

Because few people sit down and explicitly review with themselves the values they are pursuing, the pursuit of conflicting values is not uncommon. Since planning and problem solving deal with the pursuit of *valued* goals, value-clarification skills are essential to becoming self-directed in planning and problem management.

Self-management skills.   I have already noted that competence is a lifelong developmental task. Bandura (1977a) talks of competence in terms of "self-efficacy," or self-responsibility. If people are to move toward what Williams and Long (1979) call a "self-managed life-style," they need the kinds of life skills that enable them to engage in life planning. These include decision-making, goal-setting, program-development, and problem-solving skills. Planning and problem solving are similar processes. Since they are so essential to the development of autonomy and responsibility, it is amazing that people are not given systematic training in these skills from their earliest years, training that would include practical applications. Methodologies have been elaborated to do precisely this (Shure & Spivack, 1978; Spivack, Platt, & Shure, 1976; Spivack & Shure, 1974).

Early in their marriage Andy and Leslie found themselves facing a problem that afflicts many couples in the early years of marriage—the management of money. It seemed to be tearing their marriage apart. They went to a counselor who did not focus on their "relationship" so much as on their lack of certain skills. In the counseling sessions they learned basic planning and cooperative problem-solving skills and how to apply them to the management of money. As they became more skillful and tensions about finances eased, their relationship improved. They still had to face other problems in learning how to adjust to each other, but the reduction of tension over money freed them to do so. The skills they learned not only helped them to face their financial crisis but could now be used in facing their other problems.

Helping is a lifeless thing if it does not lead to action on the part of clients. However, helpers should encourage clients to pursue any given course of action only if they are sure the clients have the skills and other resources needed to do so.

Interpersonal communication skills.   People's lives are defined in significant ways by their relationships. Although clients come with a variety of problems, most come with problems in their relationships with others. Deficiencies in interpersonal skills are such a common part of the psychopathology of the average that they go almost unnoticed. Children learn how to relate to others by observing and imitating adult models (Bandura, 1977b). However, often such learning is haphazard and, if the models are poor, leads to self-defeating patterns of relating. Schools have traditionally done little or nothing to help students reflect in any systematic way on their interpersonal styles.

Janice, a nurse, was about to quit her job at the hospital because her immediate supervisor was "an impossible person." One day the director of patient support services, after listening to her woes, asked her to describe as concretely and fairly as possible the communication styles each of them used in their encounters with each other. The director asked Janice to defer quitting until she had taken a six-week course in communication skills that the director was offering for staff members. She also managed to get Janice's supervisor to take the same course but in a different training group. After the course Janice and her supervisor agreed to a couple of meetings with the director. They explored their differences in style but did so now using the skills they had learned. They listened to each other, and when they did confront, they did so with respect. After the meetings, although they still had no desire to go on a vacation together, they found that they could work together even though it still took a fair amount of effort to use the skills they had learned.

If many of the problem situations in people's lives center on interpersonal relationships, then direct training in the skills of relating seems to be called for.

Small-group skills.   Much of contemporary life involves living and working together in groups—families, discussion groups, work teams, committees, church groups, clubs, peer groups, and the like. Special skills beyond one-to-one communication skills are called for (Egan, 1970, 1976, 1977, in preparation). These include the ability to identify what needs are being met by belonging to a group, the ability to clarify the mission and goals of the group, the ability to cooperate and to use communication skills assertively, the ability to understand one's own role in the group and to relate it to the roles that others have, and the ability to share information and give feedback.

Roberta, a first-year college student, had a problem with "loneliness." She had a couple of acquaintances who were close to becoming friends, but generally Roberta lived on the margin of the social life of the school. She attended classes and occasionally socialized with her acquaintances, usually in one-to-one situations, but participated in no other school activities. In classes where participation was urged or demanded, she tended to do poorly. Instead of urging Roberta to "get involved," the counselor invited her to join a group at the counseling center that dealt with both "assertiveness" and "group involvement" skills. Although Roberta joined the group with some misgivings, she soon found that she was not the only person who felt isolated at school. Instead of merely discussing their isolation, group members learned skills and put them into practice in the training group itself. Later on they began systematically to transfer these skills to situations outside the group. Learning these skills and using them in the group helped Roberta become much more self-confident. She felt better about herself and gradually ended her self-imposed isolation. The counselor had been wise in not asking Roberta and the others to do things they were not prepared for.

The use of small groups to train people in the kinds of life or coping skills discussed here is now being urged (Gerler, 1980; Muro & Engels, 1980; Nelson, 1980; Robinson, 1980; Rotter & Wilson, 1980; Wilson & Canada, 1980).

Systems-involvement skills. As we have seen, people are members of a variety of social systems and are both affected by and, in turn, affect these systems. For example, a typical married man in his forties may be involved, in the course of any given week, in family, peer group, work setting, church group, community organization, bowling league, and county political organization. He is affected by the neighborhood in which he lives, the educational policies of the local school district, the workings of local, state, and national government, and both the nation's economic system and the current state of the economy in his locale. He needs skills to invest himself in these systems and to cope with them when they seem to be working against his better interests. Even though as systems grow larger, he has less and less control over them, he can still maintain some degree of control over his reactions to them, the way he invests himself in them, and the ways he copes with them. These skills include a basic understanding of how any given system works, how it is influencing him for better or for worse, and how to organize with others to help develop some degree of control over these systems.

Terry came to talk to the company counselor because he was having a great deal of trouble adjusting to his first major job. He had taken the job in an accounting firm with a great deal of enthusiasm because he liked the work, felt he was good at it, and was glad to get a job in a company with a good name in the accounting field. As he told his story to the counselor, he was depressed and had suffered a loss of self-esteem. He felt like quitting. He had entered the company naive about the business world and had got caught in the crossfire between the formal and informal structures of the company. The rules and roles and lines of authority were clear on paper (the formal organization), but there was another whole set of rules and roles and lines of authority in practice (the informal organization). In a word, Terry did not understand how the system "worked" and was being ground up by it. For instance, the work he did demanded that he report to two different persons in the organization who were political enemies. He became a pawn in that interaction.

An important part of the helping process can be a review of the clients' participation in the major social settings of their lives and their success at handling the realities of these systems. Some people seem to acquire "system smarts," while others do not. It is important to find out to what degree clients' problems are due to their being victims of forces beyond their control, as opposed to some kind of personal deficit. If an unemployed person is genuinely a victim of the current state of the economy, then the helping process need not focus on personal deficit. It is now a question of coping skills—coping with one's own frustrations with the current political and economic system and finding ways to survive.

It is not suggested in any simplistic way here that lack of life skills is the only reason that people get into trouble. However, it is suggested that it is often one of the main reasons that people do not manage problem situations creatively. Furthermore, even when a skills deficit is not the central problem, it is often a contributing factor.

Several times I have mentioned that it is surprising that people are not trained from their earliest years in the kinds of working knowledge and skills outlined here. Such a statement, however, has a degree of political naiveté in it. It is perhaps not at all surprising that the social institutions of life do not "give away" the kinds of working knowledge and skills that "empower people" (Berger & Neuhaus, 1977). People immersed in the "psychopathology of the average" fit better into many of the social settings of life.

The Hypothesis of the People-in-Systems Model

Figure 2-2 summarizes the three facets of the people-in-systems model. The hypothesis of the people-in-systems model is that people who develop a working knowledge of the stages, tasks, and crises of *human development,* both their own and those of the significant people in their lives; and who develop a working knowledge of the *social settings and systems* which constitute the context for development and which affect development in a variety of ways; and who develop

Figure 2–2

THE PEOPLE-IN-SYSTEMS MODEL: HUMAN DEVELOPMENT IN HUMAN SYSTEMS

The development of both individuals and systems depends on the quality of the following kinds of interaction:

- The individual with himself or herself $(P \longleftrightarrow Self)$
- The individual with other individuals $(P \longleftrightarrow P)$
- The individual with the social settings of his or her life $(P \longleftrightarrow S)$
- The systems of life in their interactions with one another $(S \longleftrightarrow S)$

These interactions can be expressed in the following formula:

$$HD_{P+S} = f(P \longleftrightarrow Self) \times (P \longleftrightarrow P) \times (P \longleftrightarrow S) \times (S \longleftrightarrow S)$$

that is, the full development of both people and systems is a function of these kinds of interactions.

People	Human Systems	Competencies
People benefit by a working knowledge of their own *developmental* realities and of those with whom they interact:	People benefit by a working knowledge of the systems of social settings of which they are members or leaders:	Both leaders and members of systems need personal and system-related *skills or competencies* to promote development in self and systems:
· *Life stages* (the when of human development) · *Key systems* (the where of human development) · *Developmental tasks* (the challenges of new social roles) · *Developmental crises* (developmental choice points) · *Developmental resources* (the support needed to face both tasks and crises)	· *Immediate* personal settings (family, school, workplace) · The *network* of personal settings (interactions of family, school, workplace, etc.) · *Larger systems* (government, economy, media) in their *direct* effects on people and systems · *Larger systems* (education, church) in their *indirect* effects on people and systems · *Culture* as the most pervasive system providing blueprints for interactions among people and systems	· Skills related to *physical* development · Skills related to *intellectual* development · Skills related to clarifying and constructing *values* · *Self-management* skills · *Interpersonal* skills · *Small-group* skills · The skills of designing, assessing, & running *systems*

the *life skills* needed to work through developmental tasks and involve themselves in, contribute to, cope with, and help change the social settings and systems of life—such people increase the probability of their handling whatever problems of living may arise and of moving in positive ways toward becoming "healthy," "intentional," "self-actualized," "transparent," "effective," or "mature" persons.

A comprehensive model of mature psychosocial development that is a practical, working model is not a luxury for helpers. First of all, such a model enables them to help clients identify what is going right and what is going wrong in their lives. Second, it enables them to help clients set goals that are appropriate in their developmental stage and realistic in terms of both their own inner resources and the resources and constraints of the social settings and systems of their lives. The people-in-systems model, in that it is an outline of or provides a framework for a comprehensive model of mature psychosocial development, is also a model for giving the social sciences away. Such a model is never "finished"; it needs to remain open to continual development and refinement. It also needs to be fashioned into a tool that helpers can actually use in order to deliver services more effectively to clients.

REFERENCES

American Psychiatric Association. *Diagnostic and statistical manual of mental disorders* (3rd ed.). Washington, D.C.: American Psychiatric Association, 1980.

Andrews, E. *The emotionally disturbed family and some gratifying alternatives.* New York: Aronson, 1974.

Bandura, A. Self-efficacy: Toward a unifying theory of behavioral change. *Psychological Review,* 1977, *84,* 191–215. (a)

Bandura, A. *Social learning theory.* Englewood Cliffs, N.J.: Prentice-Hall, 1977. (b)

Berger, P. L., & Neuhaus, R. J. *To empower people: The role of mediating structures in public policy.* Washington, D.C.: American Enterprise Institute for Public Policy Research, 1977.

Bibace, R., & Walsh, M. E. Clinical developmental psychologists in family practice settings. *Professional Psychology,* 1979, *10,* 441–450.

Blocher, D. H. Some implications of recent research in social and developmental psychology for counseling practice. *Personnel and Guidance Journal,* 1980, *58,* 334–336.

Caplan, N., & Nelson, S. D. On being useful: The nature and consequences of psychological research on social problems. *American Psychologist,* 1973, *28,* 199–211.

Cooney, E. W., & Selman, R. L. Children's use of social conceptions: Toward a dynamic model of social cognition. *Personnel and Guidance Journal,* 1980, *58,* 344–352.

Curran, C. A. *Counseling and psychotherapy: The pursuit of values.* New York: Sheed & Ward, 1968.

Edelwich, J. *Burn-out: Stages of disillusionment in the helping professions.* New York: Human Sciences Press, 1980.

Egan, G. *Encounter: Group processes for interpersonal growth.* Monterey, Calif.: Brooks/Cole, 1970.

Egan, G. *Interpersonal living: A skills-contract approach to human-relations training in groups.* Monterey, Calif.: Brooks/Cole, 1976.

Egan, G. *You and me: The skills of communicating and relating to others.* Monterey, Calif.: Brooks/Cole, 1977.

Egan, G. *Being in a group: Working knowledge and skills for effective group participation.* Monterey, Calif.: Brooks/Cole, in preparation.

Egan, G., & Cowan, M. A. *Moving into adulthood: Themes and variations in self-directed development for effective living.* Monterey, Calif.: Brooks/Cole, 1980.

Elkind, D. Child development and counseling. *Personnel and Guidance Journal,* 1980, *58,* 353–355.

Ellis, A. Should some people be labeled mentally ill? *Journal of Consulting Psychology,* 1967, *31,* 435–446.

Erikson, E. H. *Childhood and society* (2nd ed.). New York: Norton, 1963.

Erikson, E. H. *Identity: Youth and crisis.* New York: Norton, 1968.

Frank, J. *Persuasion and healing* (Rev. ed.). Baltimore: Johns Hopkins University Press, 1973.

Gazda, G. M., & Brooks, D. K., Jr. A comprehensive approach to developmental interventions. *Journal for Specialists in Group Work,* 1980, *5,* 120–126.

Gerler, E. R., Jr. Physical exercise and multimodal counseling groups. *Journal for Specialists in Group Work,* 1980, *5,* 157–162.

Goldenberg, I., & Goldenberg, H. *Family therapy: An overview.* Monterey, Calif.: Brooks/Cole, 1980.

Haley, J. *Problem-solving therapy.* San Francisco: Jossey-Bass, 1976.

Hall, E. T. *Beyond culture.* Garden City, N.Y.: Anchor Books, 1977.

Havighurst, R. J. *Human development and education.* New York: Longmans, 1953.

Havighurst, R. J. Social and developmental psychology: Trends influencing the future of counseling. *Personnel and Guidance Journal,* 1980, *58,* 328–333.

Heath, D. H. The maturing person. In G. Walsh & D. Shapiro (Eds.), *Beyond health and normality.* New York: Van Nostrand Reinhold, 1980. (a)

Heath, D. H. Wanted: A comprehensive model of healthy development. *Personnel and Guidance Journal,* 1980, *58,* 391–399. (b)

Hoffman, I. Psychological versus medical psychotherapy. *Professional Psychology,* 1979, *10,* 571–579.

Levinson, D. J., Darrow, C. N., Klein, E. B., Levinson, M. H., & McKee, B. *The seasons of a man's life.* New York: Knopf, 1978.

Lippitt, G. *Visualizing change.* San Diego, Calif.: University Associates Press, 1973.

Marcia, J. E. Development and validation of ego identity status. *Journal of Personality and Social Psychology,* 1966, *3,* 551–558.

Marcia, J. E. Identity six years after: A follow-up study. Mimeographed report, 1975.

Marcia, J. E., & Friedman, M. L. Ego identity status in college women. *Journal of Personality,* 1970, *2,* 249–263.

Maslow, A. H. *Toward a psychology of being* (2nd ed.). New York: Van Nostrand Reinhold, 1968.

McLuhan, M. *Understanding media: The extensions of man.* New York: McGraw-Hill, 1964.

Mills, C. W. *The sociological imagination.* London: Oxford University Press, 1959.

Mische, G., & Mische, P. *Toward a human world order: Beyond the national security straitjacket.* New York: Paulist Press, 1977.

Moore, M. Counselor training: Meeting new demands. *Personnel and Guidance Journal,* 1977, *55,* 359–362.

Morrison, J. A reappraisal of mental health education: A humanistic approach. *Journal of Humanistic Psychology,* 1979, *19,* 43–51.

Muro, J. J., & Engels, D. W. Life coping skills through developmental group counseling. *Journal for Specialists in Group Work,* 1980, *5,* 127–130.

Nelson, R. C. Coping and beyond: Choice awareness as a structured group process. *Journal for Specialists in Group Work,* 1980, *5,* 148–156.

Newman, B. M., & Newman, P. R. *Development through life: A psychosocial approach* (Rev. ed.). Homewood, Ill.: Dorsey Press, 1979.

Nisbet, R. *The quest for community.* London: Oxford University Press, 1969.

Novak, M. Rethinking social policy. *Worldview,* 1979, *22*(7–8), 40–44.

Okun, B. F., & Rappaport, L. J. *Working with families: An introduction to family therapy.* North Scituate, Mass.: Duxbury Press, 1980.

Robinson, E. H., III. Introduction: Life coping skills through the group medium. *Journal for Specialists in Group Work,* 1980, *5,* 117–119.

Rotter, J. C., & Wilson, N. C. A resource guide for life skills training. *Journal for Specialists in Group Work,* 1980, *5,* 177–184.

Rubin, L. B. *Worlds of pain: Life in the working class family.* New York: Basic Books, 1976.

Ryan, W. *Blaming the victim.* New York: Pantheon, 1971.

Sarason, S. B. *The psychological sense of community: Prospects for a community psychology.* San Francisco: Jossey-Bass, 1974.

Schofield, W. *Psychotherapy: The purchase of friendship.* Englewood Cliffs, N.J.: Prentice-Hall, 1964.

Shure, M. B., & Spivack, G. *Problem-solving techniques in childrearing.* San Francisco: Jossey-Bass, 1978.

Spivack, G., Platt, J. J., & Shure, M. B. *The problem-solving approach to adjustment: A guide to research and intervention.* San Francisco: Jossey-Bass, 1976.

Spivack, G., & Shure, M. B. *Social adjustment of young children: A cognitive approach to solving real-life problems.* San Francisco: Jossey-Bass, 1974.

Szasz, T. S. *The myth of mental illness.* New York: Harper & Row, 1961.

Szasz, T. S. *Ideology and insanity.* New York: Doubleday, 1970. (a)

Szasz, T. S. *The manufacture of madness.* New York: Delta, 1970. (b)

Szasz, T. S. *The myth of mental illness: Foundations of a theory of personal conduct* (Rev. ed.). New York: Harper & Row, 1974. (a)

Szasz, T. S. The myth of mental illness: Three addenda. *Journal of Humanistic Psychology,* 1974, *14,* 11–19. (b)

Szasz, T. S. *The myth of psychotherapy.* New York: Harper & Row, 1979.

Warnath, C. F., & Shelton, J. F. The ultimate disappointment: The burned-out counselor. *Personnel and Guidance Journal,* 1977, *55,* 172–175.

White, B. L. Primary prevention: Beginning at the beginning. *Personnel and Guidance Journal,* 1980, *58,* 338–343.

Williams, R. L., & Long, J. D. *Toward a self-managed life style* (2nd ed.). Boston: Houghton Mifflin, 1979.

Wilson, E. S., & Canada, R. M. Preschool groups: A vehicle for teaching life coping skills. *Journal for Specialists in Group Work,* 1980, *5,* 131–134.

CHAPTER THREE

Life Skills Education: A Video-Based Counseling/Learning Delivery System

Winthrop R. Adkins

Winthrop R. Adkins is professor of psychology and education and is director of the R & D Center for Life Skills and Human Resource Development at Teachers College, Columbia University. He has a bachelor's degree from Princeton and master's and doctoral degrees from Columbia. His first postdoctoral job was as a research fellow at Harvard University. He spent four years in the Bedford-Stuyvesant district of New York City as founder and vice-president of the YMCA-sponsored Training Resources for Youth, an antipoverty training center. He has also taught at the City University of New York and has been a fellow at Cornell University/New York Hospital. He is the author of numerous articles on Life Skills and the principal developer of the Adkins Life Skills Program: Employability Skills Series.

Adkins's chapter makes it clear that first-rate skills training programs are not built in a day. He details the development of his programs—one took three years and a half-million dollars. Adkins's programs have been highly successful: more than 350,000 people have participated in his Life Skills/Employability Program alone. Like Egan, Adkins works within a developmental and psychoeducational framework. His programs focus on predictable life problems and crises of particular populations, or, in his terms, "where people hurt." Particularly noteworthy is his four-stage Structured Inquiry learning model, which governs learning sequences aimed at helping people become not only more aware and insightful about their problems but also more knowledgeable and behaviorally competent in coping with them. Adkins was one of the first to make use of carefully produced, provocative video vignettes to pose dilemmas and model solutions as well as provide feedback to the learner. The programs are designed to "dignify the learner" by eliciting the client's own exploration and experimentation until behavioral mastery is achieved.

Life Skills Education (also known as Life Coping Skills or Life Skills Counseling) can best be understood as an effort to create a more effective delivery system for making counseling/learning sources available on a mass scale to large numbers of people from different target groups who are not now receiving help. It is also an effort to improve the rigor of the learning inherent in the counseling process. Like other counseling approaches, Life Skills aims at helping people clarify feelings and values, make decisions and choices, resolve conflicts, gain self-understanding, explore environmental opportunities and constraints, communicate effectively with others, and take personal responsibility for their actions. Yet, unlike those counseling interventions that rely mainly on nonstructured verbal exchanges between practitioner and client, the Life Skills approach makes use of preplanned, carefully developed learning programs using instructional as well as counseling methods to help people learn to cope more effectively with the specific psychological and social problems, crises, and developmental tasks they face throughout life.

Life Skills is part of an increasing trend in the field toward programmatic approaches to coping, exemplified by such problem-focused, structured, media-assisted, experience-based courses and workshops as Parent Effectiveness Training (Gordon, 1975), Structured Learning Therapy (Goldstein, 1973), Media Therapy (Ivey, 1973), assertiveness training, Multiple-Impact Training (Gazda, in press), Relationship Enhancement Therapy (Guerney, 1977), stress-management workshops, and career-education programs. Life Skills also makes use of methods employed by these and other approaches to counselor education (Ivey, 1971, Carkhuff, 1971, and Kagan, 1967): the use of video technology, small-group processes, the breaking down of complex problems into simpler learning tasks, and the integration of affective, cognitive, and behavioral learning.

Unlike approaches that focus on the training of the counselor, who in turn creates the learning experiences for the client, the Adkins Life Skills approach concentrates on *the direct training of the client* through the use of carefully developed sequential learning experiences and multimedia materials that counselors are trained to use. Thus, Life Skills as defined by this author is a full system consisting of a program design and learning model, a set of program development methods, a staff training program, and a series of installation, organizational development, and dissemination processes.

As a full system, Life Skills provides the means for developing programs on a large scale to implement what I have called the "fifth curriculum" (Adkins, 1974), a specific curriculum for helping people at every level of the educational system and at every stage of life learn to cope with the predictable problems of living. It also provides the basis for the design of counseling/learning services that can be transmitted through videodisk, video cassette, and cable to home learning centers.

HISTORY OF THE LIFE SKILLS PROGRAM

It is axiomatic that an intervention in its structure reflects the nature of the problem it was designed to solve. It might be useful to trace this investigator's evolving understanding of the problem and the way in which the Life Skills system was shaped by that understanding. In 1964 the national agenda for the War on Poverty aimed at finding better methods of helping disadvantaged youth and adults become self-reliant, self-directing, employable citizens. Having just completed a Ph.D. in counseling psychology at Teachers College, Columbia University, under Donald Super and having spent a year at Harvard with David McClelland, I was aware of the potential value of psychological concepts and methods for the design of manpower training programs. During my work at a YMCA youth and work program in New York's Bedford-Stuyvesant area, it became quickly apparent that counseling was one of the most critical needs in training programs, yet equally clear that the best counseling methods, as we then knew them, were based on middle-class assumptions and were not very effective in working with this population (Adkins, 1970; Adkins, Rosenburg, & Sharar, 1965). Our observation of the counseling process led to the following analysis:

- Without structure, disadvantaged clients found it difficult to sustain focused discussion on one topic and instead tended to flit from problem to problem without sufficient attention or effort on any one.
- Without an effective means of acquiring new knowledge, groups tended to share and perpetuate their misconceptions and ignorance.
- Without the opportunity to acquire new experience and reflect on it, learners found it difficult to discover new ways of handling current situations and to understand the new situations they would be confronting.
- Unless talk was related to action and an opportunity given for goal setting and reflection, clients tended to become apathetic or overenamored of discussion for its own sake.
- Without a means of practicing the application of knowledge to specific problems in living, clients did not acquire skill in doing so.

These observations suggested that a different kind of counseling program could be designed that would help educationally disadvantaged adults minimize their weaknesses and take full advantage of their strengths. The questions we asked ourselves were—

> Could we not collect and categorize the common problems of our clients and deal with them more efficiently? Could we not define learning objectives based upon what behaviors were necessary to solve the problems which we had collected? Could we not first take advantage of their preference for solving problems and for obtaining knowledge inductively from experience and then gradually introduce them to other means of learning about themselves and their opportunities? Could we not, in effect, reach our counseling goals better if we considered the psycho-social problems of our clients as our curriculum and employed a variety of teaching as well as counseling methods? Why not a curriculum for counseling which would be based upon our clients' actual and predictable developmental problems? [Adkins, 1970, p. 110].

The first Life Skills program was tested at Project Try (Adkins et al., 1965), a $4.5 million antipoverty training program in the Bedford-Stuyvesant area. It was during this period that we coined the term *Life Skills* to describe the kind of behavior-based psychological learning needed to help people cope with predictable developmental tasks. Later the term diffused into the general culture and has since acquired a variety of meanings ranging from those used by other psychologists, such as Gazda, Carkhuff, and Egan, to those used by people in other educational disciplines, such as English as a second language (Jones, 1974) and literacy (Northcutt, 1975).

The initial program made use of problem-centered, experience-based, and behaviorally oriented learning groups and employed a mixture of teaching and counseling methods to facilitate learning. Development of resources and learning activities that could structure the learning sessions was mainly the responsibility of trained teachers and counselors. It was found, however, that practitioners were not able to create the kinds of resources that would adequately meet the design requirements for effective learning. The conclusion was that the learning tasks were too complex and the learning activities and materials needed were too difficult to develop on an as-you-go basis. More experimentation was needed. My colleagues and I had, however, worked out some critical concepts and learning methods during that period that later proved useful.

In the years that followed, I moved my base of operations to Teachers College, Columbia University, and continued the development of the program design. Gradually, the present four-stage learning model was developed, incorporating video and other learning methods. A program development process was created to permit the systematic development of Life Skills units by full-time trained developers. In 1971, with funds from the U.S. Bureau of Adult Basic Education, a Life Skills Development project was established, and work began on making use of the learning model in developing a ten-unit Employability Skills Program (Adkins, Wylie, Grothe, Kessler, & Manuele, 1975) for adults dealing with the psychosocial tasks of choosing, finding, planning, and getting a job. Three years later a field-tested multimedia program with 260 learning components was completed. It was published in 1975 by the Psychological Corporation, a division of Harcourt Brace Jovanovich, which disseminated the program to many schools, training centers, and community agencies throughout the country. In 1979 the Institute for Life Coping Skills, Inc., a nonprofit organization, became the publisher of the *Adkins Life Skills Program: Employability Skills Series.* The Institute has continued to disseminate the program, has revised the videotapes in color, and is now completing a second edition of the program.

Over the past several years, steps have been taken to lay the base at Teachers College for the development of new Life Skills programs for other psychosocial problems of other populations. The R & D Center for Life Skills and Human Resource Development and master's and doctoral specialties to train counselors of adults and psychosocial program developers have been established. A research study (Adkins, Hattauer, Kessler, & Manuele, 1977) on the life-coping problems of unemployed, disadvantaged adults—documenting the psychosocial problems of career development, marriage, parenthood, relations with others, health, community living, and personal development—has been completed, and several experimental videotapes dealing with representative problems have been created. A documentary film on the Employability Skills program and the Life Skills method has been completed and distributed, and a book that will describe both the theoretical and operational aspects of a national program for Life Skills is in progress.

DESCRIPTION OF THE PROGRAM

The complete Life Skills system consists of the Structured Inquiry learning model, the program development system, a staff training program, and installation, organizational development, and dissemination processes. This system permits the development of Life Skills programs for the predictable, common life problems of a wide variety of populations facing common life situations throughout the life span. The programs are designed to be delivered by specially trained teachers as well as counselors in a wide variety of educational, training, industrial, rehabilitation, mental health, and community agency settings. Each Life Skills program consists of a cluster of Life Skills learning units, each of which focuses on a specific coping problem, such as how to present oneself effectively in a job interview, how to avoid escalating marital arguments, or how to listen responsively to children. The four-stage Structured Inquiry learning model (Adkins, 1970, 1973, 1974) serves as a guide for training program developers to create a sequence of learning activities and experiences and supporting video, print, and audio materials for each unit. The structure of each unit provides for the elicitation of feelings as well as prior experiences, the incorporation of new knowledge, and the translation of knowledge into actual behavior. Once a unit is completed, it is tested, revised, and then published. The Life Skills Educator Training Program prepares staff to deliver the Life Skills unit. The development methods and installation process ensure that excellent units are developed and installed effectively in learning centers.

The Structured Inquiry Learning Model

The Life Skills Structured Inquiry learning model is the central core of the Life Skills approach to the delivery of counseling services. Its four stages structure the sequence of learning activities and experiences for learners and the teaching and counseling functions to be performed by Life Skills Educators who will deliver the program. The model also serves as a format for program developers. What follows is a description of how a fully developed Life Skills unit would be delivered by a specially trained Life Skills Educator in a small group of 10 to 15 learners.

A Life Skills group begins with various group-forming activities and with an orientation to the program, often followed by a contracting session in which the learning objectives are explained and the roles and responsibilities of both learners and Life Skills Educators are made explicit and agreed to in advance.

Stimulus Stage.   Each learning unit begins with a provocative presentation of a problem, usually in the form of a dramatic, emotion-arousing five-minute video vignette that depicts a person like the clients confronting a difficult situation and making a number of errors. The emotional impact of the tape and the details presented are designed to stimulate and focus discussion.

Evocation Stage.   In this stage, usually lasting about 45 minutes, the Life Skills Educator (LSE) attempts, through a structured pattern of questions, to elicit from the group elements of the problem that was presented, to identify the critical issues, and to get the group members to describe similar experiences they have had. The LSE makes every effort to elicit feelings, thoughts, and experiences from all group members in order to get the group to define the problem, to suggest solutions to it, and to identify areas for further inquiry. Through convergent and divergent questioning techniques and the skills of paraphrasing, reflecting feelings, and summarizing, the LSE endeavors to *dignify the learners* by helping them realize how much they already know about the problem. As comments are made, they are recorded on flip charts in language as close as possible to that in which they were offered. By the end of the session, the group will become aware of what it feels and already knows about the problem, will have had its curiosity aroused, and will have identified further areas for inquiry.

Objective-Inquiry Stage.   Once Evocation is completed, the learners engage in a variety of learning activities to find out and experience what *others* know about the problem. Through the use of specially prepared video modeling tapes, pamphlets, audiotapes, questionnaires, rating sheets, simulation exercises, and specific learning activities, the LSE tries to expand group members' awareness about the problem conceptually and to help them gain insight into the origins of the problem, its current manifestations and consequences, and what must be done to solve the problem. Prior concepts are challenged, confirmed, and tested by new concepts presented through various exercises. Feelings are explored. Opportunities to acquire new knowledge about how others view or have solved a similar problem are also provided. The predeveloped activities and materials are designed to be used by learners individually or in dyads, triads, or large-group exercises in ways that permit individuals to move at their own pace, make their own decisions, and gain knowledge and experience in their own preferred style, whether through reading, seeing and hearing, experiencing, or discussion. Learners also engage in exercises designed to help them incorporate their new knowledge with their previous understanding and feelings and to practice specific subskills required for solving the problem. Video is used where relevant to model solutions, to present new concepts and knowledge, and to monitor and give feedback on the practice of new behavior.

Application Stage.   The purpose of this stage is to help the learner translate his new understanding, insight, feelings, and knowledge into actual behavior in a simulated or real-life situation. Learners engage in role-playing or simulation exercises that, where possible, are videotaped, rated, and critiqued by themselves, other group members, and the LSE. After feedback the learners are encouraged to repeat the behavior in simulated situations and then later in real-life situations until behavioral mastery is achieved. Throughout this stage the LSE functions as a coach, providing direction, support, and feedback as the learners try to gain increasing comfort in incorporating the new behavior into their basic repertoire. Throughout all four stages the LSE makes every effort to maintain a cohesive, supportive learning group and a nonjudgmental climate in which learners have the freedom to express their feelings, to ask questions, to disagree, and to make mistakes.

Program Development System

Life Skills units are not easy to develop; yet, once fully developed, they can be used and reused indefinitely by diverse groups of learners in many different settings. They are thus cost-effective with long-term usage. Life Skills Developers require special training, and special developmental centers must be established to facilitate the creation of learning units. If developed well, however, Life Skills units can be considerably more effective than those created by busy practitioners on the job. Their ability to be reused permits the cost per student hour to remain relatively low.

The development of Life Skills units involves the following steps or types of activity:

Needs assessment.   Using a method that I have termed "Reconnaissance" (Adkins et al., 1977), the design team tries to find out from a target population "where they hurt." The aim is to find what psychological and social problems the individuals cannot solve—the problems in living they face that cause them emotional pain and distress, such as fear, anxiety, despair, boredom, or hate. The assumption is that beneath the surface of the emotion lies a problem that cannot be solved. Through extensive group and individual interviews the design team makes a major effort to understand the problems as perceived by the person having them. Interviews are also held with significant others, such as parents, employers, and teachers. Reconnaissance interviews are held both to determine what programs should be developed and to assess the individual's competence with respect to particular problems once decisions have been made to develop programs in those areas. The output of the Reconnaissance survey is a kind of taxonomy of life coping problems of a given target group, broken down by areas such as work, marriage, parenting, and personal development.

Derivation of competencies. Problems are then expressed in terms of the behaviors necessary to solve them, and such statements are turned into learning objectives for learning units (Mager, 1962).

Program design. An architectural plan for a four-stage learning unit is then constructed, which specifies all learning activities, media, and sequences. This plan requires considerable conceptual ability to develop. It is important to see that the plan has both external and internal consistency. The plan is rechecked with learners before development.

Development of materials. Development of video, print, and audio materials is a long, time-consuming process (Popham & Baker, 1971). Each media component must be relevant, interesting, and usable by learners with different levels of ability and must perform a particular function within the unit. Video production is difficult to do well, particularly in view of the need to achieve what might be called "emotional validity" and because of the costs of actors, equipment, editing, facilities, and so on.

Test-out and evaluation. After the unit is fully developed, it is tested out in a protected setting by a Life Skills Educator (a specially trained counselor/teacher). The evaluation should at this time focus on intrinsic aspects of the learning units to gather data for subsequent unit revisions. Once revised, the unit should again be tested out in a field setting under more realistic conditions and once again revised on the basis of evaluation data. The unit is then ready for publication and use.

Installation System

Introducing a new program into an existing educational setting is a difficult task, since anything new is likely to be suspect and there are various institutional resistances to any requirements for changes in schedules, staff roles and relationships, and program rhythms.

Before installation in an existing center, administrators and supervisors must fully understand the new program and its requirements. This is usually accomplished through briefing sessions and actual tryouts of the program by the administrators. Such a session is also important because it provides the administrator with the essential criteria for selecting or hiring a staff person who will become the Life Skills Educator.

Life Skills Educator Training

Once selected, the potential Life Skills Educator is trained at a week-long training conference at which he or she is exposed to the Life Skills theory and concepts, is given information about how to install the program, is acquainted with the program activities and materials, and, most important, is specifically trained to carry out the teaching and counseling functions required to deliver effectively a Life Skills unit. The Life Skills Educator receives behavioral practice and feedback in conducting each of the Life Skills stages and specific training in particular skills such as reflecting feelings, paraphrasing comments, asking questions of a divergent or convergent nature, managing the group process, and dealing with predictable adult-student learning problems.

Once trained, the Life Skills Educator returns to his or her center (which has ordered the Life Skills Program) and establishes a Life Skills Learning Laboratory in an appropriate space for confidential small-group discussion, videotaping, and individualized learning. Installation, including recruiting students, orienting community agencies and center staff, and adapting the program to delivery patterns that make sense for a given center and a given adult population, may take several weeks. Frequently it is very helpful for a Life Skills consultant to visit a new center several weeks after initial installation to deal with whatever administrative, scheduling, training, and interpersonal problems have arisen.

THEORY AND RATIONALE

Life Skills as a counseling intervention shares many of the assumptions about the purposes, processes, and desirable outcomes of counseling held in common by theorists of different persuasions (Tyler, 1969; Bergin & Garfield, 1971; Krumboltz & Thoresen, 1969). In particular, Life Skills takes very seriously three major assumptions of counseling:

- Counseling is a process designed to help people cope more effectively with the predictable developmental problems, crises, and problems in living they confront at various stages of their lives. Such problems are those that cause emotional distress, which, if resolved effectively, can lead to satisfaction and the effective use of one's talents but which, if not resolved, can lead to patterns of anger, alienation, and despair.
- Counseling is primarily a process for facilitating personal growth, and it should therefore be available on a preventive, not just a remedial, basis for all people who need help at the various stages of their development.
- Counseling is fundamentally a learning process in which the person with the problem is helped to acquire new knowledge, attitudes, and behavior that will permit him or her to take action to resolve the problem.

What follows is a brief description of the main elements of the theory and rationale underlying the Life Skills approach.

Target Groups and Predictable Problems

One of the central assumptions behind the Life Skills approach is that large numbers of people face common life situations and are thus trying to solve similar psychological and social problems. Although the range of individual difference is great and each individual is unique, we share with significant numbers of other people the need to cope with similar tasks of development, life crises, situations, and events. Because of biological maturation and social expectation (Havighurst, 1953), the tasks of development occur and even recur with some regularity from childhood through adolescence through early adulthood, middle adulthood, and later adulthood. Various developmental theorists, such as Erikson (1956), Super (1957), Knowles (1970), Neugarten (1976), Kohlberg (1966), Sheehy (1974), Gould (1972), and Levinson (Levinson et al., 1978), have begun the process of conceptualizing and mapping the various predictable stages and tasks of personal development, career development, social development, moral development, patterns of marriage and parenthood, and so forth.

A handful of variables can describe different *target groups,* a term we have used for a group facing a common life situation. Different configurations of the following variables define different groups and present reasonably accurate hypotheses and predictions of the kinds of emotional problems people are trying to solve. *Age* is the primary determinant of the kinds and stages of developmental tasks a person is confronting (or reconfronting) at any given time. *Sex* is a variable that modifies age. Although increasingly men and women are facing similar developmental tasks at similar times in their lives, historical/cultural patterns have led to very different developmental tasks, and indeed there will always be some major task/stage differences between the sexes based on biological differences. *Socioeconomic status* is generally a fairly accurate predictor of not only the number and complexity of problems that people have to solve but also the quality and availability of the resources they have to solve them with. Generally, occupational level, educational level, and the availability of problem-solving resources vary directly with socioeconomic status. *Ethnicity* can often indicate the kinds of special cultural influences that help to define both the problems and the resources. *Geographical location* is a variable that operates in a similar fashion to define problems and resources. *Special conditions of life* is a term referring to such variables as being chronically ill, having six children and an unemployed husband, having just been released from prison, or being exceptionally attractive or unattractive.

These variables can help us pinpoint the problems that various people have at various stages of their lives. There are also other problems that we can predict significant numbers of people will have, on the basis of their frequency of occurrence, such as being unjustly accused of a crime, having one's house burn down, being rejected in love, being terminated from a job, or becoming the parent of a physically handicapped child.

A basic assumption of Life Skills is that if a problem is experienced by a number of people in similar ways, a common learning program can be developed that will reflect not only the particular structure of the problem but also the special experiences and learning styles of the target group or subgroup. A second assumption is that there is not an infinite array of solutions to problems, but rather a limited number of workable ones representing different combinations of different solution elements. Several of these solutions can be understood, defined, parsed, and made available to people to select from. A third assumption is that the individuality of learners can be protected and enhanced by a program model that encourages each one to take responsibility for his or her own learning through a process of inquiry that helps learners make their own value choices and create their own syntheses at their own pace. In summary, if similar problems are held in common by large numbers of people, then similar resources are likely to be needed, and it is practical and economically feasible to create common programs for the common problems of particular target groups.

Psychosocial Competence

As Robert White (1966) says,

> Every interaction with another person can be said to have an aspect of competence. Acts directed toward another are said to be, consciously or unconsciously, to have an effect of some kind, and the extent to which they produce this effect can be taken as the measure of competence. . . . When matters of importance are at stake, the aspect of competence is bound to be larger. If we are seeking help or offering it, trying to evoke love or giving it, warding off aggression or expressing it, resisting influence by others or trying to exert influence, the effectiveness of our behavior is a point of vital concern [p. 74].

Each psychosocial task, whether a developmental task, a common life crisis, or the kind of interpersonal or intrapersonal task of everyday life indicated above, requires a behavior or set of behaviors for its solution, and these behaviors can be performed well or poorly. The learning problem ultimately, then, is to help people acquire understanding and knowledge that will lead them to new behaviors that can be tried out and practiced until they achieve competence in the performance of those behaviors.

Acquisition of competence also requires learning of an affective nature, since a task of importance will often generate anticipatory emotional states such as fear of the unknown, anxiety over performance, or apathy resulting from previous failure. These feelings may precede behavioral attempts or accompany them and may be increased or diminished based on the perceived effectiveness of the effort. It is for these reasons that many developmental problems are often considered to be emotional problems, thus obscuring the need for the more competent behaviors.

The effectiveness of behavior in attempting psychosocial tasks is directly related to the quality of cognitive learning. Knowledge influences the formation of working concepts, which, in turn, influence what is perceived and how it is perceived. Perceptions, in turn, expand or limit behavioral possibilities and arouse or diminish emotional states. The knowledge required to solve problems, particularly those that are developmental tasks, does not come neatly from single disciplines but is truly cross-disciplinary. Accomplishment of developmental tasks thus involves complex operations. Whether the task involves making a career choice, taking personal responsibility for avoiding the escalation of a marital argument, or disciplining children, all these aspects of human functioning—the behavioral, the affective, and the cognitive—come into play at every stage of learning about the task and with every successive attempt to accomplish it. Moreover, every problem solution has its own special requirements for knowledge, particular behaviors, and likely accompanying emotional states. The range of concepts, the richness of the repertoire of behaviors, and the emotional flexibility required for effective development in all life areas are enormous.

Most people learn about developmental tasks and other predictable psychosocial problems through processes of socialization in the home, in the school, in the church, and in the community. This kind of learning, however, often perpetuates ignorance across generations. The accident of birth will help or hinder a person's development, depending on who one's parents are. There is often an unfairness of learning opportunity based on socioeconomic level. Persons coming from more advantaged communities tend to have access to better sources for learning how to cope. As Strodtbeck (1964) notes, there is a kind of "hidden curriculum" in the middle-class home that helps people become competent in accomplishing psychosocial tasks.

In today's society most people are experiencing problems in coping regardless of their socioeconomic background. Rapid social change has brought with it changed concepts of work, marriage, parenthood, sexuality, and personal freedom. Parents and members of the older generation, who traditionally have been the transmitters of the intimate knowledge of how to cope, find themselves sometimes more bewildered than the younger generation. Previous cultural solutions passed along through the generations no longer seem to apply in a world of rapidly changing values and assumptions. The major institutions of socialization—family, community, school, church—appear less able to offer solutions to developmental problems than in previous eras. Television has, if anything, increased our sense of the severity of the problems without providing a direction or means for their solution.

Many people today find themselves incompetent in coping with the predictable problems of modern life. Many people face the problems of development alone, as if no one else had ever confronted similar problems. They often struggle without direct access to the experience and knowledge of others and without the benefit of any direct educational efforts. The resulting sense of incompetence experienced by many persons has serious consequences for the individual and for society.

Benefits and Limitations of Counseling

The most frequently prescribed intervention for helping people with emotion-laden problems in living is counseling. In the course of working with many kinds of people over the years, the field of psychology has developed an impressive array of theories, methods, research findings, and concepts that have greatly improved our understanding of the problems of people. These concepts have begun to permeate society and whetted the appetites of many previously ignored groups for personal growth and development.

Although there will always be a need for counseling as we know it today, there are two major limitations of counseling as a delivery system. The first limitation is that there are not, and there are not likely to be, enough trained counselors to meet the demand. In the early 1970s there were about 70,000 counselors (Ginzburg, 1971; Flanagan, 1969), of whom 46,000 worked in schools and colleges serving a student population of about 60 million. (For yardstick purposes, there were 42,000 airline flight attendants in those same years.) In poorer areas the ratio of students to counselors was 2000 to 1, and on the average the ratio was 500:1, the wealthier schools having ratios of 300:1. Similar figures could be given for the 1980s. Without a sufficient number of trained counselors, counseling cannot continue to be the main provider of the learning essential for coping with developmental tasks. The Life Skills approach makes the assumption that by making use of well-designed programs and accompanying training efforts, other kinds of practitioners, such as teachers, nurses, and clergy, can help people learn to cope.

A second limitation of counseling is that the more complex the life problem, the less likely it is that a counselor will be able to create a sufficiently powerful learning experience to help the client achieve behavioral competence in mastering the task. The more needy the learner, the more powerful the learning intervention must be, and the more the intervention will require carefully planned, time-consuming media-based learning methods and materials, which the counselor does not have sufficient resources or skills to develop. To the extent that counseling as a field pays sufficient attention to the cognitive, affective, and behavioral learning processes involved in achieving developmental-task competence, it will inevitably turn its attention toward finding more powerful learning methods. Many of these methods will involve the use of instructional technology and, in particular, video. The Life Skills approach pays particular attention to this issue of learning, which is so inherent in the counseling process.

Design of Problem-Centered Life Skills Units

Unlike several of the efforts at psychological education that aim at helping learners understand the subject matter of psychology, Life Skills adopts the problem-centered focus of counseling itself and a learning process adapted from the behavioral and pedagogical sciences. The life-problem focus of Life Skills is intended to engage learners in problems they themselves want to solve. The Reconnaissance method for determining what problems should be programmed is a way of systematically preplanning the typical kinds of problems that would normally come up during counseling sessions. Motivation remains high, as in counseling, because the learner has a real stake in finding the solution and because every element of the learning process is related to the learner's acquisition of knowledge and skill and demonstrations of his or her competence. Thus, the overall organization of a Life Skills unit focuses the learner's attention, pays attention to issues of learning readiness, keeps the learner involved in the process, and leads to results that the learner can value. One of the reasons that the Life Skills model works is that it makes a specific effort to help the learner derive knowledge and understanding from his or her own experiences. This inductive mode of learning (Taba, 1932; Stratemeyer, Forkner, McKim, & Passow, 1947; Wolsch, 1970) is used throughout the four stages but in particular during the Evocation Stage. In that stage a specific effort is made to help each person realize that he or she has already been a learner and thus to dignify his or her prior learning. We assume that each person already possesses a substantial amount of the knowledge and experience necessary to solve the problem at hand. The main problem is that often learners do not know what they know, and they do not know how to use it, nor do they know how to identify what else they need to know and then how to use that.

Inductive processes are frequently followed by deductive processes in which the learner is exposed to what other people know and is helped to reason from that knowledge to the solution of the problem. These processes take place particularly during the Objective-Inquiry Stage. It is significant also that new knowledge and experience provided during this stage is made available in small steps that can be understood, easily mastered, and rapidly reinforced (Tyler, 1971; Glaser, 1966), thus encouraging further efforts and inquiry. Another principle for the organization of knowledge and experience during this stage is that it should move from concept gradually toward behavior. In addition, although there is a planned sequence of learning activities, there are a variety of options on how that sequence can take place, and there is considerable variety among the activities, using various kinds of media. The learning-style preferences of the learner (Tannenbaum, in preparation) can be accommodated. In the acquisition of new information, special provision is made for learners to proceed at their own pace, either alone or in dyads and triads. Thus, it is possible to group learners with similar abilities within a larger group of learners with higher or lower abilities. The sharing of what has been learned, however, through either discussion or demonstration, can occur within a group with very heterogeneous abilities.

Throughout the unit, but primarily during the Objective-Inquiry Stage, the shaping of behavior occurs by a variety of means. The initial posing of the problem in the Stimulus Stage delimits the problem behaviors to be addressed in the unit. In the Evocation Stage, feelings related to those behaviors are specifically elicited, as is knowledge pertinent to particular behaviors. To distinguish maladaptive behaviors and facilitate acquisition of more adaptive behaviors, modeling, role playing, simulation games, and behavioral rehearsal methods are used (Skinner, 1957; Hubbel, 1957; Lazarus, 1966; Glaser, 1966; Bandura, 1969). Potentially, all kinds of behavioral techniques, such as systematic desensitization, flooding, implosion, and various forms of conditioning and imitation, could be used. It is also likely that the principles and practices of learning that are suited to microcomputers and inter-active video will find effective use in a Life Skills unit.

Video plays a central role in a Life Skills unit. The vignette that poses the initial problem legitimizes the situation the learner finds himself in and gives him permission to recognize his negative feelings about that situation. In addition to illustrating the interaction between behavioral, affective, and cognitive components of the problem, the vignette also aims to stimulate, in the discussion that follows, the learner's awareness that others share a similar problem. The modeling tapes show people like the learners actually changing their behaviors and deriving various benefits from those changes. These tapes help to pinpoint particular aspects of performance that need attention. The positive modeling tapes vicariously convey to learners information and experience they have not been directly exposed to. Video is also used to allow students to monitor and observe their own behavior, and it provides a means for the objective analysis of that behavior within the group. The use of video playback as part of the feedback process is enormously beneficial. Although video is very important, it needs to be used within a planned learning sequence together with other media and specifically designed learning exercises that will create awareness about the problem, insight into its origins, knowledge pertinent to the solution, and an opportunity to translate knowledge into actual behavior that can be practiced to mastery.

APPLICATIONS

It should be clear that Life Skills is essentially a generic system for the design, development, and delivery of psychosocial learning programs applicable to a wide variety of target groups for an almost infinite array of emotion-laden life problems. As I indicated earlier, the most extensive application of the Life Skills approach has been what is called the Adkins Life Skills Program: the Employability Skills Series for disadvantaged adults and youth. The ten-unit Employability Skills Program, described next, deals with the psychosocial problems of choosing, finding, getting, and holding a job and preparing for a career.

It is well known that many educationally disadvantaged persons have limited exposure to the world of work. Many of them come from homes with no role model of a worker, from inadequate schools, and from disorganized communities. Many are women who found themselves performing homemaker roles and consequently did not prepare for the demands of the world of paid work. With limited knowledge about work, little awareness of the vocational choice process, low levels of aspiration for themselves, and a basic belief that they must take whatever they can get, the poor are ill equipped to cope with the predictable tasks of vocational development. Since vocational development is a longitudinal process (Super, 1957; Crites, 1975; Osipow, 1975) that starts in childhood and continues into adulthood, the years of deprivation have also limited their knowledge of themselves as workers—their interests, their abilities, their values, and their possession of various interpersonal, social, and self-management skills needed to succeed in educational and training institutions as well as in the workplace. In effect, many have missed confronting a majority of the developmental tasks of vocational development.

The Employability Skills Series is based on the tasks of vocational development (Super, Crites, Hummel, Moser, Overstreet, & Warnath, 1957) and vocational enjoyable, and competence-building way, with the vocational development tasks they never had an opportunity to learn. At the same time, this confrontation helps learners to realize that they already know a lot more about the problem than they think they do.

The Employability Skills Series is based on the tasks of vocational development (Super, Crites, Hummel, Moser, Overstreet, & Warmuth, 1957) and vocational maturity. These tasks were further specified and defined in terms of additional tasks and problems, alternative conceptions, and strengths and skill deficiencies of disadvantaged adults identified during the Reconnaissance process. The individual Life Skills unit definitions, the learning objectives, and the activities represent a specification and a refinement of the tasks of vocational development. The Life Skills unit titles reflect these tasks: *Who I Am and Where I Want to Go* (self-exploration), *Ten Occupational Fields: How Do I Explore Them* (occupational information and vocational exploration), *Jobs and Training: Beginning the Search* and *Employment Agencies and Personal Contacts* (both these units focus on formal and informal resources and networks for exploration), *Choosing a Good Job for Myself* (developing alternatives for vocational choice and decision making), *Planning for Personal Goals* and *Developing a Vocational Plan* (both these units deal with setting goals and making plans to achieve goals), *Looking Good on Paper* and *The Job Interview: How to Be Effective* (both these units deal with applying for and obtaining employment), and *Keeping My Job: Habits That Help* (identifying and confronting work-adjustment problems).

This application of the Life Skills approach, the Employability Skills Series, includes over 265 video, print, and audio components. The learning activities, sequences, and materials in this program are specifically developed for the reading level and the learning styles of disadvantaged and underprepared adults and youth. For example, all written materials are also available in an audiotape version, and there is a significant reliance on video to pose problems, model solutions, and monitor the acquisition of behavior. The program is too extensive to describe fully here. A more complete description can be obtained from the author.

Applications of the Employability Skills Program

Since 1975 over 300 Life Skills Laboratories using the Employability Skills Program have been established. Although the concentration is mainly on the East Coast, the program is being used in 35 states by the following kinds of organizations: CETA (Manpower Training), Adult Basic Education, community colleges, high schools, prisons, drug rehabilitation programs, vocational/technical schools, YMCAs, OICs, Urban Leagues, hospitals, and community agencies specializing in women returning to the labor force, displaced homemakers, alcoholics, former mental patients, Vietnam veterans, Indochinese and Spanish-speaking immigrants, and the physically handicapped. It is estimated that over 350,000 people have participated in the Life Skills/Employability Skills Program. The program has been used with people as young as junior high school students during summer youth programs and with senior citizens in programs run by the Urban League. Most participants are from the intended population, the educationally disadvantaged and underprepared, but some have been former teachers and social workers needing to brush up their employability skills before obtaining employment.

In a majority of the centers and institutions, Life Skills has been installed in conjunction with other programs such as basic education (reading and math), vocational training, English as a second language, high school equivalency preparation, and leisure activities. It works most effectively when schedules are carefully planned so that students can have a combination of different kinds of educational activities in a given week. Delivery patterns vary considerably from institution to institution. A most desirable pattern is to deliver Life Skills in two two-hour blocks each week for several successive weeks. This kind of spaced learning interspersed with other life and educational activities tends to facilitate lasting acquisition and incorporation of new attitudes and behaviors. Another pattern is to give Life Skills for intensive seven-hour days, five days a week, for two or three weeks in succession. This produces a kind of immersion learning, but it is often too intense for some learners, who find it difficult to spend that amount of concentrated time thinking about themselves and their future. Another pattern is to give it in a workshop format in one or two all-day sessions periodically. Generally a unit can be given in a day. The workshop format fits in with most institutional schedules, but generally most groups need more than just one or two units. Another pattern is to try to fit Life Skills into a 50-minute hour once a week. This has the advantage of not disrupting sacred schedules, but it has the disadvantage of never having sufficient time for small-group learning activities. We have generally found that less than an hour and a half per session or more than 15 members in the group effectively prevents the building of essential group rapport, trust, and spirit of cooperation.

Other Life Skills Learning Units

Since the initial conception of Life Skills in 1964, numerous professionals have been trained at Teachers College and in workshops to develop Life Skills units for a variety of populations and problems. Programs have been developed for disadvantaged adults and adolescents in rural Canada, for Native American parents in Head Start programs, and in a variety of urban school systems. Students as well as staff and other professionals have designed Life Skills units to deal with problems of marriage, parenthood, separation and divorce, depression, problems on the job, career development in business and industry, health, death and dying, teacher and counselor training, supervisory and management training, and many others. A wide variety of units have been designed in the process of learning program-design skills, but their full development and utilization have so far been limited by a lack of funds.

Limitations

On the surface, the Life Skills approach would appear to have a number of limitations: it is expensive, it uses video and audio as well as print, programs are expensive to produce and require equipment. Staff development requires attention, and the program takes more time to deliver than is usually allocated to counseling services. It may be that these factors are obstacles that initially prevent some institutions from installing it. It has been our experience, however, that these really are not limitations but in fact may be advantages. Once an administrator begins to understand what Life Skills will do, somehow he or she finds the money for the program, equipment, and training and the time for the delivery. This generally occurs in institutions that are held accountable for placement rates, such as employment and training programs and, increasingly, community colleges. The reason the cost of the program is sometimes an advantage is that it often ensures that the program will be used. The video will often be one of the most welcome supports for an administrator and a Life Skills Educator who must convince a board of education or a funding agency that learning is in fact taking place in the institution. Because of the emotional appeal of the Life Skills tapes and learning processes, video is a very effective public-relations device. In addition, the size of the program and the space it occupies can often dramatize the importance of human development learning much more effectively than a counseling office or a counselor can. It is simply more to point to, more to use to demonstrate that 200 hours are required for this important kind of learning.

With regard to the overall Life Skills system itself, the expense and time required to develop high-quality learning units seem to be obstacles. Our Employability Skills Series took three years and almost a half-million dollars to develop. However, when one considers the number of years such a well-developed program can be used, the number of learners who can make use of it, and the cost of the alternatives, the cost is not great. New units would take less time and money because we now know what we are doing, but still the cost is considerable. Another limitation is that systematic program development requires carefully trained personnel to design and develop the units, sufficient time, and the appropriate setting. All these factors may have the disadvantage of concentrating the development of the Life Skills learning units in the hands of a few institutions. This could increase the dangers of central-ized control, insidious orthodoxy in program development, and an increasing remoteness from the real needs of the learner. These results need not occur, however; the same kinds of checks and balances that now exist in other areas of professional activity can be instituted here as well, provided the counseling profes-sions are alert to the dangers.

Video Applications

We are about to enter a new era in which the video cassette and the video disk, the cable, the computer, and the satellite will transform the American home into a learning center. The capacity for storing and playing fast-action and slow-action dramatic material on video will have a profound effect on the technology for teaching Life Skills. It will be possible to break complex behaviors into increasingly minute segments for analysis, modeling, and replication and to draw on a vast variety of modeling sources and experts at the push of a button. The programming required will be complex, and the attendant development systems, or scaffolding, for those program development efforts will be extensive. They are clearly within the technological possibilities that are known today and even now are being readied for mass use.

In the days of the horse it was inconceivable that there would one day be millions of miles of macadam roads, thousands of gas stations, hundreds of corporations producing cars and parts for cars, specialized finance systems, legal systems, and technologies devoted specifically to the automobile. It is similarly difficult now to conceive that one day soon there will be thousands of Life Skills units available for many life problems of many target groups. There will be ways of tailor-making specific programs for persons at different developmental stages, from different socioeconomic groups, and with different learning styles. There will be provisions for rapid access to continuously updated knowledge contained in a wide variety of materials and formats. In addition to psychological knowledge and the personal experiences and behavioral models of other similar and different people, the learner will have access to relevant poetry, literature, history, sociological and economic theory, and the like as resources for understanding options and fashioning solutions to his or her own problems. With the world's resources at their fingertips, no longer will individuals have to solve their problems as if no one in the world had ever had them before. They will be able to draw on the human experience, formulating their alternatives and perfecting their moves.

RESEARCH

My major focus over the last 18 years has been on the development of the Life Skills concept, learning model, and development systems and the Employability Skills Series rather than on research. In recent years, however, a number of research studies have investigated the primary and secondary effects of the intervention on clients. Other studies have used the Life Skills design and development concepts for defining developmental tasks in greater specificity and for designing Life Skills learning units to address specific coping problems of different target populations. Another research direction has been initiated with studies that extend Life Skills as a development system.

Field Tests of the Life Skills System

As has been discussed, the Employability Skills Program aims at providing a different kind of counseling system for disadvantaged adults and adolescents experiencing, as LoCascio (1964) has called it, late, delayed, or impaired vocational development. To assess the effectiveness of this intervention as a means of modifying the vocational maturity of disadvantaged learners, Manuele (1980) developed a measure of vocational maturity appropriate for use with a disadvantaged adult population. The measure was based on existing vocational development theory (Super et al., 1957) and on the extension of that theory represented in the Life Skills intervention. The measure consists of a structured in-depth interview schedule with accompanying detailed content-analysis scoring procedures. Manuele administered the instrument as a pretest to a group of unemployed adults aged 25–53, who then participated in an intensive ten-week Life Skills/Employability Skills Program. After the intervention, Manuele readministered the vocational maturity measure. The results showed that the Life Skills Program was effective in modifying the subjects' overall vocational maturity. Significant differences were found between pretest and posttest scores on each of the following eight scales included in Manuele's measure: Orientation to Education; Orientation to Work; Concern with Choice; Self-Appraisal: Interests and Abilities; Self-Appraisal: Personality Characteristics; Self-Appraisal: Values; Exploring Occupations; and Use of Resources. Significant gains were also found on attitudinal variables related to subjects' belief in the value of accomplishing vocational development tasks and to their confidence in their own ability to master these tasks. This most comprehensive study points the way toward similar kinds of studies that need to show linkages among the theory of a particular set of developmental tasks, a specific population, special assessment techniques, and a particular kind of intervention.

Wald (1981) examined the relationship between the stated behavioral objectives for a number of Life Skills learning units and the actual behavioral outcomes of each of these units. Using an adolescent Black high school dropout population, he found significant changes in the subjects' ability to describe their vocationally related personal characteristics, to describe appropriate occupational alternatives related to these characteristics, to complete employment application forms effectively, and to conduct employment interviews that, in the judgment of fellow students, the LSE, and independent observers, would have effectively impressed an employment interviewer. Wald made use of specially constructed criterion-referenced measures in a post-only control design and established that these Life Skills units were effective in producing the intended behavioral change.

Grothe (1974) examined the effectiveness of the Life Skills Program in helping welfare recipients acquire essential job-interviewing skills. His study also examined the separate and combined contributions of video modeling and print-based information on the acquisition of interview behaviors. His major hypothesis that the program would be successful in modifying complex interviewing behaviors was confirmed. However, he also found that video-based modeling was as effective a learning tool as a combination of video and print-based materials, thus raising questions that need to be pursued with further research on the particular contribution of video, print, audio, and other means for learning behavior-oriented knowledge.

In 1978 a study was conducted in New York State at 11 Adult Basic Education learning centers across the state to determine whether the Life Skills Program had been successful in modifying specific vocational knowledge and behavior and what effect it had had on the overall performance of students in the learning centers

(Adkins, Carr, Epifania, & Shaeffer, 1982). Two hundred twenty-seven students were rated by their LSE's before and after the program and also rated themselves on a number of characteristics. There were consistent gains in every learning center on such vocationally related tasks as learning about one's interests and abilities, exploring occupational fields, finding out how to get into training programs, learning how to use employment services, writing business letters, completing a job application form, completing a successful job interview, and learning responsibilities as an employee. Changes were reported across all 11 centers for members of many special groups served by the program in the four months when the study was conducted: women reentering the labor market, addicts and former addicts, offenders and ex-offenders, welfare mothers, Vietnam veterans, migrant laborers, manpower program trainees, handicapped students, high school dropouts, the elderly, and recent immigrants.

The students enjoyed the program: 97.3% would recommend it to their friends, 47.8% said "one of the best," and 50% said "a good program." It is noteworthy that 50.9% attended all sessions during the four months of the study, 39.5% missed occasionally, and only 9.5% missed frequently. This is particularly striking because inconsistent attendance is one of the major problems experienced by learning centers with this population. Other results of the study were that students improved their ability to express themselves orally and in writing as well as to participate in groups, according to the instructors: 72.7% improved in self-confidence and their ability to speak in a group, 62.2% improved in their ability to express ideas in writing, 64.4% showed improved motivation for learning. In self-ratings, 79.9% of the students reported that their Life Skills experience caused them to work harder in their other Adult Basic Education classes, 67.4% said they learned more about themselves, and 74.7% reported increased motivation for employment by the end of the program. The results of this study, which took place in centers that had been operating Life Skills Programs for about five years, indicate that Life Skills is successful as an intervention and as an ongoing part of the Adult Basic Education program in New York State.

Joseph (1980) studied posttraining outcomes of the Life Skills Program. Her samples included 257 out-of-school, out-of-work Black youths between ages 16 and 19 enrolled in ten-week Employability Skills Programs conducted over a ten-year period by the Urban League in Newark, New Jersey. She found that 77% of the students were successfully placed in schools or in unsubsidized employment: 20.6% returned to high school, 16.0% went on to higher education, 13.6% were placed in technical training programs, and 32.0% were placed in unsubsidized employment (some were placed both in employment and in educational programs). The rate of employment/educational placements ranged from 58% to 92% in individual cycles. These figures compare very favorably with placement figures from other programs in the same area, which show that without help only 20% of this population attain work or education and, with some formal CETA training, 40% are positively placed.

Williams (1975) made use of the Life Skills model and design processes in developing a program for Native American parents of Head Start children in the Dakotas. Her program was aimed at helping mothers in particular understand the operation of the Head Start center sufficiently well to play a participative role as parents, members of advisory committees, and members of the community. Life Skills learning units were developed to train parents in various evaluative and leadership functions. Williams found that the methods were successful in increasing parents' competence and in producing the kind of attitudinal change essential in making them feel comfortable with their role. Friedman (1980) used the Reconnaissance method in defining the range of potential learning units and objectives for a program designed to help Jewish high school students cope more effectively with the problems of transition in choosing, gaining admission to, and getting established in a college. His study has helped identify the range of problems as perceived by high school seniors and college freshmen and sophomores as they move toward further independence. Tester (1981) used the four-stage learning model as a means of structuring workshop training of disadvantaged college students in person-perception skills and student/teacher interactions. Because the units were not fully developed with all the appropriate learning activities and materials, their effectiveness as an intervention was limited. The treatment group did, however, exhibit more internal responsibility for academic performance than the control group. Several hypotheses related to the attribution of hostility to teachers were not confirmed.

Studies for Developing the Life Skills System

It has long been our aim to help to establish procedures for mapping the psychosocial problems faced by different target groups at different stages of their lives. The purpose of this effort is to be able to describe client needs more effectively as well as to provide the basis for the design of learning units that can meet those needs. We felt that a taxonomy of psychosocial needs, however crude, would help to dramatize the possibilities of psychosocial programming in adult education centers. In 1976 the Life Skills Center at Teachers College conducted a survey in five representative cities in New York State. This preliminary study, using the Reconnaissance method, inventoried the kinds of emotional problems faced by disadvantaged adults in major areas of living. Problems were grouped according to categories related to work, marriage, parenthood, personal development, and so on. One result of this study is that it led to the development of 20 illustrative videotapes depicting such problems as coping with test anxiety, conflicts between younger and older students, dealing with bureaucratic problems, expressing oneself politically, disciplining children, managing home and work responsibilities, and coping with escalating marital arguments.

In 1977 a similar and much more extensive Reconnaissance study entitled *Where They Hurt: A Study of the Life Coping Problems of Unemployed Adults* (Adkins et al., 1977) was conducted. As the name implies, the study aimed at identifying the psychosocial coping problems experienced by such unemployed and underemployed persons as welfare mothers, high school dropouts, Vietnam veterans, single parents, the foreign born, native-born illiterates, unemployed blue-collar workers, ex-offenders and ex-addicts, and Blacks. Group and individual interviews were conducted with 258 persons. The interviews were directed at helping the subjects describe the problems they were experiencing, the consequences, what they perceived to be the underlying causes, and what they had attempted to do to solve them. The problems collected were grouped according to seven categories: occupational and career problems, problems of living in the community, problems of personal growth and development, problems in relating to others, medical and health problems, marriage and family problems, and problems of being a parent. The problems so identified are very familiar to practicing counselors and psychologists. They are not, however, sufficiently well known by educators, administrators, and policy makers who determine what resources are going to be available for the solution of such problems. It is hoped that studies like this will be extended further so that these problems can be normed on a national basis across different target groups.

The studies described represent a beginning of the research needed to evaluate the effectiveness of the various programs, to extend the Life Skills concept to other populations and problems, and to create the kind of taxonomic systems that will lead to the design of better interventions. What has been established to date is that the Employability Skills Series, as the first of, we hope, several carefully developed Life Skills interventions, is effective in producing changes in knowledge, attitudes, and behavior. Other studies also suggest that changes in these behaviors produce very interesting secondary changes in learners that improve their overall performance in educational and work programs. These studies also indicate that the design concepts in the Life Skills system can be transmitted to other professionals through training and can be applied to a wide variety of problems and populations.

CONCLUSION

Throughout this chapter I have tried to emphasize the importance of predesigned counseling/learning programs for helping people learn to cope with complex, predictable problems of development throughout the life span. I have argued that predesigned and prepackaged Life Skills Programs are necessary (1) to make counseling/learning available on a mass scale to the many groups that need help but are not now getting it and (2) to increase the power of counseling/learning beyond what can be achieved by talking and listening, by incorporating a variety of pedagogical methods such as modeling, simulation, small-step learning with immediate reinforcement, and behavioral rehearsal, while retaining the emphasis of counseling on psychological content and attention to feelings and on interpersonal and group processes.

I have also described the theory and rationale, the four-stage learning model, and the program development infrastructure for a Life Skills system that has evolved over the past 18 years from our first attempt to find more effective counseling methods for disadvantaged learners.

It is gratifying that many of the predictions we made years ago about learning, programming, and the use and acceptance of technology in the service of counseling goals were correct. As we look toward the future, it is clear that we are now in the midst of what an earlier Carnegie Commission report (1972) called the "fourth revolution" in education, the electronics revolution, which is expected to have an impact similar to those produced by the invention of the printing press and the movement of education from the home to the school. Television and the computer are already beginning to intrude on the consciousness of the education and counseling professions, even though today they are used minimally. Other trends in education, such as the movement toward competency-based education (Burns & Klingstedt, 1973), behavioral objectives (Krathwohl & Payne, 1971), criterion-referenced measurement (Popham, 1971), individualization of instruction (Gibbons, 1971), and the affective curriculum (Borton, 1970), signal an awareness that the instructional process is much more complex than previously believed and makes the development of predesigned curricula virtually inevitable. The day is almost here when we will no longer rely on overworked teachers and counselors to create *ad hoc* learning programs with minimal assistance from curriculum consultants, publishers, and universities.

Both these trends—the greater availability of electronic media and a greater awareness of the complexities of instruction—will, I predict, accelerate the development and use of Life Skills programs and what I have described elsewhere as the "fifth curriculum" for schools, colleges, and lifelong-learning centers (Adkins, 1974). Whether we succeed as a society in developing the necessary linkages between the mass needs of people for learning coping skills, the requirements of learning, and the opportunities for delivery of that learning will depend on the quality of our educational designs and the ways in which programs are developed. It is my hope that the Life Skills system of design and delivery will make a contribution toward that effort.

REFERENCES

Adkins, W. R. Life skills: Structured counseling for the disadvantaged. *Personnel and Guidance Journal,* 1970, *49*(2), 108–116.

Adkins, W. R. Life skills education for adult learners. *Adult Leadership,* 1973, *22*(2), 55–58, 82–84.

Adkins, W. R. Life coping skills: A fifth curriculum. *Teachers College Record,* 1974, *25,* 509–526.

Adkins, W. R., Carr, N. W., Epifania, C., & Shaeffer, M. *Life skills education in New York State.* Albany: New York State Department of Education, 1982.

Adkins, W. R., Hattauer, E., Kessler, M., & Manuele, C. Where they hurt: A study of the life coping problems of unemployed adults. Unpublished manuscript, Teachers College, Columbia University, 1977.

Adkins, W. R., Rosenburg, S., & Sharar, P. *Training resources for youth: A comprehensive operational plan for a demonstration research training center for disadvantaged youth.* New York: Training Resources for Youth, 1965.

Adkins, W. R., Wylie, P., Grothe, M., Kessler, M., & Manuele, C. *Adkins Life Skills Program: Employability Skills Series.* New York: Psychological Corporation, 1975.

Bandura, A. *Principles of behavior modification.* New York: Holt, Rinehart & Winston, 1969.

Bergin, A. E., & Garfield, S. L. (Eds.). *Handbook of psychotherapy and behavior change: An empirical analysis.* New York: Wiley, 1971.

Borton, T. *Reach, touch and teach.* New York: McGraw-Hill, 1970.

Burns, R. W., & Klingstedt, J. L. (Eds.). *Competency-based education: An introduction.* Englewood Cliffs, N.J.: Educational Technologies Publications, 1973.

Carkhuff, R. R. *Development of human resources: Education, psychology and social.* New York: Holt, Rinehart & Winston, 1971.

Carnegie Commission on Higher Education. *The fourth revolution: Instructional technology in higher education.* New York: McGraw-Hill, 1972.

Crites, J. O. Foreword. In J. S. Picou & R. E. Campbell (Eds.), *Career behavior of special groups.* Columbus, Ohio: Charles E. Merrill, 1975.

Erikson, E. H. Growth and crises of the "healthy personality." In C. Kluckhohn & H. A. Murray (Eds.), *Personality in nature, society and culture* (2nd ed.). New York: Knopf, 1956.

Flanagan, J. C. The implication of project talent and related research for guidance. *Measurement and Evaluation of Guidance* 2(2), Summer 1969, 116-123.

Friedman, J. L. A life coping skills approach to guiding college-bound Jewish students. Unpublished doctoral dissertation, Teachers College, Columbia University, 1980.

Gazda, G. M. Multiple Impact Training: A model for teaching training in life skills. In G. M. Gazda (Ed.), *Innovations to group psychotherapy* (2nd ed.). Springfield, Ill.: Charles C Thomas, in press.

Gibbons, M. *Individualized instruction.* New York: Teachers College Press, 1971.

Ginzburg, E. *Career guidance: Who needs it, who provides it, who can improve it?* New York: McGraw-Hill, 1971.

Glaser, R. The design of instruction. *Bulletin,* Learning Research and Development Center, University of Pittsburgh, 1966.

Goldstein, A. P. *Structured learning therapy.* New York: Academic Press, 1973.

Gordon, T. *Parent Effectiveness Training.* New York: New American Library, 1975.

Gould, R. The phases of adult life: A study in developmental psychology. *American Journal of Psychiatry,* 1972, *129*(5), 521-531.

Grothe, M. Training welfare recipients in adult education programs in the acquisition of employment interviewing skills. Unpublished doctoral dissertation, Teachers College, Columbia University, 1974.

Guerney, B. G., Jr. *Relationship enhancement: Skill-training programs for therapy, problem prevention, and enrichment.* San Francisco: Jossey-Bass, 1977.

Havighurst, R. J. *Human development and education.* New York: Longmans, Green, 1953.

Hubbel, A. Two person role playing for guidance in social adjustment. *Group Psychology,* 1957, 249-254.

Ivey, A. *Microcounseling: Innovations in interviewing training.* Springfield, Ill.: Charles C Thomas, 1971.

Ivey, A. Media therapy: Educational change planning for psychiatric patients. *Journal of Counseling Psychology,* 1973, *20,* 338-343.

Jones, M. N. Relevant English for the foreign born. Unpublished manuscript, Columbia University, 1974.

Joseph, R. W. The youth employability skills program of the Urban League of Essex County. Unpublished report, 1980.

Kagan, N. I. *Studies in human interaction: Interpersonal process recall stimulated by videotape.* East Lansing: Education Publication Services, College of Education, Michigan State University, 1967.

Kohlberg, L. Moral education in the schools: A developmental view. *School Review,* Spring 1966, *74*(1), 1-30.

Knowles, M. S. *The modern practice of adult education: Andragogy versus pedagogy.* New York: Association Press, 1970.

Krathwohl, D. R., & Payne, D. A. Defining and assessing educational objectives. In R. L. Thorndike (Ed.), *Educational measurement.* Washington, D.C.: American Council on Education, 1971.

Krumboltz, J. D., & Thoresen, C. E. (Eds.). *Behavioral counseling: Cases and techniques.* New York: Holt, Rinehart & Winston, 1969.

Lazarus, A. A. Behavioral rehearsal vs. non-directive therapy vs. advice in effecting behavior change. *Behavior Research and Therapy,* 1966, *4,* 200–212.

Levinson, D. J., Darrow, C. N., Klein, E. B., Levinson, M. H., & McKee, B. *The seasons of a man's life.* New York: Knopf, 1978.

LoCascio, R. Delayed and impaired vocational development: A neglected aspect of vocational development theory. *Personnel and Guidance Journal,* 1964, *42,* 885–887.

Mager, R. F. *Preparing instructional objectives.* Belmont, Calif.: Fearon, 1962.

Manuele, C. The definition, assessment and modification of vocational maturity in disadvantaged adults. Unpublished doctoral dissertation, Teachers College, Columbia University, 1980.

Neugarten, B. L. Adaptation and the life cycle. *Counseling Psychologist,* 1976, *6*(2), 16–20.

Northcutt, N. *The adult performance level study.* Austin: University of Texas at Austin, 1975.

Osipow, S. The relevance of theories of career development to special groups: Problems, needed data, and implications. In J. S. Picou & R. E. Campbell (Eds.), *Career behavior of special groups.* Columbus, Ohio: Charles E. Merrill, 1975.

Popham, W. J. (Ed.). *Criterion-referenced measurement: An introduction.* Englewood Cliffs, N.J.: Educational Technology Publications, 1971.

Popham, W. J., & Baker, E. L. *Planning and instructional sequence.* Englewood Cliffs, N.J.: Prentice-Hall, 1971.

Rugg, H. *Curriculum-making: Past and present.* New York: Arno Press, 1969.

Sheehy, G. *Passages: Predictable crises of adult life.* New York: E. P. Dutton, 1974.

Skinner, B. F. *Verbal behavior.* Englewood Cliffs, N.J.: Prentice-Hall, 1957.

Stratemeyer, F. B., Forkner, H. L., McKim, M. G., & Passow, A. H. *Developing a curriculum for modern living.* New York: Teachers College Press, 1947.

Strodtbeck, F. L. The hidden curriculum of the middle class home in Hunnicutt. In C. William (Ed.), *Urban education and cultural deprivations.* Syracuse, N.Y.: Syracuse University Press, 1964.

Super, D. E. *Psychology of careers.* New York: Harper & Row, 1957.

Super, D. E., Crites, J., Hummel, R., Moser, H., Overstreet, P. L., & Warnath, C. *Vocational development: A framework for research.* (Monograph.) New York: Teachers College Press, 1957.

Taba, H. *The dynamics of education: a methodology of progressive educational thought.* London: Trench, Trubner, 1932.

Tannenbaum, A. J. Taxonomic instruction for disabled learners. New York. In preparation for publication, Teachers College, Columbia University.

Tester, L. Academic coping-skills training and the attribution-related motivation of disadvantaged college students. Unpublished doctoral dissertation, Teachers College, Columbia University, 1981.

Tyler, L. *The work of the counselor.* New York: Appleton-Century-Crofts, 1969.

Tyler, R. W. Some persistent questions on the defining of objectives. In M. B. Kapfer, *Behavioral objectives in curriculum development.* Englewood Cliffs, N.J.: Educational Technology Publications, 1971.

Wald, A. The effects of life skills education on the employability and locus of control of unemployed minority youth. Unpublished doctoral dissertation, Teachers College, Columbia University, 1981.

White, R. W. Sense of interpersonal competence: Two case studies and some reflections on origins. In R. W. White (Ed.), *The study of lives.* New York: Atherton Press, 1966.

Williams, L. R. Mending the hoop: A case study of roles, desired responsibilities and goals for parents of children in tribally sponsored head start programs. Unpublished doctoral dissertation, Teachers College, Columbia University, 1975.

Wolsch, R. A. *Poetic composition through the grades: A language sensitivity program for teachers.* New York: Teachers College Press, 1970.

CHAPTER FOUR

Structured Learning Therapy: Background, Procedures, and Evaluation

Arnold P. Goldstein

Arnold P. Goldstein earned his Ph.D. at Pennsylvania State University. He is a professor of psychology at Syracuse University, where he directs the University Counseling and Psychotherapy Center as well as the Center for Research on Aggression. His career-long concern, both as a researcher and as a clinician, has been to enhance the effectiveness of psychotherapy. Dr. Goldstein is the author or editor of 21 books and over 60 articles on active therapeutic ingredients, research methods, behavior-change procedures, aggression control, and the teaching of prosocial skills. His books include *Therapist-Patient Expectancies in Psychotherapy, Psychotherapy and the Psychology of Behavior Change, Psychotherapeutic Attraction, The Lonely Teacher, Police Crisis Intervention, Hostage, Structured Learning Therapy,* and *Skill Training for Community Living.*

N. Jane Gershaw

N. Jane Gershaw earned her Ph.D. from Syracuse University. She is a clinical psychologist at the Syracuse Veterans Administration Mental Hygiene Clinic and is assistant professor of psychology at Syracuse University and clinical assistant professor of psychiatry at the State University of New York, Upstate Medical Center. Gershaw specializes in group psychotherapy. She has been active in training professional and paraprofessional group psychotherapists and in developing psychoeducational and group-therapy techniques for psychiatric and nonpsychiatric populations.

Robert P. Sprafkin

Robert P. Sprafkin earned his B.A. at Dartmouth College, his M.A. and Professional Diploma at Columbia University Teachers College, and his Ph.D. at Ohio State University. He directs the Day Treatment Center for the Syracuse Veterans Administration Hospital and is adjunct associate professor of psychology at Syracuse University and clinical assistant professor of psychiatry at the State University of New York, Upstate Medical Center. He has written numerous journal articles and is coeditor of *Working with Police Agencies* and coauthor (with Goldstein and Gershaw) of *Skill Training for Community Living: Applying Structured Learning Therapy* and *I Know What's Wrong but I Don't Know What to Do about It.*

Structured Learning Therapy, according to Goldstein, Gershaw, and Sprafkin, was designed to "meet the needs, life-styles, and environmental realities of the lower class, since traditional methods of treatment have proved grossly inadequate and inappropriate for this population." Attacking the Procrustean tendency to make the patient fit the therapy (a "conformity" prescription), the authors set out to reformulate psychotherapy to fit the patient (a "reformity" prescription). The major components of Structured Learning Therapy are modeling (using audio-cassette performances of 59 living skills), role playing, performance feedback, and transfer of training. The authors' attention to transfer of training methods in the Structured Learning model is impressive and accounts in large part for the high levels of skill transfer shown by SLT trainees.

In most nations, the implications of a patient's social class for his or her psychotherapeutic treatment destiny are numerous, pervasive, and enduring. If the patient is lower-class, such implications are decidedly and uniformly negative. It has been consistently shown that, in comparison with patients at higher social-class levels, the lower-class person seeking psychotherapeutic assistance in an outpatient setting is significantly more likely to—

1. be found unacceptable for treatment,
2. receive a socially less desirable formal diagnosis,
3. drop out (or be dropped out) after initial screening,
4. spend considerable time on the clinic's waiting list,
5. be assigned to the least experienced staff members,
6. hold expectations incongruent with those held by his or her therapist,
7. form a poor relationship with his or her psychotherapist,
8. terminate or be terminated earlier, and
9. improve significantly less from either his or her own or the therapist's perspective.

Analogous dimensions relevant to mental-hospital settings yield an even grimmer pattern for the lower-class inpatient. As but one example, in the United States, Canada, and other nations involved in the deinstitutionalization movement, this has been a decade during which the rate of mental-hospital discharges has increased significantly. But the proportion of lower-class inpatients still hospitalized has *increased*. In a ten-year follow-up of Hollingshead and Redlich's (1958) research, Myers, Bean, and Pepper (1965) discovered that significantly more middle- and upper-class patients had left the hospital, compared with those of lower social-class standing. Furthermore, the likelihood of rehospitalization was significantly greater for those lower-class patients who had been discharged.

At the broadest level of generalization, we would assert that the lower-social-class patient had fared so poorly in psychotherapy because the kind of psychotherapy we are most prone to offer—traditional, verbal, insight-oriented psychotherapy—is almost singularly a middle-class enterprise. It is middle-class in its underlying philosophies of human nature, in its theoretical rationales, and in its specific therapeutic techniques. Schofield (1964) has taken an analogous position by suggesting that most psychotherapists prefer to work with what he describes as the

Sections of this chapter are excerpted from *Psychological Skill Training,* by A. P. Goldstein (New York: Pergamon Press, 1981). Permission to do so from Pergamon Press is gratefully acknowledged.

YAVIS patient: Young, Attractive, Verbal, Intelligent, and Successful—and most typically middle- or upper-class. Mr. YAVIS seeks psychotherapy voluntarily; he does not wish drug or physical therapy, but, as his therapist prefers, he expects to explore his inner world and actively participate in seeking insight. He tends to form a favorable therapeutic relationship and remain in treatment for a long time; and in about two thirds of such therapist/patient pairings, Mr. YAVIS derives apparent psychotherapeutic benefit.

Our own clinical and research interest lies more with a contrasting type of patient, whom we might term Mr. or Ms. Non-YAVIS. He or she is typically lower- or working-class, is often middle-aged, physically ordinary or unattractive, verbally reticent, intellectually unexceptional or dull, and vocationally unsuccessful or marginal. In our own studies, Mr. Non-YAVIS has been formally diagnosed as schizophrenic, psychoneurotic, inadequate personality, drug addict, retarded, or alcoholic, although we consider his social-class level and its associated life-style of greater consequence than his diagnosis itself. How else might we describe the Non-YAVIS patient? He seeks psychotherapy often not with full volition. He expects not introspective behavior on his own part but advice and active guidance from his psychotherapist. Since Mr. Non-YAVIS often views his problems as physical in nature, physical or drug therapies are also consistent with his expectations and even preferences. As noted earlier, he tends to remain in treatment very briefly, forms a poor therapeutic relationship, and derives minimal benefit from psychotherapy. In the United States, 50% of the psychotherapies involving Non-YAVIS patients at community mental health centers last but one or two sessions—clearly a less successful effort than is therapy with middle-class clients.

How are we to more effectively help the lower-class patient? Four approaches can be identified. The first consists of simple admonitions in the psychiatric, social-work, and psychological literatures urging therapists to "be more directive, concrete, specific, advice-giving" and the like. Although this is indeed good prescriptive advice, like most advice, it is rarely followed. Perhaps one reason is that the training analysts, psychology professors, and psychiatrists writing these articles rarely see such patients in their own private therapy practices. Instead, while they write of Mr. Non-YAVIS and urge us on in his direction, they treat Mr. YAVIS themselves! They ask us to do as they say, not as they do. Young therapists respond to their model's behavior, not his words. Thus, this approach, consisting of admonitions and beseeching in the literature, has essentially failed. The gap between the typically middle-class therapist and the lower-class patient—a gap in values, language, beliefs about psychopathology and its remediation—is simply too great to close in this manner.

Accordingly, many have held that a second and viable solution to the psychotherapeutic needs of low-income patients is to employ therapists who share values, language, and therapy beliefs with the low-income, non-YAVIS patient—that is, lower-class or working-class psychotherapists. If such therapists could be found, this position held, then congruent therapist/patient expectancies, a positive relationship, and a favorable outcome might well ensue. It was this set of assumptions and hopes that, in the United States, led to the "paraprofessional therapist" movement of the late 1960s and early 1970s. Persons of lower- and working-class status were identified and (briefly) trained to function as what were termed paraprofessional, nonprofessional, indigenous, neighborhood, or community thera-pists. And, in fact, a great many indeed proved to be therapeutic. Unfortunately, a series of subsequent economic and political events (Vietnam War, recession, tax-payers' revolts) have combined to keep this an underfunded movement, one yet to reach its full therapeutic potential.

CONFORMITY AND REFORMITY PRESCRIPTIONS FOR THE LOWER-CLASS PATIENT

If admonitions are not enough, and paraprofessionals are too scarce, what solutions remain? There are two, and both are what we have termed prescriptive. The first seeks to "make the patient fit the therapy"; it is a conformity prescription that seeks to alter the patient, his expectancies, relatability, or similar therapy-readiness characteristics, in order that he will more adequately fit the patient role appropriate to whatever (unchanged) psychotherapy we are offering.

Conformity

Our own earlier research program is one example of such a conformity prescription for the lower-class patient (Goldstein, 1971). Our broad goal was to implement and evaluate procedures designed to enhance the favorableness of the psychotherapeutic relationship. Social psychologists have focused a great deal of research attention on procedures predicted to increase what they term interpersonal attraction—that is, the degree to which one member of a dyad likes or is attracted to the other. Working in laboratory settings, usually with college-student subjects, researchers have devel-oped several procedures for reliably enhancing interpersonal attraction. These procedures were extrapolated from laboratory to clinic as a means of seeking to increase the attraction of patients to their psychotherapists. Concretely, the proce-dures were these:

- Direct structuring, in which the patient is directly led to believe that he or she will like the therapist.
- Trait structuring, in which the patient is given information about the therapist, such as that the therapist is "warm" or "experienced."
- Status, in which both verbal and physical information is used to lead the patient to believe his or her therapist is of high status.
- Effort, in which the therapeutic interaction itself is deliberately made more effortful for the patient.
- Modeling, in which the patient is given the opportunity to view a model who is highly attracted to the psychotherapist.
- Matching, in which therapist and patient are paired on the basis of test results concerning their interpersonal needs or therapy-relevant attitudes.
- Conformity pressure, which presents both an attractive model and confeder-ates rating him or her as attractive.

In a series of investigations, we examined each of these procedures with separate middle-class and lower-class patient samples. Almost every one of our procedures worked successfully with the middle-class patient samples. Almost every procedure failed to do so with our lower-class samples. This failure is not an uncommon outcome. Most efforts to teach low-income patients "good patient" skills, to socialize them into traditional, verbal, insight-oriented therapy, to have them play the therapeutic game as it is usually structured, have not been successful.

Reformity: Structured Learning Therapy

In response to both these findings and the literature summarized earlier, an alternative approach to the lower-class patient seemed appropriate. Rather than make the patient fit the therapy, rather than a conformity prescription, we chose to try to develop a therapy to fit the lower-class patient, to try to alter or reformulate our psychotherapeutic offering to more adequately correspond to or be consistent with the patient's style. Stated otherwise, we sought what might be termed a reformity prescription. To design such an approach, we turned this time primarily to developmental psychology research on child rearing and sociological writing on social class and life-styles. These bodies of literature consistently reveal that middle-class child rearing and life-style, with their emphasis on intentions, motivation, inner states, self-regulation, and the like, are excellent "basic training" for participation in traditional, verbal psychotherapies should such persons become emotionally disturbed in later life. Lower-class child rearing and life-style, with their emphasis on action, motor behavior, consequences rather than intentions, reliance on external example and authority, and a restricted verbal code, ill prepare such persons for traditional psychotherapy but, we speculated, might prepare them very well for a treatment that *was* responsive to such life-style characteristics—that is, a treatment which was brief, concrete, behavioral, actional, and authoritatively administered and which required imitation of specific, overt examples, taught role-taking skills, and provided early, continuing, and frequent reinforcement for enactment of seldom-used but adaptive skill behaviors.

Borrowing liberally from and building on the work of Bandura (1969), Lazarus (1966), and others, we have constructed and tested such a therapy, a class-linked therapy that we have shown over the course of several dozen investigations to be optimally appropriate for the lower-class patient. We call this approach Structured Learning Therapy (Goldstein, 1973). Its major components are modeling, role playing, performance feedback, and transfer of training. That is, the patient is provided with specific, detailed, frequent, and vivid displays of adaptive behavior or of specific skills in which he or she is deficient (modeling); given considerable opportunity and encouragement to behaviorally rehearse or practice such modeled behavior (role playing); provided with positive feedback, approval, or reward for successful enactments (performance feedback); and required to engage in a number of behaviors (described later in this chapter) that enhance the likelihood that the behaviors taught in the therapy room will be used reliably in the community and other application settings (transfer of training).

At the very time that we were formulating Structured Learning Therapy, a major movement was developing in the United States—the deinstitutionalization movement. This is the transfer from public mental hospital to community of chronic, adult mental patients—85% of whom are socioeconomically lower- or working-class. In the United States, in the last 20 years, the mental-hospital patient census has decreased from 550,000 to 150,000. Judged by the movement of people out of institutions, the deinstitutionalization movement seems a marked success.

For many of the people thus moved, however, very major problems have occurred. Years and years of colonization—of increasing hospitalization; of an unskilled, chronic ward existence; of an existence far removed in its demands from the demands of adequate community functioning—left thousands of these ex-patients ill prepared for what was to confront them. As they moved from hospital to group home, welfare hotel, or halfway house, many proved too deficient in daily living skills to remain out of hospitals. They too often had moved from "back ward" to "back alley" and could not make it. It was this challenge to which we sought to respond by the full development, investigation, and dissemination of Structured Learning Therapy.

ELEMENTS OF STRUCTURED LEARNING THERAPY

Modeling

Structured Learning Therapy requires first that the patients—called trainees in this approach—be exposed to expert examples of the behaviors we wish them to learn. The 6–12 trainees constituting the Structured Learning group are selected on the basis of their shared skill deficiencies, essentially independent of their formal diagnoses. Each potentially problematic behavior is referred to as a skill. We developed a library of audio-cassette modeling displays, one for each skill. Each of the 59 tapes in the series of displays depicts a different daily-living skill (see Figure 4-1, pp. 76–77). Each skill is broken down into four to six behavioral steps. The steps constitute the operational definition of the given skill. Each tape deals with one skill and consists of ten vignettes in which actors expertly portray the steps of that skill in a variety of hospital, community, and transitional settings. Trainers describe the first skill to be taught and hand out to all trainees "Skill Cards" (see Figure 4-2, p. 77) on which the name of the skill and its behavioral steps are printed. The first modeling tape is then played (or the trainers present live modeling). Trainees are told to listen closely to the way the actors in each vignette follow the behavioral steps.

Role Playing

A brief, spontaneous discussion almost invariably follows the presentation of a modeling display. Trainees comment on the steps, on the actors, and, very often, on how the situation or skill problem portrayed occurs in their own lives. Since our primary goal in role playing is to encourage realistic behavioral rehearsal, a trainee's statements about his or her individual difficulties using the skill being taught can often develop into material for the first role play. To enhance the realism of the portrayal, have him or her (now the main actor) choose a second trainee (coactor) to play the role of the significant other person in his or her life who is relevant to the skill problem. It is of crucial importance that the main actor seek to enact the steps he or she has just heard modeled. To be sure that all participate about equally, one trainer should be responsible for keeping a record of who has role-played, which role, and for which skill.

The main actor is asked to briefly describe the real skill-problem situation and the real person(s) involved in it, with whom he or she could try these behavioral steps in real life. The coactor should be called by the name of the main actor's significant other during the role play. The trainer then instructs the role players to begin. It is the trainers' main responsibility, at this point, to be sure that the main actor keeps role-playing and that he or she attempts to follow the behavioral steps while doing so. If the main actor "breaks role" and begins making comments or explaining background events, for example, the trainers should firmly instruct him or her to resume the role. One trainer should be positioned near the chalkboard and point to each step, in turn, as the role play unfolds, being sure none is either missed or enacted out of order. If the trainers or actors feel the role play is not progressing well and wish to start it over, this is appropriate. Trainers should make an effort to have the actors complete the skill enactment before stepping down. Observers should be instructed to hold their comments until the role play is completed.

The role playing should be continued until all trainees have had an opportunity to participate—even if all the same steps must be carried over to a second or third session. Although the framework (behavioral steps) of each role play in the series remains the same, the actual content can and should change from role play to role play. It is the problem as it actually occurs, or could occur, in each trainee's real-life environment that should be the content of the given role play. When the role plays are completed, each trainee should be better armed to act appropriately in the given reality situation.

Feedback

On completion of each role play, a brief feedback period should ensue. The goals of this activity are to let the main actor know how well he or she followed the skill's steps or in what ways he or she departed from them, to explore the psychological impact of the main actor's enactment on the coactor, and to provide the main actor with encouragement to try out his or her role-play behaviors in real life.

In these critiques, it is crucial that the behavioral focus of Structured Learning be maintained. Comments must point to the presence or absence of specific, concrete behaviors and not take the form of general evaluative comments or broad generalities.

Transfer of Training

Several aspects of the training sessions described above have as their main purpose increasing the likelihood that learning in the therapy setting will transfer to the trainee's real-life environment.

Provision of general principles. Transfer of training has been shown to be facilitated by providing trainees with general mediating principles governing successful or competent performance on the training and criterion tasks. This procedure has typically been operationalized in laboratory contexts by providing subjects with the organizing concepts, principles, strategies, or rationales that explain or account for the stimulus-response relationships operative in both the training and application settings. The provision of general principles to SLT trainees is being operationalized in our training by the presentation in verbal, pictorial, and written form of information governing skill instigation, selection, and implementation principles.

Figure 4-1

STRUCTURED LEARNING SKILLS FOR ADULTS

Basic Skills

Series I	**Conversations: Beginning Skills**
	Skill 1. Starting a Conversation
	Skill 2. Carrying On a Conversation
	Skill 3. Ending a Conversation
	Skill 4. Listening
Series II	**Conversations: Expressing Oneself**
	Skill 5. Expressing a Compliment
	Skill 6. Expressing Appreciation
	Skill 7. Expressing Encouragement
	Skill 8. Asking for Help
	Skill 9. Giving Instructions
	Skill 10. Expressing Affection
	Skill 11. Expressing a Complaint
	Skill 12. Persuading Others
	Skill 13. Expressing Anger
Series III	**Conversations: Responding to Others**
	Skill 14. Responding to Praise
	Skill 15. Responding to the Feelings of Others (Empathy)
	Skill 16. Apologizing
	Skill 17. Following Instructions
	Skill 18. Responding to Persuasion
	Skill 19. Responding to Failure
	Skill 20. Responding to Contradictory Messages
	Skill 21. Responding to a Complaint
	Skill 22. Responding to Anger
Series IV	**Planning Skills**
	Skill 23. Setting a Goal
	Skill 24. Gathering Information
	Skill 25. Concentrating on a Task
	Skill 26. Evaluating Your Abilities
	Skill 27. Preparing for a Stressful Conversation
	Skill 28. Setting Problem Priorities
	Skill 29. Decision Making
Series V	**Alternatives to Aggression**
	Skill 30. Identifying and Labeling Your Emotions
	Skill 31. Determining Responsibility
	Skill 32. Making Requests
	Skill 33. Relaxation
	Skill 34. Self-Control
	Skill 35. Negotiation
	Skill 36. Helping Others
	Skill 37. Assertiveness

Overlearning. Overlearning is a procedure whereby learning is extended over more trials than suffice to produce initial changes in the subject's behavior. The overlearning, or repetition of successful skill enactment, in the typical SLT session is quite substantial. The skill taught and its behavioral steps are (1) modeled several

Figure 4-1 *(continued)*

STRUCTURED LEARNING SKILLS FOR ADULTS

Application Skills[a]

Skill 38. Finding a Place to Live (through formal channels)
Skill 39. Moving In (typical)
Skill 40. Moving In (difficult)
Skill 41. Managing Money
Skill 42. Neighboring (apartment house)
Skill 43. Job Seeking (typical)
Skill 44. Job Seeking (difficult)
Skill 45. Job Keeping (average day's work)
Skill 46. Job Keeping (strict boss)
Skill 47. Receiving Telephone Calls (difficult)
Skill 48. Restaurant Eating (typical)
Skill 49. Organizing Time (typical)
Skill 50. Using Leisure Time (learning something new)
Skill 51. Using Leisure Time (interpersonal activity)
Skill 52. Social (party)
Skill 53. Social (church supper)
Skill 54. Marital (positive interaction)
Skill 55. Marital (negative interaction)
Skill 56. Using Community Resources (seeking money)
Skill 57. Using Community Resources (avoiding red tape)
Skill 58. Dealing with Crises (inpatient to nonpatient transition)
Skill 59. Dealing with Crises (loss)

[a]Each application tape portrays a model enacting three to eight basic skills in a sequence and combination chosen to deal completely with a real-life problem.

Figure 4-2

EXAMPLES OF STRUCTURED LEARNING SKILL CARDS

Negotiation
Learning points
1. State your position.
2. State your understanding of the other person's position.
3. Ask if the other person agrees with your statement of his/her position.
4. Listen openly to the other person's response.
5. Propose a compromise.

Listening
Learning points
1. Look at the other person.
2. Show your interest in the other's statement; for example, nod your head.
3. Ask questions on the same topic.
4. Add your thoughts and feelings on the topic.

times, (2) role-played one or more times by the trainee, (3) observed live by the trainee as every other group member role-plays them, (4) read by the trainee from a blackboard and on the Skill Card, (5) written by the trainee in his or her Trainee's Notebook, (6) practiced *in vivo* one or more times by the trainee as part of the formal homework assignment, (7) practiced *in vivo* one or more times by the trainee in response to adult and/or peer-leader coaching, and (8) practiced *in vivo* one or more times by the trainee in response to skill-oriented, intrinsically interesting stimuli introduced into his or her real-life environment.

Identical elements. In perhaps the earliest experimental concern with transfer enhancement, Thorndike and Woodworth (1901) concluded that when there was a facilitative effect of one habit on another, it was to the extent that, and because, they shared identical elements. Ellis (1965) and Osgood (1953) have more recently emphasized the importance of transfer of similarity between stimulus and response aspects of the training and application tasks. The greater the similarity of physical and interpersonal stimuli in the Structured Learning Therapy setting and the home or other setting in which the skill is to be applied, the greater the likelihood of transfer.

The "real-lifeness" of SLT is operationalized in a number of ways. These operational expressions of identical elements include (1) the representative, relevant, and realistic content and portrayal of the models, protagonists, and situations on the modeling tapes, all designed to be highly similar to what trainees are likely to face in their daily lives, (2) the physical props used in, and the arrangement of, the role-playing setting to be similar to real-life settings, (3) the choice, coaching, and enactment of the coactors or protagonists to be similar to real-life figures, (4) the manner in which the role plays themselves are conducted to be as responsive as possible to the real-life interpersonal stimuli to which the trainee will actually respond with the given skill and to provide behavioral rehearsal of that skill as he or she actually plans to use it, (5) the *in vivo* homework—coached, practiced, and intrinsically interesting skill-relevant stimuli described earlier, and (6) the training of living units (all the members of a given ward) together.

Stimulus variability. Callantine and Warren (1955), Duncan (1959), and Shore and Sechrest (1961) have each shown that positive transfer is greater when a variety of relevant training stimuli are used. Stimulus variability is implemented in our SLT studies by use of (1) rotation of group leaders across groups, (2) rotation of trainees across groups, (3) having trainees role-play a given skill repeatedly with several coactors, (4) having trainees role-play a given skill repeatedly across several relevant settings, and (5) use of multiple homework assignments for each skill.

Real-life reinforcement. Given successful implementation of both appropriate SLT procedures and the transfer-enhancement procedures examined above, positive transfer may still fail to occur. As Agras (1967), Gruber (1971), Tharp and Wetzel (1969), and literally dozens of other investigators have shown, stable and enduring performance of newly learned skills in application settings is very much at the mercy of real-life reinforcement contingencies.

We have found it useful to implement several supplemental programs, outside the Structured Learning Therapy setting, that can help provide the rewards or reinforcements trainees need so that their new behaviors are maintained. These programs include provisions for both external social reward (provided by people in the trainee's real-life environment) and self-reward (provided by the trainee himself or herself).

In several hospitals and agencies, we have actively sought to identify and develop environmental or external support by holding orientation meetings for hospital staff and for relatives and friends of trainees—that is, the real-life reward and punishment givers. The purpose of these meetings is to acquaint significant others in the trainee's life with Structured Learning Therapy theory and procedures. Most important in these sessions is the presentation of procedures whereby staff, relatives, and friends can encourage and reward trainees as they practice their new skills. We consider these orientation sessions for such persons to be of major value for transfer of training.

Environmental support is often insufficient to maintain newly learned skills. In fact, many real-life environments in which trainees work and live will actively resist a trainee's efforts at behavior change. For this reason, we have found it useful to include in our transfer efforts a program of self-reinforcement. Trainees can be instructed in the nature of self-reinforcement and encouraged to "say something and do something nice for yourself" if they practice their new skill well.

APPLICATION TO DIVERSE TRAINEE GROUPS

We have described the history of SLT, its rationale, its procedures, and its application with chronic, adult trainees seeking to function in community settings. It is the natural development of most therapies, however, that a therapy developed for one population is applied in a testing-the-limits way to a number of other populations. This has been the case with Structured Learning Therapy. Our research and clinical work have extended its demonstrated applicability to geriatric trainees, child-abusing parents, aggressive adolescents, disturbed preadolescents, and such other trainees as industrial managers, police officers, teachers, and hospital personnel.

Since the components of Structured Learning are commonly used didactic techniques, our skill-training success with such diverse trainees is no surprise. Of special importance to our skill-acquisition and skill-transfer success, however, has been our continued and energetic concern with prescriptiveness. In keeping with our "reformity prescription" belief, with our effort to make the therapy fit the patient, we have consistently adapted all aspects of Structured Learning to fit salient trainee characteristics. For example, our special interest during the last few years has been to use Structured Learning for teaching prosocial skills to antisocial and aggressive adolescents (Figure 4-3, pp. 80-81, lists the Structured Learning skills for adolescents). Our own interactions with such youngsters and consultations about them reveal a number of training-relevant characteristics to which our efforts had to be responsive.

Audio-only modeling displays hardly seemed appropriate for this group, raised on TV, low in imaginal patience. Therefore, with such trainees, skills are modeled live by the trainers or a filmstrip or videotape. If one observes such youngsters and, in a Premackian sense, sees what they choose to do given freedom of choice, one finds that they will often listen to rock music, play board games, or read comic books. To capture such interests, to prescriptively use their preferred channels of influence, our filmstrip and videotape displays have rock-music themes that reflect the behavioral steps of the skill to be learned. We have a Structured Learning board game ("Making It") and have Structured Learning comic books in development.

Our strategy may be summarized as "Study your trainees, learn how they learn, and prescriptively reflect these insights in your behavior-change efforts."

Figure 4-3

STRUCTURED LEARNING SKILLS FOR ADOLESCENTS

Series I	**Beginning Social Skills**
	Skill 1. Listening
	Skill 2. Starting a Conversation
	Skill 3. Having a Conversation
	Skill 4. Asking a Question
	Skill 5. Saying Thank You
	Skill 6. Introducing Yourself
	Skill 7. Introducing Other People
	Skill 8. Giving a Compliment
Series II	**Advanced Social Skills**
	Skill 9. Asking for Help
	Skill 10. Joining In
	Skill 11. Giving Instructions
	Skill 12. Following Instructions
	Skill 13. Apologizing
	Skill 14. Convincing Others
Series III	**Skills for Dealing with Feelings**
	Skill 15. Knowing Your Feelings
	Skill 16. Expressing Your Feelings
	Skill 17. Understanding the Feelings of Others
	Skill 18. Dealing with Someone Else's Anger
	Skill 19. Expressing Affection
	Skill 20. Dealing with Fear
	Skill 21. Rewarding Yourself
Series IV	**Skill Alternatives to Aggression**
	Skill 22. Asking Permission
	Skill 23. Sharing Something
	Skill 24. Helping Others
	Skill 25. Negotiating
	Skill 26. Using Self-Control
	Skill 27. Standing Up for Your Rights
	Skill 28. Responding to Teasing
	Skill 29. Avoiding Trouble with Others
	Skill 30. Keeping out of Fights
Series V	**Skills for Dealing with Stress**
	Skill 31. Making a Complaint
	Skill 32. Answering a Complaint
	Skill 33. Sportsmanship after the Game
	Skill 34. Dealing with Embarrassment
	Skill 35. Dealing with Being Left Out
	Skill 36. Standing Up for a Friend
	Skill 37. Responding to Persuasion
	Skill 38. Responding to Failure
	Skill 39. Dealing with Confusing Messages
	Skill 40. Dealing with an Accusation
	Skill 41. Getting Ready for a Difficult Conversation
	Skill 42. Dealing with Group Pressure

Figure 4-3 (continued)

STRUCTURED LEARNING SKILLS FOR ADOLESCENTS

Series VI	**Planning Skills**
	Skill 43. Deciding on Something to Do
	Skill 44. Deciding What Caused a Problem
	Skill 45. Setting a Goal
	Skill 46. Deciding on Your Abilities
	Skill 47. Gathering Information
	Skill 48. Arranging Problems by Importance
	Skill 49. Making a Decision
	Skill 50. Concentrating on a Task

CASE EXAMPLE: MARY G.

The case presentation that follows describes one kind of client for whom the Structured Learning approach has been particularly effective—the institutionalized adult psychiatric patient. In Mary G.'s case, Structured Learning in the context of a day treatment program committed to the idea of teaching a broad spectrum of community-living skills enabled her to maintain herself outside a psychiatric hospital despite her need for a variety of support services.

Mary G. is a 51-year-old woman, mother of six children, all of whom have been brought up largely in foster homes. Mary's husband, a chronic alcoholic and father of three of her children, has not been heard from in many years. Mary's psychiatric career began after the birth of her first child, when she was 17 years old. Mary's mother brought her to a hospital, tearful and withdrawn, unable to perform even the most basic aspects of self- and child care. The hospitalization was brief and Mary returned home.

Later hospitalizations became more and more prolonged and frequent. During them Mary carried diagnoses from manic-depressive illness, depressed type, to inadequate personality, to chronic undifferentiated schizophrenia. Neither medication nor psychotherapy appeared to have much effect on her symptoms of withdrawal and passivity. The effects of institutionalization began to mount with Mary's increasing dependence on others to take care of her. Between hospitalizations her ability to maintain herself independently greatly diminished, and Mary was placed in a variety of boarding homes and proprietary homes. Outpatient follow-up consisted largely of biweekly or monthly clinic appointments during which she spoke briefly with a social worker about her progress. Rarely did periods between hospitalizations exceed a year.

Following her last hospitalization 12 months ago, Mary was discharged to a boarding house and sent to a community outreach clinic with an affiliated day treatment program. At a treatment-planning session, the day treatment staff decided (with Mary's consent) to enroll her in an Independent Living Skills program whose goal was to work on increased socialization, activities of daily living, and some rudimentary prevocational skills. The socialization skills were taught at the center, using a Structured Learning approach. With staff help, Mary filled out a skill-survey questionnaire specifying the skills she needed to work on. She agreed that her ability to "make friends" and "talk to other people" was quite limited and that she should enter a basic Structured Learning class.

*The first class session began with teaching the skill "Starting a Conversation."
The trainer played a modeling audiotape depicting a number of people effectively
starting conversations on a variety of topics. The steps for the skill were listed, and
each vignette portrayed actors using the steps successfully. Then each trainee was
given the opportunity to role-play the skill, using content relevant to his or her own
life. Mary reluctantly role-played a scene at the boarding house in which she
introduced herself to another boarder. Following positive feedback from the group,
she was instructed to do a homework assignment, introducing herself to another
boarder in real life.*

*In subsequent classes, Mary began to emerge as a quiet but friendly person. She
brought in a sports magazine for a trainee who had said he liked sports. She showed
sincere concern for one trainee who was sick. Her social skills began to improve, and
she became increasingly proficient at such skills as "Asking for Help" and "Expressing a Compliment." The boarding-house proprietor, along with the day treatment
staff, began to notice a change in Mary's out-of-class behavior. The staff provided
much positive reinforcement for Mary and encouraged the boarding-house manager to do the same. Mary was showing real gains. As her skills increased, the staff
felt that Mary might be able to function in a sheltered-workshop setting. Mary's
progress in the center, her very limited financial resources, and her expressed
interest in making money were the major reasons for this decision. The new
treatment plan included an increased emphasis on prevocational activities and, in
Structured Learning class, gearing role playing to situations Mary might encounter
at the workshop. She practiced such skills as negotiation, concentrating on a task,
apologizing, and following instructions. Finally, the day arrived when she was to
start. She agreed to attend the workshop three days a week and the day treatment
program twice a week. On her days at the day treatment center she continued to
attend Structured Learning class and worked on various socialization problems
that had emerged at work.*

*Although Structured Learning was not the only therapeutic intervention in
Mary's case, it was certainly an important one. The Structured Learning approach
provided an important method through which Mary's difficulties could be understood and behavior changes made.*

EVALUATION

Starting in 1970, our research group has conducted a systematic research program
oriented toward evaluating and improving the effectiveness of Structured Learning.
About 50 investigations have been conducted, involving a wide variety of trainee
populations. These include chronic, adult schizophrenics (Goldstein, 1973; Goldstein, Sprafkin, & Gershaw, 1976, 1979; Liberman, 1970; Orenstein, 1969; Sutton-
Simon, 1974), aggressive and other behavior-disordered adolescents (Goldstein,
Sprafkin, Gershaw, & Klein, 1979, 1980; Greenleaf, 1977; Litwack, 1976; Trief,
1976; Wood, 1977), geriatric inpatients (Lopez, 1977; Lopez, Hoyer, Goldstein,
Gershaw, & Sprafkin, in press), child-abusing parents (Solomon, 1977; Sturm,
1980), young children (Hummel, 1977; Swanstrom, 1974), and such change-agent
trainees as mental hospital staff (Berlin, 1974; Goldstein & Goodhart, 1973; Lack,
1975; Robinson, 1973), police officers (Goldstein, Monti, Sardino, & Green, 1978;
Goldstein, Hoyer, & Monti, 1979; Miron & Goldstein, 1978), teachers (Gilstad,

1976; Goldstein, 1973; Schneiman, 1972), and persons employed in industrial contexts (Goldstein & Sorcher, 1973a, 1973b). The major findings of this lengthy series of studies, reported in comprehensive form in *Psychological Skill Training* (Goldstein, 1981), as well as in the sources above, may be summarized as follows:

1. *Skill acquisition.* Across diverse trainee populations and target skills, skill acquisition is a reliable training outcome—occurring in well over 90% of Structured Learning trainees. Though pleased with this outcome, we are acutely aware that therapeutic gains demonstrable *in the training context* are rather easily accomplished, given the potency, support, encouragement, and low threat value of trainers and therapists in that context, but that the more consequential outcome question by far pertains to trainee skill performance *in real-world contexts*—that is, skill transfer.

2. *Skill transfer.* Across diverse trainee populations, target skills, and applied (real-world) settings, skill transfer occurs with about 50% of Structured Learning trainees. Goldstein and Kanfer (1979) have indicated that, across several dozen kinds of psychotherapy involving many kinds of psychopathology, the average transfer rate on follow-up is between 15% and 20% of patients seen. The 50% rate consequent to Structured Learning is a significant improvement on this collective base rate, although it must immediately be underscored that this cumulative-average transfer finding also means that the gains shown by half our trainees were limited to in-session acquisition. Of special consequence, however, is the consistently clear manner in which skill transfer in our studies was a function of the explicit implementation of laboratory-derived transfer-enhancing techniques—such as those described earlier in this chapter.

3. *Prescriptiveness.* A prescriptive research strategy is, at heart, an effort to conceptualize, operationalize, and evaluate potentially optimal trainer × trainee × training method matches. Before constituting such combinations, trainer, trainee, and training characteristics that may be active contributors to such matches must be examined singly and in combination. Stated otherwise, active and inert ingredients must be identified. A small and continuing series of multiple regression investigations conducted by us have begun to point to state, trait, cognitive, demographic, and sociometric predictors of high levels of skill acquisition and transfer (Anderson, 1981; Hoyer, Lopez, & Goldstein, 1981). More such research on prescriptive ingredients seems worthy of pursuit.

FUTURE RESEARCH

Where is Structured Learning heading? In several directions, we hope—some already under way, some yet to be pursued. We hope, in particular, that our own efforts, as well as others', will be successful in preventive directions. As we have commented elsewhere:

> We hope investigators go beyond the remedial strategy implicit in certain of our studies—in which we focused upon persons already displaying long-term skill deficiencies—and respond more to a preventive strategy by seeking to identify persons at risk and training them in a preparatory manner to confront future skill demanding situations as they arise. Concretely, we refer here to . . . young children, adults in need of pre-marital training, adults profitably taught parenting, pre-retirement or other developmental stage relevant skills, and so forth [Goldstein, 1981].

REFERENCES

Agras, W. S. Transfer during systematic desensitization therapy. *Behavior Research and Therapy,* 1967, *5,* 193–199.

Anderson, L. Role playing ability and young children. Unpublished master's thesis, Syracuse University, 1981.

Bandura, A. *Principles of behavior modification.* New York: Holt, Rinehart & Winston, 1969.

Berlin, R. J. Training of hospital staff in accurate affective perception of fear-anxiety from vocal cues in the context of varying facial cues. Unpublished master's thesis, Syracuse University, 1974.

Callantine, M. F., & Warren, J. M. Learning sets in human concept formation. *Psychological Reports,* 1955, *1,* 363–367.

Duncan, C. P. Recent research on human problem solving. *Psychological Bulletin,* 1959, *56,* 397–429.

Ellis, H. *The transfer of learning.* New York: Macmillan, 1965.

Gilstad, R. Acquisition and transfer of empathic responses by teachers through self-administered and leader-directed structured learning training and the interaction between training method and conceptual level. Unpublished doctoral dissertation, Syracuse University, 1976.

Goldstein, A. P. *Psychotherapeutic attraction.* New York: Pergamon Press, 1971.

Goldstein, A. P. *Structured Learning Therapy: Toward a psychotherapy for the poor.* New York: Academic Press, 1973.

Goldstein, A. P. *Psychological skill training.* New York: Pergamon Press, 1981.

Goldstein, A. P., Gershaw, N. J., & Sprafkin, R. P. Structured Learning Therapy: Skill training for schizophrenics. *Schizophrenia Bulletin,* 1975, *14,* 83–88.

Goldstein, A. P., & Goodhart, A. The use of Structured Learning for empathy-enhancement in paraprofessional psychotherapist training. *Journal of Community Psychology,* 1973, *1,* 168–173.

Goldstein, A. P., Hoyer, W., & Monti, P. J. *Police and the elderly.* New York: Pergamon Press, 1979.

Goldstein, A. P., & Kanfer, F. *Maximizing treatment gains.* New York: Academic Press, 1979.

Goldstein, A. P., Monti, P. J., Sardino, T. J., & Green, D. J. *Police crisis intervention.* New York: Pergamon Press, 1978.

Goldstein, A. P., & Sorcher, M. Changing managerial behavior by applied learning techniques. *Training & Development Journal,* March 1973, pp. 36–39. (a)

Goldstein, A. P., & Sorcher, M. *Changing supervisor behavior.* New York: Pergamon Press, 1973. (b)

Goldstein, A. P., Sprafkin, R. P., & Gershaw, N. J. *Skill training for community living: Applying Structured Learning Therapy.* New York: Pergamon Press, 1976.

Goldstein, A. P., Sprafkin, R. P., & Gershaw, N. J. Structured Learning Therapy: Training for community living. *Psychotherapy: Theory, Research & Practice,* 1979, *16,* 199–203.

Goldstein, A. P., Sprafkin, R. P., Gershaw, N. J., & Klein, P. *Skillstreaming the adolescent.* Urbana, Ill.: Research Press, 1979.

Goldstein, A. P., Sprafkin, R. P., Gershaw, N. J., & Klein, P. Structured learning and the skill deficient adolescent. In G. Cartledge & J. Millburn (Eds.), *Teaching social skills to children.* New York: Pergamon Press, 1980.

Greenleaf, D. Peer reinforcement as transfer enhancement in Structured Learning Therapy. Unpublished master's thesis, Syracuse University, 1977.

Gruber, R. P. Behavior therapy: Problems in generalization. *Behavior Therapy,* 1971, *2,* 361–368.

Hollingshead, A. B., & Redlich, F. C. *Social class and mental illness.* New York: Wiley, 1958.

Hoyer, W. J., Lopez, M. A., & Goldstein, A. P. Predicting social skill acquisition and transfer by psychogeriatric inpatients. *International Journal of Behavioral Geriatrics,* 1981, *1,* 43–46.

Hummel, J. W. An examination of Structured Learning Therapy, self-control, negotiations training and variations in stimulus conditions. Unpublished doctoral dissertation, Syracuse University, 1977.

Lack, D. Z. Problem-solving training, structured learning training, and didactic instruction in the preparation of paraprofessional mental health personnel for the utilization of contingency management techniques. Unpublished doctoral dissertation, Syracuse University, 1975.

Lazarus, A. A. Behavioral rehearsal vs. nondirective therapy vs. advice in effecting behavior change. *Behavior Research and Therapy,* 1966, *4,* 209–212.

Liberman, B. The effect of modeling procedures on attraction and disclosure in a psychotherapy analogue. Unpublished doctoral dissertation, Syracuse University, 1970.

Litwak, S. E. The use of the helper therapy principle to increase therapeutic effectiveness and reduce therapeutic resistance: Structured Learning Therapy with resistant adolescents. Unpublished doctoral dissertation, Syracuse University, 1976.

Lopez, M. A. The effects of overlearning and prestructuring in Structured Learning Therapy with geriatric patients. Unpublished doctoral dissertation, Syracuse University, 1977.

Lopez, M. A., Hoyer, W. J., Goldstein, A. P., Gershaw, N. J., & Sprafkin, R. P. Effects of overlearning and incentive on the acquisition and transfer of interpersonal skills with institutionalized elderly. *Journal of Gerontology,* in press.

Miron, M., & Goldstein, A. P. *Hostage.* New York: Pergamon Press, 1978.

Myers, J. K., Bean, L. L., & Pepper, M. P. Social class and psychiatric disorders: A ten-year followup. *Journal of Health and Human Behavior,* 1965, *6,* 74–79.

Orenstein, R. The influence of self-esteem on modeling behavior in a psychotherapy analogue. Unpublished master's thesis, Syracuse University, 1969.

Osgood, C. E. *Method and theory in experimental psychology.* New York: Oxford University Press, 1953.

Patterson, G. R., & Gullion, M. E. *Living with children.* Champaign, Ill.: Research Press, 1972.

Robinson, R. Evaluation of a Structured Learning empathy training program for lower socioeconomic status home-aide trainees. Unpublished master's thesis, Syracuse University, 1973.

Schneiman, R. An evaluation of Structured Learning and didactic learning as methods of training behavior modification skills to lower and middle socioeconomic level teacher-aides. Unpublished doctoral dissertation, Syracuse University, 1972.

Schofield, W. *Psychotherapy: The purchase of friendship.* Englewood Cliffs, N.J.: Prentice-Hall, 1964.

Shore, E., & Sechrest, L. Concept attainment as a function of number of positive instances presented. *Journal of Educational Psychology,* 1961, *52,* 303–307.

Solomon, E. Structured Learning Therapy with abusive parents: Training in self-control. Unpublished doctoral dissertation, Syracuse University, 1977.

Sturm, D. Therapist aggression tolerance and dependency tolerance under standardized client conditions of hostility and dependency. Unpublished master's thesis, Syracuse University, 1980.

Sutton-Simon, L. The effects of two types of modeling and rehearsal procedures upon schizophrenics' social skill behavior. Unpublished doctoral dissertation, Syracuse University, 1974.

Swanstrom, C. Training self-control in behavior problem children. Unpublished doctoral dissertation, Syracuse University, 1974.

Tharp, R. G., & Wetzel, R. *Behavior modification in the natural environment*. New York: Academic Press, 1969.

Thorndike, E. L., & Woodworth, R. S. The influence of improvement in one mental function upon the efficiency of other functions. *Psychological Review,* 1901, *8,* 247–261.

Trief, P. The reduction of egocentrism in acting-out adolescents by Structured Learning Therapy. Unpublished doctoral dissertation, Syracuse University, 1976.

Wood, M. Adolescent acquisition and transfer of assertiveness through the use of Structured Learning Therapy. Unpublished doctoral dissertation, Syracuse University, 1977.

CHAPTER FIVE

Multiple Impact Training: A Life Skills Approach

George M. Gazda

George M. Gazda is research professor of education, Department of Counseling and Human Development Services, and director of counseling psychology, University of Georgia, and is clinical professor, Department of Psychiatry, Medical College of Georgia. Gazda is author, coauthor, or editor of 12 books and over 100 articles, chapters, and monographs. Among the more recent books are *Group Counseling: A Developmental Approach; Interpersonal Communication: A Handbook for Health Professionals; Human Relations Development: A Manual for Educators; Innovations to Group Psychotherapy; Basic Approaches to Group Psychotherapy and Group Counseling; Realtalk: Exercises in Friendship and Helping Skills; Theories of Learning; Human Relations for Criminal Justice Personnel;* and *Strategies for Helping Students.* Gazda is on the editorial boards of *Journal of Group Psychotherapy, Psychodrama, and Sociometry; Personnel and Guidance Journal;* and *Small Group Behavior.* He is past president of the American Personnel and Guidance Association, the Association for Specialists in Group Work, and the Association of Counselor Education and Supervision.

In this chapter, we see the skills training approach applied within a traditional psychiatric setting as both a remedial and a preventive intervention strategy. Gazda's recognition that psychiatric patients, because of their multiple "problems" (skills deficits), needed training in multiple skills led him to develop Multiple Impact Training (MIT). His model is also equally applicable to educational and community mental health settings, and pilot projects have produced promising results in these sectors. In his approach, Gazda goes beyond the training of individual subskills (for example, stress management) and trains clients in more comprehensive generic life skill models (for example, health maintenance). Gazda makes clear how a "developmental" and "problem-solving" skills training approach like MIT corrects many of the weaknesses of traditional therapeutic approaches, including poor generalization, poor maintenance, poor cost-efficiency, and infringement of patients' rights. In addition, Gazda's model escapes the stigma of "medical models" because it conceptualizes personal dysfunction as specific gaps in life skills learning rather than as trauma-induced blockages in functioning.

Multiple Impact Training (MIT) is therapy, but not in the traditional sense of symptoms being diagnosed, treatment being administered, symptoms being amelio-

David K. Brooks, Jr., provided extensive editorial assistance in the preparation of this chapter.

rated, and the therapeutic relationship being terminated. In MIT, clients are active participants in a psychoeducational, developmentally oriented, "training-as-treatment" approach. Presenting symptoms are viewed not as pathology to be labeled but as deficits in life-skills. Once the deficits are identified (as well as the life-skills that have been mastered), clients join one or more training groups in which life-skills are taught directly. The focus of a particular group may be interpersonal communication skills, physical fitness/health maintenance skills, skills related to defining purpose in life, marital/family relationship skills, or other life-skills that have been identified as deficient.

People seeking professional help, especially those admitted to inpatient psychiatric care, are rarely deficient in only one area of life-skills. For treatment to be effective, the regimen must address multiple deficits. Furthermore, if clients are to achieve lasting benefits from the therapeutic experience, they must be more than the passive recipients assumed by most modalities based on the medical model. Hence, the name Multiple Impact Training describes an approach to treatment which is specifically educational in intent and which views clients as whole persons whose life-skills deficits are most effectively remediated by multiple interventions.

Multiple Impact Training has been most completely implemented in a program at the Psychiatric Division, Veterans Administration Medical Center, Augusta, Georgia. An observer seeking information about this program would witness a high level of involvement of staff members representing a variety of health-related disciplines, as well as a number of group activities occurring simultaneously. The observer would see patients entering the program first being referred to a screening group. Eligibility for the program is limited to patients who are not suffering from organicity and who are in good contact with reality. Patients attend the screening group for one hour a day, four days a week, until they are referred to one or more Life-Skills Training (LST) groups. In the screening group, the LST options are described to the patients, who are encouraged to discuss the kinds of problems they are experiencing and to select one or more LST groups for intensive training.

It is important to note that patients are encouraged to become involved in making decisions about the course of their treatment from the very beginning. The observer would see the screening group performing a diagnostic function, but by no means in the traditional sense of nosology. The screening group is much like any other interview-counseling group in format and procedure, except that the goal is appropriate self-referral to the LST groups. Life-Skills Training groups from which patients may currently choose are Interpersonal Communications, Physical Fitness/ Health Maintenance, Purpose in Life, Problem Solving, Vocational/Career Development, and Leisure Time. Other options are also available, such as Relaxation Therapy (a subgroup of Physical Fitness), Assertiveness Training (a subgroup of Interpersonal Communications), Problem Drinking, and a traditional interview-therapy group, plus occupational therapy, corrective therapy, and recreational therapy. The LST groups run for approximately two hours a day, four to five days a week, and may last for two or three weeks.

In addition to the screening group, other assessment devices are frequently administered. In an experimental study recently completed (May, 1981), patients were administered the Purpose in Life test (Crumbaugh & Maholick, 1976) to assist in determining their eligibility for the Purpose in Life training group. For admission to the Physical Fitness/ Health Maintenance group, patients were given the Health

Hazard Appraisal (Robbins & Hall, 1970). The computer feedback on this instrument also served as a motivator for treatment because it points out patients' health deficits and prescriptions for alleviating them. The third LST group to which patients in the study were referred was the Interpersonal Communications group. The experimental screening for this group involved patients playing a "helper" role in a three- to five-minute standard role session. They were rated on their level of communication skill by expert judges using the Global Scale (Gazda, Walters, & Childers, 1975).

The LST groups are facilitated by a number of staff members. The Purpose in Life groups are usually led by a chaplain, with the focus on Viktor Frankl's logotherapy/logoeducation approaches most recently described in *The Pursuit of Meaning* (Fabry, 1980). The Physical Fitness/Health Maintenance group consists of nutrition, fitness, and relaxation/stress-management segments. The nutrition segment is led by a dietitian and focuses on basic food groups, balanced diet, effects of drugs on the body, and the like. The corrective therapist develops a separate fitness program for each patient and monitors stress, blood pressure, weight, and so on. A clinical nurse specialist teaches the Interpersonal Communications group, following the model of Gazda et al. (1975). This group also makes frequent use of video feedback.

CASE EXAMPLE: MR. BROWN

If our observer chose to "shadow" an individual patient during the course of treatment, something like the following actual case example[1] might be noted. The patient's name has been changed and minor details of the case have been altered in the interest of protecting the patient's privacy.

Presenting history.   *Mr. Brown, a 32-year-old White Vietnam War veteran, was admitted to the hospital by his wife because he had been depressed over the loss of his job (plumber's assistant) and had taken an overdose of sleeping pills. His wife reported that Mr. Brown had had several serious episodes of drinking and that he had been fired from his last job because of drunkenness.*

Mr. Brown was a high school graduate with some vocational training. He had entered night school in a vocational/technical school following his military discharge, but he had dropped out after getting married. He felt that he had made a mistake in quitting school and that he had no options but to take whatever job came along.

Mr. Brown described himself as a loner. He had few friends (and no close friends at all), and he frequently had to rely on his wife for nurturance and financial support when he was out of work. His wife was employed as a beautician. They had a daughter, 8, and a son, 7.

Mr. Brown also reported that he found release from his troubles through heavy drinking. He had begun drinking in Vietnam. He also had used other drugs briefly while in the service. Mr. Brown's stated concern was the lack of progress in his life. He said "I'm not getting anywhere and I'm not getting any younger. Time is running out on me."

During his four meetings in the screening group before his referral for Life-Skills Training, Mr. Brown repeated the concerns cited above and requested assignment

[1]Provided by Mildred Powell, R.N.

to the following groups: Purpose in Life, Interpersonal Communications, and Vocational/Career Development. He was interviewed by the leader of the Problem Drinking group and was also accepted into that group.

Mr. Brown and his therapists identified the following life-skills deficits:

Interpersonal Communications—*had difficulty initiating conversations and sharing his problems; was lonely and nonassertive.*

Purpose in Life—*felt he was drifting, with little meaning and no meaningful goals; attempted suicide because he felt he was a hopeless failure.*

Vocational/Career Development—*had not followed through on his vocational plans; work record was spotty, with frequent unemployment.*

Physical Fitness/Health Maintenance—*frequent episodes of drunkenness; poor diet and exercise habits.*

Leisure Time—*few hobbies or leisure activities outside of going to taverns and bars.*

Problem Solving—*used avoidance behavior; alcohol abuse frequently involved.*

Family/Marital Relationship—*resented his dependence on his wife and often felt inadequate as a father.*

On the positive side, Mr. Brown had at least average intelligence, was willing to seek help with his problems, had a supportive wife, was physically able, and did not expect the government to support him, and this was his first hospitalization.

Patient progress. *Mr. Brown remained in the hospital for five weeks. During the first two weeks he participated in the following LST groups: Purpose in Life, Interpersonal Communications, and Vocational/Career Development. Concurrently he participated in the Problem Drinking group and remained in it for an additional two weeks.*

After completion of the three LST groups, Mr. Brown volunteered for three more LST groups: Leisure Time, Problem Solving, and Physical Fitness/Health Maintenance, thereby participating in the entire set of LST groups then available, plus the auxiliary Problem Drinking group. On discharge he also agreed to marital counseling at a community mental health clinic.

The following progress report illustrates Mr. Brown's behavioral changes:

Interpersonal Communications—*was able to self-disclose personal feelings and to be concrete in his communications; felt more comfortable initiating conversations on the ward; was more assertive in seeking things for himself and in giving his opinions.*

Purpose in Life—*participated in group attempts to seek meaning from both the good and the bad things that happen in life; began attending religious services regularly and had several talks with the chaplain.*

Vocational/Career Development—*took interest and aptitude inventories; explored vocational options; was admitted to night school to resume studies in drafting.*

Physical Fitness/Health Maintenance—*attended every group session and developed a regimen of physical exercise, including jogging and weightlifting; modified his diet to reduce sweets, alcoholic beverages, and junk food.*

Leisure Time—*began a regular reading program in* Popular Mechanics *and worked regularly in the hospital garden; planned to start a small vegetable garden at home on discharge.*

Problem Solving—*used a problem-solving model to decide to reenter night school and to seek marital counseling on discharge.*

Family/Marital Relationships—*(This LST group was not available in the hospital at the time of Mr. Brown's treatment; as mentioned above, he planned to seek counseling at a community mental health clinic.)*

Since Mr. Brown's is a fairly recent case, there are no follow-up data to present that might indicate the posttreatment impact of MIT in terms of successful adjustment or readmission to the hospital. The results of research studies to be presented later in this chapter indicate, however, that patients participating in MIT are readmitted less frequently and adjust to the demands of everyday life more satisfactorily than those receiving traditional treatment only.

THE DEVELOPMENTAL HISTORY OF A DEVELOPMENTAL APPROACH

Before I present the theoretical background of Multiple Impact Training, the reader may find it helpful to understand how MIT came to be. Its history is so closely intertwined with my own professional development that I find it easiest to describe using the first person singular.

My primary professional activities during the 1960s centered on a variety of pursuits related to group counseling. In these endeavors I certainly had company during this decade! The sixties were probably the high-water mark of intense interest and experimentation in group counseling and psychotherapy. My students and I conducted groups with schoolchildren of all ages, with professional educators, with psychiatric patients, with recovering alcoholics, with juvenile delinquents, with convicted felons, and with adults seeking personal growth, among others. Many of our activities were the subjects of doctoral dissertations and other research projects, while others were performed for the purpose of providing clinical training opportunities or community service.

During this same time I was becoming more convinced of the validity and utility of theories of human development expounded by such writers as Erik Erikson (1950, 1963), Robert J. Havighurst (1953, 1972), and Donald E. Super (1963). These writers and others assumed that normal development proceeded along a path from the simple to the complex, that development was more or less orderly, predictable, and age- and stage-related, and that progress from one developmental stage to the next depended on mastery of appropriate developmental tasks. Their terminology and the finer points of their theories varied somewhat, but it seemed to me that psychosocial development (Erikson, 1950, 1963; Havighurst, 1953, 1972) and vocational development (Super, 1963; Super, Crites, Hummel, Moser, Overstreet, & Warnath, 1957) could be used as an organizing framework from which the coping skills appropriate to the tasks of normal development could be abstracted.

Synthesizing my experiences and research in group counseling with my growing conviction of the importance of developmental theories, I wrote the first edition of *Group Counseling: A Developmental Approach* (Gazda, 1971). My primary thesis was that the group-counseling modality was applicable to a wide range of settings and client concerns and that it was most effective if the developmental needs of the particular age group being served were taken into account. I hypothesized that preventive measures could be better effected if deficits in coping skills could be regularly monitored. Remedial efforts therefore need not wait until clients were well beyond the optimum age for learning developmentally appropriate coping skills.

In the second edition of this text (Gazda, 1978), I broadened my view of the developing person, adding to the existing psychosocial and vocational perspectives the additional dimensions of physical/sexual development (Gesell, Ilg, & Ames, 1956; Gesell, Ilg, Ames, & Bullis, 1946), cognitive development *à la* Piaget (Flavell, 1963; Wadsworth, 1971), and moral development (Kohlberg, 1973; Kohlberg & Turiel, 1971). More recently I have incorporated the stages of ego development (Loevinger, 1976) and of affective development (Dupont, 1978, in press) into what I believe is a conceptualization of the whole developing person. From this model can be abstracted coping skills, or, as I have more recently come to call them, life-skills, appropriate to all ages and stages of human development. These life-skills are directly related to the successful accomplishment of developmental tasks appropriate to age and stage. Failure to learn relevant life-skills at various stages may result in inappropriate behavior patterns at least and in the onset of psychopathology at worst.

A concurrent influence on my thinking during the late 1960s and early 1970s was Robert Carkhuff's work in Human Relations Development. My students and several colleagues joined me in the experimental application of interpersonal communication skills training to a variety of groups. On the basis of these training experiences we developed training manuals for educators (Gazda, Asbury, Balzer, Childers, Desselle, & Walter, 1973; Gazda, Asbury, Balzer, Childers, & Walters, 1977, 1982; Gazda, Duncan, Maples, & Brown, 1976), health practitioners (Gazda, Walters, & Childers, 1975, 1982), adolescents (Gazda, Walters, & Childers, 1980), and criminal justice personnel (Sisson, Arthur, & Gazda, 1981). Having used the training approaches outlined in these materials for more than a decade, I have come to the belief that the *whole* person can be treated through *direct* training.

Yet another influence that has helped me arrive at this somewhat radical position has been my work over the last decade as a consultant to the psychiatric division of the Veterans Administration Medical Center, Augusta, Georgia. My early work there focused on interpersonal communication skills training, first with staff members and later with patients. This single intervention has been shown to have profound positive effects on a variety of patients (Powell & Clayton, 1980), not to mention the changes it has made in staff attitudes and effectiveness. Powerful as this modality proved to be, my VA colleagues (especially Mildred Powell) and I gradually realized that no *single* intervention could be expected to ameliorate what we now viewed as *multiple* life-skills deficits in patients who showed only modest gains after communication skills training. We hypothesized that multiple deficits should be addressed with multiple interventions. After recruiting staff expertise from across disciplines, we developed Life-Skills Training intervention modules, used an interview group for screening purposes, employed the other resources of the VA mentioned previously, and began to work with patients within this new framework. Without fanfare and with the involvement of a number of dedicated professionals who were willing to risk, Multiple Impact Training slowly came into existence as an effective alternative to traditional patient care.

The reader may be slightly confused at this point by the seemingly interchangeable use of the terms *Multiple Impact Training* and *Life-Skills Training*. Life-Skills

Training groups represent the heart of the Multiple Impact Training model. In addition to the LST groups, the MIT program also includes the screening group, the traditional interview-therapy group(s), and auxiliary institutional supports such as occupational therapy, corrective therapy, and recreation therapy. A patient's individualized treatment program might include these elements in any combination, the goal being to address identified life-skills deficits with multiple training interventions.

THEORETICAL RATIONALE

The rationale for MIT and for LST applications in other settings and with other populations rests on the following assumptions:

1. Within the multiple dimensions of human development (the seven developmental perspectives mentioned earlier), there are *stages* through which all persons must progress if they are to lead effective lives. Some of these are age-related; some are not.
2. Satisfactory progression through the stages depends on the successful accomplishment of *developmental tasks*[2] that are specific to the stages.
3. Accomplishment of the developmental tasks is dependent on mastery of *life-skills* appropriate to stage and task.
4. Each person encounters many agents (parents, siblings, teachers, peers, social institutions, and so on) through which life-skills may be learned.
5. There are certain age ranges during which certain life-skills can be most easily learned.
6. Individuals inherit their capacity for learning, but the degree to which they are able to achieve their maximum potential is the result of their environment and/or life experiences.
7. Individuals achieve optimal functioning when they attain operational mastery of fundamental life-skills.
8. Neuroses and functional psychoses result from failure to develop one's life-skills. Persons experiencing such dysfunctions are usually suffering from multiple life-skills deficits. Within the context of an interview-counseling group or in individual consultation with a therapist, such persons are able to identify their life-skills deficits as well as the areas in which life-skills mastery has been reached.
9. Life-skills can be taught most effectively through the medium of the small group, provided members are developmentally ready. Therefore, the most satisfactory means of ensuring positive mental health and of remediating psychological dysfunction is through direct teaching/training in life-skills, especially if two or more areas of life-skills deficits are addressed concurrently.

At this point in its development, the training model of the Life-Skills Training group does not lend itself to elegant description. Limitations of space in this chapter prohibit presentation of the "syllabi" of the LST groups described earlier. The

---

[2]Havighurst (1972) defines a developmental task as "a task which arises at or about a certain period in the life of the individual, successful achievement of which leads to his happiness and to success with later tasks, while failure leads to unhappiness in the individual, disapproval by the society, and difficulty with later tasks" (p. 2).

assumptions on which MIT/LST is based are obviously the result of a process of empirical eclecticism. The same process is operating in the development of the training model, but it is not quite so far along.

Even though MIT/LST has not reached the stage of a full-blown training paradigm, it is both possible and desirable to comment on the training philosophy that has evolved so far. Fundamental to the success of the program has been its reliance on the small group as the primary training modality. The LST groups are similar in composition, structure, and dynamics to structured groups described frequently in recent literature (for example, Drum & Knott, 1977). Although the topical focus of LST groups necessitates a certain amount of didactic presentation of information, such activity is kept to a minimum. Leader/facilitators model the target skills/behaviors, often demonstrating them in structured simulations. Group members frequently role-play new behaviors, followed by feedback from the group and from the leader. At least half of each session is devoted to practicing the skills, interspersed with feedback. Homework is regularly assigned, with the beginning of the following session devoted to individual reporting. Some aspects of each LST group are idiosyncratic to the leader and the members of the group, but the elements of brief didactic instruction, modeling, simulations, role playing, practice, feedback, and homework constitute the underlying training approach.

THE TRAINING PROCESS

Essential Elements

The following are the essential elements incorporated in the Life-Skills Training model:

- The life-skills are generated from the coping behaviors appropriate to the developmental tasks of a given age/stage (and sex, where applicable) across the seven dimensions of human development described previously.
- A mastery learning model (see Bloom, 1976) is implemented whenever the life-skills are hierarchical or progressive in nature.
- Activities are utilized throughout training to accommodate the three basic modes of learning: auditory, visual, and kinesthetic.
- Generic life-skills are assumed to be a family of related skills that can be taught much like other subject-matter areas according to the developmental readiness of the client/trainee/student.
- The same training procedures are applied wʰ ₋n teaching the life-skills for prevention as when teaching them for remediation.
- Extensive supervised practice is the core of training, using role rehearsal and simulation to ensure skill development.
- Homework assignments are used to facilitate transfer of learned skills into everyday living for trainees.
- Peer trainers are used whenever possible to increase transfer of learning and the credibility of the training process.
- Self-monitoring is emphasized and, where possible, scales for self-rating are employed.
- Trainees may repeat portions of training (or, if necessary, the entire training program) to increase and to solidify skills development.

- Training is based on an educational/instructional mode rather than a treatment approach.
- A wide variety of training materials and methods, including extensive use of audiovisual media, are employed.
- The most theoretically sound and operationally efficient model for teaching a given life-skill is used.
- Cotrainers are used in many instances to increase individualization of training.
- Training time, including length of sessions, spacing of sessions, and duration of training, is flexible to accommodate needs of trainees at different levels of readiness.
- Training is conducted in small groups of 6 to 12 clients/trainees.
- Clients/trainees are taught in a four-step pyramid sequence during which they move from the role of trainee to that of trainer. The steps in the pyramid sequence are described below.

Pyramid of Training

All trainers are expected to achieve mastery of the generic life-skill(s) that they are to teach. They must have developed the family of skills that make up the generic life-skill in order to model the skills effectively and to monitor skills development by trainees. Trainers assume a range of roles, including teacher, modeler, monitor/evaluator, motivator, encourager, facilitator, protector, and training-media developer. The training activities most frequently used in each step of the training pyramid include the following:

> *Step 1:* Training in generic life-skills.
> 1. Didactic presentation of the rationale for the model of the generic life skill to be taught—"tell."
> 2. Modeling or demonstration of the behavior(s) or response(s) to be mastered—"show."
> 3. Practice by trainees/students of the skills to be mastered—"do."
> 4. Homework application of new skill to daily living—"transfer."
> 5. Self-monitoring/assessment (as well as monitoring/assessment by trainer and fellow trainees) of skill level achieved—"feedback."
> 6. Trainees assist one another in developing skills—"peer bonding."
> *Step 2:* Cotraining with "master" trainer (usually staff member but may be fellow client/trainee who has "graduated" from Step 4).
> *Step 3:* Training under supervision of "master" trainer.
> *Step 4:* Training alone.

Steps 2, 3, and 4 contain within them the six elements of Step 1, but in each case the former trainee is gradually progressing through the status of cotrainer to becoming able to train without supervision.

MIT AND OTHER APPROACHES: SIMILARITIES AND DIFFERENCES

There are obviously many similarities between *elements* of MIT/LST and other training-oriented approaches to treatment. The efficacy of interpersonal communication skills training as a treatment intervention was established more than a decade ago (Pierce & Drasgow, 1969) and has received consistent experimental and clinical support since then (for example, Pierce, Schauble, & Wilson, 1971; Vitalo, 1971). Theoretical articles and literature reviews (for example, Authier, Gustafson, Guerney, & Kasdorf, 1975; Guerney, Stollak, & Guerney, 1971) have persuasively argued for a shift from psychotherapeutic to psychoeducational modalities. Other studies have found positive relationships between physical-fitness training and improved psychological functioning (Brown, 1978; Collingwood, 1976). D'Zurilla and Goldfried (1971) were among the first to argue for a problem-solving approach to therapy, using language that is descriptive of the MIT/LST view of etiology and is applicable to other recent approaches as well (for example, Brown, 1980):

> Much of what we view clinically as "abnormal behavior" or "emotional disturbance" may be viewed as ineffective behavior and its consequences, in which the individual is unable to resolve certain situational problems in his life and his inadequate attempts to do so are having undesirable effects, such as anxiety, depression, and the creation of additional problems [p. 107].

Just as the treatment approaches above have much in common with certain elements of MIT/LST, there are at least two systems that are somewhat similar in structure. One is Arnold Lazarus's Multimodal Behavior Therapy (MBT). Lazarus (1975) defined MBT as "a systematic problem-solving process that examines and, if necessary, endeavors to remedy maladaptive responses across six separate but inter-related modalities—behavior, affect, sensation, imagery, cognition, and interpersonal relationships" (p. 150). The seventh dimension, diet and physical functioning, permits the formation of the familiar acronym BASIC ID. In describing the thrust of MBT, Lazarus states "The multi-modal behavior approach stresses the fact that the patients are usually troubled by a multitude of specific problems that should be dealt with by a similar multitude of specific treatments" (1975, p. 165).

There are, however, some basic differences between MIT/LST and MBT, the central one being the conceptualization of the human dimensions subject to deterioration or ineffective functioning and consequently needing improvement. Another difference is in Lazarus's emphasis on locating deficits, in contrast with the MIT/LST emphasis on locating areas of strength as well as areas of weakness.

The other system that is similar in structural respects to MIT/LST is Arnold Goldstein's Structured Learning Therapy (Goldstein, Sprafkin, & Gershaw, 1976). This approach also advocates direct training of specific target behaviors and has both preventive and remedial applications. The chief differences are in the theoretical base and in the way the target life-skills were derived. Whereas MIT/LST draws on human development theory, Goldstein and his colleagues used patient and staff surveys, clinical observations, reviews of relevant professional literature, and research on Structured Learning Therapy to develop a list of 59 life-skills areas involving social, personal, and interpersonal functioning.

The MIT/LST model outlined here is unique in several respects. First, it is solidly grounded in human development theory. It therefore lends itself equally well to preventive and remedial applications. Second, it emphasizes the small group as the modality of choice in all phases of training. Third, it places major responsibility on the client/patient for determining the course of training/treatment. Fourth, it is firm in insisting that training aimed at remediating life-skills deficits must take full account of existing areas of life-skills mastery. Finally, it is an open system that permits endless permutations of training experiences in the course of individualized education/treatment.

LIFE-SKILLS TRAINING: AN OUNCE OF PREVENTION

Thus far in this chapter, Life-Skills Training has been discussed almost exclusively as the key element of Multiple Impact Training. Primary emphasis has been on the application of MIT/LST with populations of psychiatric inpatients. To limit LST to a remedial mode is to ignore its potential as a preventive intervention strategy.

Before the publication of the second edition of the developmental group-counseling text (Gazda, 1978), I began to argue for inclusion of Life-Skills Training as a "fourth R" in public school curricula. Again, I was certainly not alone! I was influenced in part by the work of Norman Sprinthall and Ralph Mosher (Mosher & Sprinthall, 1970, 1971; Sprinthall & Mosher, 1969) in Deliberate Psychological Education. As I studied reports such as one by the National Assessment of Educational Progress (1975), my hunches were confirmed concerning how poorly our nation's schools were preparing students for the business of effective living. In speeches before professional audiences (Gazda, 1977), I began to call for attention to Developmental Education. Concurrently, the Minnesota Department of Education (Miller, 1976) was also pioneering a similar form of Developmental Education. Shortly after I began to use the term *life coping skills,* I encountered Adkins's (1974) work with disadvantaged youth and adults that used the same terminology. Eventually I settled on *Life-Skills Training* (Gazda & Brooks, 1980) as descriptive of my ideas in the broadest sense. Regardless of the setting, the main objective of LST is the teaching/training of critical life-skills related to the tasks and stages of various areas of human development.

It was my good fortune during the 1970s to become involved as a consultant to an alternative education program at an elementary school in Joliet, Illinois. This program was the first attempt on the U.S. mainland to implement Corsini's (1977) Individual Education (IE) approach, developed earlier in Hawaii. Although my work initially involved communication skills training for faculty and staff, I later had the opportunity to experiment with some of the developing LST group interventions that my colleagues and I were working on at the Veterans Administration Medical Center. The setting, the population, and the intention were dramatically different here, but the feedback from students and faculty indicated real promise for LST as a part of the curriculum.

Most recently I have been involved with a rural school health project in northern Georgia. The intention of this project is to use Life-Skills Training on a schoolwide basis as the primary preventive modality in a program designed to reduce the incidence of substance abuse. Any statement I might make about expected outcomes would be premature at this point, but again the receptiveness to LST by students and faculty has been encouraging. I am optimistic that inclusion of Life-Skills Training in public school curricula, for preventive purposes, can exert a powerful positive influence on the future mental health of our citizens.

In a recent article (Gazda & Brooks, 1980), I argued that Life-Skills Training should be considered as an organizing framework for service delivery in both university counseling centers and community mental health centers. To my knowledge no such programs have been implemented to date. Since I believe that one of the benefits of LST is that it makes more effective use of staff time and talents, it is possible that cuts in human services budgets will hasten the time when LST or a similar approach may be implemented by these agencies.

EVALUATION

A recent research study of the effectiveness of the MIT/LST approach with psychiatric patients (May, 1981) showed that the experimental group made significant gains over a group of patients receiving traditional treatment. The experimental group received 12 hours of training in Interpersonal Communications skills, 6 hours in Purpose in Life, and 10 hours in Physical Fitness/Health Maintenance, which included instruction on diet and nutrition as well as practice in an exercise program. A standard role play was used to assess interpersonal communication skills. Responses were rated on the Global Scale (Gazda et al., 1975). The experimental group increased communications skills significantly ($p < .001$) over the traditional-treatment control group. Change on purpose in life was measured by the Purpose in Life test (Crumbaugh & Maholick, 1976). Again the MIT/LST group was significantly ($p < .025$) higher than the control group. Both experimental and control groups made significant pre/post physical-fitness improvements on forced vital capacity, blood pressure, and heart rate. Both groups also showed a pre/post decrease in psychopathology as measured by ward staff on the Nurse's Observation Scale for Inpatient Evaluation (NOSIE-30) (Honigfeld, Gillis, & Klett, 1966). The MIT/LST group also showed a trend ($p < .10$) toward satisfaction with treatment over the control group as measured on a semantic differential scale.

A study by Powell and Clayton (1980) dealt with the effects of training in a single life-skills area—interpersonal communications. They reported 50% fewer hospitalizations and more gainful employment or productive volunteer work two years after treatment for patients who received this training, compared with a Hawthorne treatment control group that received an equal amount of attention. Other studies (Bixler, 1972; Childers, 1973; Robinson, 1976) of the effects of interpersonal communication skills training with a variety of teacher groups showed significant positive gains for the teachers and/or their students.

When applied in the cause of prevention, the LST model has also shown encouraging results even though the model has not been fully implemented. In a study by Krebs (1981), three experimental classrooms, one each from the third, fourth, and fifth grades, were compared with three control classrooms. The students were posttested on the Barclay Classroom Climate Inventory (BCCI) (Barclay, 1978). The experimental classrooms showed statistically significant ($p < .020$ to $.001$) gains over the controls on Achievement Motivation, Control Stability, Energy Activity, Sociability-Affiliation, and Enterprising-Dominance and significant decreases on Introversion-Exclusiveness ($p < .025$ to $.046$). In addition, the fifth- and sixth-grade experimental classrooms made educationally and statistically significant gains on all scales of the Iowa Test of Basic Skills: Vocabulary, Reading, Language Skills,

Work/Study Skills, Mathematics, and Composite scores. The experimental students also scored significantly higher ($p < .01$ to $.04$) on teacher ratings of responsibility, respect, resourcefulness, and responsiveness (Pratt & Mastroianni, 1981).

The studies cited are admittedly few at this point. Several others are under way or are in the planning stages. I hope in the next few years to see experimental and clinical applications of the MIT/LST model that will further confirm its efficacy. All present signs are certainly pointing in that direction.

Mahoney and Arnkoff (1978) reviewed the "cognitive and self-control" therapies for a recent clinical handbook (Garfield & Bergin, 1978). Their reviews and conclusions lend considerable support to MIT/LST and related models. Their description of the "problem solving" approaches appears consistent with my definition and rationale for MIT/LST. They state: "With the problem-solving approaches, clients are not only taught specific coping skills, but also the more general strategies of assessment, problem definition, and so on. In a sense, the therapist is sharing years of professional training by making the client an apprentice in therapy—a student of effective self-regulation . . ." (p. 709).

In this review, Mahoney and Arnkoff summarize the criticisms leveled at contemporary approaches in psychotherapy as follows:

1. *Ineffectiveness,* particularly as defined by the client.
2. *Poor generalization* to problems and situations outside those specifically addressed by the therapist.
3. *Poor maintenance* [of therapeutic gains] over time.
4. *Poor cost-efficiency* as measured by both monetary and personal effort standards.
5. *Ethical dilemmas* in which the client's rights and responsibilities are not respected [p. 709].

A comparison of the features and initial research support for MIT/LST against the list above may help the reader to understand my excitement over the potential of this approach. Although it is premature to compare client ratings of MIT/LST with ratings of contemporary therapies, the May (1981), Krebs (1981), and Pratt and Mastroianni (1981) studies represent promising first efforts. Because of the strong emphasis on practice and homework in the teaching/training of generic life-skills, one can predict excellent transfer, or generalization, of training. To the extent that generalization of training is accomplished, the level of maintenance of therapeutic gains over time, as measured by adjustment to the demands of everyday living and by a lower incidence of readmission to treatment, should also be more than satisfactory. Since the training is based on effective models of life-skills, trainees *understand* the process and rationale for the model they are using. This level of trainee investment in the learning process should be far more beneficial than if trainees were just conditioned to give certain responses. Regarding cost-efficiency/ effectiveness, MIT/LST is equally applicable to the prevention and remediation of life-skills deficits. Preventive programs based on this approach should, over the long term, reduce the need for remedial interventions, which are inherently more costly in all cases. An added beneficial feature is, of course, its reliance on the small group as the primary modality; the more expensive individual treatment intervention simply does not work as well in MIT/LST. Finally, since this is an educational intervention, ethical issues should be minimized because participants are actively involved in their own learning and behavior change.

Mahoney and Arnkoff conclude their review with this optimistic assessment:

> Despite its broad therapeutic goals . . . this approach allows substantial room for the uniqueness of individual clients. . . . Moreover, it might be argued that the problem-solving therapies add substantial humanism to their empirical commitment. . . . If the problem-solving therapies [I maintain that MIT/LST is included under this rubric] continue to demonstrate therapeutic power, they may pose one of the most promising hybrids in clinical science [p. 709].

PROBLEMS, PROSPECTS, AND CONCLUSION

Multiple Impact Training/Life-Skills Training has been shown to be an appropriate model for both preventive and remedial mental health interventions. It was developed primarily on an adult psychiatric population, but it is equally effective when used as a curricular modality with schoolchildren. To date it has not been applied to mentally retarded or brain-damaged populations, but because it shares a number of characteristics with programs specifically designed for these persons, it should be applicable for adaptation to such groups.

Research and development efforts are under way to address the present "soft spots" of the model, some of which have been acknowledged earlier. For example, there is no currently accepted taxonomy of generic life-skills. A Delphi survey of experts in human development and skills training is being conducted in an effort to reach professional consensus on the elements of a comprehensive life-skills taxonomy. In the context of training itself, my colleagues and I have developed a number of effective approaches and useful materials. We are refining these and experimenting with new modules as we move toward a comprehensive training paradigm, which we expect will be applicable to LST in all settings and with all populations. Materials that can be disseminated on a broad basis are also under development. We know we are on solid ground, and we are satisfied that our approaches are effective. We expect to be able to share the results of our efforts with the professional community in the not-too-distant future.

Obstacles may, of course, hinder such efforts. One of these is an attitude that the mission of education should be limited to the traditional "three Rs" and that everything else is a "frill" that drains the taxpayer's pocket. Incorporating Life-Skills Training as an integral curricular component at all levels of the educational system will take time, imagination, and fortitude, but it must and will be accomplished. As computers take over teaching of the "three Rs," teachers will be relieved to teach life-skills. Skills training is already rapidly becoming the "preferred mode of treatment."

The attitude of the mental health community regarding "treatment" is another potential obstacle. Professional status is, unfortunately, still determined by the level of diagnosable pathology of the "patients" one treats. Educational interventions are not quite "respectable." We are confident that the steady stream of research supporting the efficacy of such interventions and the oppressive financial burden of traditional treatment approaches will gradually change these attitudes. Within the next century, positive mental health based on educational and training foundations will be as much a part of our society's commitments as universal literacy is today.

REFERENCES

Adkins, W. R. Life-coping skills: A fifth curriculum. *Teachers College Record,* 1974, *75,* 507–526.

Authier, J., Gustafson, K., Guerney, B., & Kasdorf, J. The psychological practitioner as a teacher: A theoretical-historical and practical review. *Counseling Psychologist,* 1975, *5,* 31–50.

Barclay, J. R. *Manual of the Barclay Classroom Climate Inventory.* Lexington, Ky.: Educational Skills Development, 1978.

Bixler, J. Influence of trainer-trainee cognitive similarity on the outcome of systematic human relations training. Unpublished doctoral dissertation, University of Georgia, 1972.

Bloom, B. S. *Human characteristics and school learning.* New York: McGraw-Hill, 1976.

Brown, R. S. Jogging may be therapeutic for the psychiatric patient. *Clinical Psychiatry News,* 1978, *6,* 1.

Brown, S. D. Coping skills training: An evaluation of a psychoeducational program in a community mental health setting. *Journal of Counseling Psychology,* 1980, *27,* 340–345.

Childers, W. C. An evaluation of the effectiveness of a human relations training model using in-class student teacher observation and interaction analysis. Unpublished doctoral dissertation, University of Georgia, 1973.

Collingwood, T. R. Effective physical functioning: A pre-condition for the helping process. *Counselor Education and Supervision,* 1976, *15,* 211–215.

Corsini, R. J. Individual Education: A system based on Individual Psychology. *Journal of Individual Psychology,* 1977, *33,* 295–349.

Crumbaugh, J. C., & Maholick, L. T. *PIL.* Munster, Ind.: Psychometric Affiliates, 1976.

Drum, D. J., & Knott, J. E. *Structured groups for facilitating development: Acquiring life skills, resolving life themes, and making life transitions.* New York: Human Sciences Press, 1977.

Dupont, H. Affective development: A Piagetian model. Paper presented at the UAP-USC Eighth Annual Interdisciplinary Conference "Piagetian Theory and the Helping Professions," Los Angeles, February 3–4, 1978.

Dupont, H. Affective development: Stage and sequence (A Piagetian interpretation). In R. L. Mosher (Ed.), *Adolescent development in education.* Berkeley, Calif.: McCutchan, in press.

D'Zurilla, T. J., & Goldfried, M. R. Problem solving and behavior modification. *Journal of Abnormal Psychology,* 1971, *78,* 107–126.

Erikson, E. H. *Childhood and society.* New York: Norton, 1950.

Erikson, E. H. *Childhood and society* (2nd ed.). New York: Norton, 1963.

Fabry, J. A. *The pursuit of meaning.* New York: Harper & Row, 1980.

Flavell, J. H. *The developmental psychology of Jean Piaget.* Princeton, N.J.: D. Van Nostrand, 1963.

Garfield, S. L., & Bergin, A. E. (Eds.). *Handbook of psychotherapy and behavior change: An empirical analysis* (2nd ed.). New York: Wiley, 1978.

Gazda, G. M. *Group counseling: A developmental approach.* Boston: Allyn & Bacon, 1971.

Gazda, G. M. Developmental education: A conceptual framework for a comprehensive counselling and guidance program. *Canadian Counsellor,* 1977, *12,* 36–40.

Gazda, G. M. *Group counseling: A developmental approach* (2nd ed.). Boston: Allyn & Bacon, 1978.

Gazda, G. M., Asbury, F. R., Balzer, F. J., Childers, W. C., Desselle, E., & Walters, R. P. *Human relations development: A manual for educators.* Boston: Allyn & Bacon, 1973.

Gazda, G. M., Asbury, F. R., Balzer, F. J., Childers, W. C., & Walters, R. P. *Human relations development: A manual for educators* (2nd ed.). Boston: Allyn & Bacon, 1977.

Gazda, G. M., Asbury, F. R., Balzer, F. J., Childers, W. C., & Walters, R. P. *Human relations development: A manual for educators* (3rd ed.). Boston: Allyn & Bacon, 1982.

Gazda, G. M., & Brooks, D. K., Jr. A comprehensive approach to developmental interventions. *Journal for Specialists in Group Work,* 1980, *5,* 120–126.

Gazda, G. M., Duncan, J. A., Maples, M. F., & Brown, J. L. *The heart of teaching applications handbook: A training manual for enhancing the human relations skills of educators.* Bloomington, Ind.: Agency for Instructional Television, 1976.

Gazda, G. M., Walters, R. P., & Childers, W. C. *Human relations development: A manual for health sciences.* Boston: Allyn & Bacon, 1975.

Gazda, G. M., Walters, R. P., & Childers, W. C. *Realtalk: Exercises in friendship and helping skills.* Atlanta: Humanics, 1980.

Gazda, G. M., Walters, R. P., & Childers, W. C. *Interpersonal communication: A handbook for health professionals.* Germantown, Md.: Aspen Systems Corporation, 1982.

Gesell, A., Ilg, F. L., & Ames, L. B. *Youth: The years from ten to sixteen.* New York: Harper, 1956.

Gesell, A., Ilg, F. L., Ames, L. B., & Bullis, G. E. *The child from five to ten.* New York: Harper, 1946.

Goldstein, A. P., Sprafkin, R. P., & Gershaw, N. J. *Skill training for community living: Applying Structured Learning Therapy.* New York: Pergamon Press, 1976.

Guerney, B., Stollak, G., & Guerney, L. The practicing psychologist as an educator: An alternative to the medical practitioner model. *Professional Psychology,* 1971, *2,* 271–283.

Havighurst, R. J. *Human development and education.* New York: Longmans, Green, 1953.

Havighurst, R. J. *Developmental tasks and education* (3rd ed.). New York: McKay, 1972.

Honigfeld, G., Gillis, R., & Klett, C. NOSIE-30: A treatment-sensitive ward behavior scale. *Psychological Reports,* 1966, *19,* 180–182.

Kohlberg, L. Continuities and discontinuities in childhood and adult moral development revisited. In P. L. Baltes & K. W. Schaie (Eds.), *Lifespan developmental psychology: Personality and socialization.* New York: Academic Press, 1973.

Kohlberg, L., & Turiel, E. Moral development and moral education. In G. Lesser (Ed.), *Psychology and educational practice.* Glenview, Ill.: Scott, Foresman, 1971.

Krebs, L. L. The effects of the Individual Education system on grade school children on selected variables in the social and affective areas. Unpublished master's thesis, DePaul University, 1981.

Lazarus, A. A. Multimodal behavior therapy in groups. In G. M. Gazda (Ed.), *Basic approaches to group psychotherapy and group counseling* (2nd ed.). Springfield, Ill.: Charles C Thomas, 1975.

Loevinger, J. *Ego development: Conceptions and theories.* San Francisco: Jossey-Bass, 1976.

Mahoney, M. J., & Arnkoff, D. Cognitive and self-control therapies. In S. L. Garfield & A. E. Bergin (Eds.), *Handbook of psychotherapy and behavior change: An empirical analysis* (2nd ed.). New York: Wiley, 1978.

May, H. J. The effects of life-skill training versus current psychiatric methods on therapeutic outcome in psychiatric patients. Unpublished doctoral dissertation, University of Georgia, 1981.

Miller, G. D. (Ed.). *Developmental education and other emerging alternatives in secondary guidance programs.* St. Paul: Pupil Personnel Services, Division of Instruction, Minnesota Department of Education, 1976.

Mosher, R. L., & Sprinthall, N. A. Psychological education in secondary schools: A program to promote individual and human development. *American Psychologist,* 1970, *25,* 911–924.

Mosher, R. L., & Sprinthall, N. A. Psychological education: A means to promote personal development during adolescence. *Counseling Psychologist,* 1971, *2*(4), 3–82.

National Assessment of Educational Progress. Draft of basic skills objectives. Unpublished paper. Denver: National Assessment of Educational Progress, Education Commission of the States, 1975.

Pierce, R., & Drasgow, J. Teaching facilitative interpersonal functioning to psychiatric inpatients. *Journal of Counseling Psychology,* 1969, *16,* 295–298.

Pierce, R., Schauble, P. B., & Wilson, R. R. Employing systematic human relations training for teaching constructive helper and helpee behavior in group therapy situations. *Journal of Research and Development in Education,* 1971, *4,* 97–109.

Powell, M. F., & Clayton, M. S. Efficacy of human relations training on selected coping behaviors of veterans in a psychiatric hospital. *Journal for Specialists in Group Work,* 1980, *5,* 170–176.

Pratt, A. B., & Mastroianni, M. Summary research on Individual Education. *Journal of Individual Psychology,* 1981, *37,* 232–246.

Robbins, L. C., & Hall, J. H. *How to practice prospective medicine.* Indianapolis, Ind.: Methodist Hospital, 1970.

Robinson, E. H., III. Students' perceptions of teachers' abilities to provide certain facilitative conditions and their relationship to language arts achievement gains. Unpublished doctoral dissertation, Duke University, 1976.

Sisson, P. J., Arthur, G. L., & Gazda, G. M. *Human relations for criminal justice personnel.* Boston: Allyn & Bacon, 1981.

Sprinthall, N. A., & Mosher, R. L. *Studies of adolescents in the secondary school.* Monograph No. 6. Cambridge, Mass.: Center for Research and Development, Harvard Graduate School of Education, 1969.

Super, D. E. Vocational development in adolescence and early adulthood: Tasks and behaviors. In D. E. Super, *Career development: Self-concept theory.* New York: College Entrance Examination Board, 1963.

Super, D. E., Crites, J. O., Hummel, R. C., Moser, H. P., Overstreet, P. L., & Warnath, C. F. *Vocational development: A framework for research.* Monograph No. 1. New York: Teachers College Press, 1957.

Vitalo, R. Teaching improved interpersonal functioning as a preferred mode of treatment. *Journal of Clinical Psychology,* 1971, *27,* 166–171.

Wadsworth, B. J. *Piaget's theory of cognitive development.* New York: McKay, 1971.

CHAPTER SIX

Social Skills Training

Eileen Gambrill

Eileen Gambrill is professor of social welfare at the University of California at Berkeley. She has also taught at the University of Michigan and at the University of Wisconsin at Madison. Her fields of interest include social skills training, decision making in foster care, and training professionals using a competency-based approach. Her research in social skills training has focused on the development of programs that help people increase their frequency of enjoyable social contacts and the development of social skills training programs for people over 65 who live in the community. She was a visiting scholar at the National Institute for Social Work, in London, during 1978 and 1979. A return visit in the summer of 1981 offered valuable opportunities to become acquainted with work in England concerning social skills training. Her publications include books as well as articles in a variety of journals.

In this chapter Eileen Gambrill provides an introduction to the rapidly expanding field of social skills training. Gambrill identifies issues in this field as she discusses recent conceptual, research, and applied developments. Her presentation of methods of assessment and her overview of applications can be profitably studied by all skills trainers and can serve as a reference source for the reader to locate more detailed information. Throughout, Gambrill underlines the complexity of social skills—emphasizing both behavioral and cognitive components—and of social skills training.

Social skills training programs have been developed for a range of situations and populations. One of the first areas to receive attention was interpersonal skills of professional helpers, including supervisors and teachers. A great deal of attention has been devoted to identifying the ingredients of effective helping behavior. Chapters in Part Two of this book illustrate this interest. Another general area to receive attention concerns social skills of subgroups of the general population—for example, youth, psychiatric patients, people who complain of depression (see Part One of this book). The ubiquitous feature of social interaction in getting along well in everyday life and the increasing evidence that degree of social competence is related to a variety of presenting concerns have encouraged research in this area (for example, Wine & Smye, 1981).

Additional information is now available concerning skills required for success, reactions that lead to failure, and related factors such as expectations. Theory and research related to social behavior should be considered in the conceptualization of social competence, the identification of component skills, and the construction of successful programs. Researchers in Britain have been more attentive to the integration of this material into training programs than those in the United States (see, for example, Argyle & Kendon, 1967; Trower, Bryant, & Argyle, 1978). Efforts to assess social skills within the United States have typically progressed in an atheoretical fashion, and they fall into two major categories: those that approach social skills as a trait and attempt to assess behavior over a range of situations and those that attempt to identify the verbal and nonverbal skills related to a particular situation (McFall, 1982; Trower, 1982). A major problem with the first kind of effort is failure to take into account the situational specificity of social behavior. A problem with the latter kind is failure to take into account a wide range of factors that may influence social behavior—for example, individual goals or cognitive factors such as expectations, attributions, and self-evaluations. The failure of many investigators to consider the unique value systems of individuals has been described by Wine (1981).

The term *assertion training* is used either to refer to training in specific kinds of social behaviors, such as refusing unwanted requests, or, as synonymous with *social skills training,* to embrace all social behaviors. For example, Wolpe (1958) uses the term *assertion* to refer to the expression of both positive and negative feelings. Great efforts have been made to distinguish among "aggressive," "assertive," and "passive behaviors." *Assertion* refers to the appropriate expression of social behaviors. Aggressive behavior entails self-enhancement at the expense of others. Submissive behavior entails reactions that allow other people to choose what is done. For example, if someone steps ahead of you in line, you might do nothing (passive), politely ask the person to step to the back of the line (assertive), or issue an implied threat, such as "Hey, if you don't . . ." (aggressive). Passive and aggressive behavior thus represent two global ways in which behavior can be ineffective. Gradually, these three terms are being replaced by the term *social skill.* One reason is the increasing recognition that this tripartite division of social behavior is a gross oversimplification.

This chapter offers an overview of social skills training. A process model of social behavior is described, including components of such a model. Important distinctions among terms used in the field are noted, and criteria for judging effective behavior discussed. Sources of assessment information and components of training programs are described, and examples of programs are given. The importance of planning for generalization and maintenance of gains is emphasized, and the effectiveness of social skill training is briefly discussed.

A PROCESS MODEL OF SOCIAL BEHAVIOR

The most satisfying empirical and theoretical views of social behavior attend to cognitions and emotions as well as overt behavior (for example, Argyle, Furnham, & Graham, 1981; Trower, 1982). People are considered to be active in the creation of their social environments, monitoring their performance and adjusting it according to the rules and constraints imposed by social situations (Harre & Secord, 1972; Mischel, 1973). Within this view, the person is not only an agent of action but a "watcher, commentator and critic as well" (Trower, 1982, p. 412). This is a *transactional model* that acknowledges the mutual influence between persons and environmental factors. Thus, people in part create their environments and, in turn, are influenced by them. It is a process model in which "the individual consciously monitors the immediate situation and his or her behavior and modifies his or her performance in the light of continuous external feedback and internal criteria such as a desired outcome" (p. 418). This view of social behavior emphasizes the importance of cognitive processes "by which rule-following action sequences are generated" (Trower, 1982, p. 413). That is, appropriate sequences of action related to particular situations are stored in our memory; socially competent people possess scripts for thousands of situations and employ them as relevant under the constraints of particular contexts—for example, initiating a conversation at a party. Our emotional reactions may alter the replay of these scripts.

Criteria for judging effective behavior have included the ratings of professionals based on observation of interaction in simulated situations, peer ratings, the reactions of significant others, and the occurrence or nonoccurrence of criterion behaviors, such as refusing a request. Definitions of socially effective behavior differ in the extent to which they consider the interests of others. For example, Argyle (1980) defines social competence as "the ability, the possession of the necessary skills, to produce the desired effects on other people in social situations" (p. 123). Spence (1981) defines social skills as "those responses that elicit reinforcing consequences from a given social interaction, in a manner that is socially acceptable and does no harm to others" (pp. 159–160). Trower (1982) distinguishes between "social skills" and "social skill." The former term refers to the "normative component behaviors or actions—single elements (looks, nods, lexical items, etc.) or identifiable sequences of elements, or acts or scripts (greetings, etc.) that ordinary people use in social interaction and that are governed by rules" (p. 418). These are acquired by experience, retained in memory, and retrieved as necessary. The particular meaning of any one component depends on its meaning in the context of a larger episode. Social skill is defined as "the process of generating skilled behavior directed toward a goal" (p. 418) (see also Argyle & Kendon, 1967; Argyle et al., 1981). Social competence is defined as "possession of the capability to generate skilled behavior"; social performance is "the actual production of skilled behavior in specific situations" (p. 419), which requires appropriate expectancies, subjective values, and other elements described in the next section.

Trower argues correctly that the bulk of work in the area of social skills training in the United States has emphasized social skills rather than this process model of social skill, with its much heavier emphasis on the cognitive components of socially effective behavior. The components of this model are described below.

COMPONENTS OF A PROCESS MODEL OF SOCIAL SKILL

A process model of social skill includes cognitive, physiological, and overt components. These components correspond to ways in which social behavior may be deficient (Furnham & Argyle, 1981). Important cognitive processes include valid inferences about self and others and relatively realistic self-standards. These cognitive processes are in addition to a repertoire of behavioral skills (Trower, 1982).

Goals/Plans/Feedback

Social situations permit the pursuit of goals, and different goals are achievable in different situations (Argyle et al., 1981; Graham, Argyle, & Furnham, 1980). Examples of goals include initiating a conversation, sharing a funny story, and obtaining advice or reassurance. People may be ineffective by having inappropriate goals in a situation, by not identifying clear goals, or by failing to plan how to achieve these. Or they may be unresponsive to feedback about the effects of their behavior.

Perception

Effective social behavior requires attention to and accurate observation of other people. We rely on the verbal and nonverbal behavior of others as feedback to modify our behavior. People who are not very effective in social situations often make errors in their perception of others. They may, for example, not notice that a person rarely smiles or rarely looks at them. Or they may not notice that a person does not ask them any questions. Inaccurate stereotypes cause a great deal of trouble. Viewing people in terms of poles such as "good or bad" encourages incorrect perceptions because variations in behavior are less likely to be noticed. It is important to have both the ability and the motivation to seek out and use social information.

Translation

We must not only perceive the behavior of others accurately, we must also interpret their behavior correctly. For example, is a smile a sign of friendliness in a particular situation or a sign of hostility? Social interaction involves a process in which we are constantly making decisions; we are aware of only some of these decisions. People differ in their accuracy of perception and translation and in the extent to which they "monitor" their behavior. People who attend more to external cues are more socially effective than people who attend more to internal cues (Snyder & Monson, 1975). Low-assertive people do not use the same information as people who are more effective. They may be extracting information that is less useful in social situations. Accuracy of perception and translation is partly dependent on knowledge of the language, values, and frameworks used by others as well as rules and roles related to particular situations. It is also influenced by attributions and self-efficacy (see, for example, Snyder & Swann, 1978), which, in turn, are influenced by the results of our past performance.

Taking the Role of Others

People who are more skilled in perceiving others' points of view are more effective in social tasks than people who are less skilled (Feffer & Suchotliffe, 1966). It is thus important to accurately perceive the perceptions as well as the reactions of others (Argyle, 1981).

Situations

Effective social behavior is situationally specific. As with all other competencies, effective use of skills requires "the ability to identify when certain skill conditions should be offered such as communicating interest, understanding, empathy, and perhaps even more important, when not to" (Strupp, 1976, p. 99). The particular behaviors that will be successful will be highly dependent on the interpersonal situation. Each situation can be considered in terms of the *goals* that are attainable, the *rules* about what may or may not be done, and the special *skills* and *knowledge* that may be required. Universal rules include being polite, being friendly, and avoiding embarrassing people (Argyle, 1981). The physical context within which an exchange occurs will pose structural barriers to certain types of exchanges, as will role differences between participants.

Verbal and Nonverbal Behaviors

Socially effective behavior requires the ability to initiate, sustain, and end conversations. Ineffective behavior is often related to *too little* verbal and nonverbal behavior rather than an excess of behaviors. Socially inadequate people have lower rates of smiling and looking, compared with "normals" (Trower, 1980). Speech and gaze have been found to be highly related to judgments of social skill (Conger & Conger, 1982; Trower, 1980). Males who are not shy respond more rapidly, speak more frequently, and break a larger percentage of silences than men who are shy (Pilkonis, 1977). Recent studies show that timing of responses is especially important (Fischetti, Curran, & Wessberg, 1977). Behavioral excesses are often related to deficiencies. For example, someone who monopolizes a conversation may not possess effective listening skills. Nonverbal signals are more important than verbal behaviors in expressing attitudes such as friendliness or assertion (Furnham & Argyle, 1981). Facial expression and tone of voice are especially important channels for indicating emotions and attitudes; however, gestures, posture, and gaze are also relevant (Harper, Wiens, & Matarazzo, 1978). Nonverbal behaviors help to "frame" verbal statements—that is, to indicate how a message should be viewed. Characteristics such as warmth and friendliness are made up of *many* small verbal and nonverbal components, such as gaze, smiles, facial expression, and appropriate questions.

Self-Presentation

We offer information to others about our role, status, and claimed social identities. What people wear, their gestures, facial expressions, and posture, as well as what they reveal about themselves through their statements offer information to others that will influence their reactions. Self-presentation "can go wrong in several ways—too little information, too much, bogus, too 'gray,' and misleading self-presentations" (Furnham & Argyle, 1981, p. 128; see also Schlenker, 1980).

Feedback

Socially effective people make accurate use of feedback. They pay attention to how others respond to their actions, and they modify subsequent behaviors in view of these reactions. People who are not effective in social interactions often fail to attend to feedback, misinterpret reactions, or do not modify their behavior to obtain more positive reactions. In turn, they may also fail to *offer* feedback or may offer inappropriate feedback. Failure to respond appropriately to feedback may be due to a number of factors, including perceptual and interpretive problems or interfering emotional reactions. Some people are overly vigilant to negative feedback from others and are not aware of occasions when they are successful. Others may attend to social feedback and have the skills to change their approach but fail to do so because of high anxiety.

Both verbal and nonverbal behaviors are involved in offering rewarding feedback. Nonverbal behaviors associated with liking include (1) closer interpersonal distances, (2) touching, (3) forward lean during encounters, (4) body and head orientations that face others, (5) moderate body relaxation, (6) "open" body positions with arms unfolded and legs uncrossed (for females only), (7) eye contact, (8) positive facial expressions, smiling, (9) affirmative head nods, (10) moderate amount of gesturing and animation, and (11) pleasant and supportive "paralanguage" that signals interest in what others are saying—for example, minimal verbal cues such as "um-hum" (Schlenker, 1980, p. 257).

Rewardingness and Reinforcement

We influence each other by offering small reinforcements, showing our approval or disapproval, our pleasure or displeasure. If we fail to use these, we forfeit a critical source of influence. Offering high levels of positive rewards will encourage people to like us, whereas low levels of positive rewards will have the opposite effect (see, for example, Willner, Braukmann, Kirigin, Fixen, Phillips, & Wolf, 1977).

Flexibility, Creativity, and Coping Skills

The effectiveness of social behavior is related to flexibility in choosing from a variety of options as well as skill in generating new options and skills in specific situations. Establishing helping relationships, for example, requires flexibility in adjusting behavior to the unique behavior and interests of each person within the situational constraints and possibilities of particular contexts. In some situations, taking direct action, such as requesting or negotiating changes, may be most effective; in others, indirect actions, such as calming self-talk, reframing the situation, or delaying a reaction, may be most effective.

In novel situations or those that present conflicting demands, available skills may not be satisfactory. Such situations require problem-solving behavior to review or increase possible options and to select one that is likely to be effective. "On the spot" cost/benefit analyses will often be required for planning social strategies in which both short-term and long-term outcomes related to given actions are considered, including personal outcomes (effects on oneself) and social outcomes (effects on others) (Nezu & D'Zurilla, 1979). Certain rules of thumb will be useful in planning, such as the rule to use the most positive response (or the minimally negative response) whenever possible and the rule to ignore minor annoyances that do not really matter. A troubled interpersonal situation or one requiring the regulation of emotion associated with this calls for a coping response (Wrubel, Benner, & Lazarus, 1981). Coping options will be influenced by personal characteristics as well as by the situation involved and by related alternatives, resources, and consequences. Options may include *seeking information, using direct action* in which the environment or personal reactions are altered, *inhibiting action* (choosing to do nothing), or selecting a *cognitive coping* strategy in which attention and/or the way events are viewed is altered (Lazarus & Launier, 1978). Examples of cognitive coping strategies include denial and intellectual detachment. For example, an imagined interpersonal slight may be viewed as irrelevant to the task at hand. There is increasing evidence that these strategies are frequently used in everyday life by well-functioning people (Lazarus, 1982). People who are skilled avoid many situations that would require a coping reaction if they did occur.

Relation between Thoughts and Social Behavior

Goals, plans, expectations, appraisals of situations, attributions of outcomes, how attention is focused, and how social signals are interpreted influence social behavior. These, in turn, are influenced by our performance—that is, what we actually do and what outcomes result. A situation may be appraised as irrelevant, as benign, or as stressful—that is, as having some actual or potential outcome considered already or potentially harmful or some threatening harm or challenge (Wrubel et al., 1981). Just as with anxiety in noninterpersonal situations, negative self-instructions may occur in anticipation of, during, and/or after encounters. Relevant cognitive skills include those that allow us to manage our emotional reactions, such as anxiety or anger, and to "take the role of the other." If we know how a person thinks about herself and what she thinks she can accomplish in certain situations, we are more likely to accurately predict what she will do. There is increasing evidence supporting the influence of cognitive events in social behavior (see, for example, Glass & Merluzzi, 1981) and increasing information on how to "tap" the internal dialogue in order to identify what thoughts occur (Merluzzi, Glass, & Genest, 1981).

People with high or moderate social anxiety, in contrast to those with low anxiety, interpret the same feedback as more negative and have a greater expectancy that others will evaluate them negatively (Smith & Sarason, 1975). The importance of self-evaluations is highlighted by the finding that socially anxious men underestimate positive aspects of their performance and overestimate negative aspects, compared with less socially anxious men (Valentine & Arkowitz, 1975). They also have a more accurate memory for negative information and a less accurate one for positive information (O'Banion & Arkowitz, 1977), and this kind of selective memory is likely to be associated with negative self-evaluations as well as with infrequent self-reinforcement for social behaviors.

Significant relationships have been found between scores on the Social Interaction Self-Statement Test and social anxiety and social skill (Glass, Merluzzi, Biever, & Larsen, in press). Self-statements were also related to self-evaluations. Subjects who had a high frequency of negative self-talk tended to rate their tension level higher and their skill level lower following interactions. These findings point to the importance of cognitive factors in relation to effective social skills and the need to assess the nature of a person's internal dialogue in social situations. If negative thoughts are found, intervention should include a focus on altering them. Perceived self-efficacy influences what will be attempted in a given situation and how long efforts will be sustained in the face of difficulties (Bandura, 1977). Research to date suggests that successful performance is the most effective way to alter related thoughts.

ASSESSMENT

Social skills training is a competency-based approach to social interaction, in contrast to a deficiency-based approach. It includes an emphasis on determining people's ability to construct competencies (Mischel, 1981) and on offering them additional skills. Situations of concern must be identified during assessment, and the adequacy of relevant repertoires examined in relation to the requisites for effective behaviors in these situations. The components of effective social behavior indicate personal and situational characteristics that should be attended to. Careful assessment is necessary to identify relevant situations, to determine whether required skills are available, to find out whether there are discrimination problems in relation to when behaviors can most profitably be displayed, and to determine whether negative thoughts or anxiety interferes with effective behavior (Gambrill, 1977). It is thus important not only to identify the person's ability to construct effective behavior but also to identify factors that may interfere with effective social behaviors that are potentially available, such as negative expectations. People may or may not have any notion that their social skills are related to a presenting concern such as depression or substance abuse. Relevant information can be gathered through a variety of means, including self-report, written measures, self-monitoring, analogue or role-play situations, and observations in real-life situations. Ideally, multiple sources of information should be used, because one alone may not offer accurate information. These are briefly described below.

Self-Report

A person may offer examples of interactions that indicate a lack of effective social behavior. He may report that it is only after a supervisor unjustly criticizes him or his wife arranges social events he does not like that he starts to "feel depressed." The interview can be used to determine the range of situations in which interpersonal difficulties are experienced and the consequences that follow both adaptive and inappropriate social behaviors. Descriptions of exactly what is done, said, thought, and felt in relevant situations should be obtained. It is often useful to check a person's report against information gained during interviews with significant others such as a spouse, or against data from other sources, because often an individual will not be able to identify important deficits or surfeits in his or her social behavior and may misinterpret the reactions of others.

Written Measures

Self-report paper-and-pencil inventories, such as the Assertion Inventory (Gambrill & Richey, 1975), may be used to gain an overview of degree of comfort in various social situations as well as information on how the person usually handles a situation. Respondents indicate degree of discomfort (on a scale from 1 to 5), as well as how likely they are to carry out a given behavior if the opportunity arises (on a scale from 1 to 5), in relation to 40 situations. Examples include initiating a conversation with a stranger and requesting the return of borrowed items. A 55-item Interpersonal Situation Inventory has been developed for psychiatric patients (Goldsmith & McFall, 1975). Patients respond to each situation with one of five alternatives, ranging from being able to handle a situation and feeling comfortable to not being able to handle a situation and feeling uncomfortable. Another alternative permits respondents to indicate that the situation is not personally relevant. Written measures related to particular kinds of situations have been developed, such as the Survey of Heterosexual Interactions (Twentyman & McFall, 1975), which describes 20 situations. Respondents indicate their ability to initiate or carry on a conversation on a 5-point scale.

Paper-and-pencil inventories can be used as screening devices to identify social situations that are difficult, and they are useful to find out whether a person can identify appropriate behaviors. More specific information must be gained by other methods, such as behavioral interviews, self-monitoring, role playing, or observation in the natural environment.

Self-Monitoring

Self-monitoring, in which a person keeps track of some behavior, thought, or feeling in certain situations, can offer helpful information for assessment as well as evaluation of progress. For example, a person may keep a log of relevant situations in the natural environment, noting the situation, what was said or done, satisfaction with the response, subjective rating of discomfort, what he would have liked to say or do, and what he thought about and felt. It is also helpful to ask people to write down what they think an effective response would be, to determine whether they are aware of effective reactions.

Analogue Situations

Observation of relevant behaviors in real-life settings is often difficult. Analogue measures, in which situations in the natural environment are simulated, are often used instead. A person can be asked to role-play behavior in situations of concern, such as beginning an employment interview, with reciprocal roles assumed by the counselor after determining how significant others may act. This information may be gained by first asking the person to role-play the part of a significant other. Reciprocal roles may be played by other persons who are available, such as secretaries.

Video or audiotape can be used to record interactions. It is important to make the role play as lifelike as possible, carefully describing the context, so that both nonverbal and verbal behaviors can be accurately assessed. If a person has difficulty expressing complaints to his employer, for example, the role play should be initiated with the person leaving the room and then reentering it so that posture, eye contact, and gait can be assessed when he first presents himself. Perhaps he avoids looking at the counselor, enters the room with drooped shoulders, and shuffles his feet uncertainly. It is important to evaluate nonverbal as well as verbal behaviors.

Role-playing situations have been developed for a number of populations, including psychiatric patients (Goldsmith & McFall, 1975; Goldstein, Sprafkin, & Gershaw, 1976), adolescents (Freedman, Donahue, Rosenthal, Schlundt, &

McFall, 1978; Goldstein, Sprafkin, Gershaw, & Klein, 1980; Hazel, Schumaker, Sherman, & Sheldon-Wildgen, 1981), children (Reardon, Hersen, Bellack, & Foley, 1979), the elderly (Berger & Rose, 1977; Edinberg, Karoly, & Gleser, 1977). Audiotape has often been used to present situations (see, for example, Perri & Richards, in press; Warren & Gilner, 1978). One scene is presented at a time, and the person's responses are recorded for later review. Videotape scene presentation has also been used, as well as live confederates. For example, Arkowitz, Lichtenstein, McGovern, and Hines (1975) asked their subjects to interact with a confederate and get to know her. They assessed duration of gaze and talk, number of silences, verbal reinforcements, and head nods and smiles as well as speech content. Asking people to verbally describe their thoughts and feelings during the role-played interactions, as well as their perception of what others were thinking and feeling, can be helpful in identifying constructive and dysfunctional feelings and thoughts. Paper and pencil as well as behavioral analogues may be used as described above under the description of self-report measures (see Nay, 1977).

Observation

Role-playing methods are artificial and may not reflect behavior in real-life situations. For this reason, role playing may be supplemented by observation of interaction with significant others either in the office or at home. Lewinsohn (1974), for example, observed depressed clients interacting with family members at home. He also used observation during group meetings. Observation of interaction is used extensively in behavioral marital counseling, where the main aim may be to enhance interaction. Valuable information can be gained by observing people in real-life situations. It is often easy to arrange this. If a person has difficulty in service situations, she can be accompanied to a store and her behavior observed to identify effective and ineffective components. As with simulated situations, asking people to share their thoughts will be helpful in identifying how these should be altered.

Physiological Measures

Little attention has been devoted to measuring physiological changes that may accompany social interaction. Heart-rate and pulse measures have been used to assess anxiety during exchanges (for example, Twentyman & McFall, 1975). Portable, unobtrusive measurement instruments will facilitate gathering such information (see also Kiritz & Moos, 1974; Lynch, 1977).

COMPONENTS OF SOCIAL SKILLS TRAINING

Social skills training is designed to enhance observational, performance, and cognitive skills related to effective social behaviors in particular situations. As noted in the section on assessment, deficiencies in skilled behavior may involve inappropriate goals, inaccurate perception or translation, or deficient performance, as well as a variety of other factors, including anxiety in social situations. Social skill training consists of a variety of components, including model presentation or demonstration, behavior rehearsal or role playing, feedback, guidance, and homework assignments. Textual material may be used to offer information. For example, written material was employed in a study designed to increase initiation of social contacts by women (Gambrill, 1973). With undergraduates, instructional control coupled with guided practice (coaching and behavior rehearsal) may be sufficient to increase effective behaviors (for example, McFall & Twentyman, 1973); however, with other populations, such as psychiatric patients, modeling has been required to achieve effects with behaviors such as resisting pressure (see Hersen, 1979).

The nature of each person's goals and related cognitive, physiological, and behavioral assets, deficits, and surfeits should be considered in the design of intervention procedures. If appropriate behaviors exist but, because of anxiety, are not performed, intervention focuses on offering training in behavioral and cognitive stress-management skills. If skills are absent, a procedure designed to develop them, including model presentation and behavior rehearsal, should be selected. Discrimination training is required when skills are available but not performed at appropriate times. For example, appropriate ways of refusing requests of a spouse may be of value in work situations but not be employed there. Thus, the selection of procedures flows directly from assessment. Like any helping endeavor, assessment is an ongoing process, since more information is gathered during intervention, and assessment is a reactive process in that changes may occur during that stage as a result of clearly defining goals and identifying helpful verbal and nonverbal behavior. Assessment should sharpen observational skills and discourage the use of global labels. Participants should learn to discriminate between effective and ineffective behavior in relation to desired goals. This training is continued during intervention through guidance, model presentation, practice, and feedback.

In our work concerning social skills training with the elderly here at Berkeley, we first identified situations of concern to a population of people over age 65 who attended senior and nutrition centers (Gambrill & Barth, 1981). Situations of greatest concern were then used in a training program carried out in a group format. These included ending conversations, refusing unwanted requests, asking favors, initiating conversations, telling a significant other about a bothersome behavior, and asking someone who is annoying you in a public situation to stop. Participants were given task cards related to each situation, which included descriptions of important behaviors related to the skill and the situations in which it could be used. Weekly, individually tailored homework assignments related to each skill were agreed upon.

Guidance

Instructions, prompting, and programming of change are used to ensure successful acquisition of skills. Each skill to be learned, including the exact verbal and nonverbal behaviors that constitute the skill as well as situations in which the skill can be used to attain certain outcomes, should be described. Important components and their sequence may be noted on task cards or checklists (see, for example, Spiegler & Agigian, 1977), and participants can refer to these during rehearsal and model presentation. Thus, instructions can be used to "prompt" behaviors—to encourage people to engage in certain behaviors rather than others. Use of guidance in this manner offers participants suggestions for attaining social goals such as refusing an unwanted request or initiating a conversation. It is important to clearly describe relevant verbal and nonverbal behaviors and when these should be used.

Specific goals should be established for each training session. Perhaps only one or two behaviors will be the focus of any one session. Or the initial repertoire might be such that all required behaviors can be practiced. Assessment should reveal competencies that are available, and training should build on these. Thus, goals are established for each person during each session. Guidance is also provided by prompting during rehearsal and feedback, as discussed below. Participants are coached to develop responses that are as positive as possible. Such behaviors are more likely to be effective.

Demonstration

Demonstration (model presentation) and rehearsal are usually employed when assessment indicates that a person lacks requisite behaviors to achieve certain goals. The advantage of model presentation is that an entire chain of behavior can be demonstrated and the person asked to imitate it. Nonverbal as well as verbal behaviors can be demonstrated and attention drawn to those that are especially important. The effectiveness of model presentation in establishing new behaviors, in decreasing avoidance behaviors, and in facilitating behaviors is well documented (Bandura, 1969). Models are more effective if they are similar to the person in sex and age, if they are perceived to have a high status, if their reactions are followed by positive consequences, and if attention is drawn to desired response elements (Bandura, 1969). For example, a person may be asked to notice the model's eye contact, his hand motions, and the orientation of his posture toward others. The model may verbalize appropriate positive thoughts during the role play if effective social skills are hampered by negative thoughts. At first, helpful self-statements can be spoken out loud when imitating the model's behavior and then, by instruction, gradually moved to a cognitive level. The effects of modeling are enhanced if observers have opportunities to practice the observed behavior and if they are asked to identify important components of, and general rules associated with, the modeled behavior. For example, observers who summarize the model's behavior are more able to learn and retain information (see, for example, Bandura, Grusec, & Menlove, 1966). Imagining multiple models and favorable consequences is more effective than imagining only one model or a lack of positive effects.

Effective behaviors may be demonstrated by the counselor or other group members, or written scripts, audiotape, videotape, or film may be used. The advantage of written material is that it can be referred to on an as-needed basis. Essential elements of responses can be highlighted. A checklist can be provided for each situation, so that participants can review their own behavior, thoughts, and feelings against it to assess their responses and the outcomes that result. People can be instructed to observe others in similar roles who are effective and to write down in a log the situation, what was done, and what happened. This increases exposure to a variety of effective models, offers examples to use during rehearsal, increases discrimination concerning when to employ certain behaviors, and permits vicarious extinction of anxiety reactions through observation of positive reactions.

Practice

Following model presentation, participants are requested to practice the modeled behavior. This provides an opportunity to practice new behaviors in a safe environment. It also allows others present, such as a counselor or other group members, to observe behavior, noting appropriate nonverbal or verbal components and those that still require some work. The contexts focused on should be clearly described and realistically arranged so that behavior is practiced in a situation that is similar to the real-life context. Guidelines for rehearsal have been discussed by many authors (for example, Jakubowski & Lange, 1978). Coaching or prompting may be used during rehearsal to encourage appropriate behaviors. Hand signals can be used to "prompt" reactions. Their advantage is that the scene can be continued while coaching is provided in relation to specific behaviors. More direct communication may be arranged by use of the "bug in the ear," a remote-control device that allows the trainer to speak to one person unheard by others. If the reciprocal role is being played by the counselor, such prompts may be more difficult to give unless their precise meaning is arranged beforehand. Prompts should be gradually faded out as skills increase.

Covert modeling or rehearsal, in which a person imagines herself or someone else acting effectively in social situations, can be used to offer additional practice. Covert rehearsal has been found to be as effective as overt rehearsal in increasing skills in some populations (Kazdin, 1973). Hierarchies ranked in terms of the degree of anxiety or anger that situations induce can be used to gradually establish new skills. Rehearsal should start with situations that result in small degrees of arousal, and as these are mastered, higher-level scenes can be introduced. Escalation of scenes should be carefully programmed in accord with the skill and comfort level of each person. Rehearsal may be required for each item in the hierarchy. If a person is too uncomfortable to engage in a role play, a script may be provided and responses read from this, rather than asking the person to ad lib an imitation of a model. As comfort increases, role playing can be introduced.

McFall and Lillesand (1971) used model presentation, coaching, and rehearsal to increase refusal of unreasonable requests. Assessment included recording the student's responses to nine prerecorded stimulus situations. During training, a tape-recorded narrator first described the scene. The student then responded covertly or overtly to the scene, then listened to one male and one female model, and was coached regarding the components of an effective reaction. Covert rehearsal produced greater improvement than overt rehearsal. Imagery during covert modeling can be checked by asking the person to verbalize what she is imagining.

Constructive Feedback

Positive feedback should be offered following each rehearsal. Previously established criteria should be used, and checklists describing these can be referred to during feedback. For instance, perhaps a person was smiling and nodding while saying no. After praise for appropriate behaviors, she could be given feedback saying so and then coached to try again without smiling and nodding. Positive aspects of the performance are carefully noted and praised, including small improvements. Critical comments, such as "You can do better" or "That wasn't too good," should be avoided. Such feedback helps people to discriminate behavior that they should increase, decrease, or vary. It is important to give clear instructions, identifying specific behaviors. It is more helpful to point out lack of eye contact and lack of "I" statements than to tell a person she was "evasive" or "hostile." Reinforcement for improvement should be in relation to a person's past performance rather than in terms of comparisons with others. This offers people a model of how to alter their own behavior (to identify small, achievable desired changes, to practice them, and to offer praise for improvements).

A structured format for feedback in a group setting has been developed at the Oxnard Mental Health Center (Oxnard, California) to promote systematic feedback and to ensure involvement of all group members (Liberman, King, DeRisi, & McCann, 1975). Group members are asked to rate behaviors in each role play on a scale from 1 (very poor) to 5 (excellent; little or no room for improvement). These include facial expression, use of hands, voice loudness, posture, eye contact, voice fluency, and content. The rating is offered in comparison with a person's last role play. The "average" rating of the group members is placed on a blackboard beside each behavior. Group members who gave high ratings or whose ratings deviated from those of the others can then be asked to offer reasons for their ratings. Liberman and associates have found that even withdrawn clients tend to carefully monitor the rehearsals of the other participants with this system of feedback. Modeling effects are enhanced, because attention to rehearsals is heightened. Models are represented as needed, and rehearsal, prompts, and feedback are continued until desired outcomes and comfort levels are demonstrated.

Homework Assignments

Much of the important work in social skills training is carried out in real-life settings. After required skill and comfort levels are attained, new behaviors can be tried out in the natural environment through assignments. Initial assignments are tasks that have a high probability of being followed by positive consequences and entail minimal discomfort. Negative consequences can often be avoided by understanding the relationships and interpersonal dynamics of the situations in which new behavior is proposed (Wolpe, 1958). If negative reactions may occur, a person should be prepared by having a variety of options available, including positive self-instructions (see, for example, Meichenbaum & Turk, 1976) and self-reinforcement skills (Gambrill & Richey, in press). Skills for coping with anger and potential aggression may also be required. Ideally, significant others should be involved in the intervention program; however, this is not always possible. With many goals, such as those related to service situations, dealing with professionals, or increasing social contacts, strangers may be involved. People should be trained to identify individuals who are likely to offer positive reactions. Training should also be provided in *when* to seek certain social goals, such as initiating a conversation with a stranger. Checklists or task cards related to assignments provide reminders of important components related to particular situations (see, for example, Hazel et al., 1981; see Shelton & Levy, 1981, for further discussion of assignments). The first instance of effective behavior may not be an exact replica of one that has been rehearsed. Guidance, model presentation, practice, and feedback provide information about important elements of effective behavior, and people are encouraged to vary their reactions in appropriate ways.

EXAMPLES OF SOCIAL SKILLS TRAINING PROGRAMS

Social skills training has been carried out with a wide variety of populations; however, only in some instances has a behavior-analytic approach been used in which situations of concern to a particular population are identified by asking members of that population and in which response options are systematically identified and evaluated (Goldfried & D'Zurilla, 1969).

Social Skills Training with Psychiatric Patients

Social competence has been found to be more important than psychiatric diagnosis in discriminating people who are hospitalized from those who are not (Zigler & Phillips, 1961). In a study by Goldsmith and McFall (1975), 80% of a sample of psychiatric patients reported some difficulty in interpersonal situations. Social skill training has been used with inpatient populations as well as with outpatients. Goldsmith and McFall (1975) used the behavior-analytic process recommended by Goldfried and D'Zurilla (1969) to develop a social skill training program for male psychiatric patients. The first step was to identify situations that were difficult for this population. A group of outpatients were asked to give specific examples of interpersonal situations that were difficult for them. They were asked to describe the context, to identify the participants and purpose of each interaction, and to describe the flow of interaction—that is, who said what to whom. Situational contexts reported included dating, making friends, having job interviews, interacting with authorities, interacting with service personnel, and interacting with people whom patients viewed as more intelligent or attractive or who appeared in some way different. Interpersonal contexts most frequently mentioned included initiating and terminating interactions, making personal disclosures, handling conversational silences, responding to rejection, and being assertive. The 55 problem situations generated were then presented on audiotape to 20 male inpatients, who indicated which of five alternatives best described the way they would respond in the situation. An item was retained only when more than 80% reported some difficulty, more than 20% reported both discomfort and inability to handle the situation, and fewer than 25% indicated that the item was not relevant. Additional steps included obtaining information on appropriate and inappropriate reactions to each situation and evaluating the effectiveness of these reactions.

Social skill training programs for psychiatric patients have also been developed by Spiegler and Agigian (1977), by Goldstein et al. (1976) (see Chapter 4 in this book), and by Anthony, Pierce, Cohen, and Cannon (1980). See also Hersen (1979), Monti, Corriveau, and Curran (1982), and Trower et al. (1978).

Social Skills Training for Children and Adolescents

Increasing attention has been devoted to enhancing children's interpersonal skills, especially those that concern peer interactions (Asher & Hymel, 1981; Cartledge & Milburn, 1980). In addition to observation and role playing, sociometric ratings are used. These offer information about the extent to which children have friends or are accepted by their peers. They do not indicate the behaviors that are related to sociometric status (Asher & Hymel, 1981). Work in this area has resulted in identification of two types of low-accepted children: (1) children who are neglected by their peers—that is, they receive few or no positive nominations—and (2) those who are rejected by their peers—they receive several negative nominations in addition to few or no positive nominations. Thus, some children without friends are openly rejected by their peers, whereas other children are merely neglected. Differences have also been found between likability and friendship (Asher & Hymel, 1981). Other programs that involve interpersonal skills of children include those in which children are trained to prompt more frequent positive feedback from parents (for example, Fedoravicius, 1973) and/or teachers (Graubard, Rosenberg, & Miller, 1971) and to initiate more mutually interesting conversations with parents (Jewett & Clark, 1979).

Freedman and her colleagues (1978) used a behavior-analytic approach to identify situations of concern to delinquent youth and effective response options in these. This information was then employed in a social skill training program. Goldstein et al. (1980) developed a social skills training program for adolescents that includes 50 skills, such as convincing others, giving instructions, introducing oneself, gathering information, and setting goals (see also Hazel et al., 1981; Shure, 1979). Adolescents have been trained to encourage more positive feedback from staff in residential settings (Seymour & Stokes, 1976). Programs have been developed to offer children more effective self-protective skills to use when approached by a potential kidnapper or child molester (Poche, Brouwer, & Swearingen, 1981).

Social Skills Training Related to Family Interaction

An extensive literature exists describing communication training programs for couples with relationship problems (for example, Birchler, 1979; Jacobson, 1982). Programs have been developed to help couples learn more effective problem-solving, decision-making, and conflict-resolution skills, as well as how to offer a higher frequency of positive verbal and nonverbal behaviors on an everyday basis (for example, Stuart, 1980). Parent-training programs include an emphasis on enhancing parents' skills in using effective instructions and increasing positive feedback for appropriate behaviors (see, for example, Dangel & Polster, in press; Forehand & McMahon, 1981). Shoemaker and Paulson (1976) used assertion training in a group context with 16 mothers who reported child-rearing difficulties and who showed an unassertive style of communication. Appropriate behaviors were encouraged through the use of tokens distributed by the trainer and by other group members. Tokens provide a source of immediate feedback for behavior in a manner that does not require interruption of ongoing conversation. White tokens were offered for assertive behaviors or reports about these. Red tokens were given for aggressive statements such as threatening or provoking comments, sarcasm, malicious joking, insults, blaming, name calling, and interrupting someone unless the other person had interrupted the speaker or was trying to change the topic. Blue tokens were given for submissive reactions such as overapologies, extreme or continual self-criticism, inappropriate changing of the topic, interjected laughter or joking to release tension if avoiding a question, refusal to speak when spoken to, or curt answers to avoid issues, such as "I don't know." The mothers increased effective and decreased aggressive statements and reported positive changes in their children's behavior. Husbands, although not participating in training, also showed increases in assertive statements and decreases in aggressive statements.

Assertion training of husbands has been found to lead to changes in the behavior of their wives (Eisler, Miller, Hersen, & Alford, 1974). Here, too, training was followed by a decrease in the frequency of negative expression by both partners and an increase in the frequency of positive expressions. Thus, an increase in the assertive behavior of one family member has been found to result in positive changes in other family members. Significant increases in effective behaviors (for example, nonattacking requests) and decreases in verbal behaviors coded as aggressive (for example, disparagement) have also been found following conjoint assertion training with couples (Epstein, DeGiovanni, & Jayne-Lazarus, 1978). Landau and Paulson (1977) employed assertion training with 16 Spanish-speaking mothers referred by welfare or probation departments. Situations of interest to the mothers included giving positive messages, giving and receiving criticism, and limiting what they agreed to do for others. Social skill training is often used in programs with parents who abuse and/or neglect their children (for example, Stein, Gambrill, & Wiltse, 1978).

The area of family interaction is a good example of the intimate concern with social skills of a wide variety of intervention areas that are not usually categorized under social skills training but do involve interpersonal skills. Programs in these other areas include components of social skill training packages, such as guidance, demonstration, practice, feedback, and homework assignments.

Social Skills Training with Other Populations/Situations

A handful of studies have devoted attention to social skills training with elderly populations, and some of these have used a behavior-analytic approach to identify situations of concern and effective response options. Berger and Rose (1977), for example, identified situations of concern to elderly people living in residential settings. They then identified effective response options and used these as a basis for a social skills training program. Programs have also been carried out with people living in the community (for example, Edinberg, Karoly, & Gleser, 1977). Social skills training programs have been designed for homosexual persons (for example, Duehn & Mayadas, 1976; Russell & Winkler, 1977), for disabled people (for example, Dunn, Van Horn, & Herman, 1981), for people with substance-abuse problems (for example, Callner & Ross, 1978; Chaney, O'Leary, & Marlatt, 1978), for the retarded (for example, Bates, 1980; Bornstein, Bach, McFall, Friman, & Lyons, 1980), and for people with overly aggressive reactions (for example, Bornstein, Bellack, & Hersen, 1980; Foy, Eisler, & Pinkston, 1975). Much attention has been devoted to enhancing social skills of women (for example, Brockway, 1976; Gambrill & Richey, 1980) as well as enhancing heterosexual skills, especially of men (for example, Conger & Conger, 1982; Curran, 1977). Some programs have focused on enhancing social contacts of both men and women (for example, Gambrill, 1973; Gambrill & Richey, in press). Social skills training has also been employed in altering sexual behavior (for example, Edwards, 1972). Programs have been developed to teach community members how to participate more effectively at board meetings (Briscoe, Hoffman, & Bailey, 1975) and how to be more effective during employment interviews (for example, Azrin & Besalel, 1980; Kelly, Wildman, & Berler, 1980).

One of the most promising characteristics of social skills training is the potential for *prevention* of problems. Offering people effective social skills not only enhances the quality of their social life but also influences their physical well-being, as suggested by studies finding a relationship between social support and physical health (for example, Kiritz & Moos, 1974; Lynch, 1977). Other examples of preventive programs include social skills training related to preventing unplanned pregnancies (Schinke, Gilchrist, & Blythe, 1980) and offering self-protective skills to children (Poche et al., 1981).

As mentioned in the introduction and as illustrated in Part Two of this book, social skills training has also been used to enhance the skills of professionals and paraprofessionals (for example, Flowers & Goldman, 1976; Jansen & Litwack, 1979; Mathews & Fawcett, 1979). Attention has also been devoted to this important area by British investigators (for example, Ellis & Whittington, 1981; Hargie, Saunders, & Dickson, 1981).

GENERALIZATION AND MAINTENANCE

It does little good to develop appropriate behavior in the training setting without the display of this behavior in relevant situations. And little has been accomplished if changes are not durable (maintained over time). Generalization may occur across behaviors (response generalization) or across situations (stimulus generalization). Changes in one kind of social behavior do not tend to generalize to changes in other kinds of behavior. That they do not would be expected, given the situational specificity of social skill. More investigation is needed concerning how to increase generalization and maintenance of new competencies. A concern for the persistence of change should be an integral aspect of selection of intervention strategies. Whenever possible, programs should be carried out in the natural environment, involving persons who influence relevant behaviors. This is often not possible initially, and training is accordingly carried out in some artificial setting, such as the trainer's office. Whenever the natural environment is not the locus for change efforts, a program should be designed to arrange the display of appropriate behaviors in real-life settings. Research clearly shows that a "train and hope" approach cannot be relied on (Stokes & Baer, 1977). Careful planning is called for, including the use of multiple training agents, so that behavior will not be under the influence of only one person; multiple settings, so that it will not be limited to one setting; and multiple kinds and sources of reinforcement. The relevance-of-behavior rule should be followed—teach only behaviors that will continue to be reinforced after training (Ayllon & Azrin, 1968). Other strategies include the use of homework assignments and problem-solving training designed to help people to generalize skills to new situations and to create new options (see, for example, Goldstein & Kanfer, 1979; Monti et al., 1982).

Persistence of behavior change may be enhanced by increasing self-reinforcement skills (Kanfer, 1971), by occasional self-monitoring or meetings with a "buddy," and by "relapse training," which has been found to be helpful in maintaining controlled alcohol consumption (Marlatt & Gordon, 1980). This training includes identifying social situations that may lead to resumption of drinking, such as being pressured to drink, and learning effective behaviors for handling such situations. Other strategies include development of attributions that increase the probability of the persistence of change (Devoge, 1980) and creation of new social settings that will encourage maintenance, such as Hunt and Azrin's (1973) social club.

HOW EFFECTIVE IS SOCIAL SKILLS TRAINING?

The literature on social skills training is so diverse that there is no single answer to the question "How effective is it?" Studies vary in their quality of design, length of follow-up, and attention to generalization across behaviors and settings. Single-case as well as group studies have been used to evaluate the effectiveness of programs. For example, Hersen and Bellack (1976) used a multiple baseline across four behaviors in which intervention was applied to one behavior at a time, while information was gathered on the frequency or duration of all behaviors. The behaviors included eye contact (the client did not look at his partner when speaking to him), voice loudness (one could barely hear what he said), speech duration (responses consisted of one- or two-word replies), and requests of his partner (he did not ask his partner to change his behavior). Each response increased after specific instructions about it were given, and effects generalized to situations that were problematic for this client.

There is no doubt that social skill training is a promising approach that also has the advantages of clear description of methods, ongoing evaluation of progress, and a systematic approach to desired outcomes, making it potentially suitable for self-management programs for many people. It is well suited for use in a group format, which will reduce costs and provide partners for new social adventures. More information is needed about the relative importance of components of skill training programs, such as frequency of practice and kinds of demonstration. Some studies confine their attention to changes that occur in analogue situations. This does not offer information about whether changes also occur in real-life situations. Developmental factors that may influence the acquisition of competencies are often neglected. Greater attention should be paid to how significant others evaluate changes that occur (see Van Houten, 1979; Wolf, 1978). More information is also required about the relative contributions of individual skills to successful performance. Continued developments within social psychology should enhance the effectiveness of programs that are developed. This should, among other contributions, offer greater knowledge of the "roles, props, event-sequences, standard entering conditions and standard outcomes" (Bower, Black, & Turner, 1979, p. 212) related to such activities as eating in a restaurant. (See also literature on social networks and social support systems—for example, Gottlieb, 1981.) Helping people achieve their goals will require knowledge about obstacles faced by particular groups of people in certain situations (for example, Smith and Grenier, 1982), as well as a sensitivity to possible biases in selection of goals to pursue and component behaviors to employ to achieve these (for example, Blechman, 1980).

It is important to remember that altering social behavior may be accomplished in a variety of ways other than social skills training programs. Changes in physical arrangements can often result in marked changes in social behavior at a minimal cost in terms of time and effort, such as serving meals to residents "family style" rather than filling plates before serving (VanBiervliet, Spangler, & Marshall, 1981). The physical environment should always be carefully examined to determine whether modifications could be made that would enhance desired behaviors. Social problems will not always require social solutions.

SUMMARY

Social skills training should be grounded in a transactional model of behavior in which the mutual influence between people and their environments is acknowledged. Increasingly, attention is devoted to a process model of social behavior in which characteristics of the situation, goals, plans, motivations, expectations, and attributions are considered, as well as component verbal and nonverbal skills such as gaze, smiles, and sequences of interaction. A variety of sources of assessment information are available, including self-report, written measures, self-monitoring, analogue measures, and observation in real-life settings. This information should be used to design individually tailored programs based on each person's unique assets, deficits and surfeits, and goals and environments. Training programs consist of a package of procedures, including guidance, demonstration, practice, feedback, and homework assignments that offer opportunities to practice new skills in real-life settings. Measurable, relevant indicators should be selected to assess progress. Programs have been developed for a variety of populations, including psychiatric patients, adolescents, people with developmental disabilities, the elderly, and women, as well as for a variety of behaviors such as refusing unwanted requests and initiating conversations. The focus on constructing repertoires of behavior highlights the importance of clear identification of component skills related to effective performance in particular situations as well as interfering factors. Many of the chapters in this book illustrate applications of a social skill training approach to enhancing interpersonal competencies.

Research indicates that social skill training is effective in increasing competent behavior. Additional efforts should yield information on how to encourage generalization and maintenance of change and on what particular components of training are necessary, which are merely facilitative, and which are unrelated to outcome. Adoption of a process model of social behavior increases the likelihood that cognitive, overt, and physiological responses will be considered. This emphasizes the importance of identifying the goals that people have in social situations, the components of skilled behaviors in each situation, clear criteria for distinguishing between effective and ineffective reactions, and cognitive, physiological, and environmental factors that may influence performance. Research in this area should offer information that will help people to enhance the quality of their social environments as well as to offer higher-quality social environments to others.

REFERENCES

Anthony, W. A., Pierce, R. M., Cohen, M. R., & Cannon, J. R. *The skills of diagnostic planning. Psychiatric Rehabilitation Practice Series: Book 1.* Baltimore: University Park Press, 1980.

Argyle, M. Interaction skills and social competence. In P. Feldman & J. Orford (Eds.), *Psychological problems—the social context*. Chichester, England: Wiley, 1980.

Argyle, M. The contribution of social interaction research to social skills training. In J. D. Wine & M. D. Smye (Eds.), *Social competence*. New York: Guilford, 1981.

Argyle, M., Furnham, A., & Graham, J. A. *Social situations*. Cambridge: Cambridge University Press, 1981.

Argyle, M., & Kendon, A. The experimental analysis of social performance. In L. Berkowitz (Ed.), *Advances in experimental social psychology* (Vol. 3). New York: Academic Press, 1967.

Arkowitz, H., Lichtenstein, E., McGovern, K., & Hines, P. The behavioral assessment of social competence in males. *Behavior Therapy,* 1975, *6,* 3–13.

Asher, S. R., & Hymel, S. Children's social competence in peer relations: Sociometric and behavioral assessment. In J. D. Wine & M. D. Smye (Eds.), *Social competence*. New York: Guilford, 1981.

Ayllon, T., & Azrin, N. H. *The token economy: A motivational system for therapy and rehabilitation*. New York: Appleton-Century-Crofts, 1968.

Azrin, N. H., & Besalel, V. A. *Job club counselor's manual: A behavioral approach to vocational counseling*. Baltimore: University Park Press, 1980.

Bandura, A. *Principles of behavior modification*. New York: Holt, Rinehart & Winston, 1969.

Bandura, A. Self-efficacy: Towards a uniform theory of behavior change. *Psychological Review,* 1977, *84,* 191–215.

Bandura, A., Grusec, J. E., & Menlove, F. L. Observational learning as a function of symbolization and incentive set. *Child Development,* 1966, *37,* 499–506.

Bates, P. The effectiveness of interpersonal skills training in the social skill acquisition of moderately and mildly retarded adults. *Journal of Applied Behavior Analysis,* 1980, *13,* 237–248.

Berger, R. M., & Rose, S. D. Interpersonal skill training with institutionalized elderly patients. *Journal of Gerontology,* 1977, *32,* 346–353.

Birchler, G. R. Communication skills in married couples. In A. S. Bellack & M. Hersen (Eds.), *Research and practice in social skills training*. New York: Plenum, 1979.

Blechman, E. A. Behavior therapies. In A. M. Brodsky and R. Hare-Mustin (Eds.), *Women and psychotherapy: An assessment of research and practice*. New York: Guilford, 1980.

Bornstein, M., Bellack, A. S., & Hersen, M. Social skills training in highly aggressive children in an in-patient psychiatric setting. *Behavior Modification,* 1980, *4,* 173–186.

Bornstein, P. H., Bach, P. J., McFall, M. E., Friman, P. C., & Lyons, P. D. Application of a social skills training program in the modification of interpersonal deficits of retarded adults: A clinical replication. *Journal of Applied Behavior Analysis,* 1980, *13,* 171–176.

Bower, G. H., Black, J. D., & Turner, T. J. Scripts in memory for texts. *Cognitive Psychology,* 1979, *11,* 177–220.

Briscoe, R., Hoffman, D., & Bailey, J. Behavioral community psychology: Training a community board to problem solve. *Journal of Applied Behavior Analysis,* 1975, *8,* 157–168.

Brockway, B. S. Assertion training with professional women. *Social Work,* 1976, *21,* 498–505.

Callner, D. A., & Ross, S. M. The assessment and training of assertive skills with drug addicts: A preliminary study. *International Journal of the Addictions,* 1978, *13,* 227–239.

Cartledge, G., & Milburn, J. D. (Eds.). *Teaching social skills to children*. New York: Pergamon, 1980.

Chaney, E. F., O'Leary, M. R., & Marlatt, G. Skill training with alcoholics. *Journal of Consulting and Clinical Psychology,* 1978, *46,* 1092–1104.

Conger, J. C., & Conger, A. J. Components of heterosexual competence. In J. P. Curran & P. M. Monti (Eds.), *Social skills training.* New York: Guilford, 1982.

Curran, J. P. Skills training as an approach to the treatment of heterosexual-social anxiety: A review. *Psychological Bulletin,* 1977, *84,* 140–157.

Dangel, R. F., & Polster, R. A. (Eds.). *Parent training: Foundations of research and practice.* New York: Guilford, in press.

Devoge, J. T. Reciprocal role training: Therapeutic transfer as viewed from a social psychology of dyads. In P. Karoly & J. J. Steffen (Eds.), *Improving the long-term effects of psychotherapy.* New York: Gardner Press, 1980.

Duehn, W. D., & Mayadas, N. S. The use of stimulus/modeling videotapes in assertive training for homosexuals. *Journal of Homosexuality,* 1976, *1,* 373–381.

Dunn, M., Van Horn, E., & Herman, S. H. Social skills and spinal cord injury: A comparison of three training procedures. *Behavior Therapy,* 1981, *12,* 153–164.

Edinberg, M. A., Karoly, P., & Gleser, G. C. Assessing assertion in the elderly: An application of the behavioral-analytic model of competence. *Journal of Clinical Psychology,* 1977, *33,* 869–874.

Edwards, N. B. Case conference: Assertive training in a case of homosexual pedophilia. *Journal of Behavior Therapy and Experimental Psychiatry,* 1972, *3,* 55–63.

Eisler, R. M., Miller, P. M., Hersen, M., & Alford, H. Effects of assertive training on marital interaction. *Archives of General Psychiatry,* 1974, *30,* 643–649.

Ellis, R., & Whittington, D. *A guide to social skill training.* London: Croom Helm, 1981.

Epstein, N., DeGiovanni, I. S., & Jayne-Lazarus, C. Assertion training for couples. *Journal of Behavior Therapy and Experimental Psychiatry,* 1978, *9,* 149–157.

Fedoravicius, A. S. The patient as shaper of required parental behavior: A case study. *Journal of Behavior Therapy and Experimental Psychiatry,* 1973, *4,* 395–396.

Feffer, M., & Suchotliffe, L. Decentering implications of social interactions. *Journal of Personality and Social Psychology,* 1966, *4,* 415–422.

Fischetti, M., Curran, J. P., & Wessberg, H. W. Sense of timing: A skill deficit in heterosexual-socially anxious males. *Behavior Modification,* 1977, *1,* 179–194.

Flowers, J. V., & Goldman, R. D. Assertion training for mental health paraprofessionals. *Journal of Counseling Psychology,* 1976, *23,* 147–150.

Forehand, R. L., & McMahon, R. J. *Helping the noncompliant child: A clinician's guide to parent training.* New York: Guilford, 1981.

Foy, D. W., Eisler, R. M., & Pinkston, S. Modeled assertion in a case of explosive rages. *Journal of Behavioral Therapy and Experimental Psychiatry,* 1975, *6,* 135–137.

Freedman, B. J., Donahue, C. P., Rosenthal, L., Schlundt, D. G., & McFall, R. M. A socio-behavioral analysis of skills deficits in delinquent and nondelinquent adolescent boys. *Journal of Consulting and Clinical Psychology,* 1978, *46,* 1448–1462.

Furnham, A., & Argyle, M. The theory, practice and application of social skills training. *International Journal of Behavioural Social Work and Abstracts,* 1981, *1,* 125–144.

Gambrill, E. D. A behavioral program to increase social interaction. Paper presented at the 7th annual convention of the Association for Advancement of Behavior Therapy, Miami, December 1973.

Gambrill, E. D. *Behavior modification: Handbook of assessment, intervention, and evaluation.* San Francisco: Jossey-Bass, 1977.

Gambrill, E. D., & Barth, R. Social situations of concern to the elderly. Unpublished manuscript, University of California, Berkeley, November 1981.

Gambrill, E. D., & Richey, C. A. An assertion inventory for use in assessment and research. *Behavior Therapy,* 1975, *6,* 550–561.

Gambrill, E. D., & Richey, C. A. Assertion training for women. In C. L. Heckerman (Ed.), *The evolving female: Psychosocial perspectives.* New York: Human Services Press, 1980.

Gambrill, E. D., & Richey, C. A. *Why be shy? It's up to you* (2nd ed.). New York: Harper & Row, in press.

Glass, C. R., & Merluzzi, T. V. Cognitive assessment of social-evaluative anxiety. In T. V. Merluzzi, C. R. Glass, & M. Genest (Eds.), *Cognitive assessment.* New York: Guilford, 1981.

Glass, C. R., Merluzzi, T. V., Biever, J. L., & Larsen, K. H. Cognitive assessment of social anxiety: Development and validation of a self-statement questionnaire. *Cognitive Therapy and Research,* in press.

Goldfried, M. R., & D'Zurilla, T. J. A behavior-analytic model for assessing competence. In C. D. Spielberger (Ed.), *Current topics in clinical and community psychology* (Vol. 1). New York: Academic Press, 1969.

Goldsmith, J. B., & McFall, R. M. Development and evaluation of an interpersonal skill-training program for psychiatric patients. *Journal of Abnormal Psychology,* 1975, *84,* 51–58.

Goldstein, A. P., & Kanfer, F. H. (Eds.). *Maximizing treatment gains: Transfer enhancement in psychotherapy.* New York: Academic Press, 1979.

Goldstein, A. P., Sprafkin, R. P., & Gershaw, N. J. *Skill training for community living: Applying Structured Learning Therapy.* New York: Pergamon Press, 1976.

Goldstein, A. P., Sprafkin, R. P., Gershaw, N. J., & Klein, P. *Skillstreaming the adolescent: A Structured Learning approach to teaching prosocial skills.* Champaign, Ill.: Research Press, 1980.

Gottlieb, B. H. *Social networks and social support.* Beverly Hills, Calif.: Sage, 1981.

Graham, J. A., Argyle, M., & Furnham, A. The goal structure of situations. *European Journal of Social Psychology,* 1980, *10,* 345–366.

Graubard, P. S., Rosenberg, H., & Miller, M. B. Student applications of behavior modification to teachers and environments or ecological approaches to social deviancy. In E. A. Ramp & B. L. Hopkins (Eds.), *A new direction for education: Behavior analysis* (Vol. 1). Lawrence: Department of Human Development, University of Kansas, 1971.

Hargie, O., Saunders, C., & Dickson, D. *Social skills in interpersonal communication.* London: Croom Helm, 1981.

Harper, R. G., Wiens, A. N., & Matarazzo, J. D. *Nonverbal communication: The state of the art.* New York: Wiley, 1978.

Harre, R., & Secord, P. F. *The explanation of social behavior.* Oxford: Blackwell, 1972.

Hazel, J. S., Schumaker, J. B., Sherman, J. A., & Sheldon-Wildgen, J. *Asset: A social skills program for adolescents.* Champaign, Ill.: Research Press, 1981.

Hersen, M. Modification of a skill deficit in psychiatric patients. In A. S. Bellack & M. Hersen (Eds.), *Research and practice in social skills training.* New York: Plenum, 1979.

Hersen, M., & Bellack, A. S. A multiple baseline analysis of social-skills training in chronic schizophrenics. *Journal of Applied Behavior Analysis,* 1976, *9,* 239–246.

Hunt, G. M., & Azrin, N. H. The community reinforcement approach to alcoholism. *Behaviour Research and Therapy,* 1973, *11,* 91–104.

Jacobson, N. S. Communication skills training for married couples. In J. P. Curran & P. M. Monti (Eds.), *Social skills training*. New York: Guilford, 1982.

Jakubowski, P., & Lange, A. J. *The assertive option*. Champaign, Ill.: Research Press, 1978.

Jansen, M. S., & Litwack, L. The effects of assertive training on counselor trainees. *Counselor Education and Supervision, 1979, 19,* 27–34.

Jewett, J., & Clark, H. B. Teaching preschoolers to use appropriate dinner-time conversation: An analysis of generalization from school to home. *Behavior Therapy, 1979, 10,* 589–605.

Kanfer, F. H. The maintenance of behavior by self-generated stimuli and reinforcement. In A. Jacobs and L. B. Sachs (Eds.), *The psychology of private events: Perspectives on covert response systems*. New York: Academic Press, 1971.

Kazdin, A. E. Court modeling and reduction of avoidance behavior. *Journal of Abnormal Psychology, 1973, 81,* 87–95.

Kelly, J. A., Wildman, B. G., & Berler, E. S. Small group behavioral training to improve the job interview skills repertoire of mildly retarded adolescents. *Journal of Applied Behavior Analysis, 1980, 13,* 461–471.

Kiritz, S., & Moos, R. H. Physiological effects of social environments. *Psychosomatic Medicine, 1974, 36,* 96–114.

Landau, P., & Paulson, T. Group assertion training for Spanish-speaking Mexican-American mothers. In R. E. Alberti (Ed.), *Assertiveness: Innovations, applications, and issues*. San Luis Obispo, Calif.: Impact Press, 1977.

Lazarus, R. S. The costs and benefits of denial. In S. Breznitz (Ed.), *Denial of stress*. New York: International Universities Press, 1982.

Lazarus, R. S., & Launier, R. Stress-related transactions between person and environment. In L. A. Pervin & M. Lewis (Eds.), *Perspectives in interactional psychology*. New York: Plenum, 1978.

Lewinsohn, P. M. Clinical and theoretical aspects of depression. In K. S. Calhoun, H. E. Adams, & K. M. Mitchell (Eds.), *Innovative treatment methods in psychopathology*. New York: Wiley, 1974.

Liberman, R. P., King, L. W., DeRisi, W. J., & McCann, M. *Personal effectiveness: Guiding people to assert themselves and improve their social skills*. Champaign, Ill.: Research Press, 1975.

Libet, J., & Lewinsohn, P. M. The concept of social skills with special references to the behavior of depressed persons. *Journal of Consulting and Clinical Psychology, 1973, 40,* 304–312.

Lynch, J. J. *The broken heart*. New York: Basic Books, 1977.

Marlatt, G. A., & Gordon, J. P. Determinants of relapse: Implications for the maintenance of behavior change. In P. O. Davidson & S. M. Davidson (Eds.), *Behavior medicine: Changing life styles*. New York: Brunner/Mazel, 1980.

Mathews, R. M., & Fawcett, S. B. A community based information and referral system. *Journal of the Community Development Society, 1979, 10,* 13–25.

McFall, R. M. A review and reformulation of the concept of social skills. *Behavioral Assessment, 1982, 4,* 1–33.

McFall, R. M., & Lillesand, D. B. Behavior rehearsal with modeling and coaching in assertion training. *Journal of Abnormal Psychology, 1971, 77,* 313–323.

McFall, R. M., & Twentyman, C. T. Four experiments on the relative contributions of rehearsal, modeling, and coaching to assertion training. *Journal of Abnormal Psychology, 1973, 81,* 199–218.

Meichenbaum, D., & Turk, D. The cognitive-behavioral management of anxiety, anger, and pain.

In P. O. Davidson (Ed.), *The behavioral management of anxiety, depression and pain.* New York: Brunner/Mazel, 1976.

Merluzzi, T. V., Glass, C. R., & Genest, M. (Eds.). *Cognitive assessment.* New York: Guilford, 1981.

Mischel, W. Toward a cognitive social learning reconceptualization of personality. *Psychological Review,* 1973, *80,* 252–283.

Mischel, W. A cognitive-social learning approach to assessment. In T. V. Merluzzi, C. R. Glass, & M. Genest (Eds.), *Cognitive assessment.* New York: Guilford, 1981.

Monti, P. M., Corriveau, D. P., & Curran, J. P. Social skills training for psychiatric patients: Treatment and outcome. In J. P. Curran & P. M. Monti (Eds.), *Social skills training.* New York: Guilford, 1982.

Nay, W. R. Analogue measures. In A. R. Ciminero, K. S. Calhoun, & H. C. Adams (Eds.), *Handbook of behavioral assessment.* New York: Wiley, 1977.

Nezu, A., & D'Zurilla, T. J. An experimental evaluation of the decision-making process in social problem solving. *Cognitive Therapy and Research,* 1979, *3,* 269–277.

O'Banion, K., & Arkowitz, H. Social anxiety and selective memory for affective information about the self. *Social Behavior and Personality,* 1977, *5,* 321–328.

Perri, M. G., & Richards, C. S. The empirical development of a behavioral role-playing test for the assessment of heterosexual skills in male college students. *Behavior Modification,* in press.

Pilkonis, P. A. The behavioral consequences of shyness. *Journal of Personality,* 1977, *45,* 596–611.

Poche, C., Brouwer, R., & Swearingen, M. Teaching self-protection to young children. *Journal of Applied Behavior Analysis,* 1981, *14,* 169–176.

Reardon, R. C., Hersen, M., Bellack, A. S., & Foley, J. M. Measuring social skill in grade school boys. *Journal of Behavioral Assessment,* 1979, *1,* 87–105.

Russell, A., & Winkler, R. Evaluation of assertive training and homosexual guidance service groups designed to improve homosexual functioning. *Journal of Consulting and Clinical Psychology,* 1977, *45,* 1–13.

Schinke, S. P., Gilchrist, L. D., & Blythe, B. J. Role of communication in the prevention of teenage pregnancy. *Health and Social Work,* 1980, *5,* 54–59.

Schlenker, B. R. *Impression management: The self-concept, social identity, and interpersonal relations.* Monterey, Calif.: Brooks/Cole, 1980.

Seymour, F. W., & Stokes, T. F. Self-recording in training girls to increase work and evoke staff praise in an institution for offenders. *Journal of Applied Behavior Analysis,* 1976, *9,* 41–54.

Shelton, J. L., & Levy, R. L. *Behavioral assignments and treatment compliance.* Champaign, Ill.: Research Press, 1981.

Shoemaker, M. E., & Paulson, T. L. Group assertion training for mothers: A family intervention strategy. In E. J. Mash, L. C. Handy, & L. A. Hamerlynch (Eds.), *Behavior modification approaches to parenting.* New York: Brunner/Mazel, 1976.

Shure, M. B. Training children to solve interpersonal problems: A preventative mental health program. In R. F. Muñoz, L. R. Snowden, J. G. Kelly, & Associates, *Social and psychological research in community settings: Designing and conducting programs for social and personal well-being.* San Francisco: Jossey-Bass, 1979.

Smith, H. L., & Grenier, M. Sources of organizational power for women: Overcoming structural obstacles. *Sex Roles,* 1982, *8,* 733–746.

Smith, R. E., & Sarason, I. G. Social anxiety and the evaluation of negative interpersonal feedback. *Journal of Consulting and Clinical Psychology,* 1975, *43,* 429.

Snyder, M., & Monson, T. C. Persons, situations, and the control of social behavior. *Journal of Personality and Social Psychology*, 1975, *32*, 637–644.

Snyder, M., & Swann, W. B. Hypothesis-testing processes in social interaction. *Journal of Personality*, 1978, *36*, 1213–1220.

Spence, S. H. Validation of social skills of adolescent males in an interview conversation with a previously unknown adult. *Journal of Applied Behavior Analysis*, 1981, *14*, 159–168.

Spiegler, M. D., & Agigian, H. *The community training center.* New York: Brunner/Mazel, 1977.

Stein, T. J., Gambrill, E. D., & Wiltse, K. T. *Children in foster homes: Achieving continuity of care.* New York: Praeger Special Studies, 1978.

Stokes, T. F., & Baer, D. M. An implicit technology of generalization. *Journal of Applied Behavior Analysis*, 1977, *10*, 349–367.

Strupp, H. The nature of the therapeutic influence and its basic ingredients. In A. Burton (Ed.), *What makes behavior change possible?* New York: Brunner/Mazel, 1976.

Stuart, R. B. *Helping couples change: A social learning approach to marital therapy.* New York: Guilford, 1980.

Trower, P. Situational analysis of the components and processes of behavior of socially skilled and unskilled patients. *Journal of Consulting and Clinical Psychology*, 1980, *48*, 327–339.

Trower, P. Toward a generative model of social skills: A critique and synthesis. In J. P. Curran & P. M. Monti (Eds.), *Social skills training.* New York: Guilford, 1982.

Trower, P., Bryant, B., & Argyle, M. *Social skills and mental health.* London: Methuen, 1978.

Twentyman, C. T., & McFall, R. M. Behavioral training of social skills in shy males. *Journal of Consulting and Clinical Psychology*, 1975, *43*, 384–395.

Valentine, J., & Arkowitz, H. Social anxiety and self-evaluation of interpersonal performance. *Psychological Reports*, 1975, *36*, 211–221.

VanBiervliet, A., Spangler, P. F., & Marshall, A. M. An ecobehavioral examination of a simple strategy for increasing mealtime language in residential facilities. *Journal of Applied Behavior Analysis*, 1981, *14*, 295–305.

Van Houten, R. Social validation: The evolution of standards of competence for target behaviors. *Journal of Applied Behavior Analysis*, 1979, *12*, 581–591.

Warren, N. J., & Gilner, F. H. Measurement of positive assertive behaviors: The behavioral test of tenderness expression. *Behavior Therapy*, 1978, *9*, 169–177.

Willner, A., Braukmann, C. J., Kirigin, K. A., Fixen, D. L., Phillips, E. L., & Wolf, M. M. The training and validation of youth-preferred behaviors of child-care personnel. *Journal of Applied Behavior Analysis*, 1977, *10*, 219–230.

Wine, J. D. Perspectives on social competence: Background, central issues, and conceptual models. In J. D. Wine & M. D. Smye (Eds.), *Social competence.* New York: Guilford, 1981.

Wine, J. D., & Smye, M. D. *Social competence.* New York: Guilford, 1981.

Wolf, M. M. Social validity: The case for subjective measurement; or, how applied behavior analysis is finding its heart. *Journal of Applied Behavior Analysis*, 1978, *11*, 203–214.

Wolpe, J. *Psychotherapy by reciprocal inhibition.* Stanford, Calif.: Stanford University Press, 1958.

Wrubel, J., Benner, P., & Lazarus, R. S. Social competence from the perspective of stress and coping. In J. D. Wine & M. D. Smye (Eds.), *Social competence.* New York: Guilford, 1981.

Zigler, E., & Phillips, L. Social competence and outcome in psychiatric disorders. *Journal of Abnormal and Social Psychology*, 1961, *63*, 264–271.

PART TWO

TEACHING HELPING SKILLS

CHAPTER SEVEN

Skilled Helping: A Problem-Management Framework for Helping and Helper Training

Gerard Egan is professor of psychology at Loyola University of Chicago. He is program coordinator for the Program in Community and Organizational Development at Loyola and is a member of the editorial review board of *Group and Organization Studies.* He is the author of *The Skilled Helper, Interpersonal Living,* and (with Michael Cowan) *People in Systems* and *Moving into Adulthood.* Forthcoming books are *Systematic Helping* and *Change Agent Skills.*

Gerard Egan

In this chapter Gerard Egan presents a four-stage, eight-step problem-management framework as a way of conceptualizing the helping process itself and as a step-by-step blueprint for training helpers in the methods and skills of helping. Because clients need to become more effective in managing the problem situations of their lives, this model, together with the methods and skills that make it operative, can be "given away" to clients as an integral part of the helping process. Egan suggests that in all effective helping, irrespective of the approach or "school" used by the helper, the eight steps of the model are accomplished by clients either in conjunction with helpers or on their own. The problem-management framework can therefore become a tool for mining, from virtually any approach to helping, strategies for helping clients achieve each of the eight subgoals of the model. That is, the framework becomes "an instrument for systematic and integrative eclecticism." The model and its steps form a tool for helping clients identify, develop, and use personal and environmental resources in the management of problem situations.

This chapter describes a problem-solving or, perhaps more accurately, a problem-management approach to helping that is based on and permeated by the people-in-systems framework (see Chapter 2). This means, first of all, that helpers approach their clients in the spirit of the people-in-systems model. That is, they see their clients in terms of the stages, tasks, and crises of normal human development; they try to understand and help them understand themselves and their concerns in terms of the social settings of their lives; and they are sensitive to the level of working knowledge and life skills development of their clients.

This chapter is based on Gerard Egan's forthcoming book *Systematic Helping: An Integrative Problem-Management Approach to the Stages. Techniques, and Skills of Helping,* to be published by Brooks/Cole, Monterey, California.

Second, it means that helpers take an education/training-as-helping approach to providing human services. Anthony (1977, 1978, 1979), Carkhuff (1969a, 1969b, 1971; Carkhuff & Berenson, 1976), Egan (1982; Egan & Cowan, 1979), Gazda and Brooks (1980), and Muro and Engels (1980), among others, suggest that educating clients in the kinds of working knowledge and training them in the kind of skills they need to work through and cope with problems in living are central to the helping process. The people-in-systems model provides a framework for this kind of "giving psychology away." Many, if not most, approaches to helping have education and/or training components, even though that is not stated explicitly in the descriptions of these approaches. The problem-management model of helping outlined in this chapter makes education and training dimensions explicit.

It goes without saying that making clients dependent on helpers is not one of the aims of helping. The problem-solving approach to helping provides both counselors and clients with a practical framework for helping, but clients should do as much of the work as possible. They will more likely do so if they are trained in the kinds of working knowledge and skills needed to be effective collaborators. In one sense, what Bandura (1977a) calls "self-efficacy" is at the heart of helping. Some clients find it difficult to take responsibility for their behavior and their emotions. This difficulty must then be seen as part of the problem situation and treated like any other problematic issue. One of the aims of counseling, then, is to help clients to take more responsibility for themselves, their behavior, and their emotions.

An education/training-as-helping approach makes most sense in group rather than one-to-one settings because in the group each person can pick up the kinds of working knowledge and skills, including the skills of the problem-management process discussed in this chapter, that he or she needs to cope with problems in living. Obviously the same thing can be done in one-to-one settings, but with less efficient use of resources. The group setting is therefore preferred unless there are strong reasons that any particular client should be seen alone. Much of the work to be outlined in this chapter may well start in a one-to-one setting, but in many, if not most, cases it would seem preferable for it to be carried on in a group (see Egan, 1982, pp. 25–26).

PROBLEM SOLVING—A FRAMEWORK FOR HELPING

Helpers are skilled if they actually help others manage their lives a bit (or a great deal) more effectively. To be helpful, they need a systematic and congruent model of helping and the skills and techniques that make this model operative. Since there are dozens of models or approaches to helping, both neophyte and established helpers may well ask themselves what approach or combination of approaches has the most to offer. Or, if they choose to be eclectic, they may wonder how they might pursue an integrative and systematic rather than a hodge-podge eclecticism (Brammer & Shostrom, 1977; Dimond, Havens, & Jones, 1978).

Mahoney and Arnkoff (1978) suggest that problem-solving approaches to helping offer a great deal of promise in the helping professions.

> Among the cognitive learning therapies, it is our opinion that the problem-solving perspectives may ultimately yield the most encouraging clinical results. This is due to the fact that—as a broader clinical endeavor—they encompass both the cognitive restructur-

ing and the coping skills therapies (not to mention a wide range of "noncognitive" perspectives) [p. 709].

The problem-solving model of helping can be called a "folk" model in that, in one form or another, it can be found even in early philosophical writings and in the very bones of people. It has the advantage of belonging to no specific "school" of helping and thus avoids some of the unfortunate limitations of school approaches (for instance, overconcern with the writings and helping style of the founder of the school and a reluctance to assimilate other useful approaches into the theory and methodologies of the school).

I prefer to call the problem-solving approach to helping a "framework" rather than a model. This framework outlines in a logical and directional way the goals that are related to successful helping. The framework provides the "geography" of helping, as it were. A skilled helper is one who "knows the territory" of helping and who can, therefore, provide direction for the client. Another way of putting it is that a problem-solving framework outlines the *tasks* of helping and indicates the relationships that exist among these tasks.

In the model or framework I presently use both to train helpers and to provide help for clients, I have four stages, and since each stage is divided into two parts, there are a total of eight steps, or tasks, in the helping process. My hypothesis is this: In all effective helping, no matter what model or school of helping is being used, the goals of all eight of these tasks are achieved by clients either on their own or in collaboration with the helper. I see helpers as *consultants* to their clients; that is, they help their clients accomplish one or more of the eight tasks of the problem-solving process. With this help, clients finish the rest of the process either on their own or by using resources in their day-to-day environments. It goes without saying that some clients need more help, others less. Skilled helpers are capable of determining, in consultation and collaboration with their clients, precisely *where* (what step) and *to what extent* their help is needed.

Prehelping: Problem Awareness

Helpers cannot be of service to clients if the latter are unaware of problems or difficulties in their lives. Presumably most people grapple with most problems in living, with whatever degree of success, by themselves or with the informal help of family and friends. They live without professional help. However, people who find that they are not coping with their problems and either do not want to share them with family or friends or feel that family and friends are not competent enough to help them might turn to some kind of helper—pastor, teacher, coach, supervisor, doctor, counselor, social worker, nurse, psychologist, psychotherapist, psychiatrist, and the like—for help. They will usually turn to such a person (1) if the problem is serious or disturbing enough and (2) if they have some expectation that the person to whom they are turning can actually help them.

"Problem Situation" Rather Than Problem: The "Messiness" of Human Problems

Obviously, problems in living are quite different from mathematical or engineering problems. Dyer and Vriend (1975) state this quite forcefully:

People don't have problems, and problem-centered counseling more often than not is

> trapped by being dependent on solutions. What people do have are difficulties, concerns, situations, and conditions with which they are living. And they currently behave, mentally, emotionally, and physically, in certain ways and at certain levels of effectiveness in response to whatever is in their lives [p. 33].

Dyer and Vriend are urging that helping be a *human* process that deals realistically with *human* problems.

D'Zurilla and Goldfried (1971), in discussing problems in living, prefer the term *problem situation*.

> The term *problem* will refer here to a specific *situation* or *set of related situations* to which a person must respond in order to function effectively in his environment. . . . The term *problematic situation* will be used in most instances in place of "problem." In the present context, a situation is considered problematic if *no effective response alternate is immediately available to the individual confronted with the situation* [pp. 107–108].

Problems in living are "messier" than mathematical problems with clear-cut solutions. One of the main reasons, of course, is that strong human feelings are often involved. Further complexity arises from the fact that problem situations exist between people and between people and the social settings and systems of their lives. Because of this complexity, helpers face a difficult task. On the one hand, they need to understand and appreciate the complexity of any given problem situation and help clients do the same. Oversimplification of problems followed by superficial solutions helps no one. On the other, they need to avoid being overwhelmed by the complexity of clients' problem situations and help their clients do the same. Even in the face of chaos, they must be able to help the client do *something*.

If helpers are successful as consultants to clients and their problem situations, their clients *manage* the problem situations of their lives a bit (or a great deal) more effectively. That is the goal of helping. "What is possible for any client as a result of counseling is that in any dimension of existence he can upgrade his level of performance or learn alternate behaviors which are more effective and self-enhancing" (Dyer & Vriend, 1975, p. 33). Helpers do well if they neither underestimate nor overestimate what clients can do to help themselves and if they help clients set reasonable goals.

The Helping Relationship

Much has been written about helping relationships. The kinds of relationships that are advocated are described variously as personal, warm, caring, deep, understanding, challenging, neutral, and so forth. The kind of relationship advocated here is the kind that will contribute best to clients' taking responsibility for themselves and the kind needed to help clients to get on with the work of managing problem situations. It is suggested that helpers should not first determine the kind of relationship that should characterize all helping and then try to fit the work of helping into it. Sometimes a deep and warm relationship might well contribute to getting the work done; at other times, however, it might not. The degrees of warmth, depth, and challenge are relative to each relationship and should be geared to getting the work of helping done (accomplishing as many of the eight tasks as are necessary), not simply to relating. Sometimes a relationship that is less warm or less deep or less challenging than either client or helper might want it to be can contribute more to achieving the goals of helping than one that is deeper, warmer, or more challenging.

Another way of putting this is that helpers need to *respect* their clients and be *genuine* (Egan, 1982) in the relationship. These are *foundational* qualities that should permeate the entire helping process. They are qualities, however, that need to be expressed behaviorally. If they remain locked up inside helpers as mere attitudes, they do little good. But both respect and genuineness can be expressed in different ways at different stages of the helping relationship. For instance, initial warmth may eventually give way to a kind of "tough love" that helps clients place demands on themselves.

The Stages of Helping

The four stages of the helping process are these:

I. *Problem identification and clarification.* Problems cannot be coped with if they remain vague and nonspecific. They need to be spelled out in terms of the client's specific experiences, behaviors, and feelings.

II. *Goal setting.* Once a problem is seen clearly or at least more clearly than it was before, clients can be helped to decide *what* they want to do about it.

III. *Program development.* Once clients decide what they want to do, they must then determine precisely *how* they are going to do it. That is, they must, in concrete and specific ways, spell out the step-by-step behaviors that will get them to their goals.

IV. *Implementation.* Finally, clients need to act; that is, they need to put their programs into effect in order to reach their goals.

In its briefest outline, the problem-management process is a fairly simple and straightforward program for facing up to problem situations and doing something about them. It is perhaps part of the perversity of human nature that most people do not seem either to think about or to use this logic when actually confronted with problem situations.

> In ordinary affairs we usually muddle ahead, doing what is habitual and customary, being slightly puzzled when it sometimes fails to give the intended outcome, but not stopping to worry much about the failures because there are . . . too many other things still to do. Then circumstances conspire against us and we find ourselves caught failing where we must succeed—where we cannot withdraw from the field, or lower our self-imposed standards, or ask for help, or throw a tantrum. Then we may suspect that we have a problem. . . . *An ordinary person almost never approaches a problem systematically and exhaustively unless he has been specifically educated to do so* [Miller, Galanter, & Pribram, 1960, pp. 171, 174; emphasis added].

Paradoxically, if the rudiments of problem solving are explained to people, they often react by saying something like "Oh, sure, I know that." The logic of problem solving seems to be embedded in our brains and bones (and that makes it a "folk" model), but somehow this logic does not always make its way into our behavior. Still, the fact that the logic of problem solving is embedded in people is one of the advantages of using a problem-solving framework with clients. At some level of their being they understand the model. In fact, at the beginning of the helping process, when a contract is being drawn up between helper and client, this framework can be shared with clients in a way that does not confuse or overburden them.

It is a way of preparing the client for the "movement" of the helping process. What follows is an expanded, eight-step version of the basic problem-management process.

THE EXPANDED PROBLEM-MANAGEMENT FRAMEWORK

Earlier in this chapter it was suggested that each of the four problem-solving stages can be divided into two steps. The first in each stage can be seen as an *expanding,* or data-gathering, step, while the second is more or less a *contracting,* decision-making step. Let's see how this works at each stage.

Stage I: Clarifying the Problem Situation

John Dewey once suggested that a question well asked is half answered. If the same logic is applied to helping, it may be said that clients who have a clear idea of precisely what is going wrong in their lives are in a better position to discover ways of managing their lives more effectively.

Step 1: General or current life-style assessment

When clients first come to helpers, they may come with very specific problems:

- "My drug habit and drinking are messing me up in school, at work, and with my family."

or with general feelings of dissatisfaction:

- "I just seem so tired and listless lately. I'm depressed, but I don't know why."

Whether the problems presented are specific or general, it can help both counselor and clients to see them in wider perspective. An analogy might help. If a person goes to a doctor with a pain in her chest, the doctor does not merely deal with that particular pain but rather gives her at least a brief physical examination in order to assess the pain in the *context* of her present state of physical functioning. A life-style assessment—that is, an assessment of current personal, interpersonal, and social functioning—whether relatively brief or quite detailed, provides background or a context that helps clarify the client's problem situation. In Gestalt terms, the presenting problem situation is the "figure," and the client's current life-style is the "ground" against which it is seen. The ground serves to highlight and clarify the figure. Assessment, then, can be considered an "expanding" step in the helping process, for it deals with life-style, the context of problem situations, the "bigger picture." An initial assessment can serve several purposes:

- *Identifying the real problem.* When clients are helped to place their concerns in some kind of perspective, they sometimes come to realize that the presenting problems are really symptoms of more fundamental problems.

Cora came to the counseling center complaining of headaches and poor "motivation" in school. A brief general assessment soon made it clear that her struggle for independence from her parents probably had a great deal to do with both headaches and motivation.

- *Clarifying problem situations.* If the client's problems are vague, some kind of life-style assessment can help the client become much more concrete and specific.

Jethro talked to his clergyman about losing interest in almost everything, including participating in church activities. A brief assessment indicated that he was in a job and a marriage that depressed him, and now that he was 39, he was beginning to face some of the common issues associated with the midlife crisis.

· *Helping put order in chaos.* Sometimes clients will come to helpers and pour out long and highly emotional stories of the difficulties they are facing. They present not just one problem but rather a whole series of either interrelated or seemingly disconnected problems. In this case the assessment step provides an initial way of putting some kind of order into what might otherwise seem like chaos.

In the helping process, the people-in-systems model can be used as an assessment instrument. Assessment models and instruments (structured interviews, tests of various types) are, at their best, not ways of categorizing, stereotyping, or pigeon-holing clients but rather filters that enable helpers to listen to clients *in focused ways.* That is, helpers listen to the problem situations of their clients in terms of developmental stages, tasks, and crises, in terms of interactions with the social settings of life, and in terms of the strengths, deficits, and unused potential in the area of life skills. In a giving-psychology-away approach to helping, clients can be taught how to listen to themselves in terms of developmental stages, tasks, and crises, in terms of strengths and deficits in life skills, and in terms of how they are participating in and being affected by the social settings of their lives.

Step 2: Focusing and exploration

Since it is impossible to deal with all problems at once, it is necessary to *focus* on issues that seem to need immediate attention or seem to be common to a number of the client's problems or can be handled in view of available resources. For instance, if an assessment reveals that Vincent is having trouble with his wife, his children, his boss, those who work under his direction, and the fellows at the bar, it might make sense not to consider each of these as a separate problem but to focus on the behavioral characteristics of his interpersonal style and the patterns of his interpersonal communication.

Focusing means helping clients choose to explore an issue or an interrelated group of behaviors that seems central, in one way or another, to the presenting problem situation. This is a "contracting" step, for it moves away from a considera-tion of a person's total life-style and away from a general consideration of a complex problem situation and concentrates, in concrete ways, on specific areas and issues. Obviously helpers do not decide by themselves what issue or issues are to be explored further and what issue seems to be most important to consider first; they do so in consultation with their clients. Effective helpers provide *direction* for their clients, but in flexible rather than rigid ways.

Defining and clarifying the problem situation.   The second part of Step 2

is to help clients explore and clarify the issue or issues that seem most worthy of attention. Once it is determined what area needs investigation, the counselor helps the client spell out the problem situation as concretely and specifically as possible— that is, in terms of concrete and specific experiences (what the client does or does not *do*), and concrete and specific feelings (the client's *emotional* reactions to his or her experiences and behaviors) as these are related to the problem situation. At this stage the goal is to help clients get as concrete and as clear a picture as possible of the problem situation, *at least from the client's point of view.*

If a client were to say to a helper "I've had a messy week," he would be stating the problem situation in very vague terms. However, suppose the client said:

- "I was talking to one of my coworkers last Tuesday when my boss comes into the room and chews me out right in front of this other person. I really felt foolish and embarrassed, but I played it cool for the moment and didn't let on. But inside I was steaming. Later I went into my boss's office and blew my stack and told him just what I thought of him. He fired me on the spot. Ever since then that whole scene has been haunting me. I keep trying to think of ways of getting my old job back or what to do about getting a new one. It's all very depressing."

This obviously is a much more concrete, clear, and specific description of the problem situation. It is important to note precisely what makes it concrete and specific.

Problem clarification deals with both overt and covert experiences, behaviors, and feelings in the client's life insofar as these are specifically related to the problem situation.

- *Experiences.* As noted, experiences are the things that happen to the client. They may be *overt,* capable of being seen by others—for instance, a factory closes and a person loses her job— or *covert,* related to the inner physiological, cognitive, or fantasy life of the client—for instance, obsessive thoughts, a headache, daydreams that a client sees as happening to him rather than the kind that he directs.
- *Behavior.* Overt behaviors are the things clients do (or fail to do) that are capable of being observed by others (whether they actually happen to be observed or not). Kissing one's spouse and drinking excessively are examples of overt behavior. *Covert* behavior is part of the client's "inner life"—that is, the client's thoughts, imaginings, attitudes, opinions, and the like insofar as the client chooses to engage in and actually directs these. For instance, harboring a grudge would be an example of a covert behavior.
- *Feelings and emotions.* Sometimes people hide their emotions from others (and even from themselves). Feelings and emotions that a person experiences but does not express in such a way that they are capable of being noticed by others (whether they actually happen to be noticed or not) can be considered *covert.* A person who feels hurt but doesn't let anyone notice it is involved with covert emotion. *Overt* emotions are those which are expressed, with varying degrees of intensity, and which are therefore capable of being noticed by others (whether they are actually noticed or not).

Let's return to the man fired from his job and see how these three categories help make his statement of the problem situation clear.

- "I was talking to one of my coworkers last Tuesday" (overt behavior), "when my boss comes into the room and chews me out right in front of this other person" (overt experience).
- "I really felt foolish and embarrassed, but I played it cool for the moment and didn't let on. But inside I was steaming" (covert emotion, covert behavior of holding back the expression of the emotions he was feeling).
- "Later I went into my boss's office and blew my stack and told him just what I thought of him" (overt behavior, overt emotion).
- "He fired me on the spot" (overt experience).

- "Ever since then that whole scene has been haunting me" (covert experience, with implied emotion, whether covert or overt).
- "I keep trying to think of ways of getting my old job back or what to do about getting a new one" (covert behavior).
- "It's all very depressing" (emotion that could at times be overt, at times covert).

Clients' experiences, behaviors, and feelings relate to developmental stages, tasks, and crises ("I'm scared to death of turning 30 without knowing what I want to do with my life"), to the social settings of life ("I'm more appreciated outside the family than inside"), and to the kinds of working knowledge and skills needed for both ("My brothers seem to know how to make friends, but I don't"). It seems that often clients get involved in self-defeating patterns of thinking (covert behavior or a combination of covert experiences and behaviors) about themselves, others, and their environments. In a variety of ways they keep telling themselves that they are no good or that they are incapable of coping with crisis situations or that situations such as the ones they face cannot be managed. As we shall see, once such patterns are uncovered and clarified, they need to be challenged.

Training clients in the skills of Stage I. The skills helpers need in order to be effective consultants at this stage are principally active listening, the communication of empathy, and probing. These skills do not exist for themselves; they are, rather, tools for achieving the goals of Stage I—that is, the establishment of a working relationship with the client and the clarification of the problem situation. Skilled helpers not only listen well, but they can interweave various degrees of both probing and empathy to help clients define and clarify their problem situations.

The skills of Stage I, especially attending, active listening, empathy, and the behavioral expression of the foundational qualities of respect and genuineness, are also the kinds of skills clients need in order to relate to others more effectively. Most of the problem situations discussed by clients include elements of disordered interpersonal relationships. Training clients in these skills can help them manage interpersonal relationships more effectively.

Stage II: Goals—Deciding What to Do to Manage the Problem Situation

Once clients get a clear picture of what is going wrong, they need to determine what can be done to manage better. By the end of Stage I they should have a clearer picture of the problem situation or of one or more of the major issues of the problem situation. However, they still may not have a picture that is *complete* enough to decide what they are going to do. If not, they must still work with the helper in getting the kind of clarity needed to set reasonable situation-managing goals.

Step 3: Acquiring the kinds of new perspectives needed to set meaningful goals

Quite often clients do not manage problem situations well because they view both themselves and their relationship to the problem situation too narrowly or even in distorted ways. Their inability to see the whole problem situation clearly and their distorted thinking about self and others keep them locked into either inaction or uncreative and futile ways of trying to manage the problem situation. Clients often need to develop *new and perhaps more objective and realistic perspectives* on themselves, others, and the world around them if they are to make a reasonable decision about what to do in order to manage their lives more effectively.

If clients are not developing the kind of perspectives they need to see their problem situations more clearly—that is, clearly enough to set reasonable goals— then in Step 3 they are *challenged* to develop the kinds of new perspectives that help them see the kind of action they need to take. Ideally helpers are consultants who aid clients in a process of self-challenge. However, when clients do not challenge themselves or when they are unsuccessful in their attempts to develop more objective views of their problems, challenges from the helper and from others can be very beneficial.

Step 3 is an "expanding" step in that it encourages the client to reach out for new and more objective perspectives on his or her problems. A sign that this step is successful is that clients begin to take more and more responsibility for challenging themselves and begin to see, at least in general ways, things they must do to handle the problems they are exploring. For instance, Jane, in exploring her relationship with her fiancé, talks about her "inability" to communicate her anger to him directly—she communicates it in oblique, obstructive ways. The counselor, who has been listening carefully not only to what Jane is saying but also to what she is only half saying or implying, may help her see that it is her *hurt* that she finds difficult to discuss with her fiancé, not her anger. Discussing her hurt with her fiancé would make her feel very vulnerable. She disguises her anger because if she did not, she would be forced to deal with her hurt. Once this is clear and she sees the problem situation more objectively, she makes the decision to talk to her fiancé about this entire self-defeating pattern.

Training clients in the skills of challenging. The skills needed by helpers to be effective consultants at this stage can be called "challenging" skills. Effective helpers are capable of using the following challenging skills, when they are called for, in order to help clients move toward the kind of problem clarification that leads to meaningful goal setting. Giving these skills away to clients can help them in two ways. First of all, these skills can help clients challenge themselves. Second, since these are also the skills of more intensive kinds of mutuality (Egan & Cowan, 1979, Chapter 11), they are the kinds of skills clients need in order to cope with problems in interpersonal relationships.

· *Information as challenge.* Counselors can help clients find the kind of information needed to see the problem situation more clearly and more fully. Note that helping clients acquire information needed to get a fuller understanding of the problem situation is not the same as giving advice. Better yet, helpers can train clients to be better information seekers, to be able to ask themselves "What do I need to know in order to handle this situation better?"

· *Advanced empathy.* This skill enables helpers to share "hunches" of varying degrees of probability about the-client-in-this-problem-situation. These hunches, if solidly based on cues found in the clients' experiences and behavior, help them see dimensions of themselves and/or of the problem situation that they have been overlooking. In the example cited earlier, once Jane realized it was her hurt that she was afraid to talk about and not just her anger, she made a decision to share this "bigger picture" with her fiancé in order to open up clearer channels of communication between them. Clients can be trained to make the same kind of hunches about themselves. For instance, Jane could ask herself "What's missing in this picture? What's going on below the surface?"

• *Confrontation.* Clients sometimes fail to understand their problem situations clearly because they fail to see that they are incapacitated by certain *discrepancies* in their lives. For instance, parents would like to see their 25-year-old son get a job and move toward more independent living, and yet they provide him with whatever funds he needs, discourage him from taking jobs that are "below his level," and so forth. Once they see that they are actually reinforcing his dependence, they are in a better position to do something about it. At least they now see the problem situation more clearly.

• *Helper self-sharing.* Helpers can, with discretion, share their own experiences with clients *if* they do so in such a way as not to distract clients from their own problem situations, if this self-sharing does not merely add another burden to an already overburdened client, and if what they share is so related to a client's problem situation that it actually helps the client see his or her own situation with the kind of clarity that suggests some kind of useful action. At this stage of the process, helper genuineness can be expressed through appropriate self-disclosure (Egan, 1976). Clients can be trained to recognize the difference between self-centered self-disclosure and the kind of self-disclosure that fosters mutuality.

• *Immediacy.* Effective helpers are capable of discussing with clients what is happening between them in the helping relationship itself if it helps clients understand the problem situation more clearly or if it helps them understand and collaborate with the helping process more fully. Sometimes the kinds of interpersonal problems that plague clients in their day-to-day relationships arise, too, in the counseling relationship. For instance, a client may be having trouble discussing his problems with a helper because he is afraid of the intimacy this entails. The helper explores with him the fear of intimacy that is blocking the counseling process itself. Understanding his fear of intimacy in the counseling relationship helps him see more clearly the ways in which he fears intimacy in his day-to-day life. It goes without saying that the skill of immediacy is critical in human relationships outside the helping encounter. Training clients in this skill and helping them transfer it to their everyday lives can help them make relationships at least more decent.

As noted, clients can first of all be taught how to use these skills "on themselves." Once they develop some competence in self-challenge, then they can be taught how to use them with others. Mutuality includes the ability to provide *both* support *and* challenge. It is not that people do not confront and challenge one another in everyday life. They do. However, they often do so in such a self-defeating way that challenge becomes part of the problem rather than a means of handling it.

It is most important to note that neither problem clarification nor challenging is a goal in itself in the helping process. Rather, these are subgoals. Challenging as it is described here is effective if it enables clients to understand critical areas of problem situations more clearly, but problem clarity itself (insight, if you wish) makes sense only insofar as it enables a client to make an informed decision about *what to do* to manage a problem situation more effectively.

Step 4: Setting problem-related goals

Steps 1, 2, and 3 are all related to problem definition and clarification, but once a client is helped to handle whatever blind spots he or she might have with respect to the problem situation (Step 3), it is time to move on. The problem-solving process is organic and cumulative. It is successful only if it leads to *problem-handling action.*

Steps 1, 2, and 3 are successful if they lead to the kind of problem clarification that contributes to setting realistic, problem-handling *goals*. Some clients, once they are helped to overcome the kind of blind spots that inhibit effective action, know precisely what they want to do. It is as if they were to say "Now that I see the problem situation this clearly, I know what I have to do to manage it better." Other clients at the end of Step 3 realize that they need to act, but they still are not sure *what* to do. That is, they need help in setting goals.

Training clients in the skills of goal setting. The skills discussed in Steps 1, 2, and 3—assessment, active listening, accurate empathy, probing, and all the challenging skills—are all useful and needed throughout the rest of the helping process. The particular mix of skills needed at any given moment depends on the client, the problem situation, the relationship between helper and client, and similar variables.

As to goal setting, while it is evident that *clients* need to decide what they are going to do about problem situations once they see them with the kind of clarity and understanding that makes some kind of action reasonable, it is also evident that counselors can help clients make these decisions both directly, by helping them set goals, and indirectly, by training clients in the goal-setting process. The following are characteristics of effective goals.

• *Accomplishments.* Goals are best differentiated from programs if they are stated as accomplishments rather than processes. "To become a nurse" is a process, while "nursing degree conferred within three years" is an accomplishment that meets a vocational need.

• *Clear, specific.* Vague goals are like New Year's resolutions—they are never achieved. Clients can be trained to move from the more general (mission statements) to the more specific (clear, behavioral goals). "I want to get into physical shape" is not as clear as "Within six months I will be running a mile under nine minutes at least four times a week." The former is a mission statement; the latter is a goal.

• *Measurable or verifiable.* A goal is effective only if the criteria for its achievement are clear to the client. "I want to have a better relationship with my wife" is a mission statement or aim, not a goal, because, as stated, it cannot be verified.

• *Realistic.* Goals are realistic if they are within the client's resources and if external circumstances do not make their achievement overly difficult or impossible. Another way of saying this is that the achievement of goals must be under the *control* of the client.

• *Adequate.* Goals are adequate if their achievement would contribute in some *substantial* way to managing the problem situation. If a client drinks two fifths of gin a week and one can of beer, her drinking problem will not be effectively handled if she eliminates the can of beer.

• *In keeping with the client's values.* Although helping is, to a degree, a process of social influences, it remains ethical only if it respects the values of the client. Although helpers may challenge clients to reexamine their values, they should in no way encourage clients to do things that are not in keeping with their values.

• *Set in a time frame.* Reasonable time frames for the achievement of goals need to be determined. Goals that are to be reached "sometime or other" never seem to be achieved.

Training in goal setting.   It is essential that the goals chosen be the client's rather than the helper's goals. Various kinds of probes can be used to help clients discover what *they* want to do in order to manage some dimension of a problem situation more effectively. For instance, Carl Rogers, in a film of a counseling session, says to the client "I think you've been telling me all along what you want to do." At another time he asks "What is it that you wish that I would tell you to do?" This puts the responsibility for goal setting where it belongs—that is, on the client's shoulders.

In a more direct way clients can be trained to shape their own goals—that is, to move from such statements as "I know I have to do something about this" to more and more specific statements. Some suggest that the client's goals be allowed to "emerge." This, they say, is a more natural process. It is not clear, however, what this process of emergence is, and, in addition, the assumption is that "emergence" has not been working for the client. Clients who have goal-setting skills have more freedom; that is, they can decide whether to set specific goals or to let them emerge. The problem with leaving goal setting to chance is that people skip goal setting entirely and keep trying one program after another. Failure to set goals can lead to a kind of "tyranny of programs." The client who says "I've tried everything and nothing works" may well be quite active but lack *direction*. Specific goals provide direction for clients who probably lack a sense of direction in their lives.

In a sense, goal setting is the central point of the helping process. Everything done to this point is done to set problem-managing goals, and everything that takes place from this point on is done to see that these goals are actually achieved. A goal is a client's way of saying "This is *what* I want to do in order to manage the problem situation more effectively." The client still might not know exactly *how* he or she is going to do it, but at least the *what* is clear.

Stage III: Program Development

Whereas goals deal with *what* is to be done to handle a problem situation, programs deal with *how* these goals are to be carried out. Goals are ends; programs are the means for achieving these ends. Some clients, once they establish clear and reasonable goals, know exactly what to do to carry them out. For instance, a father might say "I know precisely how I must rearrange my work schedule in order to keep three nights per week and two weekends per month free for my children." Many clients are not so fortunate and still need some help to fashion reasonable programs.

Step 5: Helping clients discover program possibilities

In this step counselors help their clients develop a list of concrete, realistic steps or courses of action that will lead to the achievement of the goal or goals set in Step 4. One reason people fail to achieve goals is that they do not explore the different ways in which the goal can be achieved. They choose one means or program without a great deal of exploration or reflection and try it, and when it fails, they conclude that they just can't achieve that particular goal. At this stage of the problem-solving process, as many means as possible (within time constraints) should be uncovered.

For instance, a person who wants to stop drinking may be helped to come up with the following possibilities:

- Join Alcoholics Anonymous and follow out their set program.
- Get rid of all the alcohol in the house.
- Stop "cold turkey."
- Gradually reduce daily or weekly alcohol consumption.
- Take Antabuse, a drug that causes headaches and/or nausea if followed by alcohol.
- Find activities that can be substituted for drinking.
- Find ways of handling stress other than the ingestion of alcohol.
- Rearrange social life—for example, do not go to bars after work, avoid the three-martini-lunch crowd.

The list can obviously be extended, even by adding "wild" possibilities such as moving to a deserted island. Even the wildest possibilities often contribute some element to the final program.

Training clients in the skills of divergent thinking.   In a broad sense, the skills needed at this point concern "divergent" thinking. Although both convergent (one right answer) and divergent (multiple right answer) thinking are useful in their place, many clients have allowed themselves to become victims of excessive use of convergent thinking. Helping them become divergent thinkers with respect to their problem situations can help them come up with a variety of ways of achieving their goals. Some ways of promoting divergent thinking are these:

- *Brainstorming.* Brainstorming is a well-established technique for generating practical ideas. This technique includes suspending judgment on the value of the possibilities generated.
- *Scenario writing.* Clients can be taught to use their imaginations to picture some *other* person going about achieving the chosen goal. How does this other person do it? What does the process look like?
- *Using fantasy.* Helpers can stimulate clients to use their imaginations in a variety of ways to generate program possibilities. Have them relax and imagine themselves under optimal conditions carrying out their goals.

This is obviously an "expanding," a data-gathering, step. The literature on creativity is filled with techniques for helping people to expand the ways they approach problems. Much of this, with a little ingenuity on the part of helpers, can be applied to the problem situations of clients.

Step 6: Choosing a "good fit" program
Ordinarily, helping clients generate numerous program possibilities makes it easier to help them choose a program that best fits *them*—that is, one that best fits their abilities, resources, preferences, and level of motivation *and* one that is in keeping with the constraints of their environments. This is a "contracting" step. Client and helper, in collaboration, review the programs or program elements developed in the previous step and try to choose either the best single program or the best combination.

Training clients in the skills of program choice.   The skills of program choice are similar to goal-setting skills. That is, counselors help clients learn how to choose programs that are concrete and specific, verifiable, realistic (within their resources and environmental constraints), adequate (that is, the elements of the program are actions that will actually lead to achievement of the goal), in keeping with their values, and cast in a reasonable time frame.

The second part of this skill is putting program elements chosen into some reasonable order. Programs are, ideally, *step-by-step* processes that lead to achievement of the goal. Clients must learn to see to it that no step is too large or complicated (larger steps can be broken down into smaller ones; complicated steps can be simplified). Clients should have a clear idea of precisely when they are going to do what.

It is at this stage that it is often helpful if clients know how to draw up some kind of "action contract" with themselves. Counselors can help clients draw up reasonable contracts and can also help them monitor them. Contracts can often be powerful stimuli to action because clients often find "keeping to the contract" rewarding.

Stage IV: Implementing the Program

Some clients, once they know what they want to do (goals, accomplishments) and how to do it (programs), move quickly and easily into action and need little help thereafter. However, some clients at this stage still need the kind of support and challenge that helpers can provide.

Step 7: Implementing the program

Finally, it is time to "get on with it," to turn planning into action in order to see whether what has been planned works. The fruit of helping is behavioral change that leads to valued accomplishments that contribute in some substantial way to handling a problem situation.

Training clients in the skills needed to implement programs.   Implementation has two phases. The first takes place when the client is about to put an action program into effect. The second is during the program itself.

As to the first phase, perhaps "forewarned is forearmed" might be an apt phrase. Most clients run into difficulties and obstacles of greater or lesser seriousness as they carry out the steps of a program. Clients can be taught to review the expected obstacles to the kind of program they are undertaking. To use military language, goals are *objectives,* programs are the *strategies* for achieving these objectives, and *tactics* are the ways these strategies are actually put into practice "in the field." If clients learn to identify some of the pitfalls that may be encountered in the execution of a program, they can become better "tacticians." Such previews help clients develop *contingency* plans that can be used "on the spot" if first-line plans fail. For instance, a person who wants to stop drinking and therefore chooses not to go to lunch with coworkers who drink rather heavily might find that his change of habits puzzles or upsets them. They may not accept such simple explanations as "I want to cut down on calories," "I've decided to drink less," or "Liquor is taking too much out of my budget." If no one remarks on his dropping out of the luncheon group, fine. But if he meets hostility or is pressured to drop his resolution, knowing how to deal with such difficulties can spell the difference between success and failure. *Force-field analysis* is a method clients can learn to identify both the forces that restrain them from moving toward desirable goals and the forces that facilitate movement toward goals.

There are a variety of ways in which helpers can teach clients how to find the support and challenge they need to carry out programs. They can be taught how to apply the principles of behavior, such as reinforcement, punishment, aversive conditioning, modeling, and shaping, to the implementation phase. For instance, if clients find that they are failing to participate in the programs to which they have committed themselves, it may mean that the incentives for nonparticipation are stronger than the incentives for participation. They can then search for ways of reducing the strength of restraining incentives and for more effective incentives for participation. They can be taught how to "take counsel" with friends at this stage. Sometimes simply finding a good listener, someone with whom clients can discuss the difficulties they are experiencing in trying to implement programs, can be very supportive. As in Stage I, they can help untangle themselves from self-defeating feelings and emotions.

Step 8: Evaluation

Some clients find it quite easy to monitor their progress once they embark on a program. Others need help in monitoring. Helpers can train clients to determine whether they are succeeding. There are at least three major evaluation questions that clients can ask themselves as they implement programs:

- "To what degree am I participating in the program—fully, partially, or not at all?" Counselors can help clients monitor both the degree and the quality of program participation. If clients find that they are not participating fully enough, they can fine-tune the program to fit their needs better or look for more effective incentives for program participation.
- "Am I achieving my goal by participating in the program?" If the answer here is no, then the program probably needs more than fine-tuning; that is, it needs some redoing, whether major or minor. Either it is a poor program in itself, or the "fit" for this particular client is poor. If either is the case, then the client knows that Steps 5 and 6 need some redoing.
- "Is the fact that I am achieving my goal contributing in some substantial way to managing the original problem situation?" If the answer is no, then the client needs to see that the goal was not chosen wisely and Step 4 needs to be redone. If the answer is yes, then the client must decide whether he or she is satisfied with the way the problem situation is now being managed.

There is a problem with evaluation as described here. Evaluation at its best is an ongoing process, not simply a judgment that takes place at the end of a series of actions. Although the above questions are important ones for clients to ask themselves as they are actually implementing programs, if clients know from the beginning what evaluation questions they are going to be asking themselves, these questions can somehow inform the entire planning process itself. Poorly chosen goals and programs are not only inefficient; they can also lead clients to conclude that their situations are hopeless or that helping "doesn't work."

THE RATIONAL AND THE NONRATIONAL IN HELPING AND SELF-HELP

Helping is not, of course, the completely rational, step-by-step process described here. Clients often move back and forwards in it. For instance, they explore a problem, but before it is explored sufficiently, they move into action. The course of action fails, and they find themselves back trying to get a more complete picture of the problem situation. Or they jump from problem exploration to programs ("I'll try this and see if it works"), and when the program fails, they see the need to set goals. That is to say, even though the problem-management process is a rational, step-by-step process, for a variety of reasons its logic is often violated. However, the model does provide both helpers and clients with the "geography" of helping and of problem management. It is against this "ground" that the "figure" of the actual helping or self-help process occurs. The more familiar clients are with the step-by-step logic of helping, the more capable they will be of adapting it to their own needs and style.

THE PROBLEM-SOLVING MODEL AS AN INTEGRATIVE TOOL

The problem-solving framework specifies concretely and specifically the *tasks* to be accomplished in effective helping. It places no limitations on how these tasks might be accomplished. Any technique that is ethical and suited to the needs of both client and counselor can be used to accomplish any given task. The problem-solving framework can be used both to *organize the contributions of the many approaches to helping and to mine out* from them concepts, strategies, methodologies, techniques, exercises, and skills that contribute to each of the eight helping tasks. This framework helps make sense of the "blooming, buzzing confusion" found in a helping literature that is so extensive as to be almost overwhelming. The problem-solving framework becomes the principal instrument of a systematic and integrative eclecticism. In this sense, it is not only a vehicle for giving psychology away, it is also an instrument to mine out the best in other approaches so that they, too, can be given away.

REFERENCES

Anthony, W. A. Psychological rehabilitation: A concept in need of a model. *American Psychologist,* 1977, *32,* 658–662.

Anthony, W. A. A human technology for human resource development. *Counseling Psychologist,* 1978, *7*(3), 58–65.

Anthony, W. A. *The principles of psychiatric rehabilitation.* Amherst, Mass.: Human Resource Development Press, 1979.

Bandura, A. Self-efficacy: Toward a unifying theory of behavioral change. *Psychological Review,* 1977, *84,* 191–215. (a)

Bandura, A. *Social learning theory.* Englewood Cliffs, N.J.: Prentice-Hall, 1977. (b)

Brammer, L., & Shostrom, E. *Therapeutic psychology: Fundamentals of actualization counseling and psychotherapy* (3rd ed.). Englewood Cliffs, N.J.: Prentice-Hall, 1977.

Carkhuff, R. R. *Helping and human relations.* Vol. 1: *Selection and training.* New York: Holt, Rinehart & Winston, 1969. (a)

Carkhuff, R. R. *Helping and human relations.* Vol. 2: *Practice and research.* New York: Holt, Rinehart & Winston, 1969. (b)

Carkhuff, R. R. Training as a preferred mode of treatment. *Journal of Counseling Psychology,* 1971, *18,* 123–131.

Carkhuff, R. R., & Berenson, B. G. *Teaching as treatment.* Amherst, Mass.: Human Resource Development Press, 1976.

Dimond, R. E., Havens, R. A., & Jones, A. C. A conceptual framework for the practice of prescriptive eclecticism in psychotherapy. *American Psychologist,* 1978, *33,* 239–248.

Dyer, W. W., & Vriend, J. *Counseling techniques that work: Applications to individual and group counseling.* Washington, D.C.: APGA Press, 1975.

D'Zurilla, T. J., & Goldfried, M. R. Problem solving and behavior modification. *Journal of Abnormal Psychology,* 1971, *78,* 107–126.

Egan, G. *Interpersonal living: A skills/contract approach to human-relations training in groups.* Monterey, Calif.: Brooks/Cole, 1976.

Egan, G. *The skilled helper: A model for systematic helping and interpersonal relating* (2nd ed.). Monterey, Calif.: Brooks/Cole, 1982.

Egan, G., & Cowan, M. A. *People in systems: A model for development in the human-service professions and education.* Monterey, Calif.: Brooks/Cole, 1979.

Egan, G., & Cowan, M. A. *Moving into adulthood: Themes and variations in self-directed development for effective living.* Monterey, Calif.: Brooks/Cole, 1980.

Gazda, G. M., & Brooks, D. K., Jr. A comprehensive approach to developmental interventions. *Journal for Specialists in Group Work,* 1980, *5,* 120–126.

Heath, D. H. The maturing person. In G. Walsh & D. Shapiro (Eds.), *Beyond health and normality.* New York: Van Nostrand Reinhold, 1980. (a)

Heath, D. H. Wanted: A comprehensive model of healthy development. *Personnel and Guidance Journal,* 1980, *58,* 391–399. (b)

Mahoney, M. J., & Arnkoff, D. B. Cognitive and self-control therapies. In S. L. Garfield & A. E. Bergin (Eds.), *Handbook of psychotherapy and behavior change* (2nd ed.). New York: Wiley, 1978.

Maslow, A. H. *Toward a psychology of being* (2nd ed.). New York: Van Nostrand Reinhold, 1968.

Miller, G. A., Galanter, E., & Pribram, K. H. *Plans and the structure of behavior.* New York: Holt, Rinehart & Winston, 1960.

Muro, J. J., & Engels, D. W. Life coping skills through developmental group counseling. *Journal for Specialists in Group Work,* 1980, *5,* 127–134.

CHAPTER EIGHT

Three Decades of Democratizing Relationships through Training

Thomas Gordon

Thomas Gordon is president of Effectiveness Training Incorporated, an international educational organization that designs and markets training programs for increasing people's effectiveness in interpersonal relations. More than 750,000 people have participated in Effectiveness Training programs in 14 countries. He is the author of five books: *Group-Centered Leadership* (1955), *Parent Effectiveness Training* (1970), *Teacher Effectiveness Training* (1974), *P.E.T. in Action* (1976), and *Leader Effectiveness Training* (1977). A licensed psychologist, Gordon received his Ph.D. from the University of Chicago, where he later served on the faculty for five years. He is a fellow of the American Psychological Association and a past president of the California State Psychological Association.

In this chapter, Thomas Gordon describes his personal/professional evolution from therapist to educator and from treatment specialist to prevention specialist. In so doing he captures the parallel historical developments in the skills training field. A student and colleague of Carl Rogers, Gordon has built a model incorporating client-centered principles, leadership theory, and win/win conflict resolution. He has disseminated his model widely—in the family, in the business world, and in the educational system. Gordon's methods—for example nonjudgmental listening, honest self-disclosure, problem solving, and conflict resolution—are rooted in deeply felt principles of egalitarianism and democracy. Gordon notes that in the 1960s most of the instructors he recruited and trained were from outside the helping professions. In the 1970s, that picture changed, and today, of the several thousand Parent Effectiveness instructors throughout the world, three fourths are professionals working in community mental health centers, child-guidance clinics, family counseling centers, juvenile courts, and the like. This fact speaks to the growing acceptance of skills training approaches within the traditional mental health field.

In retrospect, I'm certain that as early as my first years in high school the seeds were sown for what would later evolve into my present conviction that democratic relationships are health-giving and, conversely, that nondemocratic relationships are destructive to human well-being.

I have a clear recollection of a three-year experience in a Sunday-school class taught by a woman in her early twenties. To my knowledge Grace Cox had no formal education in human relations, although ten years later we ran into each other at a convention and discovered that both of us had become psychologists. In her role as Sunday-school teacher for a class of 20 or so teenagers (later it grew to 50 or more), Grace came across to me as some brand-new species of adult. She somehow knew how to create a special climate that made me and my classmates feel good about ourselves. I could not have described then exactly how she did this, but I was well aware of the effect of her leadership: the responsibility for managing and governing the class was transferred gradually from the leader to the kids. We elected our own officers, formed task committees, and made all the decisions about topics we wanted to discuss or projects we wanted to tackle, and some of us took turns each Sunday being the discussion leader or facilitator. In Grace's class there was nothing we felt could not be discussed openly and honestly. For the first time in my life I felt fully respected, valued, and accepted by an adult. I experienced the novelty of being a member of a self-governing group in which I had a strong voice.

I know now that this remarkable woman somehow acquired a deep understanding of participative management, student-centered teaching, and democratic leadership long before these ideas found their way into the body of knowledge of social psychology.

A second experience taught me things about democratic relationships. Here it was I who was the formal leader. My insights in this case derived from my initial failure to be democratic and person-centered. Flushed with the success of having been made the leader of a group of fellow officers in the Air Force assigned the task of designing a course to teach flight instructors more effective pedagogical techniques, I fell into the trap of taking charge—I set the goals myself (after all, I was more expert), I assigned the tasks, and I assumed sole responsibility for evaluation of how well the tasks were performed. Certainly, I did little to dispel the notion that I was the boss and the members of the group were my subordinates. To my surprise and puzzlement, within but a few months morale was bad, resistance was high, production was low, creativity was nil, and open and honest communication between me and the group members was nonexistent.

Having failed to apply what I had learned from Grace Cox, I created a climate in which my group members didn't feel anything like the students in Grace's Sunday-school class.

Fortunately, thanks to the honesty of one of the group, who was also a close friend, I was able to see the destructive effects of my authoritarian leadership soon enough to make a complete turnaround. I began to invite full participation of group members, listen to their ideas and feelings, and transfer ownership of the project and responsibility for governance of the group from me, the leader, to the group itself. The effects of this change in my leadership style were startling and enduring: creativity flourished, communication opened up, tension decreased, and the work became enjoyable and satisfying to all of us. A sick group became a healthy one. And the project became fun.

It was not until I was discharged and returned to graduate school to start my work toward a Ph.D. in psychology that I discovered that a few psychologists had done research on styles of leadership. I came across the pioneering and now-classic study of Lewin, Lippitt, and White (1939) in which they compared the effects on a group of children of three styles of adult leadership in a boys' club: authoritarian, laissez-faire, and democratic. Their results clearly favored the democratic leader with respect to such criteria as productivity (constructive activity), frequency of child/child aggression, level of motivation, maintenance of productive activity when the leader absents himself from the group, autonomy, irritability, and frequency of scapegoating. Needless to say, reading this study confirmed my earlier experiential learnings.

I remember later devouring the pages of a monograph that described a still little-known study by Baldwin, Kalhorn, and Breese (1949) conducted at the Fels Institute in Antioch, Ohio. Theirs was a longitudinal study of the effects on children of three styles of child rearing: authoritarian, permissive, and democratic. Impressive indeed were their findings that children of democratic parents year after year showed higher marks on emotional maturity, social adjustment, peer leadership, and educational achievement. Unlike the children in the other groups, the children of democratic parents showed a significant increase in IQ scores over the years!

Still later, I found a little book called *The Therapeutic Community,* written by a British psychiatrist, Maxwell Jones. He had been experimenting with introducing democracy to patients on the wards of mental hospitals in England, setting up groups in which patients were allowed and encouraged to participate with staff members in managing and governing all ward activities, including, among many other things, deciding which patients would be released from the hospital. Jones offered rather conclusive evidence that the experience of participating in these democratically run groups was truly therapeutic: more of these patients got well than those in the typical wards where the staff governed autocratically. Apathetic patients came alive, submissive patients became more assertive, silent patients began to talk. This was my first introduction to "fate control," a concept now known to be a critical component of positive mental health: the feeling of having control over one's life is a characteristic of healthy persons.

Subsequently, observing T-groups (training groups) one summer at the National Training Laboratory (NTL) at Bethel, Maine, I learned that the participants in these self-governing leaderless groups often experienced positive changes in their personality not unlike the changes people make in individual psychotherapy: losing their shyness, increasing their self-esteem, becoming less hostile toward others, trusting others more.

So impressed was I with the therapeutic potential of these egalitarian learning groups, I returned to the University of Chicago and began a three- or four-year period of conducting my own T-groups, which then were being called sensitivity training groups or, in recent years, encounter groups. These varied training experiences motivated me to write my first book, *Group-Centered Leadership: A Way of Releasing the Creative Potential of Groups* (1955). In that book I attempted to construct a model (or theory) of democratic leadership, identifying and describing the attitudes and specific skills needed by a leader to create a participative, self-directing, self-governing, problem-solving, decision-making group. And I presented some research evidence supporting the amazing therapeutic effects that this democratic style of leadership produces in individual group members.

At that time I was becoming dimly aware of a notion that by now has become a clear conviction: democracy *is* therapy. Put in somewhat different words: the experience of living or working in a democratic relationship will be health-giving, and the most effective therapy for people who are not healthy is an experience of having a democratic relationship with another.

Support for this principle began to show up with ever-increasing frequency in my professional life. I spent six health-giving years on the staff of the University of

Chicago Counseling Center, founded by Carl Rogers, whose own democratic leadership encouraged all of us to participate equally in determining the destiny of our organization and choosing the professional direction in which each wanted to go as an individual. Of the 50 or so persons I've personally known who were staff members at the center, all have said it was one of the most growth-producing, health-giving, productive, intimate, and loving periods in their lives.

In the early 1950s, I found my interests broadening. I felt the challenge of introducing democracy into the management of business and industrial organizations, schools, and hospitals. I began consuming the massive amounts of data coming steadily from the Survey Research Center at the University of Michigan. In study after study, investigators were getting consistent findings that supported the positive (therapeutic) effects of person-oriented, democratic, and participative supervisors on employees. Such leaders, compared with those less person-centered and more authoritarian, proved to have employees who were higher in productivity, job satisfaction, morale, and creativity and had lower turnover rates.

In at least one study, democratic leaders were more likely to have employees who griped a lot. The investigator found that these effective supervisors encouraged open and honest communication from employees, which could take the form of criticism and gripes as well as new ideas and constructive suggestions. In another study from the Michigan group, the more democratic and participative managers had employees whose loyalties and identification were primarily with the company, while the more authoritarian leaders had employees whose loyalties and identification were more with their union.

Over the years, the findings from these studies, as well as leadership studies at other universities, quite naturally led to the emergence of some comprehensive theories (or models) of effective management. Examples are Rensis Likert's System IV and Douglas McGregor's Theory Y, both theories that equate managerial effectiveness with the leadership style variously described as participative, person-centered, nonauthoritarian, group-centered, or democratic. Such effective leaders know how to get teamwork, build cohesive groups, encourage group problem solving, develop warm relationships with members of their work group, encourage open communication, and make work more satisfying.

Clearly the challenge now for social scientists is to try to find answers to these questions: (1) *Precisely* what does an effective leader do? (2) What *specific skills* does he or she use? (3) What *methods or procedures* does he or she employ? With better understanding of what effective leaders do, we can design training programs that will teach noneffective leaders to be more effective, train authoritarian people how to develop democratic relationships. This is what challenged me in the 1950s and has continued to be the focus of my professional life throughout the 1960s and 1970s.

TRAINING LEADERS IN ORGANIZATIONS

I was given my first opportunity to be a human-relations training consultant in 1952 when I was on the faculty of the University of Chicago. The experience was so rewarding that I decided to leave the academic life and become a full-time trainer and consultant. Over the next decade I would be doing human-relations consulting with more than 50 organizations—businesses, industrial firms, schools, hospitals, agencies. My principal role was working with supervisors, managers, and administrators and executives, either individually or in groups, to assist them in changing their leadership style from authoritarian to democratic, from leader-centered to group-centered.

I learned early that in order for leaders to change their style, they first needed the skills to develop a radically different kind of relationship with their subordinates. The most critical of these specific skills are the following:

- Listening respectfully and accurately to subordinates' feelings, opinions, and ideas—being an effective "counselor."
- Transferring to individual subordinates the responsibility to try to solve their own problems rather than be dependent on their leader for answers and solutions.
- Conducting meetings in such a way that group members will feel free to identify problems and participate in joint problem solving.
- Facilitating the group's *process* of problem solving rather than assuming full responsibility for the *content* of problem solving.
- Distributing the various leadership functions among the members of the group.
- Creating a nonthreatening, nonjudgmental, nonpunitive climate so that group members feel safe about expressing feelings, asserting themselves, and disagreeing with the leader.

I found that teaching organizational leaders these new behaviors was not as difficult as I had thought. I drew heavily on my own training as a professional counselor to teach them empathic, nonevaluative listening. I used audiotapes that demonstrated effective listening; I modeled empathic listening in the classroom; I created role-playing exercises to give them practice in counseling with subordinates; and I gave them assignments that required them to use this new skill on the job, with real problems. As for teaching the skills of conducting effective group meetings, I relied mainly on the existing technology that had been developed by the pioneering social scientists in the field of group dynamics and by Norman R.F. Maier (1952). I drew on my own early experience in teaching groups to be more self-directing and self-governing. The training methods I found most effective were (1) modeling the group-leadership skills while I was being the leader of my training classes and (2) sitting in as an observer and coach when the class participants conducted real on-the-job meetings with their own subordinates.

Though confident in knowing how to teach these new skills and behaviors, I encountered considerable resistance from some of the learners when it came to giving up their authority and power, trusting the wisdom of the group, and distributing leadership functions. Such resistance was expressed in various ways:

- "Leaders who don't give answers and solutions will be seen by their subordinates as weak or incompetent."
- "Leaders who share their authority with the group will lose their subordinates' respect."
- "Groups can't ever make decisions, so the leader has to make them."
- "Group decision making takes too much time."

I learned that such apprehensions and concerns can seldom be dispelled by logic or counterargument. Rather, it is essential that the trainer listen, show understanding and acceptance of all resistance, and give encouragement to the learners to at least give the new methods a try to discover for themselves whether their fears are justified. My experience has confirmed Kurt Lewin's principle that if people are to adopt new behaviors, they must first be given the freedom to express openly their allegiance to their old behaviors and their resistance to the new.

Despite their initial resistance to democratic leadership, I have found that leaders in organizations, by and large, are more open to these new ideas and more willing to try them out than any other group of people whom I have tried to train. Undoubtedly it is because organizational leaders have a strong economic motivation to try out whatever might increase their effectiveness—they realize that effectiveness will be rewarded with higher salaries, bonuses, or promotions. Moreover, most business leaders recognize from their experience as subordinates that coercive power, in the long run, is aversive and counterproductive.

In fact, today in business and industrial organizations we are seeing an increasing acceptance of democratic leadership, a growing recognition that employee participation brings tangible and concrete results, such as decreased costs, improved production methods, better decisions, higher morale, better quality. In the auto industry, for example, we see clear indications that companies are adopting the Japanese management philosophy that has been such an important factor in the incursion of Japanese-made cars into the American market. Top executive Dutch Landen of General Motors told a *Los Angeles Times* reporter: "I don't believe our authoritarian corporations can continue to coexist with democratic institutions in a democratic society.... In this country we must democratize our corporations" (*Los Angeles Times,* October 23, 1980). Ford, like General Motors, is now fully committed to "employee involvement," with worker management committees jointly considering decisions at every level of the corporation, from the highest executive suite to the shop floor.

From our cadre of several hundred authorized Leader Effectiveness Training instructors throughout the country, we are learning that most top executives and training directors in most organizations are more willing than ever to adopt the democratic management theories of McGregor, Likert, Herzberg, and others. During the past year, in fact, I have read at least a dozen articles in which the Japanese participative and democratic management practices have been held up as superior to the American authoritarian practices.

Consequently, it has become less and less difficult to sell organizations on the potential benefits of participative management and industrial democracy. The problem now for most organizations is finding programs that will both train and coach their supervisors and managers in the *specific skills and problem-solving methods* that will enable them to implement the more democratic philosophy of leadership. More and more companies are convinced that their traditional authoritarian leadership must be replaced, and now they want training programs to translate abstractions into specific operational skills and procedures.

This skill-training feature has been built into our Leader Effectiveness Training course and is one of the main reasons for the growing acceptance of L.E.T. by business and industrial organizations. In this 36-hour course, participants are taught the following skills and procedures:

- Empathic listening
- Confrontive and assertive communication skills
- How to conduct group problem-solving and decision-making meetings
- A no-lose conflict-resolution procedure
- How to conduct brainstorming meetings for generating creative solutions to difficult problems
- Team-building skills
- Procedures for getting employees to set their own goals and evaluate their own performance
- Procedures for getting employee participation in multilevel problem solving

Our expectation is that the L.E.T. program will play an important role in the inevitable democratization of American industry.

TEACHING PARENTS HOW TO CREATE DEMOCRATIC RELATIONSHIPS WITH THEIR CHILDREN

My understanding of the nature and workings of parent/child relationships was very limited until after I established a private practice as a clinical psychologist in the late 1950s and began to work with youngsters brought to me by their parents or referred by schools. Both parents and teachers labeled these children "emotionally disturbed," "neurotic," "maladjusted," or "predelinquent." As such, they were seen as needing counseling and psychotherapy—some form of "treatment" for their "sickness."

I was unprepared for my discovery that these youngsters seldom had any kind of emotional sickness. In fact, most of them were certain it was their parents or teachers who had the problems and needed my counseling. Nevertheless, these children talked openly about their family squabbles and conflicts, and they described incidents in which they felt unfairly treated. They complained that their parents and teachers seldom listened to them or understood them; they told about being unfairly punished; and they described incidents in which their parents or teachers had shown no respect for their needs. They felt controlled by adults who demanded obedience to their authority, and they felt they were treated like second-class citizens.

The youngsters also shared with me how they reacted to (or coped with) these conditions. It made a long list: lying, negativism, tattling, aggression, cheating, disruptive behaviors at home and in school, truancy, disobedience, poor performance at school, sexual promiscuity, bullying other children, drinking, using drugs, excessive shyness, overconforming, compulsive eating, depression, illness, suicidal thoughts.

In my later conferences with the parents, they seldom saw themselves as needing therapy or treatment. In fact, most of them appeared to be functioning rather effectively in their lives. There I was, trained to provide therapy to troubled people, but neither the children nor their parents wanted therapy or seemed to need it.

It was a sudden transformation in my thinking when I realized that these parent/child difficulties were *human-relations problems* rather than problems of psychopathology. Clearly these families were simply having difficulty living together in harmony. Few had any of the most basic human-relations skills: how to communicate openly and honestly, how to listen, how to resolve conflicts amicably, how to establish rules and standards in the home, how to show respect for each other's needs, how to make their relationships seem equitable and fair to both parent and child. What they needed was information about human relationships and competence in interpersonal skills. Training, not therapy, was the most appropriate thing I could offer them.

Drawing on my previous experience designing human-relations courses for managers and supervisors in organizations, I hastily put together a human-relations training program tailored for parents.

My first class in 1962 consisted of only 17 parents. Over the next two years I taught a dozen more classes involving several hundred parents, making constant revisions and improvements in the course during this period. So overwhelmingly favorable were parents' responses to the course, I was confident that my program was working. Quite deliberately I had designed the course to be completely different from the medical, or treatment, model with its own distinctive language (therapy, doctor, patient, treatment, fees); instead, I wanted parents to see the program as an *educational* experience. To this end I used the language of education (course, training, students, instructor, textbook, homework, tuition), and I carefully chose a name to fit this educational model—"Parent Effectiveness Training."

It was important to me that the course also attract parents who as yet were not experiencing serious problems in their family relationships. I hoped P.E.T. would be seen as a *preventive* program. This is exactly what happened. Parents enrolled in P.E.T. who never would have consulted me as a therapist. Over time, Parent Effectiveness Training dramatically changed my professional role from therapist to educator, from a treatment specialist to a prevention specialist.

To make P.E.T. widely available, I developed a program of instructor training and recruited persons whom I would train and authorize to teach the course in their own communities. Over 15,000 persons have been trained in this country alone. However, unlike the L.E.T. instructors, who found an ever-increasing acceptance in business and industry of the need for more democratic relationships between managers and subordinates, P.E.T. instructors generally found that for most parents the idea that parent/child relationships should be democratic is foreign. In fact, our instructors discovered that most parents think the concept is preposterous, ridiculous, crazy, and unbelievable. Ours is a nation of parents who are convinced that children must be coerced, restrained, directed, restricted, regimented, managed, harnessed, and inhibited. Such parental control of children is euphemistically called "discipline." And disciplining children obviously requires possessing power over them, for which parents use the term *authority*. Thus, the conventional wisdom in our country is that parents have no choice but to exercise strong authority in raising children and that the goal of these parents is to produce obedience to that authority.

The universal method parents use to produce obedience to authority is administering punishment—depriving children of something they want or need or inflicting physical pain. Just how pervasive is disciplining with physical punishment has been revealed in a recent nationwide survey of a representative sample of several thousand parents (Straus, Gelles, & Steinmetz, 1980). Straus et al. found that 86% of children 3 to 4 years old had been victims of some form of physical punishment from parents within the year in which the study was conducted; 82% of 5- to 9-year-olds; 54% of 10- to 14-year-olds; and 30% of 15- to 17-year-olds. And 61% of the parents they surveyed reported using physical punishment at least once a week!

In view of such a strong and pervasive belief in using power to coerce and control children, it is understandable why American parents are not easily convinced they should take a course to learn how to have democratic, equalitarian, nonpower relationships with their offspring. So obsessed with power are most parents that P.E.T. is sometimes seen as a program that will weaken or even extinguish any influence parents might have over their children. P.E.T. often raises the specter of permissiveness: parents fear that giving up their power over a child is tantamount to handing power over to the child, who will then become wild, unmanageable, selfish, and irresponsible—getting his or her way all the time, "ruling the roost." On the flyleaf of Fitzhugh Dodson's best-selling book *How to Parent* (1970), permissiveness is held up as the cause of all teenage problems: "Where have today's teenagers gone wrong? Why have so many turned to drugs, promiscuity, rebellion against their parents and their country? The answer lies in the extreme permissiveness taught by the leading child-raising books of the last few decades."

In P.E.T. we have found that most parents are the victims of this either/or thinking—either the parent must have the power or the child will take it. Parents have been given but two choices: parental authority or dangerous permissiveness. No wonder most parents have chosen the first, and (contrary to popular belief) very few have chosen permissiveness. Our challenge in P.E.T. has always been to show parents that they have another choice, an alternative to either authoritarianism or permissiveness.

We first help parents understand how they are locked into win/lose methods. When parents use punitive power to resolve the inevitable conflicts in parent/child relationships, the parent wins and the child loses. Being permissive, in contrast, means the parent loses and the child wins. In both approaches the relationship suffers because there is a loser—someone who feels deprived, frustrated, disappointed, resentful, angry, retaliatory, rebellious.

No-Lose Conflict Resolution

Parent Effectiveness offers parents an alternative method of resolving parent/child conflicts: the no-lose method. This involves parent and child joining together in a problem-solving process to define their conflict and search for a solution that will be acceptable to both, a solution that will result in mutual need satisfaction, a solution that leaves no one the loser (or leaves each a winner).

Actually, most parents are already familiar with the no-lose (or win/win) method, having had experience using it in solving some of their conflicts with friends, spouses, or people with whom they work. However, only a very small percentage of parents have thought of using it with their children. So to get them to use it in that relationship not only requires prior practice by means of a lot of role playing in the classroom but also requires helping them to understand that the method is *not* giving in to the child, *not* sacrificing their own needs: parents will get their needs met, but so will the child—an added benefit, to be sure.

Thus, the core of the P.E.T. course is teaching parents how to live democratically with their children by using a process that involves the participation of both parents and children in setting all rules, dividing up the household chores, and finding mutually acceptable solutions to the hundreds of conflicts (minor or major) that occur in all families over such issues as bedtime, TV, noise, cleanliness, use of the car, picking up toys and clothes, use of the phone, children's allowances, health habits, safety practices, and the like.

Communication Skills

For the no-lose method to work, however, the parent/child relationship must include an ongoing and continuous respect for each other's feelings and a mutual concern for each other's well-being. Consequently, parents must be taught how to listen and show empathy and understanding when children share their feelings and problems. P.E.T. teaches parents the skills of the professional counselor—a special kind of listening that makes children want to talk to them. In addition, P.E.T. teaches parents how to be more open, honest, and direct in sharing their own feelings and problems so that their children are more apt to listen to them.

Thus, Parent Effectiveness, in addition to giving training in democratic problem solving and conflict resolution, teaches effective interpersonal communication skills. Parents are taught and coached in empathic, nonjudgmental listening. Instructors use some of the same pedagogical techniques developed by Carl Rogers and his associates back in the late 1940s and early 1950s at the University of Chicago, where we were training graduate students to be effective helping agents, counselors, and therapists. Our aim in Parent Effectiveness is to teach parents how to provide a new and different kind of help when their children encounter problems in their own lives. With this new counseling approach, parents move away from their usual helping posture of taking control—giving advice, preaching, teaching, moralizing, warning, directing, and giving solutions. They move toward a new role that fosters a climate in which children assume ownership of their problems, take on the responsibility to begin their own problem solving, and search for their own solutions. The idea—in fact, the faith—that people have untapped capacities to solve their own problems, given a relationship with a warm, empathic, accepting, and understanding listener, is Carl Rogers's greatest contribution to the world and the clearest indication of his creative genius.

Assertive Training

Parent Effectiveness is also a kind of assertive training, in that we teach parents to acquire greater respect for their own human needs, for their right to get their own needs met. We help them understand that a healthy relationship cannot be a one-way relationship: parents must learn how to get *their* needs met, too. Parents learn how to assertively convey to the child "I have needs," "I have a problem right now," or "I need you to listen and try to understand me."

Parent Effectiveness strives to change the speaking habits of parents. Instead of the almost universal habit of sending blameful "you-messages" (*you* are a bad boy, *you* are thoughtless, *you* have ruined my day, *you* are driving me crazy, *you* stop that this instant, *you* are driving me to an early grave), parents are taught a new habit of sending I-messages (I need, I want, I have a problem, I'm bothered, I'm worried, I would appreciate, I am tired, I need help, I'm scared). In other words, Parent Effectiveness shows parents how to be more open, honest, and direct rather than manipulative; how to be self-revealing rather than blaming; how to be assertive rather than demanding or commanding; how to be self-disclosing rather than accusatory or punitive. Using this new "I-language," parents more often and more successfully influence kids to modify their unacceptable behaviors, but out of consideration for their parents' needs, not out of obedience to their authority.

Power versus Influence

We have learned that the parent/child relationship differs from the boss/subordinate relationship in another significant way. Most parents feel they "own" their children. From this it follows that they feel they have the right—in fact, the duty—to impose on their children the values, beliefs, and standards most dear to the parents. The methods most parents use to try to bring about such indoctrination of their values go far beyond teaching by example or by instruction. Most parents rely heavily on punishment or threats of punishment. Few parents realize that it is in the values arena that their power is not only most ineffective but also most destructive to the parent/child relationship. For, as children move into adolescence, they develop strong needs for independence and autonomy in choosing their own values and beliefs. Consequently, youngsters strongly resist parents' attempts to impose their values and beliefs or deny children the freedom to choose their own. In fact, some youngsters respond to coercive power by consciously adopting *the very opposite values* of their parents'. Such "rebellion" usually brings about complete alienation of parent and child, an almost irreversible deterioration of their relationship, and the resulting loss of any influence of the parent on the child. Unfortunately, few parents understand this paradox: by using *power*, parents actually lose *influence*.

Our aim in Parent Effectiveness is to show parents the critical difference between coercive control and influence. Control depends on the use of power; influence depends on the use of persuasion and education. Emphasizing that parents have the legitimate responsibility to try to influence their children's values and beliefs, we show them what they must do to be effective influencers. Here we draw principally on the body of knowledge about what it takes to be an effective consultant: (1) modeling the behaviors the influencer values, (2) verbally sharing those values and beliefs openly and honestly, (3) leaving complete responsibility with the client for accepting or rejecting the consultant's values and beliefs, and (4) refraining from hassling, cajoling, or putting down the client.

THE P.E.T. DELIVERY SYSTEM

As important as the content of Parent Effectiveness is its evolving delivery system—how we have made it widely available to parents. In the first 8–10 years, to my amazement, I found little interest in this preventive program within my own profession of psychology or from psychiatrists. Quite frankly, it was all but ignored by mental health professionals, and we found it difficult to get sponsorship of the course by any of the various agencies delivering mental health services. Although psychologists and psychiatrists sometimes talked about the importance of prevention, most were preoccupied with doing treatment. Consequently, a very large percentage of the first 1000 instructors I recruited and trained came from outside the health care field—schoolteachers, school psychologists, nursery-school directors, parent education specialists, ministers, and homemakers who, after taking the course as parents, became enthusiastic about teaching it to others.

In the second decade (during the 1970s) this picture changed gradually. Agencies began to send one or more staff members to be trained as course instructors—community mental health centers, child-guidance clinics, family counseling centers, drug-abuse centers, juvenile courts, and the like. Today, of the several thousand instructors teaching Parent Effectiveness in the United States, Canada, and 16 other countries,[1] about three fourths are professionals offering the course under the sponsorship of their agency or institution.

Although this agency-oriented delivery system has brought parent training to nearly a half-million parents, I am far from satisfied with its effectiveness, since it fails to reach a very large population of parents who need to learn alternatives to coercive discipline. I refer to the millions of parents who have not yet experienced serious enough problems in their relationships with their children to seek or require the services of treatment-oriented agencies. In communities where Parent Effectiveness is available only through one or more of these agencies, only a very small percentage of parents get to hear about the course—namely, those who are clients of such agencies.

Consequently, I have become convinced that parent education will become widely available in North America only when the course is delivered in communities by professionals who have access to all parents—as yet untroubled parents, parents of very young children, those soon to become parents, and those reasonably good parents who with training could become even better.

EVALUATION

A number of studies have evaluated the effects of Parent Effectiveness, both on parents and on their children. Although the quality and rigor of these studies varied greatly, it is gratifying to find that six parent variables showed statistically significant positive changes in three or more independent studies. These variables were confidence in the parent role, acceptance of their children, trust in their children, understanding of their children's behavior, democratic and nonauthoritarian attitudes, and parent self-esteem.

Following is a list of the various changes reported in 21 studies.

Changes in Parents after P.E.T.

1. Parents showed increased confidence in themselves in the role of parents (Aldassy, 1977; Andelin, 1975; Garcia, 1971; Larson, 1972; Lillibridge, 1971; Miles, 1974).

[1]New Zealand, Australia, South Africa, Sweden, Norway, Finland, Denmark, Belgium, France, Netherlands, Germany, Austria, Switzerland, Spain, Mexico, Japan.

2. Parents showed increased acceptance of their children (Lillibridge, 1971; Mee, 1977; Peterson, 1970; Schofield, 1976; Williams & Sanders, 1973).
3. Parents showed increased trust in their children (Aldassy, 1977; Garcia, 1971; Geffen, 1977; Hanley, 1973; Larson, 1972; Lillibridge, 1971; Schmitz, 1975).
4. Parents showed increased understanding of their children's behavior (Aldassy, 1977; Garcia, 1971; Geffen, 1977; Hanley, 1973; Knowles, 1970; Larson, 1972; Schofield, 1976).
5. Parents showed an increase in democratic attitudes and a decrease in authoritarian attitudes and practices (Knowles, 1970; Mee, 1977; Peterson, 1970; Pieper, 1977; Piercy & Brush, 1971; Stearn, 1970).
6. Parents showed improvement in overall parental attitudes and/or child-rearing behaviors, as measured by such tests as the Child Management Inventory, Parent Attitude Survey Scales, and Hereford Parent Attitude Scale (Aldassy, 1977; Haynes, 1972; Larson, 1972; Williams & Sanders, 1973).
7. Parents showed improvements in their self-esteem (Larson, 1972; Stearn, 1970; Williams & Sanders, 1973).
8. Parents showed a reduction in the number of problems with their children (Larson, 1972).
9. Parents showed a reduction in anxiety (Williams & Sanders, 1973).
10. Parents showed an increase in the use of progressive educational practices (Schofield, 1976).
11. Parents improved their scores on tests of empathy, understanding, positive regard, congruence, and acceptance (Mee, 1977; Piercy & Brush, 1971).
12. Mothers and fathers made equal gains in overall positive parental attitudes (Aldassy, 1977).
13. Parents showed more willingness to accept children's right to hold beliefs different from parents' (Peterson, 1970).
14. Parents and their children showed no significant decrease in "interpersonal distance" (Knight, 1974).

Changes in the Children of P.E.T. Parents

1. Children who participated with their parents in P.E.T. showed a progressive increase in level of moral reasoning on Kohlberg's Moral Maturity Scale (Stanley, 1978).
2. Children designated as underachievers whose parents took P.E.T. gained an average of one full grade point in school (Larson, 1972).
3. Children of P.E.T. parents perceived their parents as having increased their acceptance of them as persons (Lillibridge, 1971).
4. Children of P.E.T. parents showed increases in self-esteem (Schofield, 1976; Stearn, 1970).
5. Children of P.E.T. parents showed a decrease in inappropriate and disruptive behaviors (children were potential dropouts) (Miles, 1974).

TRAINING YOUTH IN THE SKILLS OF BUILDING DEMOCRATIC RELATIONSHIPS

As Parent Effectiveness Training spread throughout the country, several instructors found opportunities to teach its communication and problem-solving skills to groups of adolescents—often, but not always, the children of Parent Effectiveness graduates.

In 1973 two such opportunities led to our designing a special course for young people. The first was the federal funding of a juvenile diversion project through the juvenile court system in Lancaster, Ohio. Judge Farrell Jackson of the Fairfield County Juvenile Court and Marilyn Tedesco, an Effectiveness Training instructor, collaborated in the design of a program to meet the needs of youth (and their parents) who had come to the attention of the juvenile court. The Law Enforcement Assistance Administration (LEAA) funded this project, which offered Parent Effectiveness to the parents and the youth-oriented course to their kids. LEAA funding and sponsorship for this project continued from 1974 through 1978. In 1979 financial support of this unique prevention model was taken over by the Lancaster Community Mental Health Center.

The second opportunity emerged when the National Boys' Clubs of America received a grant in 1973 from the Office of Child Development to develop an Education for Parenthood program. Effectiveness Training Incorporated was asked to design a program that would teach leadership and communication skills to older Boys' Club members to help them work more effectively with younger members in the clubs.

Our work in these two projects led to the design and field testing of a course, which was named Youth Effectiveness Training (Y.E.T.). Many Parent Effectiveness instructors volunteered to receive special training to teach this course, later offering it through various agencies and organizations serving youth, such as mental health centers, schools, churches, and youth service bureaus. We also recruit instructors who are staff members of such agencies or are teachers in schools.

Y.E.T. was designed so that young people could learn communication and problem-solving skills to help them function more democratically in their relationships with peers and with parents, teachers, and other adults.

Y.E.T. is a 28-hour course, usually taught in 14 two-hour sessions. A wide variety of instructional methodologies are used—brief presentations by the instructor, class discussions, skill demonstrations, wall charts, role playing, games, at-home activities, and workbook exercises. Class size ranges from 8 to 15. The content of Y.E.T. provides the opportunity for youngsters to learn many things:

- They learn about power and authority differentials in their human relationships.
- They learn how youngsters typically respond to (cope with) adults who try to control them with power—for example, retaliation, aggression, withdrawal, submission, passive resistance, rebellion, anger, physical violence, vandalism, disruptive behaviors, forming alliances, lying.
- They learn how such behaviors can be self-defeating—can, for example, get them in more trouble, bring on more power, get them punished, get them arrested or expelled from school.
- They learn how to cope with adult controllers in less self-destructive ways—for example, communicating how the controlling behavior makes them feel, initiating conflict-resolution methodologies.
- They learn how to assess their own unique strengths and how to set goals for achieving success experiences using their special talents and abilities.
- They learn how to get in touch with their feelings and communicate them clearly to others.

- They learn how to listen with empathy and understanding to help others when they have problems.
- They learn the pitfalls of win/lose approaches to conflict resolution, and they learn how to employ the no-lose problem-solving method of resolving conflicts by negotiating an agreement.
- They learn how to introduce constructive problem-solving methods in their own families to reduce conflicts and increase enjoyment of family life.
- They learn how people hold very different values and beliefs and how they can avoid putting down others who are different from them.

Since 1977 the Y.E.T. course and Y.E.T. instructor-training workshops have been funded by several funding agencies. The Law Enforcement Assistance Administration (LEAA) has formally recognized Y.E.T. as a core program for juvenile delinquency diversion and prevention. Y.E.T. is also widely supported and funded by the Comprehensive Employment and Training Act (CETA), which has given recognition to Y.E.T. as the communications and conflict-resolution component in job-training programs. Additional support and funding have come from Title XX, the National Institute of Drug Abuse (NIDA), the Elementary-Secondary Education Act (ESEA), and the Emergency School Aid Act (ESAA).

During the summer of 1977, 530 youngsters participated in 28 Y.E.T. classes sponsored by the Youth Departments of the Lutheran Church (Missouri Synod) and the American Lutheran Church. Both participants and instructors filled out a comprehensive questionnaire that asked for evaluations of Y.E.T. The summary report of these evaluations can be made available to any interested agency.

During the 1977–78 and 1978–79 school years, over 200 youths participated in Y.E.T. groups within the Oklahoma City school system. Y.E.T. was taught by guidance counselors who had been trained as instructors. The program was assessed by the research and evaluation department of the Oklahoma City schools in 1978 and again in 1979. The report of this research can be made available.

Bennison (1979) evaluated the outcomes of Y.E.T. with a sample of 206 ninth-grade students in a Catholic high school. Contrasted with a control group of nontrained students, Y.E.T.-trained students revealed the following differences:

1. Stronger leadership potential.
2. Locus of control perceived as more internal (within the person), as opposed to external.
3. A more positive overall attitude toward their mothers.
4. A perception of their mothers and fathers as more caring and accepting toward them.
5. Higher self-sentiment.
6. More ability to function in both group and interpersonal relationships.

TRAINING TEACHERS TO DEMOCRATIZE THEIR CLASSROOMS

Although our specially designed course for teachers, called Teacher Effectiveness, is very similar to Parent Effectiveness, we have found it harder to get teachers to accept the desirability of establishing democratic relationships in the classroom. Our schools have a long and well-established tradition of teachers' relying on power (rewards and punishment) to control their students. Even more important, most school administrators strongly support their teachers' use of coercive discipline.

Consequently, we have found that, with few exceptions, schools are modeled after military organizations, with a strict hierarchy of authority in which relationships are clearly defined in terms of institutionalized dominance and subordination. Nevertheless, several hundred school districts have used our Teacher Effectiveness course for in-service training of their teachers. The total number of teachers we have trained is in excess of 30,000. Funding for the Teacher Effectiveness Training program in schools has come from district in-service budgets or from federal grants administered by the U.S. Office of Education.

The response of teachers to their training is universally positive. Most teachers are frustrated with having to spend so much of their time in discipline and enforcement of rules. (Studies have shown that teachers spend as much as 75% of classroom time on discipline.) Therefore, they welcome the opportunity to learn methods that might reduce the frequency of disruptive behaviors of their students. Teacher Effectiveness provides several nonpower methods to help teachers deal with unacceptable behavior: nonblaming I-messages for confronting students with the tangible effects of their behaviors on the teacher, mutual problem solving with teacher and student together searching for a solution acceptable to both, and the method of involving the entire class in establishing classroom rules and procedures instead of the teacher's setting down the rules unilaterally. Teachers also learn the importance of listening with empathy and understanding when students have feelings or problems, and they also learn to use this listening skill to encourage students to participate actively in subject-matter class discussions.

A study of the effects of Teacher Effectiveness Training in the Newport News, Virginia, schools found a 30% decrease in absenteeism among students of teachers who completed the T.E.T. course (Aspy, 1977).

Our experience has repeatedly shown that the impact of the T.E.T. course in a school district is greater when school principals have participated in our Leader Effectiveness Training for School Administrators, as would be expected. When their relationships with their administrators are mutually satisfying and rewarding, teachers are more apt to put energy into meeting their students' needs.

TRAINING WOMEN TO DEMOCRATIZE THEIR RELATIONSHIPS

Getting involved in the training of women was rather fortuitous for our organization, inasmuch as the impetus came from a professional woman with whom I had a close relationship and whom I later married. She also had had certain experiences in her life that had shaped her attitudes about human relationships. As a graduate student in sociology, Linda Adams had identified with, and actively worked for, the growing civil rights movement, in which Blacks were for the first time organizing as a group to demand their equal rights. When, in her graduate work, she later elected to specialize in women's studies, her consciousness was raised about the inequalities experienced by women, no less universal than the inequalities suffered by Blacks. Still in its infancy then, the women's movement nevertheless touched her closest to where she lived. Her participation in women's consciousness-raising groups led to membership in the National Organization for Women and then to the insight that mere awareness of inequality in women's relationships was not enough. She began to see that women needed some kind of training to become more effective in bringing about equality in their relationships. Of course there were the various assertive training programs, just then springing up throughout the country, but they appeared to fall far short of teaching women the full range of skills for building and maintaining equitable and democratic relationships.

It became clear that the theoretical model for mutually satisfying relationships used in our Effectiveness Training courses was a solid foundation on which to build a course for women. Moreover, Effectiveness Training as an organization seemed to provide the right vehicle for both production and delivery of the women's course.

Apart from Linda's own reasons for designing a special course for women, the staff of Effectiveness Training had been sensing a need for some kind of course as we began to realize why certain women were finding it more difficult to apply the democratic philosophy they learned in the parent program. From remarks they made in class, we could see that these women were having trouble establishing a democratic, equalitarian relationship with their husbands: they played subordinate roles in their marriages.

Some women enrolled in Parent Effectiveness alone because of their husbands' refusal to share any of the responsibility for child rearing. Others complained of their husbands' unwillingness to have their own authoritarian style of parenting challenged or questioned. Some reported that their husbands had actually admonished them never to use anything they had learned in class. We also met women who were so unsuccessful in getting their own needs met in their marriage relationship that they had little to give to meet the needs of their children. We could see that women who had never learned to be open and assertive with their husbands had difficulty being open and assertive with their children. And women who were permissive and submissive with their husbands had difficulty being anything else with their children. Another common pattern was the mother with repressed anger and hostility from an unfulfilled marriage venting these strong feelings on the children.

With few exceptions, the women in our Parent Effectiveness classes had felt the effects of their parents' strong and consistent sex-role stereotyping, which reinforced nonassertive communication, the role of ministering only to the needs of others, taking a subservient role in marriage, sacrificing their own needs, and giving in rather than standing up for their rights. And few had ever seen a democratic relationship between a man and a woman, let alone between a parent and a child.

It is not surprising, then, that we chose to commit the resources of our organization to the development of a course that might strengthen women's resolve to make their relationships with men (and others) more democratic and provide them with the interpersonal skills they needed to get their own needs met. The textbook for the course was written by Linda Adams and later published (1979).

In Effectiveness Training for Women the participants start out with a self-assessment of how much (or how little) control they have over their lives. Then they learn the skills of effective self-disclosure, which, in the language of the course, translates into four kinds of "I-messages":

- *Declarative I-messages.* Disclosures about one's beliefs, ideas, values, interests, opinions.

- *Responsive I-messages.* Responses to demands and requests one doesn't want to accept.
- *Preventive I-messages.* Disclosures of one's future needs, desires, and intentions for the purpose of preventing future conflicts.
- *Confrontive I-messages.* Disclosures that confront those whose behavior has already interfered with meeting one's needs.

Obviously the chief function of these four kinds of self-disclosures is to help women open themselves up to others—to let others know who they are, what they think and feel, what they need and want. By learning how to assert themselves in I-language (versus you-language), women greatly reduce the probability of coming across as aggressive, punitive, judgmental, angry, or retaliatory.

Because many women experience anxiety over being self-disclosing, the course also helps participants handle such anxiety more constructively, suggesting how they can increase their readiness to self-disclose, how they can rehearse and practice before self-disclosing in the real situation, and how they can relieve some of their anxiety through relaxation.

Having begun with self-disclosure, where most women feel the greatest inadequacy, the course then proceeds to teach the same skills taught in our other Effectiveness Training courses, with the emphasis, however, on the adult relationships women have—with men friends, women friends, spouses, bosses, work associates, parents, and so on. These skills are empathic, nonevaluative listening; mutual problem solving; no-lose conflict resolution; and dealing with values collisions.

The response to Effectiveness Training for Women has been overwhelmingly positive, both from instructors, who find that teaching women is exciting and rewarding, and from the participants, who report taking charge of their lives more often and making their relationships more democratic, equitable, and fulfilling.

CONCLUSION

After three decades of trying to democratize relationships, I am left with several feelings. Sometimes I am aware of feeling discouraged because so many people in our "democratic" society strongly resist giving up their authoritarian attitudes and their patterns of using power-based, coercive control in their relationships. This resistance is found more often among parents and teachers, less often among organizational leaders and women.

However, I also feel both heartened and personally rewarded when I think about the thousands of people who have expressed their gratitude to me and to our instructors for giving them the opportunity of replacing their power-based methods with democratic ones. These have been people from all walks of life, from all socioeconomic levels, and from many countries. The world is full of people who hunger for relationships that are fair, equitable, mutually satisfying, and warm.

I often feel worried that the present win/lose approach in relationships might so weaken our institutions that our society will be destroyed before we have a chance to shift human relationships to the win/win, or no-lose, posture. I am convinced that if we are to preserve the democratic principles on which our country was founded, we must have democratic institutions and democratic relationships.

At times I can be cautiously optimistic, even knowing that it will take several generations before we see a significant change in the quality of human relationships, because I have learned that once people experience democracy in their important relationships, few will want to give it up.

REFERENCES

Adams, L. *Effectiveness Training for women.* New York: Wyden Books, 1979.

Aldassy, M. The relationship of P.E.T. to change in parent attitudes. Unpublished master's thesis, California State University at Hayward, 1977.

Andelin, S. The effects of concurrently teaching parents and then their children with learning adjustment problems the principles of P.E.T. Unpublished doctoral dissertation, Utah State University, 1975.

Aspy, D. An evaluation of Teacher Effectiveness Training. Unpublished report, National Consortium for Humanizing Education, 1977.

Baldwin, A., Kalhorn, J., & Breese, H. The appraisal of parent behavior. *Psychological Monographs,* 1949, *63,* 1–85.

Bennison, W. M. The relationship of Youth Effectiveness Training to perceived locus of control, attitude toward parents and school, report of parental behavior and selected personality dimensions of male and female adolescents. Unpublished dissertation, St. John's University, 1979.

Dodson, F. *How to parent.* Los Angeles: Nash, 1970.

Garcia, J. Preventive programs in parent education: A study of P.E.T. Unpublished master's thesis, University of Southern California, 1971.

Geffen, M. The value of a course in P.E.T. for single parents. Unpublished doctoral dissertation, California School of Professional Psychology, Fresno, 1977.

Gordon, T. *Group-centered leadership: A way of releasing the creative potential of groups.* Boston: Houghton Mifflin, 1955.

Gordon, T. *Parent Effectiveness Training.* New York: New American Library, 1975.

Gordon, T. *Teacher Effectiveness Training.* New York: McKay, 1977.

Hanley, D. Changes in parent attitude related to a Parent Effectiveness Training and a family enrichment program. Unpublished doctoral dissertation, United States International University, 1973.

Haynes, S. Altering parental attitudes toward child-rearing practices using parent education groups. Unpublished manuscript, Boston University, 1972.

Jones, M. *The therapeutic community.* New York: Basic Books, 1953.

Knight, N. The effects of changes in family interpersonal relationships on the behavior of enuretic children. Unpublished doctoral dissertation, University of Hawaii, 1974.

Knowles, L. Evaluation of P.E.T.: Does improved communication result in better understanding? Unpublished manuscript, Chico State College, California, 1970.

Larson, R. Can parent classes affect family communications? *School Counselor,* 1972, *19,* 261–270.

Lewin, K., Lippitt, R., & White, R. Patterns of aggressive behavior in experimentally created "social climates." *Journal of Social Psychology*, 1939, *10*, 271–279.

Lillibridge, M. The relationship of a P.E.T. program to change in parents' self-assessed attitudes and children's perceptions of parents. Unpublished doctoral dissertation, United States International University, 1971.

Maier, N. R. F. *Principles of human relations.* New York: Wiley, 1952.

Mee, C. P.E.T.: Assessment of the developmental gains in parents' capacity to counsel their children. Unpublished doctoral dissertation, Catholic University of America, 1977.

Miles, J. A comparative analysis of the effectiveness of verbal reinforcement, group counseling, and Parent Effectiveness Training on certain behavioral aspects of potential dropouts. Unpublished doctoral dissertation, Auburn University, 1974.

Peterson, B. Parent Effectiveness Training and change in parental attitudes. Unpublished manuscript, University of Santa Clara, 1970.

Pieper, A. P.E.T. and parent attitudes about child rearing. Unpublished master's thesis, California State University at Hayward, 1977.

Piercy, F., & Brush, D. Effects of P.E.T. on empathy and self-disclosure. Unpublished manuscript, Mental Hygiene Consultation Service, Fort Benning, Ga., 1971.

Schmitz, K. A study of the relationship of Parent Effectiveness Training to changes in parents' self-addressed attitudes and behavior in a rural population. Unpublished doctoral dissertation, University of South Dakota, 1975.

Schofield, R. A comparison of two parent education programs—P.E.T. and behavior modification —and their effects on the child's self-esteem. Unpublished dissertation, University of Northern Colorado, 1976.

Stanley, S. Family education to enhance the moral atmosphere of the family and the moral development of adolescents. *Journal of Counseling Psychology*, 1978, *25*, 110–118.

Stearn, M. The relationship of P.E.T. to parent attitudes, parent behavior, and child self-esteem. Unpublished doctoral dissertation, United States International University, 1970.

Straus, M., Gelles, R., & Steinmetz, S. *Behind closed doors: Violence in the American family.* New York: Anchor Books, 1980.

Williams, B., & Sanders, B. A comparative study of the relative effectiveness of P.E.T. and a program of behavior modification. Unpublished manuscript, Alamance County, N.C., 1973.

CHAPTER NINE

Relationship Enhancement Therapy and Training

Bernard G. Guerney

Bernard G. Guerney, Jr., is professor of human development at The Pennsylvania State University and head of the Individual and Family Consultation Center, which he founded there in 1969. A Penn State Ph.D., he is a diplomate in clinical psychology and in behavioral medicine and an AAMFT-approved clinical supervisor in marriage and family therapy. He is founder and president of the nonprofit Institute for the Development of Emotional and Life Skills (IDEALS), which provides nationwide training of mental health professionals in therapeutic methods following an educational model. Individually and with others, he has produced many films and video- and audio-tapes for professional training and has written numerous articles and chapters on professional training and on individual, child, marital, and family therapy as well as four books on these subjects, the most recent of which is *Relationship Enhancement*.

The roots of Relationship Enhancement Therapy and Training can be traced to Guerney's earlier Filial Therapy. Initiated in the early 1960s, Filial Therapy was the first systematic effort to teach therapeutic skills to family members and thus served as a springboard for the psychoeducation movement. In this chapter Guerney gives detailed descriptions of individual Relationship Enhancement skills and provides an instructive case discussion illustrating the use of Relationship Enhancement approaches in an actual therapy situation. One aspect of interest about Relationship Enhancement is that it is applicable in the training of three groups: clients, families, and professionals/paraprofessionals. The wide spectrum of theoretical influences cited by Guerney—Carl Rogers, Karen Horney, Harry Stack Sullivan, Anna Freud, B. F. Skinner, and Albert Bandura—is suggestive of the powerful integrative potential of skills training models.

Relationship Enhancement (RE) methods are applicable as a therapy, as a means of problem prevention, and as a program for enrichment of personal or vocational life. RE may be conducted with a single individual, a group of individuals, members of a family, or members of a familylike group (for example, members working in one unit of an organization). The skills of Relationship Enhancement are designed to help groups achieve their goals as well as to help individuals improve their personal and interpersonal adjustment. In addition, the skills include some designed to help other people to change in therapeutic directions. Professionals-in-training can therefore benefit from learning RE skills not only because it enables them to conduct RE therapy but because it improves their generic therapy/counseling skills.

HISTORY

The roots of RE therapy go back to Filial Therapy, initiated in the early 1960s. To my knowledge, Filial Therapy was the first therapeutic method to be formulated in terms of a programmatic educational model. In Filial Therapy, parents are systematically taught the rationale, principles, and methods of child-centered (Rogerian) play therapy. The method is applicable to a parent/child dyad, a family, or a group of parents. After presenting to the parents the rationale and principles of Rogerian play-therapy techniques, the therapist demonstrates these techniques in play sessions with the children. The parents themselves then practice therapeutic play sessions under the therapist's supervision. In the next phase of the therapy, the parents conduct the play-therapy sessions at home with their children and bring reports of these sessions to the therapist, who gives them further skill training, mainly in the form of supervision. The parents also continue to be observed periodically in order to receive further supervision and training. The areas in which parents experience difficulty in learning the skills point to areas they need to work on to change their own personalities and/or habits. These difficulties are worked through in a dynamic fashion in the parent sessions. In this manner, Filial Therapy provides a blending of dynamic and didactic features. In the final stage of Filial Therapy, after the children have worked through areas of interpersonal conflict through the medium of the play sessions with their parents, the parents are taught behavioral management skills that allow them to more effectively build personal and interpersonal skills into their children's behavioral repertoire.

Over the past 20 years, a great variety of behavioral disorders in children have been treated successfully with Filial Therapy. Such cases run the gamut from extremely withdrawn through hyperactive to acting-out children. We have not used the method with psychotic children. A series of controlled and quasi-controlled studies (Guerney, 1976; Guerney & Stover, 1971; Sywulak, 1977) have yielded evidence for the effectiveness of Filial Therapy. These studies have included follow-ups several years after termination of therapy, showing that the strong initial gains held up well (Oxman, 1971; Sensué, 1981).

From the parents, we learned that the therapeutic attitudes and skills they were learning proved extremely valuable to them in their marital and work relationships in addition to being valuable in their relationships with their children. This encouraged us to establish a marital therapy program (originally called "Conjugal Therapy") in which we trained couples with marital problems in sets of skills designed to resolve those problems and to enhance their relationships. Since the late 1960s, when we began the Conjugal Therapy effort, we have broadened the skills taught and have strengthened our methods of systematic RE instruction. In the early 1970s, we broadened the population with which we worked to include parent/adolescent dyads, and in the mid-1970s we broadened further to working with entire family units (or subunits) and to working with more than one family (or family subunit) at a time.

The methods developed for therapeutic purposes have been adapted over the years for purposes of providing training to students studying counseling, to teachers, and to a variety of paraprofessional groups, such as the clergy and drug- and alcohol-abuse counselors. The RE methods have also broadened to include almost any groups that must work together closely, such as supervisors and their supervisees, and business management personnel who wish to develop better communication and interpersonal-conflict/problem-resolution skills.

In 1972 a nonprofit educational institute, the Institute for the Development of Emotional and Life Skills (IDEALS), was established in order to train professionals, paraprofessionals, and members of the public in Relationship Enhancement skills. For therapists who can work toward certification in Relationship Enhancement Therapy, or for educators and trainers who can be certified to give Relationship Enhancement prevention and enrichment programs to the general public, the training is geared toward equipping them to help others by means of this method. For the general public, the skill training is designed to help people solve problems and conflicts, to enrich their personal and vocational lives, and to prevent problems and conflicts from developing in their personal or vocational lives. Through this organization, many hundreds of professionals and members of the public have been trained in Relationship Enhancement skills.

PURPOSES OF RELATIONSHIP ENHANCEMENT THERAPY AND PROGRAMS

The following statement of purposes is general enough to encompass the application of RE not only to therapy clients but to members of the general public who wish to acquire skills to enhance their personal and professional functioning and to professionals and student-professionals. The same set of purposes pertains to all these groups, although some receive greater emphasis with one class of participant than with another. The major purposes of RE training are to impart to the participants skills that will—

1. Help the participants to find realistic ways to achieve personal and interpersonal goals and to achieve better understanding of their self-concepts, their emotions, their conflicts, their problems, and their wishes and goals.
2. Help them to better elicit help and cooperation from others that will enable them to deepen their understanding and meet their personal and vocational goals.
3. Help them to become more personally appealing to other persons who are important to them.
4. Help them to better understand others' self-concepts, emotions, conflicts, problems, desires, and goals.
5. Help them to be more effective in helping others by promoting others' self-understanding; by showing others compassionate appreciation of their needs; by offering to others, in appropriate ways and at appropriate times, insights and suggestions for constructive change.
6. Help participants to understand and resolve problems between themselves and others in a constructive and enduring way—a way that takes all realities, including emotional ones, into account and a way that comes closest to satisfying all parties.
7. Increase participants' ability to enrich their relationships with those who are important to them in love, work, and play—that is, enable them to discover

more ways to increase the enjoyment and productivity they experience in such relationships.

8. Help participants to increase their ability to generalize and to transfer these skills (and other desired skills) into their daily life and to maintain them over time.

9. Help participants to increase their ability to teach significant others the skills necessary to accomplish the above.

THEORY

What are the characteristics of RE that contribute to its effectiveness? I believe these characteristics are best considered in terms of three general categories: (1) the intervention method used, (2) the particular set of skills taught in RE, and (3) the way the skill training is conducted.

Skill Training as the Intervention Method

In my view, RE derives a great deal of its strength from its having been so deliberately based on a mass educational model, as distinct from a clinical, medical model of changing people. I believe that many methods of intervention (not, of course, including those found in the present volume) are severely weakened by their derivation from the medical model. One component of the medical model is the disease model, which carries with it the following paradigm of intervention: patient illness (or maladjustment) → diagnosis → prescription → treatment → cure.

There are many differences between the two models, which influence the process of personality change beginning before the client ever sets foot in the therapist's office and which pervade the nature of the interpersonal transactions involved in the process of change. I have explicated the disadvantages of the clinical-medicine and disease models for psychotherapy elsewhere in some detail (Authier, Gustafson, Guerney, & Kasdorf, 1975; Guerney, 1977b, 1979, 1982; Guerney, Guerney, & Stollak, 1971/72; Guerney, Stollak, & Guerney, 1970, 1971). Here I will mention only the fact that the diagnostic/genetic component of the medical and disease models implies that there is something *wrong* with the client that needs to be uncovered and eradicated. The emphasis is on correcting wrongs rather than simply on learning to do what is right. This generally creates a great deal of conscious or unconscious threat, defensiveness, and resistance to learning.

The educational paradigm in contrast to the paradigm presented above is as follows: student motivation (ambition) → course selection → teaching → skill training → goal achievement. The advantages of an educational model for psychotherapy also have been spelled out in the references mentioned above.

The particular kind of teaching on which we have based RE and which we strongly recommend is one that combines (1) cognitive instruction, which may include principles, attitudes, and/or values, and (2) behavioral instruction, which may include emotional self-reconditioning and guided practice and rehearsal of new ways of handling emotions, interpersonal interactions, and self-concept-related thoughts. This dual approach is what we call *skill training.*

Skill training is distinct from traditional, predominantly introspective and analytic insight-oriented therapies in being much more programmatic and systematic. Skill training therapy is also distinct from those types of behavior therapy which may be systematic but which (1) do not involve transformation of attitudes and values or instill an understanding of rationale and principles but rely instead on conditioning of a relatively passive client and/or (2) seek only to remedy a specific complaint and do not seek to *implant* the knowledge and skill necessary to resolve the entire *class* of problems or deficits of which the client's symptom is but one example.

I believe that RE is effective largely because it preserves many of the most important principles and advantages of the "insight" and "behavioral" approaches and yet integrates them in such a manner that the client is consciously involved in the choice of therapeutic or enrichment goals. That is, clients themselves are consciously concerned with mastering those skills that effect the personality changes. Clients themselves are in charge of the use of those skills during the intervention process as well as in daily life. They incorporate the ability to use their new knowledge and skills in *future* situations when they need to do so to resolve new problems or achieve new goals.

Choice of Skills Taught in RE

The particular skills taught to clients in RE programs arise from the following theoretical perspectives.

Personality is here defined as "relatively enduring preferred ways of dealing with emotions, people, and self-concept-related thoughts." Personality is viewed as being formed, expressed, and continually reformulated, mainly under the influence of our relationships with significant others.

Following the theories of such theoretical giants as Carl Rogers, Anna Freud, Karen Horney, and Harry Stack Sullivan, among many others, we view the nature of one's relationships with significant others as the major determinant of one's ability to avoid the reality-distorting effects of psychological defense/escape maneuvers and of one's ability to achieve self-acceptance, to win the love of others, and to achieve productivity in work.

RE is based on the belief that the ability to acknowledge our emotions and our desires concerning the way we wish to relate to others and to have them relate to us is an essential first step in avoiding the debilitating effects of psychological defense mechanisms. Such sensitivity to and understanding of our own emotions and desires are first steps toward dealing with emotional and interpersonal realities in ways that will lead to personal and interpersonal goal attainment and satisfaction.

A further assumption basic to RE is that to attain lasting satisfaction in these regards, it is necessary to be able to communicate one's thoughts, emotions, and wants effectively to other people. That is, one's self-understanding must be communicated to others in a manner that maximizes the probability that they too will appreciate one's internal realities and be willing to cooperate in helping one to achieve one's own emotional, personal, and interpersonal goals.

Many of the procedures used in RE are derived from the theories and methods of Carl Rogers, B. F. Skinner, and Albert Bandura. Freudian theory has influenced the theory underlying RE in that in RE great weight is given to the necessity of not triggering the defense mechanisms, "discovered" by the Freudians. Another major theoretical underpinning of RE is Timothy Leary's Interpersonal Theory of Personality (1957), which is, in turn, indebted to the theories of Harry Stack Sullivan (1947). One of the most important aspects of this theory for RE is the view that the interpersonal responses that people make to other people trigger certain kinds of reactions in them. Usually, this triggering action takes place automatically and unconsciously—that is, outside our awareness. The reaction of the other, in turn, automatically or semiautomatically triggers our own next response, and so on. Moreover, we often respond to others in ways traceable to an immediate unconscious goal of reducing our anxieties and allowing us to use our preferred defense mechanisms. Such unconscious tendencies often operate against our own best interests and our more fundamental, long-range goals. The theoretical perspective underlying RE holds that by learning the central roles that self-concept and psychological defense mechanisms play in such interactions, by learning to be acutely aware of what has hitherto been unconscious in these regards, and by learning to understand and to alter their responses accordingly, people can gain control over what previously has been mysterious and has worked mainly at an unconscious, "reflexive" level.

As was initially determined by Leary and essentially substantiated by Shannon and Guerney (1973), such "interpersonal reflexes," as they emerge in interpersonal interactions, are very largely reciprocal in nature. By this I mean that "like elicits like" on certain critical dimensions of attitude and behavior. Affection, openness, love, cooperativeness, and, in general, positive interpersonal responses generally elicit positive responses from others. Hostility, competitive/uncooperative, deceptive, and, in general, negative interpersonal responses likewise elicit negative responses from others. The theoretical perspective underlying RE is that people can consciously control the nature of their interpersonal relations and can better achieve their interpersonal goals by acquiring the capacity to consciously control those interpersonal behaviors that they initiate and those that they make in response to the interpersonal behaviors of others. In the long run, this capacity serves to modify personality in the desired direction.

Another factor that largely determines one's *own* ability to improve relationships and to foster one's *own* personal growth is the ability to consistently meet the emotional and interpersonal wants of significant *others*. The ability to consistently meet others' emotional needs depends on one's knowledge and appreciation of the emotional and interpersonal needs of those others. To gain such knowledge and appreciation, one must be able to generate responses from others that will reveal their needs. Generally, others will reveal their emotions and desires to us—thereby placing us in a position to meet them—only in proportion to the degree to which they trust us to understand and appreciate them. Behaviors that tend to challenge such emotions and needs or that reflect negatively on them will inhibit such self-revelation from others.

The rationale for RE rests on the view that it is generally possible to instruct people systematically and successfully in the principles, attitudes, and behavior that will foster their capacity to generate understanding, appreciation, and trust in others toward them. Similarly, we hold that it is possible to instruct people systematically and successfully in attitudes and behavior that will increase their ability to understand and to appreciate compassionately the emotions and wants of significant others.

The resolution of interpersonal problems and conflicts rests mainly on a person's capacity to generate honest and compassionate communications to and from others, as described above. However, there are additional skills needed for solving problems and resolving conflicts in realistic, sustainable ways. It is assumed within the RE rationale that these too can be clearly formulated into principles and guidelines and taught effectively.

Finally, the rationale for RE rests on the view that the principles and practices that enable people to incorporate skills into their daily lives and to maintain skills over a long period also can be taught systematically and successfully.

Choice of Training Methods

In RE the controversy over whether one should concentrate on attitudes and let behavior follow by itself or should change behavior and let attitude change follow by itself is viewed as fruitless. The most efficient and productive type of training with respect to reshaping personality and interpersonal behavior is seen as one based on trying to change both together in a reciprocally interactive manner. Some attitude shaping or reshaping is usually necessary in order to incite sufficient motivation to make people put up with the hard work of changing behavior. At the same time, one's actions and one's observations of their consequences continually reshape one's attitudes. Other guiding principles in the formulation of RE were designed to (1) make it procedurally systematic and replicable, (2) build in enough flexibility to allow the program to encompass individuals with a wide range of differences in intellectual and emotional capacities, (3) make the program psychodynamically sophisticated in terms of its power to avoid the deleterious effects of defense mechanisms, and (4) have it make use of a wide variety of instructional methods and procedures, both traditional and modern. Perhaps the most efficient way to present the rationale underlying the training methods of RE is to discuss what we see clients as needing to have in order to learn new behaviors and how these needs can be met by the therapist/leader.

The most essential ingredient is client *motivation*. We accept the proposition that personal and interpersonal functioning is best explained by viewing people as goal seekers. This means that clients are seen as having a strong need to know where they are headed in terms of the reshaping of their personality and behavior. A primary goal of the therapist/leader, therefore, is to provide the client with high expectations that when the client emits the behavior being taught, it will result in gratification of very significant client needs.

Conservation of energy is viewed as an important principle in understanding human behavior. In terms of reshaping people's functioning, this means that the leader must convince clients that the high level of energy they must expend in learning to change will be small in proportion to the gains they will experience as a result of fulfilling their life goals.

Both the preceding principles dictate that the leader take great pains to make clear to clients the causal chain between the fulfillment of their perceived wants and the new behaviors that the leader is encouraging them to adopt.

The capacity of clients to learn is considered to be greatly dependent on their faith in their instructor, especially during the early phases of learning, before the natural desirable consequences of the behaviors being learned are evident in the real world. This faith, in turn, depends largely on the clients' perceiving the instructor as competent, enthusiastic, warm, genuine, and empathic.

Clients' maladaptive and unskilled behaviors are viewed as having been developed because they provided a high level of *immediate* emotional gratification in proportion to the amount of effort the behaviors require. More skilled behaviors depend on the capacity to perceive and to experience the much greater long-term gains that come with *delaying* emotional gratification and putting forth greater emotional and intellectual effort. To prevail against the odds inherent in the first-mentioned ratio, it is necessary for clients to have a continued *feeling* of success in their ability to learn the new skills. They must feel that their level of success is high in proportion to the effort they are expending. The leader can accomplish this best if he or she (1) reduces the time spent in activities not essential to the learning process, (2) orders the client's experiences hierarchically such that the chances of client success are maximized and the chances of failure minimized, (3) gives the client a great deal of social reinforcement for the *effort* the client expends as well as for any success actually attained in learning the skill, and (4) minimizes any reactions to the client that even hint of criticisms, serious incapacities, or failure. The therapist/teacher must assiduously adhere to these procedures until clients attain a level of skill such that their natural environment affords a high level of reward in proportion to the effort they are expending.

In the final analysis, it is the natural environment that must support and sustain the new skills by providing emotional and social support to clients when they use the skills they have been taught. This means that the therapist/leader must constantly be aware of the relationship between the level of skill that the client has so far obtained in the learning process and the responses that level of skill is likely to generate in his or her environment. To maximize success and minimize failure in the client's attempts to use new skills in the natural environment, the therapist/leader should instruct the client about the appropriate times, places, and circumstances to use the skills.

In addition, this principle suggests that, wherever possible, the therapist/leader should try to teach others in the environment to react in ways that will help the learner feel that his or her skills have paid off. The opportunity to do this is one of the great advantages of a family approach to treatment. It is also possible to influence clients' feelings of success in the natural environment by preparing them for the kinds of reactions they are likely to experience at various stages of competency in using the skills being taught. Finally, clients' attitudes and feelings toward their experience in the natural environment can also be influenced by encouraging them to view their early attempts at outside use of skills more in terms of process than of outcome—that is, to view potential difficulties while they are in the phase of skill acquisition not as failures but as successes in the process of learning.

All this is part of a general principle that clients should be taught generalization and ways of maintaining their skills in the natural environment in the same way that they would be taught any other behavioral skill; that is, this task of maintenance of generalization should be approached using all the earlier-mentioned principles.

SKILLS TAUGHT IN RELATIONSHIP ENHANCEMENT

Expressive Skill

Expressive skill serves two major purposes. The first is to increase clients' sensitivity to and understanding of their own self-concept and their own emotions, conflicts, problems, desires, and goals. The second major purpose is to increase clients' ability to communicate those things about themselves to important others in ways that will increase the probability that those others will understand them better and respond to them in more compassionate and cooperative ways. The subskills for this mode of behavior, as they might be described to clients in the briefest possible way, are as follows.

· *Before you express your own point of view, show understanding—try to let the other person see that you appreciate his or her feelings, views, and circumstances.* This will make the other person more responsive to your own views and needs.

· *Be the world's leading authority on everything you say.* That is, whenever you are discussing a significant topic and there is even the remotest possibility that the other person might disagree with your views, state them subjectively ("I think," "I believe," "In my view," "It seems to me") rather than presenting them as objective, factual, morally valid, or normatively correct. Since you are the best-informed person in the world on your feelings, perceptions, and attitudes, stating things in those terms reduces argumentativeness and allows the other person to respond to your views and feelings as such. Therefore, it sharply reduces the probability that the other person will challenge your statement. It also allows the other person to respond to your needs rather than to his or her own perceptions of reality.

· *State your past, present, or anticipated feelings if they are important to the issue.* This allows the other party to concentrate on all major dimensions of the problem, and it often increases the probability that the other's response will be understanding and compassionate.

· *Be specific.* Describe the particular events and behaviors that cause you to think and feel as you do. When you are discussing your *own* attitudes or feelings, this helps prevent you from exaggerating and overgeneralizing, and it helps you to focus your attention on your problems in a more accurate way and in a way that makes it more likely that you will actually do something constructive about them. When you are discussing *another* person, this guideline is especially important. In that case, it helps to prevent you from stating generalizations and conclusions with which the other person might sharply disagree. It will help you to avoid exaggerations, digressions, recriminations, and the general deterioration of the discussion. Avoiding unnecessary generalizations and conclusions helps you to avoid impugning the other person's character or motives when those are not a necessary part of the discussion. That avoids threatening the other's self-concept and thereby greatly facilitates problem solving. When generalizations and conclusions about the other *are* a necessary part of the conversation, they should at least be documented and exemplified through citation of specific events and behaviors.

· *When you want another to change his or her views or behaviors, at the earliest feasible time state your positive assumptions, attitudes, expectations, and feelings about the other that are related to this issue.* That is, when the time is right, search for and express your implicit positive attitudes or feelings (for example, affection) toward the other person, which often are more basic than, and may even have given rise to, negative ones (for example, anger because of feeling neglected). The fact that you are requesting change from another person almost always implies certain positive attitudes, which should be placed in clear focus at some point in the discussion. Such a focus makes it likely that the other person will be more compassionate and understanding of your viewpoint, more capable of perceiving its validity, and more willing to change in accordance with your request.

· *When you want another to change, state your "interpersonal message" at an appropriate time.* By an interpersonal message, we mean a request for new, more satisfying attitudes and behaviors from the other person. Proper formulation of such a message requires many of the other skills mentioned above—for example, being positive and including important feelings, which, in this instance, means your anticipated, positive feeling that would be brought about by the other person's compliance with your request. An interpersonal message allows the other person to understand precisely what you wish of him or her. It increases the probability that the person will consider your suggestion realistically and carefully. Your expression of anticipated positive feelings upon compliance will give the other person an incentive to cooperate.

Empathic Skill

Empathic skill is designed to help the client to elicit self-revealing statements from others, with the purpose of increasing the client's ability to understand others' self-regarding attitudes, emotions, conflicts, problems, desires, and goals. Another purpose of Empathic skill is to increase the client's personal attractiveness in the eyes of others. Empathy helps the client to meet these objectives by making the recipients feel well respected, understood, and appreciated by the client. The client's increased appeal to the other person causes the other to consider the client's views, attitudes, opinions, and suggestions more carefully and cooperatively. An additional purpose of Empathic skill is an altruistic one—to help the others involved to understand themselves better and to be able to more successfully explore and select realistic courses of action with respect to attaining their goals.

To change a client into one who can effectively and permanently use empathic responding when he or she wishes to do so requires changing the client's attitudes. It is necessary for clients to be convinced, and to learn through experience, that it will operate to their *own* benefit: (1) to learn to see the world in the ways that significant others they interact with see it, (2) to try to emotionally identify with the conflicts, problems, emotions, desires, and goals of others, and, most important, (3) to respect, accept, and be compassionate toward others and appreciative of their willingness to share their views.

In an extremely abbreviated form, the following are specific guidelines that the client is given to implement these attitudes and to show others that he or she does indeed have such attitudes.

1. Listen intently.
2. Show interest and understanding while the other person is talking.
3. Absorb the other's mood.
4. Concentrate on the other's *internal* world.
5. Put yourself in the other's place by asking yourself the following questions: "If I were the other, (1) what would I be thinking pro and/or con about

myself *as a person;* (2) what would I be *feeling;* (3) what would I be *wishing;* (4) what would I be thinking about *doing;* (5) what *conflicts* would I be experiencing about any of the above?"

6. Consider possible differences between your reactions (your answers to the above questions) and the reactions of the other.
7. Formulate a tentative statement that incorporates answers to one or more of the questions outlined above.
8. Put yourself in the other's place again to hear your own tentative statement.
9. Screen out potentially threatening words and phrases.
10. Make your statement declaratively and without use of the first-person pronoun.
11. Monitor the length of your statement in accordance with the other's reactions.
12. Accept corrections readily.

Mode Switching

Mode-Switching skills are designed to give the client the ability (1) always to keep in mind which of the above modes of behavior (that is, Empathic or Expressive) is being used at any given time, (2) to use each of the modes at the appropriate time, (3) to change from one mode to the other in a manner that is coordinated with the needs and views of the other person, and (4) to understand when and how to switch from one mode to the other in order to resolve conflicts and problems most effectively, to improve self-understanding, to promote self-improvement, and to improve relationships with others.

Mode Switching may be used when only one person has RE skills ("unilateral" Mode Switching), when two persons are skilled ("dyadic" Mode Switching), or when several persons are ("multilateral" Mode Switching, as in family therapy).

Some of the guidelines are as follows:

1. An *Expresser* switches modes (1) when he has already expressed his most important thoughts, feelings, and suggestions on the topic under discussion or (2) when he wants to know the other person's views, feelings, or suggestions.
2. As an *Empathic Responder,* a client switches modes (1) when he has already repeated the other's *deepest* thoughts and feelings on an issue twice or (2) when his thoughts and feelings begin to impair his ability to be empathic or (3) when he has something to say that might *favorably* influence the other's perceptions to help the other person to resolve a conflict or problem or reach a goal of his or her own or (4) when he has something to say that might help to resolve a problem or conflict between himself and the other.
3. As *Facilitator,* a client suggests a mode switch when he thinks that any of the above things is happening to other persons whose dialogue he is trying to facilitate.

Interpersonal Conflict/Problem Resolution

Interpersonal Conflict/Problem Resolution skills are designed to enable the client to resolve problems and conflicts between himself or herself and one or more other persons. The skills are designed to see that all realities that promote resolution are taken into account, including emotional ones. Conflict/Problem Resolution skills are built on an assumption that the client must be made to fully understand—that the most realistic and enduring problem/conflict resolutions are those that come closest to satisfying the wants and goals of *all* concerned parties.

I believe the most difficult and productive part of problem solving resides in the art of finding out what truly is the problem. Through a complex dialogue in which each person continuously redefines his or her perception of his or her own needs and the needs of the other person, a problem is continually redefined until a true meeting of minds, emotions, and desires occurs. I believe a system of problem solving that attempts to solve emotionally significant conflicts between intimates efficiently and effectively must allow for such a continual revision of each party's understanding of the essential nature of the problem. A problem that starts out as a disagreement about which spouse should do the dishes may really involve underlying feelings and attitudes involving respect, love, and other basic aspects of marital commitment. If the nature of the problem as it is originally perceived by the clients is prematurely given a "fixed" status by the problem-solving system, the net result over a period of months is that much energy can be wasted rearranging the deck chairs to everyone's satisfaction while the ship continues to sink.

Therefore, in my view, the major work in the RE system occurs before formal RE "problem solving" skills themselves are called into play. The Problem/Conflict Resolution skills are more analogous to a mop-up squad than to a major task force. Often the originally perceived problem is no longer a problem once the underlying attitudes and feelings are clarified. Nevertheless, even after the parties have reached an understanding about the most fundamental issues that are at stake, there often remains the question of who will be doing the dishes. That is, the task still remains, which can be difficult at times, of nailing down exact responsibilities, times, dates, places, and the like. The agreement arrived at must be one that will not unravel or lead to further misunderstandings. It must be one that will be realistic yet flexible and so enable the participants to continue to build on the trust that their skills, including the problem-solving skills, have allowed them to establish.

In briefest form, the Interpersonal Problem/Conflict Resolution skills may be stated as follows:

1. Make sure that you and the other persons involved are satisfied that you have expressed and have had understood by the others your views, self-concept issues, emotions, conflicts, problems, desires, and goals as they relate to the issue under discussion.
2. Determine whether this is the most appropriate time and place to try to reach a solution or whether different circumstances, or allowing more time for private deliberations, would be better.
3. Try to think of solutions that will satisfy the needs of everyone involved. Do not settle for mere compromise (splitting the difference) until you have spent considerable time thinking about the possibility that more creative solutions might better meet the needs of all parties.
4. Communicate your suggested solutions, making use of all Expressive skills (as described above), with emphasis on the interpersonal message.
5. Use your Empathic skills when responding to the suggestions and reactions of others.
6. Use unilateral, bilateral, or multilateral Mode Switching frequently in discussing the solutions.

7. In *working toward* an agreement (contract), make sure you have followed the specificity guideline of the Expressive mode in such a manner as to work out the details of time, place, frequency, and so on.
8. When an agreement *has been* reached in principle, make sure the Expressive-mode guideline of specificity is used to work out all details of time, place, frequency, and so on.
9. When an agreement in principle has been reached and the details specified, consider ways in which exceptions and difficulties might arise and ways in which exceptions to and modifications of the plan might be made to rule out misunderstandings or negative feelings that might otherwise result from these exceptions or difficulties.
10. Set a follow-up time when everyone involved will meet again to evaluate the plan (contract) reached and, if necessary, to make further modificatons.
11. If at follow-up modifications do seem necessary, begin again at Step 1 and follow all the above guidelines.

Facilitation

Facilitator skills are designed to enable a client to elicit (trigger) from others those types of interpersonal reactions and statements that will help the client (1) to resolve and prevent conflict and problems, (2) to enrich relationships, (3) to foster the client's personal growth, and (4) to foster the other individual's personal growth. Facilitator skills are skills in instructing or prompting others to make responses conducive to achieving the goals just mentioned. Such instruction may be systematic or may be limited to modifying particular responses in a given situation. That is, Facilitator skills can be used with another just once—for example, in a particularly critical situation—or they can be used in a long-term systematic program to shape another's behavior.

In briefest form, Facilitator skills may be stated as follows:

1. With respect to RE skills, make yourself a model to be emulated.
2. Use Expressive skills, especially interpersonal messages, to elicit relationship-enhancing and self-concept-enhancing responses from others.
3. With a relatively unskilled partner, and frequently with a skilled partner also, link the interpersonal message with a modeling response—that is, suggest a specific response that the other can copy.
4. Request only such responses as you believe the other person is willing and able to provide at the time.
5. Use Expressive skills to express appreciation of any sincere attempt at compliance with your request.
6. Also reinforce any *un*solicited approximations of responses that meet RE guidelines.
7. When your partners are skilled and cooperative, develop nonverbal signals as quick and efficient cues to elicit responses following RE guidelines.
8. When your partners are skilled and motivated, take the initiative in setting up regular times at which to use the skills to (1) express positive perceptions and feelings and (2) work through routine or serious conflicts and problems.

Generalization and Maintenance

Generalization and Maintenance skills are designed to enable clients to make use of their RE skills in the course of daily living on a permanent basis and to provide them with some of the concepts and skills useful in similarly training themselves to incorporate other desired behaviors into their daily life patterns.

Generalization and Maintenance skills may be outlined in brief form as follows. Note that if you substitute the phrase *desired behaviors* for the word *skills* in the following, it will show the usefulness of the guidelines for incorporating new behaviors of *any* sort.

1. Recognize that all complex new skills seem unnatural, discomforting, lacking in spontaneity, awkward, non-self-expressive, and ungratifying in the initial stages of their acquisition but that later such skills become a part of the "real you" and a vehicle for spontaneous and more complete self-expression and / or gratification.

2. When acquiring a skill, practice for the sake of practice. That is, regard each failure to achieve a desired outcome not as a failure but as a source of learning in the *process* of acquiring the new skill.

3. When acquiring a skill, set aside specific regular times and / or specific types of occasions when you will practice your skill.

4. When first acquiring a skill, rearrange objects or place new ones in your surroundings or on your person to serve as reminders to use your new skill.

5. Learn to identify situations that generally trigger behaviors on your part that are contrary to skilled behaviors. Try to make conscious the previously unconscious or taken-for-granted self-statements you make to yourself at those times. Substitute new self-statements that are appropriate to the use of your skills (that is, to the attainment of your goals). This is comparable to replacing cues for unwanted behavior with cues for wanted behavior.

6. Compliment yourself and / or imagine your instructor or others complimenting you (1) for your efforts and (2) for an approximation of successful performance, regardless of whether the total performance or outcome has been successful.

7. Begin your skill practice in the situations that best assure success. As your confidence and skills grow, find new and different situations in which to practice your skills, but progress in such a manner as to always maximize your chance of success.

8. When acquiring a skill, *if appropriate,* raise questions that will encourage others to compliment you for your new behaviors and / or solicit expression of their appreciation if your use of the skill has a favorable impact on them.

9. When acquiring a skill, *raise your consciousness* of the times when you might use it by keeping a log, preferably daily and preferably in writing (but at least mentally). Look back over the day and note times when (1) you might have used your skills but did not and (2) you did in fact exercise your skills. (Don't forget to compliment yourself in the latter case.)

10. When your skill level is high enough to lead to successful outcomes in your daily life, mentally contrast each such outcome with what probably would have happened had you not used your skill. Dwell on this difference to increase your appreciation of the beneficial effects of your new behavior.

11. Recognize that entropy is a law of nature. This means recognizing that (1) skilled behaviors generally require more concentration and self-discipline than unskilled ones and (2) lures of short-range relief and quick gratification constantly operate in opposition to long-range satisfactions and long-range goal attainment. Therefore, (1) continue to set aside regular times and occasions for skill use rather than relying solely on their spontaneous use in

daily life; (2) continue to consciously monitor your skills in some regular way at regular intervals; and (3) if feasible, enlist the cooperation of others to help you to maintain your skill usage.

THE INTAKE OR INTRODUCTORY PHASE OF RELATIONSHIP ENHANCEMENT

When professionals, paraprofessionals, or coworkers come to a Relationship Enhancement *program,* they generally have an understanding of the purposes of the program and of the appropriateness of the program for their own needs—much as a group of students usually understand the general purposes and content of a course before they enroll in it. When clients come for RE *therapy,* each one during the intake phase is given the opportunity to express his or her problems and the goals he or she seeks to achieve. Any set of problems or goals in which better relationships with other people would be helpful is deemed appropriate for Relationship Enhancement therapy. (The only criteria for exclusion are severe lack of contact with reality and intellectual retardation so severe that learning any kind of complex skill is not feasible.) During this intake or enrollment phase, it is also determined whether additional types of treatment or enrichment programs might also be recommended to the clients.

After establishing that the needs of the client and the program fit together, clients are given an explanation of how RE skills will help them to resolve their problems and achieve their goals. Usually, in doing this, an illustration is provided of an attempt to try to solve a conflict or problem without the use of skills. This is then contrasted with an illustration of how the same problem can be resolved more effectively through the use of RE skills. A variety of specially prepared audio-cassette tapes containing such illustrations are available for this purpose (Guerney & Vogelsong, 1981).[1]

FORMATS

Any of the formats listed below can be used with any kind of unit: an individual, a dyad, or a group. For example, in any of the following formats, family therapy could be conducted with only one member of a family attending, with a subgroup from a family, with the entire family attending as a unit, with two or more whole family units, or with groups comprising subunits of two or more families.

Intensive Format

Intensive format refers to marathon (eight-hour or weekend-long) sessions or to minimarathon (three- or four-hour) sessions. A group of married couples or premarital couples receiving RE training during one weekend would be a typical example of a marathon format.

---

[1]The tapes can be ordered by writing to the Individual and Family Consultation Center, Pennsylvania State University, Catharine Beecher House, University Park, PA 16802.

Extensive Format

By *extensive format* we mean sessions lasting 50 or 100 minutes and spread out over many weeks at the rate of one or two a week. A typical example would be a married couple seen for a period of 10 or 15 weeks for 50 minutes each week.

Combination Format

The intensive and extensive formats may be used in combination. For example, a family could be seen for two three-hour sessions during the first one or two weeks, to be followed by weekly sessions lasting an hour and a half each for ten weeks or more. This combination format is particularly useful for clients who are in a distressed or crisis situation when they first come for help. This format allows the training stage to be completed quickly so that the clients can proceed to use their skills to work intensively to resolve the problem or crisis.

Time-Limited Format

The kind of RE programs that run a predetermined length of time are those concerned with prevention and enrichment. For example, a typical marital enrich-ment program would last for a single weekend or a weekend followed by one or two days of follow-up over the next month or two. A typical premarital training program would last for one weekend.

Time-Designated Format

The term *time-designated* has been coined to apply to the typical RE therapy program. This means that an initial informal contract about an initial time com-mitment is developed by the therapist or intake worker with the individual or family group being seen. This amount of time is not regarded as a limit to the number of sessions but rather as a time at which progress will be evaluated to determine whether further sessions are indicated. When that time is up, the therapist and client(s) discuss whether more time would be desirable to achieve the therapist's and the client(s)' goals. If it is decided that more time is needed, another designated time is set for a second evaluation.

Professional and Paraprofessional Training Formats

The typical general counseling skills training program based on RE encompasses 20 hours of classroom instruction plus additional hours of *in vivo* practice and home-work assignments. The typical training program in methods of conducting RE therapy for practicing professionals begins with a three-day workshop followed by one or more advanced training workshops lasting a day or two each. After this, there may be coleadership of groups with a trainer and/or supervision by a certified RE trainer based on audiotapes of sessions with clients mailed to the supervisor and discussed through return tapes, in person, and/or by telephone.

TRAINING PROCESSES

General Paradigm

The general paradigm of RE training procedures is (1) motivate, (2) explain, (3) demonstrate, (4) model/prompt, (5) supervise skill practice within the training sessions, (6) prepare the learner to be successful with homework, (7) supervise homework, (8) prepare the learner to use the skills spontaneously in everyday living, (9) supervise the transfer of skills into everyday living, and (10) supervise the acquisition of maintenance skills.

Motivation

Inducing and maintaining client motivation is regarded as the most fundamental part of any skills teaching process. If motivation is maintained, it is possible for every other kind of success to follow. If motivation is lost before the teaching goals are accomplished, the learning process loses momentum and stops, and even gains already attained will probably decay. In the intake or first hours of any RE training program, inducing motivation means showing the trainees how the skills would meet their specific needs and goals. It means providing examples that have meaning in the clients' lives, and at times it even means citing research evidence. Another important motivating factor is to provide clients with a thorough and convincing rationale for each of the skills they are being taught. Further, we try hard to make it clear to clients how the skills fit together to form a coherent system.

Types of Therapist/Leader Responses

All appropriate responses made by RE therapist/leaders in implementing the general paradigm outlined above, including motivation, can be readily coded into the following types.

Social reinforcement and praise.   In RE, praise is used as social reinforcement. That is, it is used *contingently* to gradually shape behavior by rewarding successive approximations of the desired behavior. However, an additional major use of praise in the RE training method is noncontingent; praise is used to provide *motivational impetus*. That is, we regard using praise and the feeling of success it generates as an important part of maintaining motivation. This distinction is important because it means that it is a major responsibility of the trainer/therapist to *seek out* and find things to praise, even when progress is not evident on the behavior that is currently the main focus of attention. We do not make up things to praise out of thin air. But when it is hard to find things to praise, we often call to mind, for our own benefit and that of the client, any related attitudes and behaviors that are praiseworthy and encouraging (for example, good effort).

Demonstration.   By *demonstration* we mean the conscious use of illustrative examples and behaviors that show in a concrete fashion the rationale, the principles, and the mechanics of the skill being taught. The illustration is nailed down fore and aft with specific analysis of the example to make its pertinence as clear as possible. It is the feature of specific exposition, breakdown into component parts, and analysis that, we say, distinguishes demonstration from modeling.

Modeling.   By *modeling* we mean not only the general use by the therapist in some of his or her own behaviors of the skills being demonstrated but, more important, providing clients with specific words they can use. The client is free to use them exactly as given or to modify them slightly to fit his or her own style. Modeling in this sense is the preferred training response whenever a client is having difficulty or, even more important, when the trainer believes the client *will* have difficulty. That is, modeling is frequently used before the trainee has had a chance to make an inadequate response, which would then require correction. This helps the client to avoid a sense of being corrected and therefore to avoid feeling inadequate.

Prompting. As we use the term *prompting* in coding RE leader responses, it designates a more open-ended way than modeling of helping the client to perform appropriately. It provides a general cue to the client rather than giving the client an exact response to make. Prompting is used only when the leader feels certain that the trainee will *immediately* be able to make an entirely appropriate response on receiving the prompt.

Structuring. By *structuring* we mean relating a particular response being demonstrated or being suggested by the leader to the guideline that underlies it. That is, structuring provides the rule or principle related to the client response that a given situation calls for. Thus, particularly early in the training process, feedback to the client is often accompanied by a statement of the appropriate skill guideline.

Troubleshooting. This technique is used mainly in two kinds of situations. The first occurs when clients question or resist the rationale, guidelines, or assignments being made. The second situation occurs when the system breaks down because one or more of the persons involved are emotionally overcome. Use in the first situation is often required in the earliest phase of therapy and seldom later. The use of troubleshooting when clients are emotionally overcome usually occurs in the middle phases of therapy, if at all. In either case, troubleshooting involves a series of empathic responses made directly to the trainee. (Normally in RE, direct empathic responses from the therapist to the trainee after intake are generally avoided in favor of prompting empathy from the natural significant others with whom the trainee interacts in the real world.) At an appropriate time, these empathic responses are followed by expressive or administrative therapist responses designed to bring the client back to the usual RE practices and procedures. A third and even rarer use of troubleshooting occurs when the therapist wishes to express to the clients some strong value or belief of his own that he believes necessary to their own welfare or to the effective continuation of the therapeutic relationship.

Doubling. RE clients, as part of their training, are taught to teach RE skills to others ("Facilitation"). Doubling is a special form of Facilitation. Instead of Modeling or Prompting the person he or she is facilitating, the leader, another group member, or, most frequently, another member of the same family plays the role of a "double." That is, the facilitator repeats the response just made by the person for whom he or she is doubling but tries to do so in a way that makes it more skillful. In addition to teaching the other person by modeling, doubling promotes empathy in the person who is doing the doubling. It also tends to equalize what would otherwise be a psychological imbalance of power and attention in the eyes of one or more group members. For these last two reasons, the technique is used most frequently when working with adolescents and their parents. When a parent doubles for the adolescent vis-à-vis the other parent, it helps balance the power equation and makes the adolescent feel less overwhelmed. Because the parent who is doubling is also expressing the adolescent's views and feelings, that parent becomes perceived by the adolescent as a sort of emotional soul mate, or ally, during that period of time.

Administrating.   Administrative responses are responses that keep the group functioning smoothly along RE lines. One of the purposes of administrative responses is to maintain psychological equality in the group. That is, administrative responses are used to make sure that each person in the group feels he or she has a fair share in the proceedings and receives an appropriate amount of attention from the trainer—for example, "Mary and Bill, sorry to say we can allow you only about five minutes more now, so that George and Elaine will be able to have their turn." Administrative responses are also used to maximize the amount of time spent in actually practicing skills. They accomplish this by virtually eliminating general discussions that do not employ RE skills—for example, "Well, I'm sure you have strong feelings about that. Instead of telling me about it, please talk directly to your husband about it, using the skills."

Administrative responses are also used to guide clients to follow the procedures that help them select for discussion the most significant issues in their lives, as distinct from issues that are merely the most salient ones. That is, administrative responses are used to help clients avoid falling into the "here and now" trap—for example, "I realize that his behavior in the car on your way here tonight made you very angry at him. But I think we'd make better progress if you could put those feelings aside and tackle one of the fundamental problems you have listed in the Relationship Questionnaire." Finally, administrative responses are used to ensure that clients do not select topics that would lead to failure because they would be too difficult for the clients' current level of skill—for example, "This first topic you've listed in the Relationship Questionnaire is too difficult for your current skill level. Let's wait a while for that one. How about discussing the second one you've listed?"

Topic Selection

With clients.   Clients are guided to select those topics that are consistent with the skill level they have acquired and that are most personally meaningful and important in the context of interpersonal relationships. Clients would likely have great difficulty mastering empathic skill if in the early stages of the skill acquisition process they were asked to deal with topics that were personally threatening. Thus, taking as an example family therapy with all members of the family present, the members begin by discussing *neutral* topics—that is, topics that do not involve other members of the family at all. Then they proceed to discuss *positive* perceptions and feelings about others in the family. Then they discuss *enhancement* or enrichment issues—issues that they do not believe are likely to lead to serious emotional discord. After they have mastered all the necessary components of problem and conflict resolution, they proceed to that type of issue and are asked to concentrate on the most fundamental and important issues, including *problems* affecting their family relationships.[2]

Topic selection may vary from the above paradigm if clients are experiencing a crisis. If clients enter therapy in a period of crisis, the preferred method is to use a

---

[2]When a single individual from a family or familylike group is being trained and not all members of that group are participating in the training, the leader/therapist plays the roles of persons not participating. If such an individual is being trained in a group format with others also in that circumstance, these other members may do such role playing instead of, or in addition to, the trainer.

marathon or minimarathon format at first so that they can reach the phase of dealing with their crisis during the first week of therapy. However, on rare occasions when time for training is literally almost nil, the therapist will use the doubling, structuring, and modeling techniques to help resolve the initial crisis, reversing the general rule that conflict/problem resolution topics should come last.

Training of Student-Professionals and Professionals

When RE principles and skills are used to train students in the mental health profession, instead of following the above paradigm for topic selection, the trainees produce a hierarchy of personal goals. These may be personal goals for which they need to enlist the help of others, goals that involve establishing or enriching a relationship, goals that involve the resolution of conflicts or problems with other people, or some combination. These goals are then arranged from the least to the most difficult, and students implement their goals in that order. The procedure used here is as follows. First, to prepare them for their attempts to implement these goals, the students complete a planning worksheet based on RE skills. Second, on the basis of this planning, the students enter into role rehearsal in which they practice using the skills to implement the goal, with the trainer and/or other group members playing the part of the significant other(s) involved. Next, the student tries to implement the goal *in vivo*. Finally, there is a recapitulation and feedback session following the student's attempt at real-life implementation. This feedback, which sometimes involves more role playing, centers on the use of the skills rather than the content and is used to further increase the student's sophistication in using the skills in an integrated and sophisticated manner in real life.

When practicing professionals are trained, they generally employ situations they have encountered or would expect to encounter with their clients. These situations are role-played with other members of the group, with the trainer acting as supervisor. Again, the situations chosen start with the least difficult and proceed to the most difficult.

CASE ILLUSTRATION

I will now use a dyadic marital case presentation to illustrate RE in action. The case began with a call by the wife, whom I shall call Ruth. She said her husband, whom I shall call Bill, had left their home a few days earlier. The wife was concerned about preserving her marriage for her own sake and for the children's (two teenagers).

Ruth and Bill were public school teachers working in different schools. Bill had taken up separate residence in a one-room apartment. Initially Ruth was doubtful whether her husband would be willing to come. The therapist convinced her that she should make every effort to persuade him and suggested that she emphasize that the first session would be mainly to inform him of the nature of RE and would carry no implied commitment that he continue to come. He agreed to come for the exploratory interview.

At the intake interview, the husband was vague about his reasons for leaving home. However, he revealed that there was no other woman involved and that he felt he needed his freedom to discover who he was and how he wanted to live his life. Living at home made him feel stifled and extremely depressed, and he could not stand another moment of it. Ruth's view was that the problem was essentially a psychological problem of the husband's, not a relationship problem. But she wanted to participate to learn whatever it was she needed to know about him to help him overcome his problems, including any problems that might, indeed, be found within the relationship. She still loved him and wanted him back as husband and father. Bill was pained at the distress he was causing his wife and children by leaving but felt it was a matter of his personal survival to remain independent. He was not yet fully committed to a legal divorce, and he wished to continue to visit his children, but he would be unwilling to attend any further sessions if the goal of the sessions was his return to the family.

The therapist explained that reconciliation in such cases was a frequent outcome of RE but that preserving the marriage was not the goal of RE. The goal was improvement of the relationship *between Bill and his wife, regardless of whether they were married, separated, or divorced. The therapist stressed that improving the relationship between them—their communication and ability to solve conflicts and problems effectively—would be of value to Bill regardless of the choice he made concerning divorce. An improved relationship would, in fact, make separation or divorce a much less devastating experience for all concerned. It was clear that Bill wanted a continuing role with the children. The therapist pointed out that an improved relationship between him and his wife would make this a much less discordant, destructive affair for him and the children as well as for his wife, even if they were to be divorced. Presenting the rationale underlying the skills they would learn, and demonstrating skilled versus unskilled interactions in a typical marital conflict, made the advantages of learning such skills clear to both participants. Finally, it was pointed out to Bill that the skills would have fringe benefits to him in the way he could interact with his children, students, and colleagues.*

Seeing these advantages and assured that there would be absolutely no pressure in the RE approach to steer him toward a marital reconciliation, Bill agreed to a further trial period of RE. Ruth, realizing that RE gave her a good chance to better understand what was going on with Bill and possibly to win him back, committed herself fully to continuing.

Bill and Ruth were seen for weekly sessions lasting an hour and a half. They learned the skills well, and except for some difficulties in getting Bill to complete the Relationship Questionnaire and the written assignments, they both cooperated well with all aspects of the treatment.

In talking about positive qualities, the major one that Bill saw in Ruth was her concern, caring, and effectiveness vis-à-vis the children. Ruth emphasized Bill's general character of caring and sensitivity toward herself and the children.

As the therapy sessions advanced into discussion and resolution of conflicts and problems, Bill discussed the following issues. He said he felt trapped, like a caged prisoner, in the presence of his wife, because of her judgmentalness about his behavior. It emerged that he felt he had negative feelings that he could not openly express because of her judgmentalness, his fear of hurting her, and his own general fear of expressing aggression. As a result of discussing this with his wife in the sessions, he came to realize that the need he felt to inhibit negative emotions made him so unassertive about his own wishes as to prevent him from freely leading the kind of life he wanted to lead vis-à-vis friends and work as well as her. He realized that this was largely responsible for his depression. He came to realize, too, that his need to repress his negative emotions and his fear of Ruth's judgmentalness had gradually killed his ability to feel and to express any affection for her. He had reached the point (still felt and openly expressed at about the sixth week in therapy) that he no longer experienced any feeling of love for her, only fear and an overwhelming feeling of being kept a prisoner by her.

In the early phases of problem discussion, Ruth's reaction to Bill's disclosures was to deny responsibility and to assert her belief that he was, in effect, projecting onto her the behaviors and attitudes he had experienced vis-à-vis his mother. At the same time, however, she continued to openly express her feeling of deep love and caring for Bill. She expressed the deep pain and sense of being treated unjustly she experienced in his leaving and in the uncommunicative, sudden way he did it.

As Bill began to make more and more use of the specificity guideline in the expressive mode regarding those behaviors of Ruth's that he regarded as judgmental and inhibiting to him, Ruth more and more accepted the responsibility for her own behavior in the interactive process, without the "psychologizing" that had characterized her first responses to this issue. She clearly expressed her wish to change those behaviors and her strong desire to be receptive and open to all his feelings, including the negative ones.

As Bill continued to express the feeling that he could not tolerate returning to Ruth because he saw her as his jailer, Ruth expressed strong hurt and frustration about his inability to recognize the changes she had made as a result of the new understandings she had achieved about him, herself, and the relationship in the RE sessions. She assured him over and over that she truly perceived things and felt very, very differently than before—that she was no longer the same person he had reacted to by leaving and that she felt the strongest desire to encourage, rather than discourage, his search for self. She felt great strength in herself and confidence in her ability to behave differently. She expressed deep hurt over his unwillingness to return home to give her the chance to demonstrate her new self to him.

In the course of all this, what was happening, of course, was that Bill was indeed expressing his negative feelings to his wife. The principles, attitudes, and skills of RE made it clear to him that it was important to do so, gave him a structure that encouraged such openness, and gave him the skills to do it in a manner that he knew would minimize any unnecessary hurt to his wife. Thus, he realized that he had indeed acquired the capacity to express his negative feelings. He was able to do so in ways that allowed him to establish psychological and personal freedom without sacrificing the relationship. Perhaps more important, he was able to achieve catharsis, or disinhibition, of negative feelings. The lifting of this inhibition enabled the disinhibition of his positive feelings toward his wife as well. His feelings of love and affection were thereby restored.

Essential to accomplishing this, of course, was the fact that, through her acquisition of the RE attitudes and skills, Ruth had demonstrated to him, first in the sessions and then outside them, that she was receptive to all his needs and feelings, including ones that might have been devastating to the relationship had they been expressed without skill (for example, that he no longer felt any love for her, that he perceived her in their relationship as no more than a jailer). With her newfound therapeutic attitudes and skills, she demonstrated the ability not only to "survive" such expressions on his part but to empathize with them. Moreover, she was able to change her style of interaction in accordance with the behaviors he wanted to see her adopt to establish the level of independence he felt he needed to have at this time (for example, not quizzing him as intensely as was her habit about his comings and goings and how he divided his time between work and family).

As Ruth empathized with his negative feelings and continued to express her own (predominantly) loving ones, his affectionate feelings and his ability to express them to her verbally and physically reemerged and grew stronger. As they did, Ruth's openness, confidence, and spontaneity with him likewise increased. (Part of the problem had been her fear of being natural and spontaneous with him, physically and otherwise, largely because she had come to fear his rejection of her feelings and of her physical advances.) Ruth's renewed confidence and spontaneity further increased Bill's feelings of love and affection.

During the course of this process, at about the eighth session, Bill's trust and affection had reached the point that he was willing—with great trepidation—to return to living at home for a trial period. This gave them more opportunity to practice generalizing their skills in everyday situations and also to increase the frequency of their regular one-hour at-home RE skill meetings to two or three times a week. As prescribed in the RE system, in addition to problem-solving discussions, these meetings regularly included the sharing of positive feelings and the exploration of changes and activities—including the area of sex—that would increase their enjoyment of each other's company. Because of the skill levels they had attained by this time, the staying-at-home test period was more than successful and, in fact, significantly accelerated the whole process described above.

By the fifteenth session, the relationship seemed to them and to the therapist to be extremely positive and strong, far exceeding the affection they had felt for each other in many, many years. They met all the criteria for termination of RE therapy: they had essentially worked through the fundamental problems that had brought them to therapy; they were able to use the skills in their everyday interactions to share promptly the positive and negative feelings that arose in the course of everyday living; they held regular meetings to continue to work through any thorny problems or conflicts and, equally important, to enrich their enjoyment of each other; the RE attitudes and skills had generalized—had become a natural part of their behavioral repertoire—as evidenced by their use and consequently enriched relationships at work and with the children. A brief follow-up meeting was scheduled for two weeks later to check whether these gains were being fully maintained (and to provide a booster if they weren't) and then again another four weeks later for the same purpose. The gains were being fully maintained. The couple attributed the restoration and revitalization of their relationship entirely to RE and were by now actively recruiting other couples they knew to come for RE sessions. A brief follow-up interview a year later indicated that the couple were still using the skills and enjoying a strong and mutually supportive marital relationship.

EVALUATION STUDIES

Group Family RE

Ginsberg (1977) was the first to study Group Family RE, working with father-and-son pairs in a program then called the Parent Adolescent Relationship Development (PARD) program. Using a format of ten sessions lasting two hours each, he worked with 14 father/son pairs randomly assigned to the experimental group. Fifteen pairs were in the no-treatment control group. This control group was later offered treatment, serving as its own control in a quasi-replication study. In discussing emotionally significant topics in the Verbal Interaction Task (Guerney, 1977a), the RE group showed more improvement in empathic acceptance as measured by the Acceptance of Other Scale (Guerney, 1977a) and in the expression of their views and feelings in ways deemed to show greater sensitivity and greater self-awareness and to be less threat-inducing as measured by the Self/Feeling Awareness Scale (Guerney, 1977a). Unobtrusively observed natural interactions between fathers and sons coded on the same scales also showed that the RE pairs gained significantly on those variables while the no-treatment pairs did not. A hypothesis that the RE-trained fathers and sons would show greater improvement in patterns of general communication as measured by the Adolescent-Parent Communications Check List (Beaubien, 1970) was also confirmed. Differences were found on all subscales of this measure, thereby indicating greater gains for RE participants in (1) transmission processes in communication, (2) feedback processes, and (3) satisfaction with communication. Also confirmed was a hypothesis that the general quality of the relationship between fathers and sons as measured by the Family Life Questionnaire (Guerney, 1977a) would show greater improvement in RE participants than in untrained fathers and sons. The quasi-replication study generally confirmed the results reported above and also showed significant improvement in the self-concepts of both fathers and sons trained in RE.

With respect to the question of specific versus nonspecific treatment effects—that is, whether suggestion, placebo, and thank-you effects might account for the results—the finding that changes occurred on unobtrusively observed behavioral interactions is of particular importance. Such a finding is not attributable to attention, placebo, or thank-you effects and the like. There also are other studies bearing on this question that compared an alternative treatment design and a PARD program. Comparisons with alternative treatment approaches which are of equal credibility and which are executed with equal competence, enthusiasm, warmth, empathy, and genuineness reveal whether the treatment of interest leads to specific treatment effects over and above any nonspecific effects, which should be equally present in both treatments.

Guerney, Coufal, and Vogelsong (1981) compared Group Family RE in a PARD program with a traditional (discussion-based) group treatment and a no-treatment control group. A total of 54 mother/daughter pairs were randomly assigned to these three conditions. The two treatment groups met two hours weekly, generally in groups of three pairs, approximately 13 times. Three basic hypotheses were confirmed on a wide variety of measures. The RE participants were superior both to traditional treatment participants and to the no-treatment subjects in (1) specific empathic and expressive communication skills as measured both behaviorally and on paper-and-pencil measures, (2) general patterns of communication, and (3) the quality of the general relationship between the mothers and daughters.

The traditional and RE methods had been carefully equalized in every way: the therapists/leaders were the same for both groups and were perceived by the clients in the two groups as showing virtually identical degrees of empathy, warmth, genuineness, enthusiasm, and competence. Thus, this study virtually rules out the possibility that generic factors (attention, placebo, experimenter demand, and so on) could fully account for any of the various kinds of improvement shown as a result of participating in RE.

In a follow-up to the above-mentioned study, Guerney, Vogelsong, and Coufal (1981) examined maintenance of gains. They found that six months after termination, mothers and daughters in the traditional treatment, in comparison with mothers and daughters who had received no treatment, showed no greater gains in specific communication skills, general communication patterns, or the general quality of their relationship. In contrast, participants in RE showed significantly greater gains in all these areas than either the traditionally treated group or the control group. In addition to demonstrating the long-term superiority of RE to a traditional, discussion-oriented approach, this finding demonstrated that, as with posttreatment gains, a significant portion of the long-range gains are treatment-specific.

Group Marital RE

Originally called "Conjugal Therapy," Group Marital RE therapy was first studied by Ely, Guerney, and Stover (1973). The couples, who were experiencing marital problems, ranged in age from 20 to 55 years and had been married for an average of ten years. They were randomly assigned to experimental and no-treatment control groups. Only the training phase of the therapy was studied. The primary objective was to determine whether the couples were able to learn the skills. As measured by verbatim responses to hypothetical critical incidents on a questionnaire and by behavioral coding of role playing, the trained couples were found to be higher in skilled communication than the control group. In a later quasi-replication study, RE clients gained more during treatment than they had during a comparable time period before treatment began. Significant gains were also found in general communication patterns as measured by Navran's Primary Communication Inventory (1967) and in the general pattern of the couples' relationships as measured by the Conjugal Life Questionnaire (Guerney, 1977a).

A study extending beyond the training phase was conducted by Collins (1977) with 45 couples. The randomly assigned RE-therapy couples showed greater gains than control couples in marital communication as measured by the Marital Communication Inventory (Bienvenu, 1970) and in marital adjustment as measured by the Marital Adjustment Test (Locke & Williamson, 1958).

The *intensive* Group Marital format of RE was studied by Rappaport (1976), using an own-control design. The 20 participating married couples were first tested and then, after two months, were tested again just before beginning the two-month, four-session RE program. The time-limited program was conducted on alternate weekends for 4- and 8-hour sessions, for a total of 24 hours.

On all variables, the clients showed greater gains during the treatment period than they had during the waiting period. In discussions of emotionally significant topics in the Verbal Interaction Task, couples expressed themselves with more sensitivity to their own feelings and in ways less likely to evoke argument from their partners as determined by the Self/Feeling Awareness Scale. Participants also showed more empathic acceptance of their partners in these discussions as determined by coding their behavior with the Acceptance of Other Scale. Clients also experienced greater improvement in marital harmony as measured by the Family Life Questionnaire. They showed greater gains in trust and intimacy as measured by the Interpersonal Relationship Scale (Guerney, 1977a). They showed a greater rate of change in their overall relationship patterns on the Relationship Change Scale (1977a). They showed greater improvement in their satisfaction with their relationships on the Satisfaction Change Scale (1977a), and they showed greater improvement in their ability to satisfactorily resolve relationship problems as measured by the Handling Problems Change Scale (1977a).

Comparison with another study (Harrell & Guerney, 1976) suggested that it was the specific nature of the RE program, and not program-extraneous or generic factors, that was responsible for the significant differences found in the earlier RE studies. The first direct comparison of Group Marital RE with another equally credible and competently administered program was conducted by Wieman (1973). He compared RE with his Reciprocal Reinforcement program, which drew heavily on principles and techniques used by Knox (1971), Rappaport and Harrell (1972), and especially Stuart (1969a, 1969b). The RE program used here was an abbreviated and time-limited one of eight weeks' duration. Participants in the two treatments, in comparison with a waiting-list control group, showed equal improvement in measures of marital communication, marital adjustment, and cooperativeness. Ratings on 16 semantic differential scales were, in general, positive for both treatments, but there were many differences between the treatments on these measures. Clients in the Reciprocal Reinforcement program evaluated their treatment as being more light, safe, easy, cold, and calm than participants in the RE program. Clients in the RE program perceived their treatment experience as being significantly more deep, good, worthwhile, exciting, strong, fair, important, comfortable, and professional than did clients in the Reciprocal Reinforcement program. Since both were highly credible treatments, these differences cannot be attributed to nonspecific treatment factors.

Jessee and Guerney (1981) also conducted a study pertinent to the question of specific versus generic treatment effects. In this study, 36 couples were randomly assigned to Group Marital RE or to a group Gestalt Relationship Facilitation treatment. Conducted in small groups, sessions lasted two and a half hours and continued for 12 consecutive weeks. Participants in both groups gained significantly on all variables studied: marital adjustment, communication, trust and harmony, rate of positive change in the relationship, relationship satisfaction, and ability to handle problems as measured by instruments mentioned in reviewing the research covered above. RE participants attained greater gains than Gestalt Relationship Facilitation participants in communication, relationship satisfaction, and ability to handle problems. Because the therapists were seen by clients as being essentially equal in their behavior toward the clients and because the treatments were designed to be equally credible, the results obtained, at least on those variables on which RE showed superior performance, must have been due to treatment-specific and not to generic treatment factors.

Ridley, Jorgensen, Morgan, and Avery (in press) compared a 24-hour Group Marital RE program with a discussion treatment of equal length that sought to improve couples' marital relationships on a wide variety of marital issues. Participants in the RE program showed significantly greater improvement in satisfaction, communication, intimacy, sensitivity, openness, and understanding in the marital relationship (as measured by their overall score on the Relationship Change Scale) than participants in the other treatment.

Maintenance of gains in Group Marital RE was studied as part of the earlier-mentioned Wieman study. That study showed that married couples in the RE program (and the other treatment also) maintained their gains well ten weeks after the close of treatment, as determined by empirical assessment of the major treatment variables.

Dyadic Marital RE

Dyadic Marital RE is RE conducted with one married or cohabiting couple, as distinct from *Group* Marital RE, which involves individuals from more than one pair, and as distinct from *Unilateral* Marital RE, which involves working individually or in groups with marital or cohabiting couples with half the dyad not attending. Only one study, by Ross (1981), has been conducted to date on Dyadic Marital RE. Five therapists participated in the study. These therapists had been conducting marital therapy from 3 to 13 years (mean = 6). During that time, they had developed eclectic methods which they felt were most effective and fitted their own personal styles and which they varied according to the needs of particular cases. Each counselor saw himself or herself as very strongly influenced by a particular theoretical orientation. Two perceived themselves as being primarily Rogerian, one relied heavily on behavior modification, another saw Harry Stack Sullivan's theory as predominant in his orientation, and the fifth therapist drew mainly on a psychoanalytic framework. (Theoretical orientations of secondary influence they cited were those of Ellis, Glasser, and Haley.) These types of therapies were called the "therapists' preferred therapy."

These therapists, all of whom worked in the same mental health/mental retardation psychiatric center, were jointly given a three-day training program in marital RE. Persons coming to the center with marital complaints were first screened as individuals to determine whether their own pathology called for immediate individual treatment instead of marital therapy. Nine potential cases were accordingly screened out. Twelve couples were randomly assigned to conjoint treatment in such a manner as to ensure that each therapist would see an equal number of couples in each treatment. Pretesting was conducted just before a couple's first marital-therapy session. Random assignment was effective in that pretesting showed no significant differences between clients in the two treatments on any of the dependent variables. Posttesting was conducted at the ten-week point.

Clients in RE showed greater improvement after ten weeks of therapy than clients treated with the therapist's preferred treatment on all variables studied: (1) marital adjustment as measured by the Marital Adjustment Test, (2) the quality of the couple's relationship as measured by the Interpersonal Relationship Scale, and (3) the quality of their communication as measured by the Marital Communication Inventory. In addition to greater relative gains, absolute differences were found. The clients in RE showed significant pretest-to-posttest gains on all measures. Those in the therapist's preferred treatment did not show such a gain on any measure. At posttest, RE clients were at significantly higher levels on all the variables than clients in the therapist's preferred treatment.

This study is of special interest for a number of reasons. First, it shows more clearly than previous research that RE therapy is effective—and for treatment-specific reasons—with extremely disturbed marriages. In fact, comparison of gains among those couples with the gains observed in previous studies with less distressed couples suggests this hypothesis: *in RE therapy, the more distressed the marriage, the greater the gains obtained.* Second, previous research with RE had usually been done with therapists who, though neophytes, had had a full program of training and supervision in RE. Such therapists obtained significant improvement with their clients. In the present study, the therapists were experienced as therapists but had very little training and no supervision in RE therapy. (The original plan, abandoned because of practical constraints, called for much more supervision of the therapists.) Despite this drawback, RE was effective. The third reason this study is of special interest is that it pitted RE against what many believe to be the most powerful type of therapy—namely, a method of therapy that an experienced therapist has maximum confidence in and enthusiasm for, has devised to suit his own theoretical preferences and personality, and is free to vary in accordance with the perceived special needs of his particular clients. The superiority of RE despite such handicaps speaks well for its potency.

Premarital RE

Group RE as an enrichment/problem-prevention program for dating and premarital couples was first studied by Schlein (1971) and reported also by Ginsberg and Vogelsong (1977). In this time-limited study, couples met over a period of 8 to 12 weeks for two-and-a-half-hour sessions. There were approximately three couples in each group. The couples, all college students, had been randomly assigned to an RE group or a waiting-list control group. The final sample consisted of 15 couples in RE and 27 in the control condition.

The RE participants showed greater gains than the untrained subjects in specific communication skills. That is, in discussing emotionally relevant topics on the Verbal Interaction Task, as coded by means of the Acceptance of Other Scale, the RE participants showed greater empathic acceptance toward their partners. They also showed greater improvement in their ability to openly express their views and feelings in ways deemed less threatening to their partners, as determined by coding the dialogues with the Self/Feeling Awareness Scale. Hypotheses that the RE couples would also show greater improvement in their general patterns of communication as measured by the Premarital Communication Inventory and by a slightly modified version of the Primary Communication Inventory (Locke, Sabagh, & Thomas, 1956) were not confirmed. The nonconfirmation may have been due to a ceiling effect, since the participants' initial scores were extremely high and the changes were in the expected direction.

We return now to hypotheses that were confirmed. The trained participants showed greater improvement in their ability to handle problems as measured by the Handling Problems Change Scale. They also showed greater improvement in the general quality of their relationship on most of the measures used to assess this variable—namely, greater improvement in empathy, warmth, and genuineness as measured by the Relationship Scale (Guerney, 1977a) and in satisfaction with their relationship as measured by the Satisfaction Change Scale.

A study by Most (1980) recently confirmed the effectiveness of group Premarital RE problem prevention/enrichment. He used an intensive time-limited (one weekend) format. The training was conducted by married lay couples who themselves had had only two weekends of training. Most found that the 12 premarital couples improved significantly in (1) their own perceptions of their skill levels in empathy, expressive skills, ability to conduct a skilled dialogue, potential capacity to use skills in everyday life, and problem solving, (2) their perceived level of confidence in their ability to handle expected problems in their future married life, and (3) their ability to handle problems constructively as measured by experimentally naive judges' coding of (a) their written responses to hypothetical marital problem situations and (b) their interaction in role-playing attempts to solve hypothetical marital problems. Improvement on the third measure involved both an increase in positive behaviors and a reduction in negative behaviors.

D'Augelli, Deyss, Guerney, Hershenberg, and Sborofsky (1974) coded the emotionally significant dialogues of the couples who had participated in the earlier-described study by Schlein (1971). Their behavior was coded on Carkhuff's (1969b) Behavior Scales, which have been used widely to assess counselor performance and the efficacy of training programs for counselors and paraprofessionals. The RE-trained group gained significantly more on these scales than the untrained group. After less than 20 hours of training, these college undergraduates—who had not been selected because of any sort of interest in counseling—had changed, in the way they dealt with emotional issues with their partner, from levels of counseling skills typical of college students to levels typical of professional counselors.

We turn now to studies comparing RE to alternative treatment approaches. Ridley et al. (in press) compared essentially randomly assigned couples trained in RE ($N = 25$) with couples in a discussion-based treatment ($N = 29$) designed to improve their relationships. The study used five measures of relationship quality: the Relationship Change Scale, the Interpersonal Relationship Scale, the Relationship Scale—Self, the Relationship Scale—Partner (Guerney, 1977a; Shapiro, Krauss, & Truax, 1969), and the Primary Communication Inventory. Compared with the couples in the discussion-oriented treatment, couples who had received RE training showed more improvement on each of these measures, thereby indicating improvement in satisfaction, communication, trust, intimacy, sensitivity, openness, understanding, empathy, warmth, and genuineness.

Avery, Ridley, Leslie, and Milholland (1980) compared group Premarital RE with a lecture/discussion program designed to improve premarital relationships. Each of the programs was conducted over an eight-week period for approximately three hours per week. Using the Acceptance of Other Scale and the Self/Feeling Awareness Scale to code the couples' discussions of significant interpersonal topics on the Verbal Interaction Task, the authors found significantly greater improvement in the RE couples on both variables assessed—empathy and appropriate self-disclosure.

Another study of premarital couples was conducted by Ridley, Avery, Dent, and Harrell (1981). They compared three groups: (1) group Premarital RE (without the problem-solving and generalization/maintenance components), (2) a Premarital Problem-Solving skills training program (Ridley, Avery, Harrell, Leslie, & Dent, in press), and (3) a non-skills-oriented Relationship Development program that the authors had developed to promote better understanding between couples. Couples in each group were assessed pre- and posttraining on the Peterman-Ridley Heterosexual Competency Scale, which assesses self-perceptions of success in relationships with the other sex. After the training, which was conducted in eight three- or four-couple group meetings each lasting three hours, the RE group showed the greatest mean gain. An analysis of covariance yielded one significant difference: couples in the RE treatment showed greater gains than couples in the Relationship Development group.

With respect to *maintenance of gains,* there has been only one study to date on Premarital RE. In the earlier-discussed study comparing group Premarital RE with a lecture/discussion Relationship Improvement program (Avery et al., 1980), there was a follow-up six months after termination. A significant decline in performance from the levels attained at the conclusion of treatment was found. Nevertheless, the RE couples still maintained their superiority on both measures studied (empathy and appropriate self-disclosure) compared with their own pretest levels and compared with couples who had been in the lecture/discussion-based treatment.

An RE-Related Program for Divorcees

Thiessen, Avery, and Joanning (1980) have developed a 15-hour, five-week communication skills training program for recently divorced women. The program is based on the authors' experience in divorce adjustment counseling, on divorce adjustment seminars conducted by Weiss (1976) and by Welch and Granvold (1977), on the work of Tubesing and Tubesing (1973), and on RE. Subjects were assigned by convenience of time scheduling to a training group ($N = 13$) or to a no-treatment group ($N = 15$). Each subgroup of trainees was composed of six or seven divorcees. The trained participants showed greater improvement in divorce adjustment as measured by the Fisher Divorce Adjustment Scale (Fisher, 1977), in self-esteem as measured by a subscale of that measure, and in empathy as measured by the subjects' responses indicating what they would say in situations that divorced women frequently must deal with, coded on the Acceptance of Other Scale. (Significant differences were not found on self-disclosure or on the social support the women perceived themselves as getting.)

RESEARCH ON TRAINING PARAPROFESSIONALS

Residence-Hall Counselors

Avery (1973) trained 22 potential residence-hall counselors in RE skills over a nine-week period in weekly meetings of two to two and a half hours. The training was done in groups of five or six trainees. The trainees conducted a 15-minute audiotaped helping interview with a confederate at the outset of the study and again after the training. An untrained control group of 15 potential residence-hall counselors also conducted such interviews before and after a comparable time period. The interviews were coded by reliable, expert coders on the Carkhuff Scale for Empathic Understanding (Carkhuff, 1969b). The RE-trained group showed significantly greater improvement.

A follow-up study (Avery, 1978) showed that the superiority of the trained to the untrained prospective dormitory counselors was maintained six months after completion of the training.

Probation Workers

An uncontrolled empirical evaluation of the effectiveness of RE administered by probation officers for juvenile offenders was conducted by Guerney, Vogelsong, and Glynn (1977). The probation officers had had one week's training in RE methods plus weekly supervision sessions. Seventeen members of five families, one member of which was a juvenile offender, were studied. Significant improvement was shown in family harmony as measured by the Family Life Questionnaire, in family satisfaction as measured by the Satisfaction Change Scale, and in participants' ability to handle family problems as measured by the Handling Problems Change Scale.

Drug Rehabilitation Staff

Cadigan (1980) adapted RE to train staff members in a residential drug-rehabilitation center. He used this modified RE program to train former drug addicts who had become staff members at the center. These staff members then trained residents of the rehabilitation center ($N = 16$) in this program. Trainees were compared with a nonrandomly assigned untrained control group ($N = 24$), which later was determined to be an equivalent group as judged by initial scores on the dependent variables. The trained residents achieved greater improvement in mean scores on every measure used. Two of these gains were statistically significant: (1) more positive interpersonal responses as determined by written responses to hypothetical peer problem situations and (2) residents' perceptions of the way staff members behaved toward them. Strong trends toward greater gains of the trained group ($p < .10$) were found on two other variables: (1) perceptions of the quality of the trainees' relationships with nonaddicts and (2) perceptions of the quality of their relationships with their peers.

Training in Public School Settings

Hatch (1973) studied elementary school teachers who had been trained in basic RE skills and in democratic classroom management (Guerney & Merriam, 1972; Merriam & Guerney, 1973) and their pupils. Tallies of various kinds of teacher behaviors were made from tape recordings of classroom meetings held to discuss classroom problems. The results confirmed hypotheses that trained teachers, compared with an untrained control group, would solicit (1) more feelings and (2) more ideas from the children. In addition, coding of pupils' statements in these meetings showed that the pupils of the trained teachers expressed their views more freely than control pupils.

Rocks (1980) trained, in an abbreviated RE program, high school teachers and students nominated by them as noncommunicative underachievers. The trained students were compared with a group of similarly selected students who, by random assignment, were not trained, along with their teachers. (The comparison group of students received only one non-RE lecture/discussion session.) The RE-trained students improved more in classroom behavior and in school attendance (though not in academic ranking). Rocks's study lent support to the anecdotal evidence of Hatch and Guerney (1975) that conducting a Peer Relationship program was both feasible and effective in a high school setting.

Vogelsong (1978) probed the lower age limits of the effectiveness of RE programs in a school setting. Vogelsong trained six boys and ten girls in the fifth grade of a rural public school in empathic skills, using appropriately simplified RE procedures and vocabulary. These pupils were compared with a randomly assigned control group, which spent an equivalent amount of time working together on arts and crafts projects. After ten 45-minute weekly meetings, the trained group showed significantly greater gains in empathy between pre- and posttesting as measured by the Acceptance of Other Scale than the control group.

Haynes and Avery (1979) developed a 16-hour training program for high school students that makes use of some RE skills and training methods. They randomly selected one of two junior English classes for training; the other served as a no-treatment control group. Twenty minutes of dialogue between two randomly assigned same-sex students in the training group were assessed by the Self/Feeling Awareness Scale to measure appropriate self-disclosure and by the Acceptance of Other Scale to measure empathy. The topics discussed in these dialogues were what the students found likable about members of their own sex and members of the other sex. The trained participants showed more pre-post improvement on both appropriate self-disclosure and empathy. To assess generalization, the above-mentioned scales were also applied to a questionnaire in which students indicated exactly what they would say when confronted with hypothetical situations involving peers, parents, and dating partners. The trained group showed more generalization on both self-disclosure and empathy.

In a follow-up to that study, Avery, Rider, and Haynes-Clements (1981) found that the superiority in empathy and in appropriate self-disclosure of the trained students over the untrained students was maintained five months after the termination of training. This maintenance of training effects was found on the behavioral measure of skills and also on the quasi-behavioral measure assessing generalization. The studies cited above lend some empirical support to the idea that Filial and RE-based programs of one kind or another can be useful in school settings from preschool on up (Andronico & Guerney, 1967, 1969; Guerney, 1979; Guerney, Stover, & Andronico, 1967).

REFERENCES

Andronico, M. P., & Guerney, B. G., Jr. The potential application of Filial Therapy to the school situation. *Journal of School Psychology,* 1967, *6*(1), 2–7.

Andronico, M. P., & Guerney, B. G., Jr. A psychotherapeutic aid in a Headstart program. *Children,* 1969, *16*(1), 14–22.

Authier, J., Gustafson, K., Guerney, B. G., Jr., & Kasdorf, J. A. The psychological practitioner as a teacher: A theoretical-historical practical review. *Counseling Psychologist,* 1975, *5*(2), 31–50.

Avery, A. W. An experimental program for training paraprofessional helpers. Unpublished master's thesis, Pennsylvania State University, 1973.

Avery, A. W. Communication skills training for paraprofessional helpers. *American Journal of Community Psychology,* 1978, *6,* 583–592.

Avery, A. W., Rider, K., & Haynes-Clements, L. A. Communication skills training for adolescents: A five month follow-up. *Adolescence,* 1981, *16,* 289–298.

Avery, A. W., Ridley, C. A., Leslie, L. A., & Milholland, T. Relationship Enhancement with premarital dyads: A six-month follow-up. *American Journal of Family Therapy,* 1980, *8,* 23–30.

Beaubien, C. O. Adolescent-parent communication styles. Unpublished doctoral dissertation, Pennsylvania State University, 1970.

Bienvenu, M. Measurement of marital communication. *Family Coordinator,* 1970, *19,* 26–31.

Cadigan, J. D. RETEACH program and project: Relationship Enhancement in a therapeutic environment as clients head out. Unpublished doctoral dissertation, Pennsylvania State University, 1980.

Carkhuff, R. R. *Helping and human relations.* Vol. 1: *Selection and training.* New York: Holt, Rinehart & Winston, 1969. (a)

Carkhuff, R. R. *Helping and human relations.* Vol. 2: *Practice and research.* New York: Holt, Rinehart & Winston, 1969. (b)

Collins, J. D. Experimental evaluation of a six-month conjugal therapy and relationship enhancement program. In B. G. Guerney, Jr. (Ed.), *Relationship Enhancement: Skill-training programs for therapy, problem prevention, and enrichment.* San Francisco: Jossey-Bass, 1977.

D'Augelli, A. R., Deyss, C. S., Guerney, B. G., Jr., Hershenberg, B., & Sborofsky, S. Interpersonal skill training for dating couples: An evaluation of an educational mental health service. *Journal of Counseling Psychology,* 1974, *21*(5), 385–389.

Ely, A. L., Guerney, B. G., Jr., & Stover, L. Efficacy of the training phase of conjugal therapy. *Psychotherapy: Theory, Research, and Practice,* 1973, *10*(3), 201–207.

Fisher, B. F. Identifying and meeting needs of formerly-married people through a divorce adjustment seminar (Doctoral dissertation, University of Northern Colorado, 1977). *Dissertation Abstracts International,* 1977, 37/11A, 7036. (University Microfilms No. 77-11, 057.)

Ginsberg, B. G. Parent-adolescent relationship development program. In B. G. Guerney, Jr. (Ed.), *Relationship Enhancement: Skill-training programs for therapy, problem prevention, and enrichment.* San Francisco: Jossey-Bass, 1977.

Ginsberg, B. G., & Vogelsong, E. L. Premarital relationship improvement by maximizing empathy and self-disclosure: The PRIMES program. In B. G. Guerney, Jr. (Ed.), *Relationship Enhancement: Skill-training programs for therapy, problem prevention, and enrichment.* San Francisco: Jossey-Bass, 1977.

Guerney, B. G., Jr. Filial Therapy used as a treatment method for disturbed children. *Evaluation,* 1976, *3,* 34–35.

Guerney, B. G., Jr. *Relationship Enhancement: Skill-training programs for therapy, problem prevention, and enrichment.* San Francisco: Jossey-Bass, 1977. (a)

Guerney, B. G., Jr. Should teachers treat illiteracy, hypocalligraphy, and dysmathematica? *Canadian Counsellor,* 1977, *12*(1), 9–14. (b)

Guerney, B. G., Jr. The great potential of an educational skill-training model in problem prevention. *Journal of Clinical Child Psychology,* 1979, *3*(2), 84–86.

Guerney, B. G., Jr. The delivery of mental health services: Spiritual vs. medical vs. educational models. In T. R. Vallance & R. M. Sabre (Eds.), *Mental health services in transition: A policy sourcebook.* New York: Human Sciences Press, 1982.

Guerney, B. G., Jr., Coufal, J., & Vogelsong, E. Relationship Enhancement versus a traditional approach to therapeutic/preventative/enrichment parent-adolescent programs. *Journal of Consulting and Clinical Psychology,* 1981, *49,* 927–929.

Guerney, B. G., Jr., Guerney, L., & Stollak, G. The potential advantages of changing from a medical to an educational model in practicing psychology. *Interpersonal Development,* 1971/72, *2*(4), 238–245.

Guerney, B. G., Jr., & Merriam, M. L. Toward a democratic elementary school classroom. *Elementary School Journal,* 1972, *72,* 372–383.

Guerney, B. G., Jr., Stollak, G. E., & Guerney, L. A format for a new mode of psychological practice; or, how to escape a zombie. *Counseling Psychologist,* 1970, *2*(2), 97–104.

Guerney, B. G., Jr., Stollak, G. E., & Guerney, L. The practicing psychologist as educator—an alternative to the medical practitioner model. *Professional Psychology,* 1971, *2*(3), 276–282.

Guerney, B. G., Jr., & Stover, L. *Filial Therapy: Final report on MH 1826401.* Mimeographed report, State College, Pa., 1971.

Guerney, B. G., Jr., Stover, L., & Andronico, M. P. On educating the disadvantaged parent to motivate children for learning: A filial approach. *Community Mental Health Journal,* 1967, *3,* 66–72.

Guerney, B. G., Jr., & Vogelsong, E. *Relationship Enhancement cassette tapes.* Individual and Family Consultation Center, Pennsylvania State University, 1981.

Guerney, B. G., Jr., Vogelsong, E., & Coufal, J. Relationship Enhancement versus a traditional treatment: Follow up and booster effects. Manuscript in preparation, 1981.

Guerney, B. G., Jr., Vogelsong, E. L., & Glynn, S. *Evaluation of the Family Counseling Unit of the Cambria County Probation Bureau.* Mimeographed report. State College, Pa.: Institute for the Development of Emotional and Life Skills, 1977.

Guerney, L. F. *Parenting: A skills training manual.* State College, Pa.: Institute for the Development of Emotional and Life Skills, 1979.

Harrell, J., & Guerney, B., Jr. Training married couples in conflict negotiation skills. In D. Olson (Ed.), *Treating relationships.* Lake Mills, Iowa: Graphic, 1976.

Hatch, E. An empirical study of a teacher training program in empathic responsiveness and democratic decision making. Unpublished doctoral dissertation, Pennsylvania State University, 1973.

Hatch, E., & Guerney, B. G., Jr. A pupil enhancement program. *Personnel and Guidance Journal,* 1975, *54,* 102–105.

Haynes, L. A., & Avery, A. W. Training adolescents in self-disclosure and empathy skills. *Journal of Counseling Psychology,* 1979, *26*(6), 526–530.

Jessee, R., & Guerney, B. G., Jr. A comparison of Gestalt and Relationship Enhancement treatments with married couples. *American Journal of Family Therapy,* 1981, *9,* 31–41.

Knox, D. *Marriage happiness: A behavioral approach to counseling.* Champaign, Ill.: Research Press, 1971.

Leary, T. *Interpersonal diagnosis of personality.* New York: Ronald Press, 1957.

Locke, H. J., Sabagh, G., & Thomas, M. Correlates of primary communication and empathy. *Research Studies of the State College of Washington,* 1956, *24,* 116–124.

Locke, H. J., & Williamson, R. C. Marital adjustment: A factor analysis study. *American Sociological Review,* 1958, *28,* 562–569.

Merriam, M. L., & Guerney, B. G., Jr. Creating a democratic elementary school classroom: A pilot training program involving teachers, administrators, and parents. *Contemporary Education,* 1973, *45*(1), 34–42.

Most, R. K. An exploratory program to train lay couples to conduct a marriage preparation intervention based on Relationship Enhancement skills. Unpublished doctoral dissertation, Pennsylvania State University, 1980.

Navran, L. Communication and adjustment in marriage. *Family Process,* 1967, *6,* 173–184.

Oxman, L. The effectiveness of Filial Therapy: A controlled study. Unpublished doctoral dissertation, Rutgers University, 1971.

Rappaport, A. F. Conjugal Relationship Enhancement program. In D. H. Olson (Ed.), *Treating relationships.* Lake Mills, Iowa: Graphic, 1976.

Rappaport, A. F., & Harrell, J. A behavioral exchange model for marital counseling. *Family Coordinator,* 1972, *21,* 203–212.

Ridley, C. A., Avery, A. W., Dent, J., & Harrell, J. The effects of Relationship Enhancement and problem solving programs on perceived heterosexual competence. *Family Therapy,* 1981, *8,* 60–66.

Ridley, C. A., Avery, A. W., Harrell, J. E., Leslie, L., & Dent, J. A. Conflict management: A premarital training program in mutual problem solving. *American Journal of Family Therapy,* in press.

Ridley, C. A., Jorgensen, S. R., Morgan, A. C., & Avery, A. W. Relationship Enhancement with premarital couples: An assessment of effects on relationship quality. *American Journal of Family Therapy,* in press.

Rocks, T. The effectiveness of communication skills training with under-achieving, low-communicating secondary school students and their teachers. Unpublished doctoral dissertation, Pennsylvania State University, 1980.

Ross, E. Comparative effectiveness of Relationship Enhancement vs. therapists' preferred therapy on marital adjustment. Unpublished doctoral dissertation, Pennsylvania State University, 1981.

Schlein, S. Training dating couples in empathic and open communication: An experimental evaluation of a potential preventive mental health program. Unpublished doctoral dissertation, Pennsylvania University, 1971.

Sensué, M. E. Filial Therapy follow-up study: Effects on parental acceptance and child adjustment. Unpublished doctoral dissertation, Pennsylvania State University, 1981.

Shannon, J., & Guerney, B. G., Jr. Interpersonal effects of interpersonal behavior. *Journal of Personality and Social Psychology,* 1973, *26*(1), 142–150.

Shapiro, J., Krauss, H., & Truax, C. Therapeutic conditions and disclosure beyond the therapeutic encounter. *Journal of Counseling Psychology,* 1969, *16,* 290–294.

Stuart, R. B. Operant-interpersonal treatment for marital discord. *Journal of Consulting and Clinical Psychology,* 1969, *33,* 675–682. (a)

Stuart, R. B. Token reinforcement in marital therapy. In R. D. Rubin & C. M. Franks (Eds.), *Advances in behavior therapy, 1968.* New York: Academic Press, 1969. (b)

Sullivan, H. S. *Conceptions of modern psychiatry.* Washington, D.C.: William Alanson White Psychiatric Foundation, 1947.

Sywulak, A. E. The effect of Filial Therapy on parental acceptance and child adjustment. Unpublished doctoral dissertation, Pennsylvania State University, 1977.

Thiessen, J. D., Avery, A. W., & Joanning, H. Facilitating postdivorce adjustment among women: A communication skills training approach. *Journal of Divorce,* 1980, *4,* 35–44.

Tubesing, D. A., & Tubesing, N. L. *Tune in: Empathy training workshop.* Milwaukee: Listening Group, 1973.

Vogelsong, E. L. Relationship Enhancement Training for children. *Elementary School Guidance and Counseling,* 1978, *12*(4), 272–279.

Weiss, R. S. Transition states and other stressful situations: Their nature and programs for their management. In G. Caplan & R. Killilea (Eds.), *Support systems and mutual help: Multidisciplinary explorations.* New York: Grune & Stratton, 1976.

Welch, G. J., & Granvold, D. K. Seminars for separated/divorced: An educational approach to postdivorce adjustment. *Journal of Sex and Marital Therapy,* 1977, *3,* 31–39.

Wieman, R. J. Conjugal relationship modification and reciprocal reinforcement: A comparison of treatments for marital discord. Unpublished doctoral dissertation, Pennsylvania State University, 1973.

CHAPTER TEN

Microcounseling: A Metamodel for Counseling, Therapy, Business, and Medical Interviews

Allen E. Ivey is professor and director of counseling psychology at the University of Massachusetts, Amherst. A Harvard University Ed.D., he has been president of the Division of Counseling Psychology of the American Psychological Association. His work in Microcounseling has taken him from the Arctic to Australia and Sweden, where he has worked with a variety of problems concerning communication among different peoples. He is the author of *Microcounseling* (with J. Drasgow and J. Authier) and six other books and more than 120 articles.

Allen E. Ivey

Maryanne Galvin is director of the School Consultation Team in the Division of Child Psychiatry, Tufts New England Medical Center, Boston. She has been an assistant professor in the Department of Counselor Education at the University of New Hampshire Graduate School. Galvin has published in the areas of creative problem solving with children, interpersonal skills training, psychoeducation, and mental health classroom consultation. She has worked as an early-childhood educator and is licensed as a school psychologist and as a counseling psychologist.

Maryanne Galvin

The Microcounseling program developed by Allen Ivey has had an enormous impact on the skills training field. Rooted in social learning theory, Microcounseling teaches specific interviewing skills ("microskills") one at a time in a workshop format. Videotaped feedback is used to enhance skill development. In this chapter Ivey and Galvin discuss the need for trainers to develop cross-cultural sensitivity. They claim that the Microcounseling model is transtheoretical and can be effectively used to train counselors operating within a variety of therapeutic frameworks. Ivey has told me that he encourages trainers to develop their own training tapes—thus he seeks to give away the training function as well as the skills of Microcounseling.

Through a step-by-step instructional program we have found it possible to teach beginning therapists and counselors high levels of functional skills in interviewing in a relatively short time. Within 45 hours of training they can engage in elementary Rogerian counseling, psychodynamic dream analysis, and assertion training. Further, we have found that the underlying structure of the interview is quite similar whether the content concerns interviewing, medicine, business, or law. We have found it possible to train business managers to conduct assertion training with their employees within a three-day program.

These are strong statements. We are impressed by the power of the Microcounseling model. We believe it raises interesting new questions for the training of interviewers, for the transfer of communication skills from field to field, and for cross-cultural communication. The purpose of this chapter is to describe the Microcounseling model, originally developed to train novice counselors and now expanded to many fields. The bulk of this discussion will focus on Microcounseling as a counseling technology and method, but some discussion will follow on the broader applications and implications of the model.

MICROCOUNSELING TRAINING

In a review of psychotherapy research (1968) Cartwright depicted the educational process for training novice clinicians as being in need of systematic evaluation. Microtraining and Microcounseling techniques, a systematic design for interviewing training, have done much to fill that vacuum; they have supplemented traditional and experiential/didactic training. The Microcounseling model is unique in that it combines theoretical and practical training techniques in a systematic way; these skills are learned not by chance but through practice of clearly delineated interviewer behaviors. The training model takes beginning counselors and therapists through a series of didactic and experiential exercises with the expectation that within 45 hours of training they will be able to engage competently in a broad base of approaches, including psychodynamic dream analysis and rational-emotive therapy. One of the major goals of the Microcounseling training is to generate multiple responses. The underlying construct of intentionality is defined as follows:

> The person who acts with intentionality has a sense of capability. He or she can generate alternative behaviors in a given situation and "approach" a problem from different vantage points. The intentional, fully functioning individual is not bound to one course of action but can respond in the moment to changing life situations and look forward to longer term goals [Ivey & Simek-Downing, 1980, p. 8].

This systematic approach to teaching basic skills in therapy begins with a simple exercise. A brief video vignette, in which a client talks directly from the screen and presents an immediate concern or problem, is viewed by all. The tape is stopped, and students are asked to respond to the question "What would you say next to this particular client?" Students propose a wide variety of responses, most of them potentially useful. We then begin our instruction with the basic and critical instruction that different people respond to the same stimulus differently and that, depending on context, *any of the responses on the part of the therapist-in-training may be appropriate.*

The course of training then moves to an in-depth examination of specific *skills* used by therapists and counselors in many domains. The very familiar skills of open and closed questions, paraphrasing, reflecting feelings, giving directives, and interpreting are each taught in a single skill approach. The Microcounseling format for one-at-a-time learning is as follows:

1. Brief introduction to the skill.
2. Viewing of a video modeling tape of an "expert" therapist demonstrating the skill.
3. Presentation of reading material elaborating on the concepts just viewed.
4. Immediate practice of that skill in small groups with video- or audiotape equipment.

That is, theory and practice of the skill are demonstrated, followed by immediate application by the student. Student groups ranging from 12 to 60 or more have participated in the single-skill training.

Figure 10-1 presents several skills of the Microcounseling paradigm. In approximately two to four hours students learn each of these skills in class workshops. Level of competency is directly correlated with the amount of time students engage in actual practice with the skill (Berg & Stone, 1980). Students also learn to focus their responses on the client in a variety of ways. For example, a client may say "I just had an abortion." The counselor may then focus on the topic or problem ("Tell me about the abortion"), on the client ("You seem to be really worried"), on others ("What do your parents know?"), and so on. What the client says next is strongly influenced by the subject or theme of the counselor's lead. The beginning student attains full mastery when he or she is able to focus the client in any of these areas at will. The microskill model goes a step beyond more traditional theoretical training models in presenting the empathy dimensions (confrontation, concreteness, respect, warmth) in more operational terms. For example, students are taught to notice client or therapist verb tense and to move toward immediacy (present tense) in their work. Interventions posed in the present tense tend to be most powerful, although not appropriate at *all* times.

In approximately half of the 45-hour training period, students are engaged in the experience of learning the basic attending skills as well as the concepts of focus and empathy in the interview. Through the use of videotape, systematic observation of the nonverbal dimensions of communication is stressed. Students use small groups to practice giving and receiving direct feedback from taped interview sessions. They learn to rate and classify specific interviewer behaviors. The combination of the clearly defined single-skill approach and the mechanics of video feedback training with a high level of observational skills provides impressive information about their own and the client's nonverbal behavior in the session.

An additional component in the Microcounseling model emphasizes utilizing the remainder of the course to apply skills in different theoretical orientations.

THE ACTIVE INGREDIENTS OF MICROCOUNSELING: APPLYING SKILLS METHODS TO ALTERNATIVE THEORIES OF THERAPY

Therapists with different orientations tend to use different skills and manifest empathy in various forms. For example, Figure 10-2 reveals that classical, nondirective therapists tend to use paraphrases and reflection of feeling, while psychoanalytically oriented therapists tend to use the skill of interpretation. In teaching the

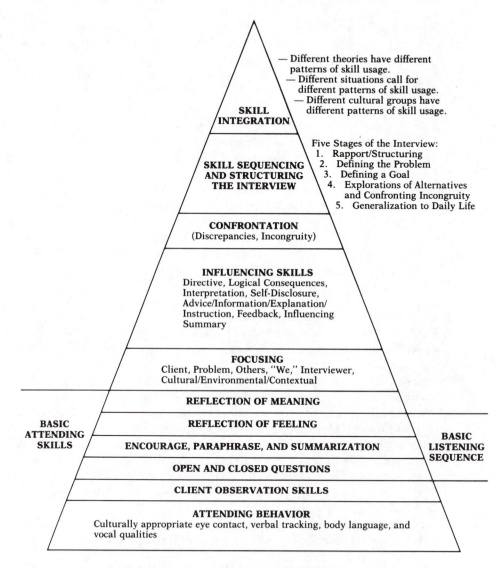

The following appears within the pyramid figure:

— Different theories have different patterns of skill usage.
— Different situations call for different patterns of skill usage.
— Different cultural groups have different patterns of skill usage.

SKILL INTEGRATION

Five Stages of the Interview:
1. Rapport/Structuring
2. Defining the Problem
3. Defining a Goal
4. Explorations of Alternatives and Confronting Incongruity
5. Generalization to Daily Life

SKILL SEQUENCING AND STRUCTURING THE INTERVIEW

CONFRONTATION
(Discrepancies, Incongruity)

INFLUENCING SKILLS
Directive, Logical Consequences, Interpretation, Self-Disclosure, Advice/Information/Explanation/ Instruction, Feedback, Influencing Summary

FOCUSING
Client, Problem, Others, "We," Interviewer, Cultural/Environmental/Contextual

REFLECTION OF MEANING

REFLECTION OF FEELING

ENCOURAGE, PARAPHRASE, AND SUMMARIZATION

OPEN AND CLOSED QUESTIONS

CLIENT OBSERVATION SKILLS

ATTENDING BEHAVIOR
Culturally appropriate eye contact, verbal tracking, body language, and vocal qualities

BASIC ATTENDING SKILLS

BASIC LISTENING SEQUENCE

1. Attending behavior and client observation skills form the foundation of effective communication, but are not always the appropriate place to begin training.
2. The basic listening sequence of attending skills (open and closed questions, encouraging, paraphrasing, reflection of feeling, and summarization) is often found in effective interviewing, management, social work, physician diagnostic sessions, and many other settings.

Figure 10-1. The microskill hierarchy. *(Copyright 1982 Allen E. Ivey, Box 641, N. Amherst, Mass. 01059.)*

Theory	Microskills: Quantitative dimensions											Focus						Empathy: Qualitative dimensions								
	Closed question	Open question	Min. encourage	Paraphrase	Reflect. feeling	Summarization	Directive	Express content	Express feeling	Inf. summarization	Interpretation	Helpee	Others	Topic	Helper	Mutual	Cultural envir.	Primary empathy	Additive empathy	Positive regard	Respect	Warmth	Concreteness	Immediacy	Confrontation	Genuineness
Psychodynamic	◑	○	○	◑	◑	○	◑	◑	◑	◑	●	●	○	◑	◑	◑	○	○	●	○	○	◑	○	P	○	◑
Behavioral	●	●	○	○	○	○	●	●	◑	○	◑	●	○	●	◑	◑	○	○	●	○	○	◑	●	F	○	◑
Nondirective	◑	◑	○	●	●	○	◑	◑	◑	◑	◑	●	◑	◑	◑	◑	◑	●	◑	●	●	●	◑	H	○	○
Modern Rogerian	◑	◑	○	●	●	○	◑	◑	◑	○	◑	●	◑	◑	○	◑	●	◑	●	○	●	●	●	◑	H	○	●
Exist.-Humanistic	◑	○	◑	○	○	○	◑	◑	◑	○	◑	●	●	◑	◑	○	○	○	○	○	●	○	◑	H	○	○
Gestalt	○	○	◑	◑	◑	◑	◑	●	○	◑	◑	●	●	◑	◑	◑	◑	◑	●	○	◑	◑	◑	H	●	○
Transpersonal	○	○	○	○	○	○	◑	●	●	○	○	●	●	○	○	○	●	○	●	●	●	○	○	F	○	●
Trait & Factor	○	●	○	○	○	○	○	◑	●	○	○	●	◑	●	◑	◑	○	○	○	○	○	○	●	F	○	○
Rational-Emotive	○	○	◑	◑	◑	◑	◑	○	●	◑	○	●	◑	●	◑	◑	○	○	●	○	○	◑	○	PH	○	◑
Trans. Analysis	◑	○	○	○	◑	○	○	●	◑	●	○	●	◑	◑	◑	◑	◑	○	●	○	◑	◑	◑	PH	●	○
Reality Therapy	○	○	○	○	○	○	○	●	○	○	○	●	◑	●	○	◑	●	○	○	●	○	○	○	PF	○	●
Strategic	○	○	◑	◑	◑	◑	●	◑	◑	◑	○	●	◑	○	◑	◑	◑	○	●	○	◑	◑	●	PH	●	◑

Legend:

● = Most frequently used dimensions

○ = Frequently used dimensions

◑ = Dimension may be used but is not a central aspect of theory

P = Primary emphasis on past-tense immediacy

H = Primary emphasis on present-tense immediacy

F = Primary emphasis on future-tense immediacy

Figure 10-2. Twelve counseling and psychotherapy theories: their use of quantitative, qualitative, and focus skills. *(From* Counseling and Psychotherapy: Skills, Theories, and Practice, *by Allen E. Ivey and Lynn Simek-Downing, © 1980, pp. 87, 454–457. Reprinted by permission of Prentice-Hall, Inc., Englewood Cliffs, N.J.)*

theoretical approach, key theoretical points are stressed, followed by observation of a therapist demonstrating that therapy. For example, the concepts of self-actualization, positive regard, and so on are presented in lecture form. Students then observe a film of Carl Rogers demonstrating these concepts, and they are then able to analyze the behavior of the therapist and note the sequence of skill use and any special techniques and sequences before breaking into small groups for video- and audiotape practice in which they attempt to play the role of Carl Rogers.

As in the fixed-role therapy of George Kelly (1955), once a particular role has been identified and the key constructs associated with that role explicated, students can test out that role in a simulated situation without endangering real clients. Furthermore, they can determine the role's appropriateness to their own role repertoire. The power and elegance of this simple social-learning model result in the production of surprising levels of competence.

For example, students given an elementary introduction to experiential Freudian techniques learn to generate on their own such concepts as unconscious material, heretofore usually "learned" in lecture. Students view a videotape about a client's dream in which the therapist uses the microskills of closed and open questions, paraphrasing and reflection of feeling, and summarization to draw out the details of the dream. The client is then directed to free-associate to a childhood memory; again, the basic listening skills are used to obtain specifics of the early experience. Trainees who role-played clients then transfer this set of theoretical constructs and skill sequences to practice sessions.

This simple but elegant model of teaching and learning allows students to master complex techniques quickly and efficiently. Interestingly, they spontaneously start generating theoretical constructs on their own that are part of the different theories. They seem to have become part of the theory, rather than mere "learners."

Yet, the ever-present question remains—is this real or is it a clinical artifact? The following statements, based on clinical experience and data from previous studies, attest to the efficacy of the Microcounseling model.

1. Students are able to recognize the various skills and behaviors of a wide range of therapists and classify them with accuracy.
2. Students are able to demonstrate a wide array of therapeutic alternatives on videotape or audiotape by the end of the course of training.
3. Students do improve and change their patterns of skill use and empathy during the training period. If they are able to practice and use learning skills in a supervised practice, they tend to increase their abilities over time. However, if skills are not practiced, they will be lost owing to lack of use.
4. The language patterns and conceptual levels of clients working with our students appear to change as a result of our training.
5. The complete training package of lecture, video model, experiential exercises, readings, and practice appears to be effective. Practice with the single skills to *mastery* levels appears to be most central to development of competence.

The last stage of the course consists of a presentation by each student of a half-hour typescript exemplifying his or her therapeutic style, classifying interviewing leads, noting focus and empathic dimensions, and discussing theoretical constructs used. A brief selection from an interview typescript presented by one of the students appears at the end of this chapter.

SKILL SEQUENCING AND THE TRANSFERRING OF MICROSKILLS TO ALTERNATIVE SETTINGS

Perhaps the most interesting and exciting applications of the Microcounseling model lie outside the field of counseling and psychotherapy. Microcounseling has been transferred, for example, to business, nursing, social work, drug education, alcohol counseling, and community hotline volunteers. The framework appears to be useful and effective in many settings.

What it is that makes for transfer? Observation of business interviews has revealed that the effective manager tends to begin discussion of a complex issue with an open question (for example, "Could you tell me about the general issues surrounding your problem on the production line?") followed by closed questions to diagnose the problem (Ivey & Litterer, 1979). Further, the manager often facilitates conversation by head nods and minimal encourages, reflection of feeling, and paraphrasing. Before coming up with a response to the employee, the manager often summarizes the discussion. In contrast, ineffective managers faced with the same production-line problem may say "Do this . . ." and fail to diagnose the problem fully.

This pattern of conversation—the basic listening sequence—appears among many counselors and therapists. They often begin their interviews with open questions followed by closed questions for diagnosis, and the same pattern of encouraging, paraphrasing, reflection of feeling, and summarization appears. Again, this pattern manifests itself in the physician's interview, in volunteer counseling, and, often, in effective sales.

Ivey and Litterer have developed a management training program, FACE TO FACE. This program takes managers through the microskills hierarchy in a three-day experiential workshop, and by the end of the third day, managers are able to diagnose their own and their employees' communication patterns and conduct assertion training sessions. Assertion training involves a basic pattern of skill sequencing. Once a person has mastered the basic skills of Microcounseling, it is possible to adapt the skills to many sequences associated with different situations. In management, for example, a disciplinary interview and a performance review require different skill sequences, and yet the underlying skill dimensions remain the same. Managers are taught to adapt the skills of communication in a variety of ways to achieve their objectives.

In a similar fashion, Microcounseling can be used as a psychoeducational program with clients. Psychiatric patients (Ivey, 1973) have participated in the microskills model. "Therapy" consists in skills training, and patients move up the skill hierarchy much as counselors and business managers do. Parents, children, and families have also participated in microskills training with demonstrable effect and impact. The communication skills of counseling and therapy are too important to be confined to helping professionals. Microskills at their best are to be shared with the lay public.

Cross-cultural implications of microskills should also be considered. Work with native populations in the North American Arctic, with Australian aborigines, with guest workers in Germany and Sweden, and with counselors and managers in Mexico and Puerto Rico has revealed that the microskills model works well across cultures (Marsella & Pedersen, 1981). However, skills and skill sequences change in different cultures. Questions, for example, are relatively ineffective with many populations. Nonverbal communication styles also vary.

TOWARD A METATHEORY OF COUNSELING AND THERAPY

In the past few pages we have tried to summarize our training program and its impact on our student populations and on others. We now turn our attention to an examination of *why* we do what we do, through a theoretical explanation of these procedures.

We have recently proposed a comprehensive model of counseling and therapy (Ivey, 1981) that underlies the training model discussed here. The major construct defined earlier as *intentionality*—that is, generating multiple responses—is the backbone of this particular approach to training. Because intentionality exists in a system, one must also have an awareness of *context,* be it cultural, environmental, or situational. Two premises demonstrate this thinking:

Premise 1. All theoretical approaches, group or individual, are ultimately concerned with developing intentionality. Each theoretical approach is concerned with freeing people from immobility (tight or excessively loose constructs, polarities, splits, irrational ideas, discrepancies between idealized self and real self, and so on).

Premise 2. Basic to understanding of the client and the psychotherapy process are the person/environment transaction and the effects that the person and the environment have on each other. The therapist serves as an environment for the client and the client as an environment for the therapist.

It is the mutual interaction between client and therapist that provides the context for the development of intentionality or immobility; such interaction, in turn, is affected by cultural, environmental, and situational concepts. What is culturally or environmentally appropriate will vary from situation to situation. Consequently, we have a strong commitment to developing increased potential for action between our students and their clients. Our students exist in a sociocultural system and provide an environment for those with whom they will work. Because we believe that no one theory provides a "true" answer, we encourage students to develop maximum options so that they can respond in ways that are culturally appropriate for clients.

An array of assumptions and accompanying corollaries has been developed (Ivey & Simek-Downing, 1980) and may be described as beginning steps toward a metatheory of counseling and psychotherapy. Drawing once again from the previously mentioned major premises, a few key points of this framework are summarized below:

Assumption 1. The major theories of individual and group psychotherapy may be considered systematic constructions for construing the world and acting more intentionally. These systematic constructions (for example, the unconscious, stimulus-response, analysis *of* the group, *in* the group, *by* the group) result in alternative actions by the therapist.

Assumption 1 clearly illustrates why the term *metatheoretical* is used to describe this approach. By using metatheoretical concepts instead of eclecticism as a background, we are given the opportunity to search for commonalities among theories and to examine why a certain theory may or may not work. But, most important, we are reminded that each theory remains as only one construction of reality and not reality itself.

Through the use of metaphor in instruction, we are able to instruct students in the key constructs or concepts of each theory. Students quickly grasp the key metaphors of transpersonal psychology, of group systems, or of psychoanalysis, for example, and are then able to generate many remaining constructs.

Clients, in fact, tend to construct reality much as therapists do. Depending on the environmental context provided by their therapist, clients may be expected to generate behavioral, existential, or group constructs. The following assumption is very important, considering this observation:

Assumption 2. The client may be expected to enter the interview or group situation with a basic construction of the situation he or she experiences. A task of the therapist is to examine both surface and deep structure for overt and covert meanings from the client's point of view.

Figure 10-2 delineates some of the process dimensions discussed in the following assumptions:

Assumption 3. Different family and cultural backgrounds will lead both clients and therapists to generate different constructs and sentences.

Assumption 4. All counselors and therapists and their clients use basic microskills of communication. Therapists of differing schools tend to use different patterns of skills, as do people from differing cultural groups.

Assumption 5. Empathy, a foundation stone of therapy, manifests itself differently among different therapists and different cultures.

Assumption 6. The structure of the interview or group process may be described as analogous to the decision-making process: defining the problem, generating alternatives, and commitment to an action or decision. Counseling and therapy may be viewed as a creative act. The therapist, with the client, examines data from the client's life, and together they reorganize pieces and create new sentences, constructs, and meanings. Different cultures, of course, will tend to make different decisions.

On mastery of the skills observed in these assumptions, students are able to proceed to direct contact with a wide array of theoretical systems. These last three assumptions are key instructional tools for assuring understanding and mastery of the underlying process of therapy. Moving one step further, as students examine the structures and methods of other cultures, they are better able to communicate effectively. For example, in many schools of psychotherapy questions are considered a basic skill. In many Asian and Arctic settings, however, questions are considered intrusive and rude. Through more thorough examination of typical help-giving patterns in different cultures, we will be able to respond with new and clearer modes of training.

Assumption 7. (May be described as an action synthesis of the preceding premises and assumptions.) Different theories of psychotherapy, group or individual, will be of varying degrees of utility for people who present alternative kinds of treatment problems, come from varying cultural backgrounds, and have special histories of person/environment transactions.

The question "Which treatment for which individual under what conditions?" has drawn an accumulation of research and theory indicating that systematic planning of appropriate treatment modalities may indeed be possible (for example, Goldstein & Stein, 1976). Once a differential diagnosis is made, certain treatment modalities may be ruled out, while others are of more promise. In response to our opening premise, it will suffice to note that data and theory are reaching a state such that chance eclectic answers to this question can no longer be considered satisfactory; nor can application of one theory to all clients be considered professionally ethical. The nature of the problem, issues of the client's individual and cultural background, and the way the client construes the problem are all important in such differential diagnosis. Space does not allow elaboration on this issue.

The preceding is a brief summary of this metatheoretical approach. Traditional diagnostic labels—"schizophrenia," "anxiety reaction," and so on—are only partly helpful in implementing a treatment plan.

Honest diagnosis requires examination of the total content of the therapist and client. We have found George Kelly's five-step model a very useful tool in developing a broad-based assessment of treatment options.

1. What is the client's problem?
2. What are the client's constructs for viewing the world?
3. What is the client's situational and environmental context?
4. What are the therapist's basic theories and constructs?
5. What is to be done?

It is obvious that a client suffering from depression who comes from a low-income area and has poor language skills is unlikely to benefit from long-term analytic therapy. Likewise, a "successful," middle-class person suffering from alienation is likely to have little interest in behavior modification techniques, with the possible exception of cognitive restructuring. Again, the basic question "What therapeutic environment, group or individual, is most appropriate given the needs of a unique client?" demands our attention and resolutions.

APPLICATIONS

The theoretical framework for the psychoeducational model of teaching emerged from a need to efficiently and effectively help people to cope with their environments and themselves (Ivey & Alschuler, 1973). It was born from the positivistic stance that all people are able to learn effective means of operating in the world and that these skills can be taught to all (Authier, Gustafson, Guerney, & Kasdorf, 1975). Carkhuff (1971) views the teaching of communication skills as an essential mode of treatment in mental health for both laypeople and professionals. Research in the psychoeducational model covers the areas of teaching communication skills to incarcerated persons, paraprofessionals, counseling students, and professional psychologists.

Donk (1972) first used a modified Microcounseling workshop to teach hospitalized inpatients the skills of attending behavior. As patients learned the new interpersonal skills of listening, questioning, and giving structured feedback, they came to be viewed as generally more positive in communication and overall ward behavior. Ivey (1973) taught attending skills to mental-hospital inpatients and found significant improvement in relational skills, lessening of depressive symptoms, and an increase in communication skills. These findings support Carkhuff's (1971) theory that teaching individual communication skills can be used as a treatment modality. Pierce and Drasgow (1969) used microtraining techniques to heighten interpersonal functioning of psychotic inpatients and found significant improvement in facilitative functioning. The group they trained in Microcounseling showed a lessening of psychotic symptoms and were vastly more communicative than the control groups treated with more traditional forms of psychotherapy, drug therapy, and group therapy.

Chilsom (1977) offered training in a systematized program of human relations both to graduate students in counseling and to public offenders in jails. There was a significant difference between the pre- and postscores of the offenders' communicational functioning. Chilsom concluded that both graduate students and public offenders can learn and can demonstrate helping skills after only 50 hours of training. Recently a correctional-officer training program for institutions has been developed by Chilsom.

Ivey and Gluckstern (1974, 1976) designed leader and participant manuals for teaching basic attending and influencing skills and created workshop designs that are easy to apply to any nonprofessional or professional setting. A comprehensive survey on the research supporting each construct and the reliability and validity of teaching each skill is available in Ivey and Authier (1978). Scoring for effective use of each skill has been researched by Sherrard (1973), who found that group leaders with different styles and orientations will use different microskills in a variety of ways.

Bizer (1972) found Microcounseling training effective in teaching communication skills to parents. Goshko (1973) taught Microcounseling skills to elementary school children to increase their communication skills. Microcounseling training was used by Andes (1974) as a teaching program for a couples' relationship-building workshop. Terrell (1977) used Microcounseling training for all the applicants for the position of orientation leader at a university and found an increase in attending behavior after training and a significant reduction in the numbers of eye-contact breaks and of arm, hand, leg, and foot movements.

This research has been validated on a population of nonprofessionals, and the results are successful. The individual skill approach is quickly becoming one of the most widely used and vital resources for professional and counselor training. The next set of studies will cover Microcounseling as applied to the training of counselors and therapists.

Bergin and Garfield (1971) have voiced concern over the lack of adequate measures for evaluating counselors' effectiveness. Many methods for training counselors and psychotherapists have emerged, including the use of group therapy (Eiben & Clark, 1973), practice experiences (Silverman, 1972), didactic and effective training (Pearson, 1973), and others that are more fully reviewed by Matarazzo (1971).

Over 150 data-based studies are available on the microskills model (Kasdorf & Gustafson, 1978). The initial thrust of microtraining research has been to prove that, indeed, counseling skills and qualities can be taught, learned, and demonstrated regardless of theoretical orientation or school of training. The first microskills study (Ivey, Normington, Miller, Morrill, & Haase, 1968) revealed that beginning counselors could learn the basic skills of attending, reflection of feeling, and summarization using this model. This kind of study has been replicated many times, illustrating the construct validity of the framework.

Higgins, Ivey, and Uhlemann (1973) instructed students in the interpersonal skill of direct-mutual communication. Direct-mutual communication is the here-and-now communication between people who are committed to the person they are communicating with and able to be truly themselves in relationship to that person. Significant results showed that Microcounseling can be used to train students in extremely complex interpersonal skills that somewhat resemble a peak experience.

Haase, Forsyth, Julius, and Lee (1971) demonstrated that clients receiving pre-counseling training in the microskill of expression of feeling expressed more feelings in an initial counseling interview than clients who had received no training. Haase and DiMattia (1970) taught Microcounseling skills to paraprofessionals to learn clinical counseling skills and demonstrated that the training was effective in teaching attending skills, reflection of feeling, and expression of feeling.

Mihalovich (1976) trained undergraduates in a beginning counseling course in the Microcounseling skills. Students trained in Microcounseling skills emitted fewer verbal responses and experienced less behavioral anxiety after training than did controls who received no training. Belle (1974) divided 30 graduate students majoring in counseling into two instructional groups, one receiving Microcounseling training and the other receiving traditional didactic training. Results showed that the Microcounseling group did significantly better in verbal response, and clients rated that group as significantly better than the didactic group.

Arnold (1976) assigned 24 graduate students to two teaching conditions; one group received traditional attention training and one received Microcounseling training. Significant results showed Microcounseling training to be the more effective method for teaching open-ended questioning techniques.

Gormally (1975) trained undergraduate students in individual skills and video feedback models and compared them with a control group receiving no training. The skills and video feedback groups showed significant increases in helper references to nonverbal behavior and empathy and in self-disclosures and questioning, compared with controls. Shea (1975) studied 30 graduate students who had received two different field practicums. One group received five weeks of Microcounseling training with supervised field work. The other group received only supervised field practice. Compared with controls, the Microcounseling training group showed increased strengths in field practice (as judged from taped interviews), in confrontation behavior, and in encouraging clients to action.

McIvroy (1976) studied 24 male undergraduates enrolled in a psychology class. They were divided into three treatment groups: one received Microcounseling instruction, one received Microcounseling instruction plus empathy training, and the third received a group-therapy experience. Significant results showed those trained in group therapy to be exceedingly high in the use of empathy, compared with the two other groups. However, the group trained in Microcounseling and empathy showed significantly higher levels of discrimination of helping responses than the group-therapy section.

CRITIQUE OF THE MICROCOUNSELING APPROACH

The studies just reviewed are but a sample of the over 150 data-based studies summarized by Kasdorf and Gustafson (1978), but they do show a positive view of the merits of Microcounseling training programs for both teaching and research. More recent studies lead to an understanding of the deficits of this training model as well as to suggestions for further development. Criticisms of this model indicate that a single-skill approach is a rather reductionist model. Further, critics claim there is an inherent danger in the Microcounseling model if people adhere too rigidly to the framework as presented without broadening to eliminate cultural biases. We agree that caution must be taken in applying this or any other model rigidly. Users must adapt and expand the model as closely to their population as possible.

At present, the majority of studies showing empirical support for the microtraining paradigm have focused mainly on its general effectiveness as a training package. Results have shown that the *multimethod training* approaches are extremely helpful in skill acquisition (Kuna, 1975; Stone & Vance, 1976; Uhlemann, Lea, & Stone, 1976). Few studies since have focused on the influence or impact of supervision on microtraining; contradictions surface among studies, some indicating that supervision is unnecessary in imparting interviewing skills (Authier & Gustafson, 1975; Frankel, 1971), while other studies support supervision as a vital factor in skill acquisition (Authier & Gustafson, 1975; McDonald & Allen, cited in Ivey & Authier, 1978).

In a recent article Berg and Stone (1980) posited several reasons for these discrepancies, including (1) neglect of the impact of individual learning styles, (2) an emphasis on quantitative behavior counts to the relative exclusion of the qualitative dimensions of interviewing skills, and (3) the multidimensional nature of the supervisory process, in which the variables of supervisor style, relationship factors, reinforcement, and amount and kind of feedback have been previously uncontrolled. It could be argued that microtraining research is, in some ways, still in its infancy. The real issue for future examination is study of the impact of skills on clients. Early data suggest that change in counselor style results in client change.

An area of further expansion that Microcounseling must soon encompass is research into the coordination of learner characteristics with instructional methods to maximize performance. Proponents of the Microcounseling model are already beginning to examine Hunt and Sullivan's (1974) Conceptual Level Matching Model, which coordinates the learner's level of conceptual complexity with the degree of structure in the teaching method.

Another commentary directed at the skills training model and motivated by concern about the "washout" over time was made by Lambert and DeJulio (1977), particularly on methodological grounds. A number of studies have demonstrated that the communication skills often "wash out" shortly after training and that, to ensure maintenance, a retraining period is necessary (Collingswood, 1971; Haase,

DiMattia, & Guttman, 1973). A recent review of the training literature by Ford (1979) indicates that only 6 of 40 microskills studies demonstrated skill maintenance at long-term follow-up. Ford stated that very few of these modified behavioral technologies are presently designed for training complex behaviors. As stated previously, one runs the risk of falling into a "technological trap" of determined training objectives if one adheres too rigidly to the microskills model.

Ford's review offers an interesting challenge to the model. Maintenance of learned skills is a critical issue in microtraining and other skills-oriented programs. The possibility of skill loss is real. In early research and training efforts, investigators were content simply to run trainees through the paradigm and observe immediate improvement in the laboratory. More recent work, only now beginning to develop, has shown the importance of skill-transfer programs wherein trainees focus on taking learned behavior out of the laboratory. Furthermore, theory-based microtraining, such as metatheoretical assumptions, is drawn on to help trainees develop a conceptual map of how to use skills and when to use them. This appears to be a most useful method of promoting skill transfer. Finally, trainees need to develop *mastery* of skills. Not all trainees can master the skill of reflecting feeling, for example, in a single workshop session. Rather than assuming that training is adequate, care must be taken to ensure that competence is achieved.

SUMMARY

Microcounseling technology combined with new theoretical assumptions should provide a system for relating many types of counseling and therapy and for passing microskills on to trainees more quickly and efficiently at higher levels of quality. A useful beginning in microskills has occurred during the last 15 years. However, it is the questions that have been unearthed that perhaps will show the real value of the framework. Microskills research and training need to move to examination of the metatheoretical assumptions that now underlie the framework. Most critical will be examination of how clients are affected by counselors' use of skills. The real issue of maintenance of behavior is the impact a person can have on someone else. A delicate balance will need to be maintained in adhering to both training methodologies *and* precise attention to human dimensions such as cultural/environmental indicators and individual learning style. Ongoing monitoring of training-process features such as client/counselor match will represent a step in the right direction in providing a road map for generating effective outcome through personal encounters in therapy and counseling.

INTERVIEW WITH MR. S.

This is a selection from an interview by Joann Griswold, one of our students who participated in the 45-hour training program in microskills. She completed the assignment as part of a final assessment. The client, Mr. S., is 72 and widowed. He is a retired postman who sought counseling in an alternative care agency and complained about depression and an "inability to get started." This is a segment of the second interview. After obtaining data and current status in the first segment of the interview, Griswold attempts an assertion exercise, which is only partly effective, and then follows this with a focused free association from a psychodynamic framework. The "Rep Test" refers to Griswold's analysis of her own counseling role constructs, according to the paradigm provided in the work of George Kelly.

Counselor or Client Statement	Focus: Main Theme of Statement	Microskill	Key Qualitative Dimensions
I want to do them rather than be pressured into "today do this and the next day do that." That's the pressure.			

Joann's analysis: Note the parallel between "break loose" and "break out." This seems to me an example of how a counselor's construction of an issue can become that of the client. I think this is OK as the client needs to find his own direction (hummmm . . . another construct of mine).

27. **Joann:** Ummmmmmmnnn . . . pressure . . . when you talk about pressure, I sense you can feel it now. How do you react to pressure? Can you tell me how pressure affects you?	Helpee, topic— pressure	Expression of content—feedback, reflection of feeling, open question	Present tense
28. **Mr. S.:** Ah, I get *depressed.* I don't sleep well. It's on my mind.	Helpee, topic	Exp. of feeling and content	Somewhat vague
29. **Joann:** So you . . . you go to bed at night and you think about your problems and you get depressed and it's a vicious cycle. (**Mr. S.:** "Right.") And instead of looking forward to a project or something you're going to enjoy, it feels more like an obligation. (**Mr. S.:** "Ummmmmnnnn.") Obligation . . . obligations to other people and things are like a leash—they seem to lead us around. I've been in that trap at times. We all get into it. I think we have to be obligated to ourselves too. "Hey, what about me?" What is the best thing that could happen if for one whole day you chucked all your other-people obligations and ...?	Helpee, topic, helper	Summary and interpretation, self-disclosure (exp. of feeling), open question	Concreteness, genuineness, present- and past-tense immediacy

Joann's analysis: Wow, when I look at my Rep Test and this statement, I see how my way of looking at the world shows in my counseling. I *hate* to be pushed by others. In this case, my urge for self-

INTERVIEW WITH MR. S.

Counselor or Client Statement	Focus: Main Theme of Statement	Microskill	Key Qualitative Dimensions
direction really shows. My desire to "have at it" is also shown in this segment. When I see a problem, I think we ought to be about solving it. Hopefully, I don't move too fast.			
30. **Mr. S.:** I sometimes like to go off by myself and just fish and fish. Other times, it is comfortable to be with some old friends I've known a long time and play cards. I like to dance.	Helpee, others, topic—positive actions	Exp. of content— sharing information and some feelings	Concreteness, present and past
31. **Joann:** Both being by yourself and with others are enjoyable. People enjoy your company. I appreciate your company, but I also like the fact that you enjoy being alone. These are some real strengths. Some people can't stand to be alone.	Helpee, others	Paraphrase, self-disclosure (exp. of feeling)	Present tense, respect, positive regard, genuineness
32. **Mr. S.:** I guess I am lucky. I still do have some real friends, but I don't want to hurt anyone's feelings . . .	Helpee, others	Exp. of feeling and content	

Over the next several interchanges, which are deleted, Joann and Mr. S. talk about how he might develop a more comfortable balance of relationship. Joann suggests that it is OK for Mr. S. to respond with a "no" and that it is "OK for you to be yourself." Joann then suggests an assertive exercise.

42. **Joann:** So you want to be yourself and stand up for what you want. Let's imagine that your friends Joe and Mary have called and want to take you to an auction, something you do enjoy. Then, imagine that I am one of your busy acquaintances and I call and say, "Say, there's a meeting and dinner at the lodge for our members' children who are graduating from college next semester. I'll plan to pick you up at 1:30." Now tell me what you are going to do.	Helpee, others	Paraphrase, directive	Concrete, respect (in that I felt that Mr. S. could do it)
43. **Mr. S.:** I should tell you "Well, I'm sorry, but I want to go with Joe and Mary." But if I had made my new	Others, helpee	Exp. of content and feeling	Concrete, some lack of genuineness

INTERVIEW WITH MR. S.

Counselor or Client Statement	Focus: Main Theme of Statement	Microskill	Key Qualitative Dimensions
friend think I was very interested, I would feel obligated to cancel the auction and go to this, even though I would prefer the auction. I don't want to hurt anyone's feelings.			

Joann's analysis: A "full blown" assertion exercise would be more helpful. I should have confronted Mr. S.'s lack of enthusiasm and low vocal tone. He wasn't very convincing.

Counselor or Client Statement	Focus: Main Theme of Statement	Microskill	Key Qualitative Dimensions
44. **Joann:** Do you feel that Joe's and Mary's feelings would be hurt?	Others	Closed question	Mild confrontation
45. **Mr. S.:** No, ah, well . . . they would understand . . . they understand that I get into these, ah . . . I guess I just feel comfortable with them and they will not think badly about me if I cancel.	Others, helpee	Exp. of content—sharing inform., exp. of feeling	Some lack of genuineness, vague

Joann's analysis: I am a little off track here. I fear I put Mr. S. against the wall with my confrontation at 44. I also wonder if perhaps I could have had Mr. S. describe in more detail how his friends understood him. This whole section started off on the right track, but I blew it partially . . . I say partially, as I think he did get some insight and ideas from this short interaction. During the session, I felt confused and changed the topic. As I look at it now, I could have stayed with it and clarified things. My next response again shows my desire for action in the interview as shown in the Rep Test.

Counselor or Client Statement	Focus: Main Theme of Statement	Microskill	Key Qualitative Dimensions
46. **Joann:** Let's go back to you. Let's try something else. Just imagine I have just arrived on your doorstep, Mr. S. I have three large plastic bags with me; one is full of polyester stuffing, the second is full of octopus legs, the third is full of octopus bodies, and I meet you at the door saying "Mr. S., I need these all put together for the lodge party. I need them a week from Saturday. I know you'll do a good job for me . . ."	Helpee, topic	Directive	Concrete
47. **Mr. S.** (Interrupts laughing): . . . and I would say yes.	Helpee	Exp. of content	Respect for others, not for self
48. **Joann:** You'd say yes. Mr. S., tell me what you feel like when you close the door.	Helpee, topic	Minimal encourage, open question	Search for concreteness

INTERVIEW WITH MR. S.

Counselor or Client Statement	Focus: Main Theme of Statement	Microskill	Key Qualitative Dimensions
What do you say to yourself and those three bags?			
49. **Mr. S.:** I would just say . . . "Well, here I go again," and I would have to push hard to get them done, and I would give up on some things that I wanted to do.	Helpee, topic	Exp. of content and feeling	Some lack of gen-uineness shown in incongruent vocal tone (anger?)
50. **Joann:** I'm thinking about how angry I would be with myself. Ohhh, I'd be so dis-gusted that I'd given in. How does it feel to be doing something like that for somebody else?	Helper, helpee	Exp. of content and feeling	Genuineness, present tense, concrete
51. **Mr. S.:** Miserable, it makes me depressed . . . unless I like the person and I'm making her happy. That isn't quite so miserable.	Helpee, others	Exp. of feeling and content	Past and present tense
52. **Joann:** I'd like you to try something. Just relax and close your eyes. Relax and think back—think about that miserable feeling just after the door was closed and you had the bags before you. Think back in life to a time when you felt miserable. Do you have an incident you can share with me?	Helpee	Directive	Concrete, past tense
53. **Mr. S.:** Oh, I have an inci-dent from way back: I bor-rowed something without telling my brother. And when he found out, he just cursed me and wished me dead and lost his temper and screamed at me. I just went into my room and cried. I was *miserable*. (Mr. S.'s voice is very sad and his eyes are moist.)	Helpee, others	Exp. of feeling and content	Concrete, past tense, genuine
54. **Joann:** I would have been miserable too. I can feel how miserable you were. I can feel it now.	Helper, helpee	Exp. of feeling	Positive regard, genuineness, present tense, warmth
55. **Mr. S.:** It seems ridiculous, but I was so miserable. He really hurt my feelings and	Helpee, other	Exp. of feeling	Genuineness, con-gruence.

INTERVIEW WITH MR. S.

Counselor or Client Statement	Focus: Main Theme of Statement	Microskill	Key Qualitative Dimensions
made me feel guilty. He hurt my feelings, but I didn't hurt his.			
56. **Joann:** What did you say to him?	Helpee, other	Open question	Search for concreteness
57. **Mr. S.:** Like I did, I said I was sorry and I did not deserve all that he said and did, but it was no use. He had a terrible temper and I just cried it out. And so it seems, Joann, that I just never hurt people from that day . . .	Helpee, other	Exp. of content	Past and present, connected
58. **Joann:** What I'm hearing (**Mr. S.:** "Ummmmmnnn") is that you are afraid you will hurt people in the same manner you were hurt.	Helpee, others	Paraphrase, ref. of feeling (some interpret.)	Present, concrete, respect, confrontation
59. **Mr. S.** (softly): That's right, that's part of the answer.	Topic	Exp. of content	

Joann's analysis: I was surprised at myself when I used the focused free-association exercise. It was the first time I had used it, and I was surprised at its power. I don't usually like to think in psychodynamic terms, but I found in this case that Mr. S. did have some long-term connections from the past which affected present functioning. However, I wonder if simple assertion training carried forward in more detail than my effort wouldn't have been equally effective.

Counselor or Client Statement	Focus: Main Theme of Statement	Microskill	Key Qualitative Dimensions
60. **Joann:** Has . . . what have you thought about how you hurt yourself?	Helpee	Open question	Confrontation, present tense, positive regard
61. **Mr. S.:** Um . . . ah . . . (tearfully) subconsciously . . . I don't dwell on myself too much.	Helpee	Exp. of feeling	Present tense, genuineness
62. **Joann:** You don't dwell on yourself too much. I'd like to dwell on you because I think you are a pretty terrific person. I think you are a courageous person.	Helpee	Minimal encourage, exp. of feeling	Present tense, genuineness, respect, positive regard, warmth

REFERENCES

Andes, D. An evaluation of a couple's relationship building workshop: The use of video and small group feedback in teaching communication skills. Unpublished doctoral dissertation, University of Massachusetts, 1974.

Arnold, W. Effectiveness of Microcounseling as a supervisory model for teaching interviewing skills. Unpublished doctoral dissertation, Texas State University, 1976.

Authier, J., & Gustafson, D. Application of supervised and nonsupervised Microcounseling paradigms in the training of paraprofessionals. *Journal of Counseling Psychology,* 1975, *22,* 74–78.

Authier, J., Gustafson, K., Guerney, B., & Kasdorf, J. The psychological practitioner as a teacher: A theoretical, historical, and practical review. *Counseling Psychologist,* 1975, *5,* 31–50.

Belle, R. The effects of Microcounseling on attending behavior of counseling trainees. Unpublished doctoral dissertation, Lehigh University, 1974. *Dissertation Abstracts International,* 1974, *37,* 2626A.

Berg, K., & Stone, G. Effects of conceptual level and supervision structure on counselor skill development. *Personnel and Guidance Journal,* 1980, *27*(5), 500–509.

Bergin, A., & Garfield, S. *Handbook of psychotherapy and behavior change.* New York: Wiley, 1971.

Bizer, L. Parent program in behavioral skills. Unpublished manual, Amherst Regional Public Schools, 1972.

Carkhuff, R. Training as a mode of treatment. *Journal of Counseling Psychology,* 1971, *18,* 123–131.

Cartwright, R. Psychotherapeutic process. *Annual review of psychology,* 1968, *19,* 387–416.

Chilsom, A. Some effects of systematic human relations training on offenders' ability to demonstrate helping skills. Unpublished doctoral dissertation, University of Georgia, 1977. *Dissertation Abstracts International,* 1977, *37,* 4857A.

Collingswood, T. Retention and retaining of interpersonal communication skills. *Journal of Clinical Psychology,* 1971, *27*(2), 294–296.

Donk, L. Attending behavior in mental patients. Unpublished doctoral dissertation, 1972. *Dissertation Abstracts International,* 1972, *33,* 569.

Eiben, R., & Clark, R. Impact of a participating group experience on counselors in training. *Small Group Behavior,* 1973, *4*(4), 486–495.

Ford, J. D. Research on training counselors and clinicians. *Review of Educational Research,* 1979, *49*(1), 87–130.

Frankel, M. Effects of videotape modeling and self-confrontation techniques on Microcounseling behavior. *Journal of Counseling Psychology,* 1971, *18,* 465–471.

Goldstein, A., & Stein, N. *Prescriptive psychotherapies.* New York: Pergamon Press, 1976.

Gormally, J. Videotape feedback in human relations training. Unpublished doctoral dissertation, Illinois University, 1975. *Dissertation Abstracts International,* 1975, *35,* 6094B.

Goshko, R. Self-determined behavior change. *Personnel and Guidance Journal,* 1973, *51,* 599–632.

Haase, R., & DiMattia, D. The application of the Microcounseling paradigm to training of support personnel in counseling. *Counselor Education and Supervision,* 1970, *10,* 16–22.

Haase, R., DiMattia, D., & Guttman, M. Training of support personnel in three human relations skills: A systematic one-year follow-up. *Counselor Education and Supervision,* 1972, *11,* 194–199.

Haase, R., Forsyth, D., Julius, M., & Lee, R. Client training prior to counseling: An extension of the Microcounseling paradigm. *Canadian Counsellor,* 1971, *5,* 9–15.

Higgins, W., Ivey, A., & Uhlemann, M. Media therapy: A programmed approach to teaching behavioral skills. *Journal of Counseling Psychology,* 1973, *20,* 101–104.

Hunt, D. E., & Sullivan, E. V. *Between psychology and education.* Hinsdale, Ill.: Dryden Press, 1974.

Ivey, A. Media therapy: Educational change planning for psychiatric patients. *Journal of Counseling Psychology,* 1973, *20,* 338–343.

Ivey, A. Counseling and psychotherapy: Toward a new perspective. In A. Marsella & P. Pedersen (Eds.), *Cross-cultural counseling and psychotherapy.* New York: Pergamon Press, 1981.

Ivey, A., & Alschuler, A. Psychological education: A prime function of the counselor. *Personnel and Guidance Journal,* 1973, *51,* 581–692.

Ivey, A., & Authier, J. (Eds.). *Microcounseling: Innovations in interviewing, counseling and psychotherapy, and psychoeducation* (2nd ed.). Springfield, Ill.: Charles C Thomas, 1978.

Ivey, A., & Gluckstern, N. *Basic attending skills: Leader and participant manuals; Basic influencing skills: Leader and participant manuals.* North Amherst, Mass.: Microtraining Associates, 1974, 1976.

Ivey, A., & Litterer, J. *FACE TO FACE.* North Amherst, Mass.: Amherst Consulting Group, 1979.

Ivey, A., Normington, C., Miller, C., Morrill, W., & Haase, R. Microcounseling and attending behavior: An approach to pre-practicum counselor training. *Journal of Counseling Psychology,* 1968, *15*(2), 1–12.

Ivey, A., with Simek-Downing, L. *Counseling and psychotherapy.* Englewood Cliffs, N.J.: Prentice-Hall, 1980.

Kasdorf, J., & Gustafson, K. Research related to microtraining. In A. Ivey & J. Authier (Eds.), *Microcounseling: Innovations in interviewing, counseling and psychotherapy, and psychoeducation* (2nd ed.). Springfield, Ill.: Charles C Thomas, 1978.

Kelly, G. *The psychology of personal constructs.* New York: Norton, 1955.

Kuna, D. Lecturing, reading, and modeling in counselor restatement training. *Journal of Counseling Psychology,* 1975, *22,* 542–546.

Lambert, M. J., & DeJulio, S. Outcome research in Carkhuff's human resource development training program: Where is the doughnut? *Counseling Psychologist,* 1977, *6*(4), 79–86.

Marsella, A., & Pedersen, P. *Cross-cultural counseling and psychotherapy.* New York: Pergamon Press, 1981.

Matarazzo, R. Research on the teaching and learning of psychotherapeutic skills. In A. Bergin & S. Garfield (Eds.), *Psychotherapy and behavior change.* New York: Wiley, 1971.

McIvroy, J. A. Comparative study of three Microcounseling models. Unpublished doctoral dissertation, University of Iowa, 1976. *Dissertation Abstracts International,* 1976, *36,* 2642A.

Mihalovich, J. Competencies in teaching counseling and interpersonal skills. Unpublished doctoral dissertation, University of Iowa, 1976. *Dissertation Abstracts International,* 1976, *37,* 2642A.

Pearson, P. The comparative effects of a cognitive and affective counselor training program on the client-counselor self-actualization. Unpublished doctoral dissertation, University of Southern Mississippi, 1973. *Dissertation Abstracts International,* 1973, *34,* 2313A.

Pierce, R., & Drasgow, J. Teaching facilitative interpersonal functioning to psychiatric patients. *Journal of Counseling Psychology,* 1969, *16,* 295–298.

Sawyer, H. Microcounseling as a training model for the rehabilitation initial interview. Unpublished doctoral dissertation, Auburn University, 1973. *Dissertation Abstracts International,* 1973, *34,* 2313A.

Shea, J. An evaluation of the effectiveness of Microcounseling in training counselors to use selected behaviors in an urban field practice. Unpublished doctoral dissertation, Columbia University, 1975. *Dissertation Abstracts International,* 1975, *36,* 3419–3420A.

Sherrard, P. Predicting group leader/member interaction: The efficacy of the Ivey taxonomy. Unpublished doctoral dissertation, University of Massachusetts, Amherst, 1973.

Silverman, M. Perceptions of counseling following practicum experiences. *Journal of Counseling Psychology,* 1972, *19,* 11–15.

Stone, G., & Vance, A. Instruction modeling and rehearsal: Implications for training. *Journal of Counseling Psychology,* 1976, *23,* 272–279.

Terrell, T. The effects of microtraining in attending behavior in response behavior of paraprofessional orientation leaders. Unpublished doctoral dissertation, Mississippi State University, 1977. *Dissertation Abstracts International,* 1977, *37,* 4149A.

Uhlemann, M. R., Lea, G. W., & Stone, G. C. Effects of instructions and modeling on trainees low in interpersonal communication skills. *Journal of Counseling Psychology,* 1976, *23,* 509–513.

CHAPTER ELEVEN

Interpersonal Process Recall: Basic Methods and Recent Research

Norman Kagan is professor in the Department of Counseling, Educational Psychology and Special Education and in the Department of Psychiatry at Michigan State University. In 1981 he was given the Distinguished Faculty Award by Michigan State University in recognition of his research on interpersonal behavior over the previous 19 years. He has served as president of the Division of Counseling Psychology of the American Psychological Association and has coordinated a three-year study of the future of counseling psychology in the next decade. Dr. Kagan is the author of a series of 21 films, which have been used worldwide in the training of people in interpersonal relations.

Norman Kagan

The Interpersonal Process Recall (IPR) method, developed by Norman Kagan over the past two decades, is a well-packaged, portable, film-based mental health skills training program that emphasizes a dynamic approach to learning. At the core of the IPR program is the recall process, in which an "inquirer" guides professionals or students as they review video- or audio-recorded sessions with clients or coworkers. I have made extensive use of the IPR method in my teaching—both to mental health professionals and to health care professionals—and have found that the versatility of the program, combined with the intrinsic power of the recall process, makes it an excellent tool for training diverse populations. The model works as well with psychiatric residents as it does with army sergeants. The "discovery" model of learning in IPR provides an alternative to approaches offering a set of prepackaged "good skills." Trainees are asked to study their own interpersonal behavior and to identify and develop skills of their own choosing. In Kagan's words, IPR "helps people do what they wish they could do with others."

Interpersonal Process Recall (IPR), a method for influencing human interaction, was first developed nearly 20 years ago to improve the reliability of training programs for mental health workers, later broadening to include teaching others to achieve improved interpersonal relations. The core of the IPR process is reviewing a videotape or an audiotape in order to recall one's thoughts, feelings, goals, aspirations, bodily sensations, and a host of other covert processes and describing these

Descriptions of the core process have appeared in print many times. This chapter contains many new elements but of necessity also contains material that has been reported elsewhere.

In developing Interpersonal Process Recall I have received help from many colleagues and students. I am especially indebted to David R. Krathwohl and to J. Bruce Burke.

processes as explicitly as possible during the tape review. The method, used in a variety of ways and for different purposes (Kagan, 1980), has received considerable attention as an aid for helping people learn to improve their interpersonal relations. It has also enabled us to identify basic recurring interpersonal fears, to identify effective and less effective interviews, to develop affective sensitivity scales, to accelerate client growth in therapy, and to study medical inquiry. Significant outcomes have been obtained with a variety of formats.

The most frequently used format follows the "developmental tasks" that a neophyte must accomplish in order to become skillful at influencing human interaction. The order in which the tasks are presented progresses from the least threatening to the most threatening process. Each unit in the series is presented by means of a 16-mm color film in which a narrator describes the unit and carries students through the various exercises. Student and instructor manuals accompany the film series. The process is complex but no more so than one would expect of a 30- to 50-hour training program. The manual and film series have been so designed that an instructor can learn to teach the methods without prior training. Most instructors prefer to attend a trainer's workshop, which is offered from time to time by professional associations or by the author.

BASIC UNITS OF THE IPR MODEL

Elements of Facilitating Communication

The first phase grew out of our early attempts to develop a counselor rating scale. We identified the scale categories by comparing videotapes of counselors whose clients indicated on recall that the session was very positive with videotapes of counselors who were seen by their clients as ineffective. We found that effective counselors *sometimes* exhibited certain behaviors that ineffective counselors *never* used. Effective counselors (1) respond to clients with exploratory questions and behave so as to encourage the client to explore further and assume an active role in the counseling process (exploratory mode), (2) listen intently and communicate to the client their attempt to understand, usually by paraphrasing or asking for clarification (listening), (3) focus much of their attention on client affect dealing with client themes that are communicated subtly (affect), and (4) can be extremely frank and honest but gentle (honest labeling). These four behaviors became the basis of the first phase in the model. Beginning students are encouraged to learn the four response modes, to practice them, and to add them to their repertoires.

A woman narrates the training film associated with this unit. Students view brief scenes in which a client or patient makes a statement and an interviewer responds to one facet (for example, cognitive) of the statement. In the next scene, the patient repeats the statement to a second interviewer, who responds to a different (for example, affective) component of the statement. Several client types and interviewer types are presented for each of the four sets of concepts. The narrator points out that the cognitive, nonexploratory, nonattentive, and avoiding response modes are usually associated with social conversation, while the other response modes are often found in professional interviewing and counseling. Students then practice each response mode by responding to simulated patients and clients on film who look directly at them and make statements varying in complexity and intensity. Various minority groups are represented in the films.

This is the only pure "skill" unit in the IPR series. That is, there are specific behaviors to be learned and practiced; there are correct and incorrect responses. The unit differs from other approaches to skill training primarily in the importance placed on the use of the skills taught. These are specific behaviors *to be added* to a student's repertoire, not "core" conditions. Students are informed that there are many situations in which use of the skills would not help achieve the goals of the interaction.

Presenting the skills as "sometime" behaviors is not simply a teaching strategy but derives from the research that led to identification of the skills. The skills were observed to be within the repertoire of effective interviewers and sometimes used by them. This emphasis on adding the knowledge, skills, or abilities learned in each unit to one's repertoire of other behaviors and to one's general professional role is an important characteristic of the entire training program and may account in part for the model's widespread use in a variety of disciplines and in numerous cultures. Teachers, for instance, do not have to feel as if they were violating the basic tenets of IPR if they discipline a child. In this skill unit and throughout the entire program, students are reminded that we are attempting to add to their abilities rather than to dictate a new interpersonal life-style.

The filmed examples, the narrator's explanation, and finally the simulated practice make it relatively easy for students to learn the skills regardless of educational or cultural background. Four to six hours is usually sufficient for most groups of students.

Affect Simulation

Helping students become competent at interpersonal skills in the training setting in no way ensures that these same skills will be used outside that setting. This is especially true if student fears of interpersonal involvement itself are not dealt with. Affect simulation was added to the model in order to help students overcome their resistance to the often intense intimate communication that the use of interpersonal skills can encourage. People often fear behaviors to which they will probably never be subjected. We were fascinated to observe that these "allergies" fell into four basic themes. "If I drop my guard, if I become psychologically intimate," then—

1. "The other person will hurt me." This fear and the others were not reality-based but were based on some vague potential sensed in other people, an "interpersonal allergy"—just a hint conjures up powerful reactions. On close examination these fears seem to be very primitive, infantile in nature—living vestiges, apparently, from one's earliest years, when one was a small person in a big people's world. Many of the fears that people expressed in recall seem to be based on things they had learned in their prelanguage days. Indeed, these fears were often expressed as "I don't know why, but I almost feel as if I'm going to be picked up and hurt. Or somehow the other person will walk out, abandon me, and I won't be able to survive on my own. I'll die."
2. "I will hurt the other person." This second concern was often expressed during recall as "If I let myself go, if I don't cover up, my angry thoughts might somehow magically hurt you."

3. "The other person will engulf me." This third concern was in the general area of intimacy, sexuality, affectionate stickiness. "If you get too close, you'll engulf me. I'll lose my identity, my separateness."

4. "I will engulf the other person." The fourth concern was that "my dependency, my sexual curiosity, my intimacy needs might be acted out on you."

It occurred to us that if we filmed actors looking directly at the camera lens so that the resulting image was talking directly to the viewer, and if the actor in each film sequence portrayed a variation on one of the universal "nightmares," it might be possible to create a reliable, efficient way of helping people face their interpersonal fears. In this second IPR unit, then, students view brief film vignettes and are asked to imagine that the actor is talking directly to them. Students are then encouraged to talk, from a position of safety and support, about their reactions to the vignettes. The film series now contains over 70 vignettes. Most are quite general, but some are designed for specific audiences, such as teachers, medical students, counselors, or physicians. Specific themes such as geriatrics, racism, and sexism have also been included. The following descriptions of several of the vignettes illustrate the range of themes included in the unit.

Middle-aged woman (round, smiling face, perceived by most people as motherly and/or patronizing):   I know I can trust you to do what's right. I know you wouldn't do anything that I wouldn't approve of . . . I know I can trust you.

Young woman (makes and breaks eye contact with viewer during early part of the scene):   [Crying] Charlie and I . . . we were walking together the other night . . . the dark street . . . and these two men stopped us. [Pause] They knocked him out . . . just beat him and knocked him out . . . and . . . they pulled me into this building and . . . beat me . . . they beat me up. [Pause] And . . . then they tore my clothes off and they raped me—both of them. [Crying] They both . . .

Elderly man: I'd be proud to be your father, any man would be. *I'd* be proud to be your father.

Young, attractive woman: Well, I don't really know how to say this, because I've never said this to anyone before, but . . . you just turn me on. And if you don't come over here and touch me, I'm going to go out of my mind.

Young, handsome man (continues eye contact with viewer):   You know, you really make me feel very, very special. I really look forward to having this time with you and to just be able to let the whole day . . . melt away. I'm really glad you're my friend. You really mean a lot to me. You really do.

Same actor as in previous vignette: I really like you. I really like . . . being with you. Uh . . . do you have any idea what you do to me? I just want to touch you. I just want to reach out and feel your warmth. I want to smell you. Just like animals.

Elderly man: Your work has been excellent. The feedback on you has been terrific. But . . . unfortunately, we've had budget cuts. We're going to have to let you go.

Man at desk: The reason I wanted you to stop by is, we've gotten into a bad situation. We just got a phone call—the little Snyder boy—his father was just in a car accident . . . killed, instantly. Now I think it's best if you tell him.

Elderly man: So . . . you've had everything you want out of me and now you're going to throw me out, now that I'm old. After all I've given you—all I've done for you. You're going to toss me out on a junk heap . . . you son of a bitch.

Older woman: What's the matter? Taken on more than you can handle? In over your head? Well, shit, grow up!

Black man (with White woman—woman turns and stares at viewer, motions to man): What in hell are you looking at?

Elderly man: Can you give me a minute? Something has been driving me *frantic*. For the last few years I've found myself . . . thinking about . . . little children. Wanting to touch them—where I shouldn't. I know it's wrong. I know it's evil, I know it's unnatural. I can't help myself. Please help me. You've *got* to *help* me.

Young woman: I don't want to talk to you. Just stay away. Just stay *away*. Just stay . . . [screaming, tears off blouse].

Young woman: Well, I'd love to, but, um . . . well, it's just that I've been so busy lately, and, um . . . well, I've just been up to my eyebrows in work . . . really, I . . . maybe some other time?

Man (mid-30s at desk): I've listened to you, and I would like you to know that I don't like your ideas one goddamn bit. I think that *you* and people like you have caused most of the misery we have around us, and I'd like to come over there and ram your fucking teeth down your *throat*.

Older woman: We've been to so many doctors who are just *awful*. But I'm sure you'll be able to help us.

Man in chair: This is very hard for me. This is hard for me to talk about. Even . . . to think about [gags, vomits].

Young woman: You're a good teacher . . . but you know Smith in English—her classes are just great. I just love them. They're so enjoyable and so interesting. Your classes are good, too. I really like them.

Young woman: [Crying] I . . . I thought you liked me. I really . . . I guess I know what you're thinking. [Sighs] I . . . um . . . I thought that you really liked me, and I, uh . . . oh, wow!

Man: I tell you, man, I can't take it much more. You can get the fuck off my back. You know what? I'm going to have to kick your ass. I'm going to kick your fucking ass.

Man in bar (continuous eye contact with viewer): If my wife wants to work . . . I mean, I don't care. I don't give a damn, but when I come home and I want dinner on the table, I don't care whether she works or not, I want dinner on the table.

Male teacher: Math teachers are always complaining about how difficult it is to make math relevant to girls. I never have that problem. For instance, when I'm teaching fractions, I say to them "Girls, how are you ever going to cook for your husbands if you don't learn fractions?"

Man at desk: What do you mean, you don't want to be promoted? You realize the organization has invested an enormous amount of money in your improvement? And now you're telling us you don't want to be promoted?

Man: Honest feedback, my ass. It's because I'm not Anglo, isn't it? If I was Anglo, you wouldn't give me feedback like this. You'd think I was great.

Students' exploration of their reactions to each vignette is focused on the following general questions:

· What did you think?
· What would you probably do?
· What did you feel?
· What did you think the person was feeling about you?
· What made the person think he or she could talk to you that way—that is, what did the person see in you or think he or she saw in you that gave the person the right?
· What did you think the person really wanted you to do or really wanted to make you feel?
· If you've never experienced that kind of interaction, have you ever felt that someone wanted to tell you what the person you were viewing told you, and what does that usually do to you?
· If that kind of situation actually does occur, do you wish you could respond differently than the way you typically do?
· What do you suppose keeps you from being able to respond the way you wish you could?

Most students are able to get involved in the process, to become more aware of their unfounded vestigial feelings of vulnerability, and then to become less frightened by psychologically intimate interactions.

A brief unit on interpersonal theory is presented to students at this point in the training. The theory involves interpersonal distancing, fears associated with intimacy, fears associated with aloneness, and assumptions about the interaction between the need for closeness and fear of closeness. Observations about fully functioning people are presented.

In this unit and in the subsequent units there are no correct or incorrect responses. Generally students begin to develop an enthusiasm for the process when they realize that we are interested in improving their interpersonal style rather than evaluating their competence or character. Students also begin to realize that they are in complete control of what they will reveal of themselves—that they are in charge of their own rate and direction of learning.

Counselor Recall

The third phase involves making a video- or audiotape of an interaction between a student and a client and then reviewing the tape with the student. The review process is unique. It is not a critique, not self-confrontation, but *stimulated recall*—hence the name of the model, "Interpersonal Process Recall." The student is given control of the playback switch and asked to stop the tape whenever he or she recalls any thoughts, feelings, goals, impressions, conflicts, confusions, images, internal dialogues, or any other covert processes that occurred during the recorded session. Only the student may stop the tape. The person who reviews the tape with the student encourages the student to elaborate whenever the student stops the tape and asks such questions as these:

· What were you thinking?
· What were you feeling?
· What pictures or memories went through your mind?

- What did you think the other person was feeling?
- What did you want the other person to think or feel?
- How did you think the other person felt about you?
- How did you want the other person to feel about you?
- Was there anything you wanted to say but couldn't find the appropriate words for?
- Do you recall how your body felt—can you recall any specific parts of your body reacting more than any other parts?
- What did the sex or physical appearance of the other do to you?
- What had you hoped would happen next?
- Did you have any goals at this point in the interview?
- Were you satisfied with your own behavior?
- Were you satisfied with the reactions of the other person? [1]

"To what end?" one might ask. Surely a neophyte needs to be told more than to recall. One of the primary assumptions underlying the counselor-recall phase is that people perceive much more of each other's messages than they acknowledge to themselves or to the other person. [2] Counselor recall is based on the assumption that counselors always have a wealth of information that they failed to acknowledge or to use productively and that sessions devoted to uncovering these clinically important impressions and making them explicit in language helps students become aware of messages that they denied or ignored. The process also helps students to identify their own previously unverbalized fears and imagined vulnerabilities in human interaction.

Equally important is that a sense of personal responsibility for one's own behavior is fostered in the student. The student is helped to assume ownership of his or her behavior. The motivation to change is then likely to be more intrinsic than extrinsic. We find that the recall process encourages students to talk about their motives and to continue pondering their own actions long after the session is over. The basic self-exploration process does not extinguish at the end of the course. Indeed, students who have been through IPR appear to continue accelerated learning months after the process has been completed (Boltuch, 1975). The recall process, then, encourages change out of a sense of personal responsibility for one's own behavior and out of a feeling that one is newly capable of determining one's own direction. Interviewer recall also gives students an opportunity to improve through *rehearsal* ("What I was tempted to say at that point, but didn't, was . . ."). Interviewer recall usually increases student confidence and risk taking in subsequent interviews.

Why does it work? What about the recall process enables people to describe so openly what they actually experienced during the recorded session? There are probably several reasons. First, the behavior is over; it is history. In face-to-face interactions one is never certain about the next moment in time, and so there is a heightened anxiety, a tenseness, which usually fosters some degree of defensiveness. During the recall process, however, the behavior has been completed—it is safely over, and it is safe to talk about. The videotape playback also provides a depiction

---

[1] A three-page list of types of leads appears in the manual.

[2] This ability to perceive may be simply a result of having survived in our society, or perhaps it is so basic to survival as to be genetically coded as a special instance of "deep grammar."

of one's self, but it is not truly oneself. Here again a certain degree of distancing and some element of objectivity can exist. It is as if the person on the screen were someone well known to the viewer but not quite the viewer. It is possible to speak knowledgeably about, and even be entertained by, the not-quite-me. The noninterpretive, nonthreatening inquirer behaviors also foster safety and stimulate openness. Finally, participants are never forced into discoveries or admissions they are not ready to make. The participant is always in control and has the ultimate power. Under those conditions people are more likely to reveal than in situations in which they have less power. During class sessions students view films depicting interviews and then interviewer recall that were made of actual interactions. The film series includes films of psychotherapists and patients, counselors and clients, dormitory advisers, and a teacher and her supervisor.

Inquirer Training

The person who reviews the videotape with a student is called the "inquirer." The inquirer role requires nonjudgmental but assertive probing and consists entirely of asking exploratory questions. The inquirer assumes that the person is the best authority on his or her own thoughts and feelings; the inquirer's task is to facilitate learning-by-discovery rather than to provide information, to give lectures, or even to share observations. The specific questions one learns to ask in the inquirer role, in addition, are very useful skills to add to one's face-to-face repertoire.

A brief history of the inquirer role might be useful for understanding this basic part of the IPR model. The role was discovered rather than designed. In 1961 Michigan State University was one of a very few institutions at that time to have professional videotaping equipment readily accessible to faculty members. I was then a young assistant professor and had been in charge of a National Defense Education Act grant. Part of the grant permitted hiring eminent psychologists as visiting lecturers. I decided to videotape the lectures to preserve the presentations for future years. Curious about the videotaping process, several of the visitors asked to review the playback immediately after their studio presentation. It was amazing to observe the extent to which the videotapes stimulated detailed recall of the experiences. Lecturers reported having forgotten passages in their prepared script and momentarily panicked; yet, the only unusual behavior on the videotape was a very slight hesitation. At other times lecturers recalled having been concerned about some activity in the control room; yet, to the casual observer, they seemed never to have taken their attention from the prepared address. Most startling was the potential of the immediate playback for recognizing and labeling covert processes associated with uncomfortable behavior. These eminent visitors made such comments as "I really seem to look down at my audience—I look haughty—but really I was feeling a bit defensive" or "I certainly behave like a stuffed shirt, don't I?" or "I may not look it, but I was frightened to death—concerned that perhaps I'm not as good as my reputation."

These people were not research subjects or supervisees. Probing or interpreting on my part would have been totally inappropriate and unacceptable. I encouraged them to elaborate on their reactions to the videotape and offered them only the most respectful inquiries. In many ways my role was that of a precocious listener. Given these conditions—immediate videotape playback and respectful probes rather than interpretations or admonitions—the guests often said critical things about themselves that others said about them only behind their backs. Yet, the visitors also claimed that the session was instructive for them. Having made what might be thought of as very critical comments about themselves they nonetheless typically left the playback session excited and enthusiastic about what they had learned.

The second serendipitous experience that led to the inquirer role grew out of research rather than status constraints. It occurred to me that we might use videotape to develop an objective measure of affective sensitivity, one component of empathy. We could use the accessibility to videotaping equipment to record actual interactions between clients and counselors, physicians and patients, and to then select dramatic moments in these indigenous interactions for presentation to viewers. The purpose was to develop an instrument in which a person would view film excerpts and then select from a list of multiple-choice items the item that most closely approximated what the client actually felt at the moment the film stopped. The number of "correct" and "incorrect" responses might reflect the person's sensitivity to others' feelings.

The research team consisted of David R. Krathwohl, William Farquhar, and me. In developing the instrument, we needed to determine what the client, student, or counselor was indeed feeling at various moments in the interaction. We decided to use stimulated recall as a vehicle for finding out. We would play back the videotape to each of the participants. In determining the researcher's role, it became apparent that we would have to teach ourselves to avoid leading the subjects, and certainly interpretations and suggestions were out of the question if we were to have any faith in the validity of subjects' comments. We carefully taught ourselves to ask a series of highly probing but noninterpretive open-ended questions. To our amazement, the process proved unusually powerful not only for obtaining data from the participants but also for fostering important learning by the participants. The inquirer role was thus discovered first because of an unusual status relationship between the participant and the reviewer and later because of an unusual research constraint. The learning-by-discovery potential of the role is the most central feature of the IPR model.

In this fourth phase of the IPR program, inquirer training, each student learns the inquirer role and then serves as inquirer for another student and for the other student's clients.[3] The inquirer role is presented on film and includes simulated practice in which a person looks up from a TV monitor at the viewer and makes comments about the tape so that the viewer can try out inquirer leads in simulation. The film and manuals then offer suggested formats for students to practice the inquirer role with each other, using audio or video recorders.

Client Recall

It is one thing to learn about client dynamics through theory and demonstration; it is quite another to learn through discovery. In this next phase students serve as

---

[3]We have found that it is possible to teach the inquirer role to students before they have engaged in the previous phase. That is, when an instructor cannot serve as inquirer for all the students in the interviewer-recall phase and cannot obtain the help of students who have previously been through the course, then students can learn the inquirer role and serve as inquirers for each other from the very start of the program. No measurable loss in skill level results (Bedell, 1976).

inquirers with each other's clients. At the end of an audio- or videotaped interview, one of the student's colleagues reviews the tape with the client alone. The client is encouraged to be as open as possible about aspirations, satisfactions, and dissatisfactions. Prior client consent is obtained. The client has been told that the process will probably be informative for the client and for the inquirer and that when the inquirer later describes how the client perceived the taped session, the client's comments will serve as a source of learning for the counselor. Students then share comments made by each other's clients. The recall sessions themselves can be recorded so that students can listen to the recalled client comments, or with client consent they may arrange to observe the recall session through a one-way mirror.

In this unit, then, students learn how they are being reacted to not from the instructor's critique but from an almost unimpeachable source, the clients themselves. In class, students have an opportunity to observe client-recall sessions in the film series. One film is of a client who had been in long-term therapy. Another is of a junior high school student's recall after a session with his school principal, with the school social worker serving as inquirer. A third film is of the separate and independent recalls of a young couple after a stressful interaction about their marital difficulties.

An almost universal outcome of this phase is an appreciation for the importance of the "here and now" of client communication and the understanding that, regardless of the content of the session, a large part of a client's attention is focused on the counselor/client interaction itself.

Mutual Recall

One of the most powerful phases of the IPR training model is mutual recall, a technique for facilitating the ability to talk openly and nondefensively about the ongoing process between the counselor and client. In the previous phases students learned experientially that an important part of a client's concerns may involve the counselor; they must then also learn to verbalize these processes in the relationship—to learn to deal directly and explicitly with the relationship itself as content. This is probably the most difficult behavior for students to learn. It is a complicated act, requiring self-awareness, sensitivity to the other person, and courage. Mutual recall provides an unusually reliable vehicle for fostering this learning.

In mutual recall, *both* counselor and client participate in the recall session with an inquirer. Counselor and client are each asked to share their recalled thoughts and feelings, paying particular attention to how they perceived each other and what meanings they ascribed to each other's behaviors. During such sessions students and clients typically become better able to tell each other about the "here and now" of their interactions.

Students view films of mutual-recall sessions that depict a variety of possible applications. One is of ongoing psychotherapy; others are of doctor/patient interactions, the mutual recall of a dating couple, the recall of a health team's interactions, recalls of entire families after a family therapy session, junior high school classes conducting mutual-recall sessions with their teachers, and a military interaction between a captain and a major followed by individual and mutual sessions with a colonel serving as inquirer.

Transfer of Learning

Students are next encouraged to experiment with the methods. They are encouraged to engage in interaction, follow it with a recall session, and then immediately conduct a second interaction with the same person they interacted with. This process of interview-recall-interview gives students an immediate opportunity to act on their own discoveries.

We also found that student skill development and transfer of learning were augmented if we shared some of the theoretical contructs underpinning the affect-simulation vignettes and other theories that grew out of experience in conducting recall sessions. Having a conceptual "road map" apparently enhances learning and transfer. Therefore, two theory sessions have been added to the course. One of the theory sessions has already been described briefly. The second is a theory of interpersonal behavioral styles similar in many ways to Karen Horney's (Horney, 1945).

Transfer of learning is also facilitated by requiring students to use the recall process in field settings. Medical students are required to interview patients and to conduct interviewer-, patient-, or mutual-recall sessions using videotape or audio cassette. Counselors are required to use the process in their clinic settings. Teachers are assigned sessions in which they conduct recall sessions with their entire classrooms. Administrators may be assigned the recording and recall of a staff meeting or a supervisory session.

APPLICATIONS

The IPR model has been extensively used to educate mental health workers and more recently has also been used by teachers, physicians, medical students, nurses, prison guards, prison inmates, undergraduate students, and military personnel. According to a national survey (Kahn, Cohen, & Jason, 1979), 27% of all medical training programs in the United States reported that they were using IPR in their training. Currently each drill sergeant in the U.S. Army completes an IPR course as part of basic drill-sergeant training. The model has been translated into Swedish, Danish, and German.[4]

DISSEMINATION

One of the unique characteristics of the IPR model is the learning-by-discovery underpinning. A second unique characteristic of the model is the delivery system itself. In the mid-1960s, to our chagrin, we observed that on the basis of written descriptions of the training model, and supplied only with the affect-simulation vignettes on film, many instructors were unable to implement the training. The

[4]Swedish edition available through Dr. Gert Wretmark, Psykiatriska Institutionen, Regionsjukhuset, 581, 85-Linkoping, Sweden. Danish edition available through Dr. Jorgen Nystrup, Nordisk Federation for Medicinsk Undervisning, Rigshospitalet, 2100 Copenhagen Ø, Denmark. German edition available through Ms. Katharina Meyer-Hartwig, KIK Klopstockstrasse 7, 3400 Gottingen, West Germany.

essential philosophy of discovery learning and particularly the assumptions and behaviors required in the inquirer role apparently were not adequately communicated by the written word alone. This led us to the development of the film series, the instructor manual, and student manuals.[5] Implementation proved to be possible with the use of the film series (Boltuch, 1975; Robbins, Kaus, Heinrich, Abrass, Dreyer, & Clyman, 1979). If a major objective of our professional efforts is to "give psychology away," then it is not enough that we design and validate our methods. We must be equally concerned about reliable dissemination.

CURRENT RESEARCH

Since 1968 my colleagues and I have worked to improve the model through the addition of a specific process in the affect-simulation phase. The work is just now bearing fruit in the form of statistically significant improvement for those students who experience the new unit over students who receive the regular course with an additional lab session of a more traditional sort. The improvement is indicated by higher "accurate empathy" scores from independent raters and by the use of a greater number of affective statements by medical students in a patient interview at the end of the course. A measure of interviewee difficulty (each patient's depth-of-self-exploration ratings) was used as a covariate. Findings have been replicated.[6]

The new lab experience was developed on the assumption that student learning would be enhanced if students were able to base their recall of events not only on the video playback but also on a playback of their physiological behavior. It seemed possible that students would then better understand mind/body interactions and the nature of psychosomatic illness.

The method that evolved is complex and currently expensive, but the history of videotape and other recorders has been one of continually shrinking cost. A student sits in a comfortable chair facing a projection screen. As the student watches each affect-simulation vignette, a video recording is made of (1) the student, (2) the vignette, and (3) the student's heart rate, respiration, and left- and right-hand skin conductance. An on-line computer also records the physiological events. After a dozen vignettes have been viewed and the student's physical and physiological reactions have been recorded, an inquirer reviews the video with the student. The recall session is conducted in the usual way except that the student can now see physical behavior (grimaces, bodily shifts, and so on), the vignette being reacted to, and a video playback of his or her physiological behavior as recorded on a polygraph. In order for the student to have even more self-information, we have now added a second video monitor, which displays, at the student's direction, an *intra*personal statistical analysis of the record. For example, if a student wishes to know how her heart rate during the second vignette compared with her heart rate on all of the other vignettes, she presses a single key, and the information is immediately displayed. Similarly, frequencies, amplitudes, slopes, and area under the curve for each physiological measure are displayed for the vignette being viewed. The new lab experience is repeated. Each of the two sessions takes about two hours.

[5]Distributed by Mason Media, Inc., 1265 Lakeside Drive, East Lansing, Michigan 48823.
[6]A project supported by NIMH Grant #ST-24-MH15473-02. Final report in press.

At the start of the Winter 1981 IPR course, 20 medical students volunteered for the four-hour "physio" labs. The process was well received by the students. Before the course was over, 50 additional students out of a class of 90 had volunteered their time. No student failed to return for the second two-hour session.

The "physio" lab experience has also been used with more advanced medical students just prior to their surgical clerkship. This lab was stimulated by the late professor of surgery Dr. Edward Coppola. We developed a series of surgical stimulus vignettes, including scenes of incisions as well as simulations of interpersonal situations such as being scolded by a scrub nurse or laughed at by a surgeon.

We now include pattern-analysis techniques applied to each student's physiological experience to enable us to inform the student about which of the many vignettes clustered together in terms of similar patterns of reactivity. This process could enable students to discover threads of personal meaning that groups of vignettes had for them. The implications for training are fascinating.

EVALUATION

In many ways the very strength of the model is also its major weakness. In fostering discovery learning it is very difficult to determine how much one has learned, and, indeed, oftentimes it is difficult to determine exactly what one has learned. Because IPR encourages people to deal with those issues that are most important for them at their current stage of interpersonal development, group evaluation is exceedingly difficult. The statistically significant findings that have occurred in numerous studies must be thought of as minimal findings. That which could be measured is not, in all likelihood, all that was learned.

An early version of the model was used in conjunction with a graduate practicum (Kagan & Krathwohl, 1967). That phase of the 1967 project was under the direction of Alan D. Goldberg and gave us the first clear-cut evidence to support the effectiveness of IPR in implementing a counselor-training program. A pre-post and between-treatment design was replicated with three different samples in each of three academic quarters. The IPR model was compared with an intensive traditional supervisory process. At the beginning of each program both IPR and traditional groups were given a common framework about the goals of the program and were given experience themselves in using the same instruments that would be used to rate them at the end of training. There were statistically significant pre-post gains. Both approaches were effective in bringing about changes in a counselor's interview behavior. There were also statistically significant differences in counseling skills between the groups, as rated on a double-blind basis by independent judges. Differences on basic counselor behaviors were found to be in favor of the IPR treatment. Client evaluation of counselors also resulted in statistically significant differences between the groups in favor of the IPR process.

Additional controlled studies (Spivack & Kagan, 1972) again provided support for the utility of the model in counselor training. Dendy (1971) found significant growth in affective sensitivity and interviewing skills and no loss of skill during a three month no-training period. It was then found that the undergraduate students trained by Dendy could, in turn, train other undergraduates and that these peer-instructed students scored significantly higher than students who experienced other forms of training (Archer & Kagan, 1973). The Archer study found that the IPR-trained students scored significantly higher on affective sensitivity and self-actualization; even more important, their roommates, who had not been included in the study, when given lists of all participants, selected the IPR-trained students as the ones they "would be willing to talk to about a personal problem" significantly more frequently than they selected students trained by other means.

Under the direction of Jason (Jason, Kagan, Werner, Elstein, & Thomas, 1971) IPR was modified for use with medical students. Evaluations of the program (Resnikoff, 1968; Werner & Schneider, 1974) found statistically significant gains in interviewing skills and in sensitivity by medical students. At UCLA Robbins et al. (1979) found that internists made significantly greater gains in interviewing skills than a control group. Statistically significant differences were also found with first-year German medical students in a controlled study in Germany (Feidel & Bolm, 1981). Novik (1978) found that third-year family-practice residents prescribed significantly fewer minor tranquilizers after IPR training than they had during the months preceding IPR training.

The addition of theory units improved the skill level of trainees (Rowe, 1972). Kingdon (1975) found that clients of counselors who received IPR supervision made significantly greater gains in the area of depth of self-exploration than clients of counselors supervised by other means.

Not all studies of the effectiveness of IPR have resulted in statistically significant gains. This is particularly true where participants are not motivated to improve interpersonal skills. For instance, Heiserman (1971) applied IPR to a population of court caseworkers and found no significant gains. Nor have we yet achieved consistent success in studies of acceleration of therapy in which client gains are used as the dependent variable (Munoz, 1971; Van Noord & Kagan, 1976). Interestingly, statistically significant differences were found with recently brain-damaged clients (Helffenstein, 1981).

An important quality of IPR is its applicability to other than middle-class populations. Singleton (1975) found small but statistically significant gains by prison inmates in their relationships with prison guards after training. Most of the inmates were of low socioeconomic status, and many were illiterate.

The basic IPR processes have been used as a research tool. The best-known of these studies is that of Elstein, Shulman, and Sprafka (1978). There has also been some research on the basic processes involved in the IPR model. Katz and Resnikoff (1977) found evidence to validate the assumption that the recall process is indeed recall rather than "rewriting history." Grossman (1975) found evidence to support the premise that the affect-simulation vignettes do indeed have an emotional impact. Further validation of the recall process was found by Young (1980).

Finally, it has been possible to influence large numbers of people through IPR. A single instructor can teach large numbers of students if other students are available to assist in the recall process or if the inquirer role is taught to all students early in the model. Many thousands of soldiers have been trained by a relatively small number of military IPR instructors. In a controlled study of large-scale implementation in a school system, junior high school teachers were rated by students as more human and more likable after teachers received training (Burke & Kagan, 1976).

The more contact hours a student had had with an IPR-trained teacher, the more positive was that student's attitude toward the teacher.

At core, IPR is a series of learning-by-discovery techniques that can be used reliably with any population. Its fundamental assumption is that life is a journey, not a destination.

REFERENCES

Archer, J., Jr., & Kagan, N. Teaching interpersonal relationship skills on campus: A pyramid approach. *Journal of Counseling Psychology,* 1973, *20,* 535–541.

Bedell, W. P. A comparison of two approaches to peer supervision in the training of communication skills using a videotape recall model. Unpublished doctoral dissertation, Michigan State University, 1976.

Boltuch, B. S. The effects of a pre-practicum skill training program; Influencing human interaction: On development of counselor effectiveness in a master's level practicum. Unpublished doctoral dissertation, New York University, 1975.

Burke, J. B., & Kagan, N. Influencing human interaction in urban schools. NIMH Grant MH13526–02, final report, 1976.

Dendy, R. F. A model for the training of undergraduate residence hall assistants as paraprofessional counselors using videotape techniques and Interpersonal Process Recall (IPR). Unpublished doctoral dissertation, Michigan State University, 1971.

Elstein, A. S., Shulman, L., & Sprafka, S. A. *Medical problem solving: An analysis of clinical reasoning.* Cambridge, Mass.: Harvard University Press, 1978.

Feidel, D., & Bolm, G. Self confrontation through video-playback in courses of medical psychology—a summary evaluation of Kagan's Interpersonal Process Recall method in a German adaptation. *Medizinische Psychologie,* 1981, *7,* 61–72.

Grossman, R. W. Limb tremor responses to antagonistic and informational communication. Unpublished doctoral dissertation, Michigan State University, 1975.

Heiserman, M. S. The effect of experiential-videotape training procedures compared to cognitive-classroom teaching methods on the interpersonal communication skills of juvenile court caseworkers. Unpublished doctoral dissertation, Michigan State University, 1971.

Helffenstein, D. A. The effects of IPR (Interpersonal Process Recall) on the interpersonal and communication skills of newly brain injured. Unpublished doctoral dissertation, University of Virginia, 1981.

Horney, K. *Our inner conflicts: A constructive theory of neurosis.* New York: Norton, 1945.

Jason, H., Kagan, N., Werner, A., Elstein, A., & Thomas, J. B. New approaches to teaching basic interview skills to medical students. *American Journal of Psychiatry,* 1971, *127,* 1404–1407.

Kagan, N. Influencing human interaction—eighteen years with IPR. In A. K. Hess (Ed.), *Psychotherapy supervision: Theory, research and practice.* New York: Wiley, 1980.

Kagan, N., & Krathwohl, D. R. Studies in human interaction: Interpersonal Process Recall stimulated by videotape. East Lansing: Michigan State University, 1967.

Kahn, G. S., Cohen, B., & Jason, H. The teaching of interpersonal skills in U.S. medical schools. *Journal of Medical Education,* 1979, *54,* 29–35.

Katz, D., & Resnikoff, A. Televised self-confrontation and recalled affect: A new look at videotape recall. *Journal of Counseling Psychology,* 1977, *24,* 150–152.

Kingdon, M. A. A cost/benefit analysis of the Interpersonal Process Recall technique. *Journal of Counseling Psychology,* 1975, *22,* 353–357.

Munoz, D. G. The effects of simulated affect films and videotape feedback in group psychotherapy with alcoholics. Unpublished doctoral dissertation, Michigan State University, 1971.

Novik, B. R. The effects of teaching interviewing skills and affective sensitivity to family medicine residents. Unpublished doctoral dissertation, Michigan State University, 1978.

Resnikoff, A. The relationship of counselor behavior to client response and an analysis of a medical interview training procedure involving simulated patients. Unpublished doctoral dissertation, Michigan State University, 1968.

Robbins, A. S., Kaus, D. R., Heinrich, R., Abrass, I., Dreyer, J., & Clyman, B. Interpersonal skills: Evaluation in an internal medicine residency. *Journal of Medical Education,* 1979, *54,* 885–894.

Rowe, K. K. A 50-hour intensified IPR training program for counselors. Unpublished doctoral dissertation, Michigan State University, 1972.

Singleton, N. Training incarcerated felons in communication skills using an integrated IPR (Interpersonal Process Recall) videotape feedback/affect simulation training model. Unpublished doctoral dissertation, Michigan State University, 1975.

Spivack, J. S., & Kagan, N. Laboratory to classroom—the practical application of IPR in a masters level pre-practicum counselor education program. *Counselor Education and Supervision,* September 1972, 3–15.

Van Noord, R. W., & Kagan, N. Stimulated recall and affect simulation in counseling: Client growth reexamined. *Journal of Counseling Psychology,* 1976, *23,* 28–33.

Werner, A., & Schneider, J. M. Teaching medical students interactional skills. *New England Journal of Medicine,* 1974, *290,* 1232–1237.

Young, D. W. Reliability of videotape-assisted recall in counseling process research. Unpublished doctoral dissertation, University of Rochester, 1980.

CHAPTER TWELVE

The Human Resources Development Model

Robert W. Cash

Robert W. Cash is a licensed psychologist and a professor in the Department of Educational Psychology and Administration at California State University, Long Beach. In addition, he has been a consultant to over 30 school districts, 10 colleges and universities, and numerous health services agencies. This involvement has resulted in the development and delivery of training programs serving over 3000 helpers. The research on these projects has contributed to establishing a criterion-referenced instructional approach to human resources development. Cash has collaborated with others in authoring book chapters, journal articles, training manuals, and video-cassette training materials on Human Resources Development programs.

In this chapter Robert Cash presents the Human Resources Development Model (HRD), originally conceived by Robert Carkhuff in the early sixties. Today the HRD model is the most widely used method in professional and paraprofessional training. Carkhuff's model expanded Carl Rogers's core conditions (empathic understanding, unconditional positive regard, and genuineness) to include many facilitative therapist skills. Cash redesigned this original "conceptual" HRD model into a criterion-referenced, instructional-based (CRI) approach. Here, Cash marshals an impressive array of research supporting the effectiveness of the HRD model with a wide range of trainee populations.

The Human Resources Development Model (HRD) evolved in response to the need to provide effective and accountable training programs in the delivery of helping services. This model was originally conceived by Robert R. Carkhuff in the early 1960s, and subsequent development, application, and research findings have made it the most influential and widely used training approach in professional and paraprofessional counselor education programs (Banks & Anthony, 1973; Ford, 1979). The model uses training methods and materials shown to be the most efficient at producing acquisition of helper skills, especially interpersonal counseling skills, identified as contributing to positive outcomes in helping relationships. This chapter will describe the HRD model as a helper skills training approach.

HISTORY AND DEVELOPMENT OF THE HRD MODEL

A systematic human-relations-development program was begun by Charles B. Truax and Robert R. Carkhuff (1967) in response to findings by Levitt (1963), Eysenck (1965), and Lewis (1965) that both adults and children treated by professional counselors and therapists did not improve, on the average, any more than untreated persons in control groups. Carkhuff's and Truax's initial efforts to identify the effective ingredients in the helping relationship drew on Carl Rogers's (1957) core dimensions of counselor interpersonal functioning. These original core conditions of empathic understanding, unconditional positive regard, and genuineness (often called "congruence") (Rogers, Gendlin, Kiesler, & Truax, 1967) were examined extensively by Robert Carkhuff, Bernard Berenson, and numerous other researchers who conducted a series of predictive studies on the helper skills and helping processes that related to helping outcomes. As a result of the findings, concreteness, confrontation, and immediacy (referred to as "initiative" or "action") were added to the initial list of core conditions (Carkhuff, 1969a, 1969b). The addition of problem-solving and program-development skills (Carkhuff & Berenson, 1976) to the training system reflects how the eclectic developmental model has continued to add counseling skills relevant to the helping process.

The current criterion-referenced instruction (CRI) HRD training model has grown out of the original pre-1974 "conceptual" systematic human-relations training program developed by Carkhuff (Carkhuff & Berenson, 1976; Cash & Vellema, 1979). This pre-1974 program can be described as a conceptual approach because the core dimensions were presented in a general form rather than as specific observable and measurable behaviors. The term *systematic* refers to the process of presentation in the training, whereby a trainee must first learn to discriminate and then communicate one concept, such as empathy, and then proceed to the next concept, such as respect. This process continues sequentially throughout the seven conditions making up the focus of the human-relations program. A complete description of the training is available in the text *The Development of Human Resources* (Carkhuff, 1971).

Figure 12-1 portrays the three stages of the helping process: self-exploration, understanding, and action. These helpee stages in the Carkhuff model are similar in the conceptual HRD approach and the competency-based CRI approach. The difference is that the post-1974 competency-based approach involves implementation of CRI principles requiring acquisition of behaviorally defined skills in the helper phases. The four phases and sets of helping skills are presented in the areas labeled "Prehelping," "Responding," "Personalizing," and "Initiating." These phases are sets of skills identified through a series of research studies and factor analyses as being the behavioral performance variables making up the original core dimensions of empathy, respect, genuineness, concreteness, and so on—the conditions involved in the pre-1974 conceptually based human-relations training (Carkhuff & Berenson, 1976). These skills have been found to facilitate the counselee's or helpee's movement through self-exploration, understanding, and action stages.

Today's competency-based training uses a criterion-referenced instruction approach that describes goals, objectives, and training activities in observable and measurable performance terms. The training uses social-learning principles to aid in the acquisition of a progressive sequence of specific, research-identified, behaviorally defined competencies (skills).

The HRD model has made immense contributions to the contemporary movement to demystify psychotherapy, especially in regard to processes operating in interpersonal communication. Its operational definitions of helping skills and its functional basis for explaining their use in the helping process provide a person with

CARKHUFF'S HUMAN RELATIONS TRAINING

Facilitative Conditions	Action Conditions
Empathy	Immediacy
Respect	Confrontation

Genuineness
Concreteness
Self-Disclosure

POST-1974 COMPETENCY-BASED HUMAN RESOURCES DEVELOPMENT MODEL

Phases of Helping

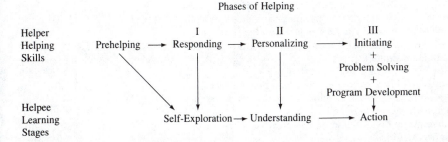

Figure 12-1.   Phases of Carkhuff's Systematic Human Relations Training (pre-1974 conceptually based human relations training) and of the post-1974 competency-based Human Resources Development Model.

tangible skills and a cognitive strategy for guiding the use of those skills in helping interactions and human relationships.

Another unique feature of the HRD model is that it allows helpers of differing theoretical orientations to bring their individual methods into the helping-interaction phases conceptualized in the model. Whereas particular helper skills are specifically prescribed in the development of the facilitation phase of the relationship, the action phase allows any technique to be applied that the helper perceives as giving direction and being relevant to meeting the needs of the helpee, assuming that the helper is competent in the technique and is following appropriate ethical standards.

The continual evolution in the HRD training model has been the result of being able to integrate contemporary instructional-technology developments to gain effectiveness in the delivery of the program (Cash & Vellema, 1979). The increased gains in interpersonal communication skills through use of the media-assisted criterion-referenced instruction (CRI) approach offer a time- and cost-efficient training program.

THE TRAINING PROGRAM

Figure 12-2 shows the 45-hour training-program schedule. The HRD model is organized into four phases, or sets of helping skills; these relate and contribute to the natural processes a helpee moves through in a constructive helping relationship

Figure 12-2

TENTATIVE TRAINING SCHEDULE (45-HOUR TRAINING PROGRAM)

	Approximate Time Involved (Hrs:Min)
1. General meeting with entire class for orientation and introduction to training program and trainers.	0:30
Administration of Communication and Discrimination Indexes. Pretraining videotaping of helping-interview interactions.	2:30
2. Large-group presentation of Prehelping Concepts and demonstration of skills.	1:00
Small-group training in Prehelping Skills: Attending, Observing, Listening (ten per trainer).	2:00
3. Large-group presentation on Responding Phase in Helping.	1:00
Small-group training in Responding Skills and Prehelping Skills.	2:00
4. Small-group training, a continuation on Responding Skills (with triads). Self-Exploration Concepts explained and demonstrated.	3:00
5. Large-group review of Responding.	0:30
Videotaped or cassette recording of a helping relationship.	1:00
Small-group review and rating of videotaped pretraining and mid-training helping interview.	1:30
6. Large-group presentation on Personalizing Phase Concepts and Skills.	1:30
Small-group training in Personalizing Skills.	1:30
7. Small-group training in Personalizing Skills.	3:00
8. Small-group training, a continuation on Personalizing Skills (with dyads).	2:00
Large-group review and discussion of live demonstration or videotaped helping relationship.	1:00
9. Large-group presentation of Initiating Phase Concepts and Skills (Part 1: Problem-Solving Steps).	1:30
Small-group training in Initiating Skills.	1:30
10. Large-group presentation of Initiating Phase Concepts and Skills (Part 2: Program-Development Steps).	1:00
Small-group training in Initiating Skills.	2:00
11. Small-group training in Initiating Skills by using the core facilitation dimensions with action dimensions in the Phases of Helping (with dyads).	3:00
12. Large-group meeting for review of concepts and applications.	1:00
Viewing and discussion of live demonstration or video-taped helping relationship.	2:00
Small-group training.	
13. Administration of Communication and Discrimination Indexes.	1:00
Videotaping or cassette recording of helping-interview interactions.	1:30
14. Small-group meetings to assess communication skills levels.	1:00
Review and rate videotapes/cassette recordings.	2:00
15. General meeting with entire class to summarize effect of skills gained, applications in respective settings, planning of follow-up and support programs. Discuss and critique aspects of the training program.	2:00

(Carkhuff & Anthony, 1979; Egan, 1975; Gazda, Asbury, Balzer, Childers, Desselle, & Walters, 1973). Module 1 provides an introduction to and overview of the
training program. Module 2, called "Prehelping Skills," focuses on attending,
observing, and listening skills. Module 3 presents the "Responding Skills," in which
the accurate response to feeling and to reasons for the feeling is learned. Module 4,
"Personalizing Skills," beginning in the sixth session, helps the trainee to learn how
to personalize the problem situation, define the helpee's problem and the deficits
that are causing the problem, respond to new feelings, and identify personalized
goal(s). The helper initiating phase is divided into two modules: Module 5, in
Session 9, develops "Problem-Solving Processes," and Module 6, in Session 10,
provides "Program-Development Steps," or planning skills that can be used to
provide direction to the helpee's progress toward reaching the personalized goal(s).

Typically, a general group session (no limit to participant numbers) is used to
present each new learning module. The module, designed on a CRI basis (Cash &
Stevens, 1980), provides an initial didactic presentation of selected concepts for
each respective phase of helping and a demonstration of how skills work in helping
interactions. Pre- and postassessments focus on content and obtain a picture of the
trainees' conceptual comprehension of the set of skills covered in each module. The
large group then breaks into small groups of 10 to 12 under the direction of a
qualified trainer to provide practice (experiential learning) of the skills being
sequentially presented. A *Trainer's Manual* (Cash, Scherba, & Mills, 1975) and a
Trainee's Workbook (Cash, 1981b) have been developed to assist in practice and
acquisition of the skills.

The "guided learning" structure followed in conducting the small group provides
systematic procedures to ensure appropriate practice and demonstration of the
skills. A structured verbal-response format is used in the initial training phases
because it assists efficiency in skill acquisition. Training procedures to assist the
individualizing and natural use of the helping skills are used later in the training of
the helping skills when the verbal-response format is dropped. Homework assignments or outside practice activities contribute to and correlate with the training
skills being learned. A log or journal filled out at the end of each small-group session
helps trainees to communicate in writing the feelings and reactions they are experiencing as a result of the training. The trainer responds to each entry in a personal
and confidential manner to assist the establishment of a facilitative relationship.
Visual aids are used as prompters for reference when introducing new skills to the
small group. These supporting materials have been developed in response to identified needs of training programs and have received highly positive responses from
trainees.

The Trainer

A trainer is a person who has successfully completed this initial training course and
possesses the interpersonal skills on which effective helping relationships are
based. This trainer has great importance, as it is in the small-group practice sessions
that the vital experiential phase of training is provided. "If the trainer is functioning
at high levels of the dimensions on which the trainee is being trained, the probability

of the success of training with any trainee population is high" (Carkhuff, 1971, p. 185).

In the program at California State University, Long Beach, trainers must complete a trainer-training program that provides an understanding of the HRD theory, research, rater training, and small-group instructional delivery skills and must have successfully conducted a supervised small group. The trainer is required to have demonstrated that he or she is living effectively in the three relevant life areas of intellectual, physical, and emotional/interpersonal skills. The "tell, show, and do" teaching strategy requires the trainer to utilize researched social-learning principles. In conducting practice activities prescribed by the manual, the trainer must be able to explain specific instructions in a positive, enthusiastic, and directive manner and must, through immediate reinforcement, provide positive support for the trainee's progress. We have found it more effective to build on positive reinforcement and "stay on task" by focusing on the training-program objective than to use negative comments and general conceptual discussions. The trainer needs to be able to model the skill, individualize practice activities, and provide continuous feedback so that each trainee is successful in acquiring the sequential skills. The trainer's responsibility for determining whether the trainee has met the criterion level of acceptability for each of the behavioral skills is important, for 90% of the trainees in the small group are required to demonstrate effective use of the skill in practice before the group moves on to the next behavioral skill objective in the training.

Assessment Measures

One of the most advantageous features of the HRD model has been its accountability procedures, which have helped to produce a substantial research base on helper skills. The CRI version of the HRD training integrates the written indexes, videotaped or audiorecorded interactions, and "live" assessment procedures. As can be noted in Figure 12-2, written indexes and videoing procedures are used before, during, and after training. Pretraining assessment provides information on levels of functioning existing before instruction so that teaching strategies can be adapted to trainees' needs. The posttraining assessment provides overall measures of gain that can be attributed to the training. The playback of the video- and audiotaped interactions to the trainee provides opportunities for feedback, modeling, individualizing input, and support for appropriate skill use. Ongoing trainer comments, other trainee input, and self-evaluation capability due to the developed comprehension of the prescribed skills provide continual feedback on progress made during the program.

Provision for observing live and videotaped models of appropriate skill use is programmed for key points in the delivery (see sessions 5, 8, 12, and 14, Figure 12-2). In addition, the module presenter and trainers continually provide modeling of the skills in the general and small-group sessions as necessary to meet individual trainees' needs.

The HRD model also provides assessment to assist selection of counselor trainees and examines levels of competence of graduates (such as for certification or licensure standards), as well as contributing a standardized data source for research. As counseling relationships also have the potential to harm clients, counselor educators need to take responsibility for ensuring that helpers have the identified basic interpersonal skills necessary for effective helping relationships. The base that the HRD research has developed provides procedures for selection and assessment of helper-training-program effects. Because we are able to establish a criterion level of acceptance for skills performance, it is our vital responsibility to use indexes of the criteria to select potential helpers in order to ensure that we have people who have the ability to provide helpful relationships.

The most commonly used instruments to measure the criterion variables are adaptations of Carkhuff's (1971) Communication and Discrimination Indexes. The Discrimination Index measures the trainee's ability to discriminate effective from ineffective use of the core dimensions in helping responses. The index presents "helpee stimulus statements" in written form and a set of four "helper responses" to each statement by the helpee. The trainee's ratings are objectively scored against preestablished experts' norms to obtain a measure of the trainee's ability.

The Communication Index evaluates the trainee's performance in using the core conditions in response to written helpee statements. The trainee's written "helper response" is judged by trained raters on a 5-point scale (Figure 12-3).

The data obtained from the use of the written indexes or videotaped helping-interaction assessments can be used also for comparison of training programs and research on selected instructional or helper-skill variables of interest.

THEORETICAL CONCEPTS

To understand how and why the HRD model has worked in the selection and training of helpers to function in dimensions that contribute to effective helping relationships, one must examine its theoretical ingredients. Recognition and credit need to be given to Robert R. Carkhuff's leadership and contribution to initially developing the HRD model. The early years of 1965–1975 are marked in the literature by his and numerous colleagues' studies and writing on the model. The text *Helping and Human Relations* (Vol. 2) (1969b) delineates the propositions, corollaries, and principles underpinning helping (pp. 4–14) and training processes (pp. 130, 182–183). An updated summary of the unique contributions of the conceptual HRD training procedures can be found in Carkhuff (1972c).

It is from these foundations that the criterion-referenced, instructional-based HRD model has been able to further the effectiveness of training delivery. Emphasis on carefully designed learning modules and on small-group instruction in developmentally sequenced sessions integrates modern learning principles and instructional technology to teach defined helping skills. The model is built on the assumptions that skills are learned through interaction with the environment and that control of these interactions can accomplish more efficient teaching. The counselor educator or trainer role demands an understanding of these principles and an ability to use them to maximize learning gains.

The learning principles used in the design are considered applicable to all levels of education. Readers who have responsibilities for developing training programs or who teach helper skills are challenged to be able to adjust them to the developmental level and needs of the learners. Instructional-technology principles have been

Figure 12-3

GENERAL DEFINITIONS OF LEVELS USED IN THE COMMUNICATION INDEX

5.0	Has 4.0 conditions plus operationalizing directional steps toward the goal. Here you will find initial suggestions or steps provided toward reaching the goal. Program development of operational steps, reinforcement, and so on, preferably with specified time line.
4.5	Dimensions that operationally define the goal into observable and measurable behaviors (problem-solving steps, skills needed, and so forth).
4.0	Has 3.5 conditions plus identification of the goal. (Personalizes the goal—that is, where the helpee wants to go.) Gives personalized understanding regarding where the helpee needs to be or where he or she wants to be.
3.5	Has 3.0 conditions plus definition of the problem, preferably with deficits that are causing the problem. (Personalizes the problem regarding where the helpee is—lack of skills, inability, and so on—from the helper's reference.) It includes personalizing the meaning it has to the helpee in order to assist him or her understand and own the problem.
3.0	Responds accurately to the helpee feeling and meaning (content/situation/reason for the feeling). Response captures helpee's expressed feeling and meaning experienced.
2.5	Expresses feeling only (accurately). Content (reason/situation/meaning) missing.
2.0	Contains only a response to situational content/situation (reason for the feeling). It has omitted feeling or missed it (demonstrates observing and listening).
1.5	Response has some relation to helpee's statement. This level could have direction, advice, or question statements (attending physically). It should not negate or "put down" the helpee.
1.0	Both feeling and content/reason/situation missing. Comment or behavior indicates helper is not attending (physically or emotionally). Makes judgmental comments that negate helpee's statement.

developed and researched from a number of areas, including educational psychology, experimental psychology, programmed instruction, and audiovisual developments. Main contributors include Eva Baker, Norman Gronlund, Robert Mager, Peter Pipe, James Popham, James Russell, and Kathleen Johanningsmeier. An important premise of the CRI model is the goal of maximizing students' effectiveness and efficiency in achieving specified interpersonal communication skill objectives.

The model functions to (1) guide trainers through the instructional steps of delivering the helper skills effectively and (2) provide an overall frame of reference for communicating future efforts to examine and expand the training model. The model, the materials, and most of the specific methods have been experimentally tested for teaching efficiency. You will probably recognize many of the learning principles and teaching procedures as methods you already use. The providing of clear descriptions in the trainer's manual assists in making explicit what goes into the CRI delivery of the HRD model. The CRI version has the potential to provide a clear format of a training-program approach that specifies the instructional objectives and the methods used to achieve them. This could be used to compare the HRD model with other training-program approaches or to analyze alternative instructional methods being considered for reaching particular instructional objectives within the HRD model. The model thus far has proved to be dynamic and continually growing, in that it provides for the continual evaluation of different training procedures, population applications, and helper skills so that innovations can have a research base and a functional rationale for use. The CRI approach can be modified for new kinds of learners and can assist an instructor to use personal preferences and capabilities with instructional methods/resources to meet learners' needs. Given that the individual instructor decides what to teach, what procedures to use, and what means of evaluation to apply, the CRI approach might be given consideration as an alternative for increasing efficiency and quality in training of helper skills.

The basic components of the instructional theory underlying CRI are derived from modern social-learning theory as reviewed by Becker, Engelmann, and Thomas (1971) or Reynolds (1968). This source of behavior theory provides principles for designing the instructional activities and procedures. These principles—practice, reinforcement, modeling, feedback, prompting, shaping, and so on—are well known and can be examined in the sources cited.

Another component of the instructional approach is a set of principles used for selecting and sequencing the objectives and the tasks chosen to teach the objectives. These programming and task-analysis principles are also usually credited to behavior theory.

The CRI design principles require that construction of the training be directed toward instructional objectives or descriptions of achievements sought that can be expressed in terms of performance. Both conceptual knowledge and performance execution of the skills are included in the training program. Certain principles inherent in the model need to be identified for understanding the operational framework:

1. CRI requires that the training have a clearly defined and limited number of specific learning outcomes. By dividing the complex learning process into manageable units, one can analyze the overall learning task and sequence the essential skills to facilitate its successful achievement.

2. CRI also requires that instructional objectives be defined in terms of observable and measurable behavioral performance. In addition, if desirable, a description of conditions when or where the performance is to occur can be included.

3. A key requirement is that a minimum standard of performance be clearly established. Ideally, there would be research establishing this criterion level of acceptability. The time allowable for attaining mastery is adjustable in this approach, not the performance standard for mastery.

4. All trainees are required to demonstrate acquisition of the performance skill. This requirement presumes that the training format provides an opportunity for the student to show appropriate use of the helper skill.

5. The direct observation and assessment of the trainee's functioning in the helper skill reflect the absolute performance standard specified in the instructional

objective. No inference or norm-referenced testing is required, as the behavior performance standard and learning tasks are clearly defined measures of the helper skill. The training approach ensures that all students will master the goal if sufficient time is available.

6. CRI requires that a scoring and reporting system describe trainee performance on the defined learning task. The development of standards for the levels of functioning (Figure 12-3) has provided a scoring procedure to report precisely at what specified level of proficiency the helpee can perform. This assessment procedure describes the trainee's level of performance without reference to the performance of other trainees. The scores can be compared for quality-control purposes or research if desired.

The theoretical principles just outlined form the basis for contemporary HRD programs and explain why the CRI model has been so effective. The evidence to date supports training programs having an operationally defined goal and skill orientation (Cash & Vellema, 1979; Cormier, Cormier, Zerega, & Wagaman, 1976). A cautionary note is added here: If an instructor's orientation and skill level are not compatible with such a rigorous instructional approach, the training effort will fail or at least will fall short of producing the gain possible. An instructor using the CRI design must be personally willing to give time and energy to make it work.

APPLICATIONS AND POTENTIALITIES

The HRD helper skills training program has shown great flexibility in its capacity to be applied to differing populations. It has an impressive capability to be modified to effectively and efficiently train individuals or groups of people needing specific skills to cope with environmental or personal living demands.

Figure 12-4 (on pp. 259–265) provides a picture of the extent and quality of applications that have been made over the past six years. Our initial studies focused predominantly on instructional variables to improve the interpersonal skill gains (outcomes) from training, but the expansion to in-service training of school-district personnel throughout California soon became the focus.

Increasing requests from sources such as other college and university training programs and nursing, psychology, physical education, criminal justice, and community human services agencies (mental health agencies, hospitals, drug-abuse programs, and so on) necessitated the construction of a "pyramiding" model to maintain effectiveness and quality control of training programs. The four phases of the "pyramid" approach provide the individual institution the capacity to offer the HRD training independently. Briefly, the first phase provides orientation, needs assessment, goals and resources identification, program planning, and organizational assistance. The second step is to conduct an initial helper skills training program of 30 to 45 hours for a limited number of institutional or agency people. From this base, the third phase repeats the initial helper skills training for a new group of participants and at the same time coordinates a trainer-training program (50–60 hours) for selected high-functioning individuals from the initial training session. The fourth stage enables the now-qualified trainers from the institution to conduct the training while outside consultants are gradually phased out. Organizational planning for management and resources support is developed so that subsequent training—offerings for additional community, agency, or school-district personnel—can be conducted without outside assistance.

The nature of the criterion-referenced instructional model, materials developed, and evaluation procedures makes it possible to use computer and data systems to monitor training progress and outcomes. The recently produced videotaped learning modules covering the main sets of helper skills can be coordinated with the *HRD Trainer's Manual* (Cash, Scherba, & Mills, 1975), *Trainee's Workbook* (Cash, 1981b), and evaluation instruments to support dissemination and effective, efficient delivery of HRD training to additional populations and settings.

The current movement is to design the HRD training for telecourses and educational television delivery. It seems quite likely that CRI delivery using small-group trainers at "on site" locations of libraries, schools, and even homes will accomplish identical high acquisition levels on execution of performance skills as well as cognitive knowledge.

Another potential area of application is the use of the CRI model for identifying needs and providing specific training in the more comprehensive "life-span development" skills (more commonly known as "life skills"). The HRD model provides a basis for examining individuals' capacities for meeting key developmental tasks and transition or crisis points in life. The instructional model has the potential to deliver the skills needed to cope with living needs and to enhance the ability to achieve human goals. Maximum human development, more than ever before envisioned, may be within the realm of possibility.

REVIEW OF RESEARCH

In examining use of the HRD model with educational populations and settings, the contributions of David Aspy, Robert Carkhuff, Robert Cash, and George Gazda merit attention.

Aspy's initial research with teachers (1969), followed up by his work with the National Consortium for Humanizing Education (Aspy & Roebuck, 1974, 1977) and the text *Kids Don't Learn from Teachers They "Don't Like"* (Aspy & Roebuck, 1977), showed that teachers who provided high levels of interpersonal communication skills contributed to significant student improvements in academic achievement, classroom behavior, and attendance.

Cash and colleagues at California State University, Long Beach, have provided the CRI version of the HRD training as on-campus preservice preparation and as in-service education of public school professional credentialed staff and paraprofessional personnel. Over 45 studies report significant pre-to-post gains by the trainees in an average training program. Improvements in academic achievement, attendance, behavior, attitude toward school, and interpersonal communication have been reported. These programs have varied from 30 to 60 hours' duration. Norms for pretraining and posttraining levels of functioning have been developed on a population of over 1500 trainees for analysis and comparison with other programs.

Gazda and his colleagues (1973) at the University of Georgia have developed human-relations training programs and materials for preservice and in-service training of teachers. Studies reported reveal significant gains in interpersonal communication and positive response in as short a training period as 15 to 20 hours.

Populations and settings where HRD training programs have been used include correctional institutions, community mental health workers, parents, and health care services. For example, use of the HRD model at the Federal Adult Correctional Center in Lompoc, California, and at the Rhode Island Training School resulted in increased functioning of staff, reduced recidivism, and improved physical, emotional, interpersonal, and intellectual functioning of inmates (Carkhuff, Devine, Berenson, Griffin, Angelone, Keeling, Patch, & Steinberg, 1974).

A number of studies have addressed themselves to the specific effects that HRD training has had on health care service workers: Carkhuff and Truax (1965a, 1965b) with psychiatric-hospital lay personnel; Pagell, Carkhuff, and Berenson (1967), along with Pierce and Drasgow (1969), studying counselor effects on outpatients; Kalish (1971) with student nurses; Deneen (1973) in the area of dentistry; Gazda, Walters, and Childers (1975) with hospital health care teams; Cash (1980) with nursing instructors and community agency personnel. Positive outcome gains in interpersonal communication skills over brief training periods of 15 to 100 hours are reported as a result of HRD training programs.

Contradictory results from follow-up studies on the retention of skills from HRD training raise more issues and questions than they provide useful guidelines for training. Pierce and Schauble (1971) report that facilitative-functioning levels of trainees tend to remain the same for a nine-month period; Holder (1969) and Renz (1970), for one- and two-month periods; Butler and Hansen (1973), for four weeks. Salcido (1975) conducted a one-year follow-up with teachers and reported that discrimination scores maintained similar levels to posttraining but that facilitative-communication levels had a significant loss. Collingwood's (1969) five-month check also indicated that most trainees slip in functioning levels after training. Both Salcido and Collingwood report that some trainees maintain and even continue to gain beyond their posttraining levels.

These inconsistent results are due to a number of factors. First, the sample sizes, from 9 to 34, do not support conclusive results. Second, there are extreme differences in the amount of training time (5 to 30 hours) and in the populations (both in type and in motivation) reported. Third, the interval between posttraining tests and follow-up was not long or systematically planned. These differences in procedures have complicated the findings and contributed to contradictory results.

The variance in amount of training time is one of the most controversial factors in the delivery of helping skills training programs. Instructors and investigators have differing views on the number and kinds of training goals or instructional objectives, which subsequently affect the amount of time taken for training. Several studies report between 1 and 100 hours of HRD training as significantly more effective than no training (Ford, 1979). The initial efforts to use the HRD model reported that up to 100 hours were used to have helpers achieve levels of facilitative functioning (empathy, positive regard, genuineness) comparable to those of experienced therapists (Carkhuff & Truax, 1965a). Truax and Lister (1971) cited 40 hours to assess effect on accurate empathy. Kelly (1972) did a study in which only 16 hours yielded significant increases in both written and videotaped responses. The training time reported appears directly related to the instructor's or investigator's choice of goals. The confusing differences require that an instructor examine closely what helping skills are to be achieved in the training program.

The current HRD program has generally established that 20 to 30 hours is required to acquire comprehension, performance execution, and transfer of responding skills by trainees into their natural environment; 40 to 45 hours for demonstrating satisfactory use of personalizing skills; and 50 to 60 hours for problem-solving and program-development skills that complete the entire skill series currently included in the HRD model (Carkhuff, 1969a; Cash, Scherba, & Mills, 1975; Egan, 1975). A key guideline is that time is adjustable according to the instructional goal and the skill criterion level desired by the trainer and trainee.

Most training models claim to be effective in assisting development of interpersonal dimensions of helping relationships. The question that Resnikoff (1972) posed ten years ago, "If the training is effective, what is it better than?" has yet to be answered in counselor education. The limited research reported to date on comparing different training approaches seems to reflect the experimenter's bias, rather than establishing whether there is a difference between training models.

Selfridge, Weitz, Calabria, Steger, Abramotwitz, and Abramotwitz (1975) compared two treatment groups, each having 16 hours of HRD, with one group having 8 hours of lectures and the other 8 hours of sensitivity encounter-group training. Results showed that clients saw the HRD/sensitivity-group training as offering more facilitative levels of interpersonal functioning. In a related study, Sawyer (1977) comprehensively examined the effect of differential sequencing of HRD training and sensitivity-encounter training. The Carkhuff Communication and Discrimination Indexes showed a significant relationship between trainee gain in level of functioning and HRD segments. When training segments were combined so that all groups had both treatments, no differences between the groups were found. Self-reports of participants implied a preference for having the HRD training before the sensitivity-encounter-group training model.

Toukmanian and Rennie (1975) compared Microcounseling with HRD training and reported that the Microcounseling-trained counselors gained significantly more on empathy functioning. Both training groups significantly improved on three other categories of counselor communication derived from the Microcounseling training paradigm, compared with no-training control groups.

Cash and Vellema (1979) compared the originally designed HRD model with the criterion-referenced competency-based (post-1974) HRD training as related to defined interpersonal communication skills and discrimination abilities. The results support the competency-based CRI approach as significantly more effective than the pre-1974 HRD-model training (Carkhuff, 1969a, 1971) in both acquisition of communication skills and improvement of discrimination skill functioning. In addition, the pre-1974 HRD training was significantly more effective in developing communication and discrimination skills than having no training.

CONCLUSIONS

In concluding this chapter, I reemphasize the basic premise that the most important single factor in effective helping is the level of interpersonal functioning of the helper (Carkhuff, 1969a, 1969b; Carkhuff & Berenson, 1976; Gazda, 1977; Rogers et al., 1967). It would seem desirable to seek counselor-training programs that most efficiently and effectively provide the highest levels of functioning in the helping relationship.

The frequency and variety of studies and of references being made in the professional literature imply a widespread use of the HRD model. The clear-cut findings from Cash and Vellema's (1979) study suggest that counselor educators might want to reexamine their training programs by considering innovations based on instructional technology. It bears mentioning that the texts and teaching materials published by the Carkhuff-sponsored HRD Press since 1975 reflect a utilization of CRI principles, or what those publications call "Human Technology" principles. Media-assisted instructional materials (Cash, 1981a) and the *HRD Trainer's Manual* (Cash, Scherba, & Mills, 1975) also provide individuals and organizations with the capacity to conduct the CRI version of the HRD training.

If, as several studies report (Egan, 1975; Hatcher, Brooks, & Associates, 1977; Horan, 1979; Jakubowski-Spector, Dustin, & George, 1971; Popham, 1973), a number of other skill areas exist that are important for effective counseling, then the CRI methodology could be a vehicle for designing effective training-delivery systems for these performance skill areas. Describing goals and objectives in behavioral-criterion terms contributes to designing evaluation procedures, thus enabling comparisons of training alternatives. Choices of training activities might be made more wisely if empirical data were available on which to base decisions.

The professional issues of accreditation and licensure have raised many questions about standards. Being able to specify competencies having direct relations to positive outcomes in counseling offers the possibility of using CRI principles to define and assess these proficiencies. One could foresee the selection of applicants for counselor training, and even endorsement of graduates, on the basis of having defined skills.

There have been a number of efforts to design interpersonal skills training programs for populations other than counselors (Aspy & Roebuck, 1977; Carkhuff, 1971; Egan, 1975; Gazda, 1977). People in such related helping service areas as nursing, teaching, and parenting are continually involved in interpersonal relationships. The use of effective training programs to assist acquisition of interpersonal skills will be in even more demand in the future.

Counseling psychologists, paraprofessionals, and everyone in the human services will be faced with the challenge of providing effective and cost-efficient programs in the delivery of helping services. The training of counselors requires methods shown to have the most impact on the acquisition of skills—especially those interpersonal counseling skills necessary to positive outcomes from helping relationships. The HRD criterion-referenced instruction approach has shown that it has potential for increasing efficiency and quality in helper skills training and counselor education programs.

Figure 12-4

HRD APPLICATIONS: POPULATIONS, OUTCOME MEASURES, AND RESULTS

Helping-Programs Study	HRD Outcome Measures	Results
Community Agency Services (racial relations, rehabilitation, and so on)		
1. Effects of trained community helpers on unemployed (Carkhuff, 1971; Carkhuff & Griffin, 1971)	Helpee employment	88% of graduates gainfully employed 1 year later
2. Effects of trained community helpers on students (Carkhuff, 1971; Carkhuff & Griffin, 1970)	Student interpersonal functioning	Improved significantly ($p < .05$)
	Parent interpersonal functioning	Improved significantly ($p < .05$)
	School staff interpersonal functioning	Improved significantly ($p < .05$)
	Teacher interpersonal functioning	Improved significantly ($p < .05$)
	Attendance officer interpersonal functioning	Improved significantly ($p < .05$)
3. Effects of trained community helpers on students (Carkhuff, 1971)	Black student classroom expression	12 of 12 students desensitized by trained community helpers expressed themselves effectively in class (mean of 4.0 on 5-point scale)
4. Effects of interpersonal skills training on rehabilitation counselors (Anthony, 1973)	Counselor interpersonal functioning	Recommends training for rehabilitation counselors
5. Effects of academic background and experience on social worker interpersonal skills (Westwood, 1972)	Social worker level of communication Social worker level of discrimination	Social work graduate students significantly higher in communication skills
6. Effects of interpersonal skills training with community members and mental health personnel (Cash, 1978)	Level of discrimination	Significantly improved ($p < .01$)
	Level of communication	Significantly improved ($p < .01$)
	Trainee self-report	100% positive
7. Effects of client/counselor interaction and patterns of service on rehabilitation clients (Bozarth, Rubin, Krauft, Richardson, & Bolton, 1974)	Self-reports Tape-recorded interviews	Higher level of interpersonal skill (above minimal facilitative level) related to higher monthly earnings, positive psychological change, greater job satisfaction at follow up

		High-level helpers	Low-level helpers
Counselor Education (training and selection of counselors)			
8. Effects of counselor level of functioning on patients (Pagell, Carkhuff, & Berenson, 1967)	Patient interpersonal functioning across 5 dimensions		
	Expert ratings	100% positive	10% positive
	Therapist ratings	100% positive	30% positive
	Tape ratings	80% positive	43% positive
	Interviewee ratings	80% positive	47% positive
	Self-ratings	30% positive	13% positive

Figure 12-4 *(continued)*

HRD APPLICATIONS: POPULATIONS, OUTCOME MEASURES, AND RESULTS

Helping-Program Study	HRD Outcome Measures	Results	
	Gross ratings of patient behavior across 4 indexes: disturbance, self-care, sociability, improvement		
	Expert ratings	88% positive	16% positive
	Therapist ratings	88% positive	29% positive
	Interviewee ratings	56% positive	27% positive
	Self-ratings	88% positive	46% positive
9. Effects of trained counselors on clients (Carkhuff, Friel, Berenson, Bebermeyer, Mahrt, & Forrest, 1972)	Student self-reports of helpfulness of counseling	Students of trained counselor groups reported guidance effectiveness from 74% to 91% against base rate of 13% and traditionally trained counselor rate of 25%	
10. Effects of supervisor on supervisee (Pierce & Schauble, 1970)	Supervisee level of interpersonal functioning	Supervisee level higher for higher-functioning supervisors ($p < .05$)	
11. Effects of supervisor on supervisee (Pierce & Schauble, 1971)	Supervisee level of interpersonal functioning	Supervisee level higher for higher-functioning supervisors 9 months later ($p < .05$)	
12. Effects of physical functioning levels on training in interpersonal skills (Cassatta, 1974)	Level of discrimination	High-level physical-fitness students significantly improved ($p < .01$ over low-level physical-fitness students	
	Level of communication	High-level physical-fitness students significantly improved ($p < .001$) over low-level physical-fitness students	
13. Effects of videotaping and written instruments on rating interpersonal skills (Hawley, 1978)	Videotaped interviews Written instruments	No differences No differences	
14. Study of advanced graduate students compared with practicing school counselors (Louscher, 1972)	Level of discrimination Level of communication	Did not differ: both groups functioned below minimal level to be effective helpers	
15. Effects of trainer training on trained counselors (Mitchell, 1974)	Level of discrimination Level of communication	Significant improvement ($p < .01$) Significant improvement ($p < .05$)	
16. Effects of sex and prior group experience on training gains (Pasley, 1973)	Student level of discrimination Student level of communication	Pretraining level of functioning affected gains; sex and prior group experience interacted and affected gains; no differences on posttest	
17. Relationship of personality characteristics and level of communication skills (Plummer, 1973)	Level of communication Omnibus Personality Inventory Eysenck Personality Inventory	No significant correlations on characteristics studied	

Figure 12-4 *(continued)*

HRD APPLICATIONS: POPULATIONS, OUTCOME MEASURES, AND RESULTS

Helping-Program Study	HRD Outcome Measures	Results
18. Relationship of social intelligence and level of communication skills (Richards, 1973)	Social intelligence Level of communication	No significant correlations
19. Follow-up study (1 yr.) on retention of interpersonal skills from training (Salcido, 1975)	Level of discrimination Level of communication	No change Significant loss ($p < .05$)
20. Effect of sequencing sensitivity-encounter training and HRD training (Sawyer, 1974)	Level of discrimination Level of communication	HRD resulted in significant improvement ($p < .001$) in discrimination and communication levels; no differences when both sequences combined
21. Study of entering graduate students compared with advanced graduate students (Scherba, 1973)	Level of discrimination Level of communication	Did not differ Did not differ Both groups functioned below minimal level to be effective helpers
22. Effect of problem and affect on development of interpersonal skills (Seaman, 1972)	Level of discrimination Level of communication	No differences No differences Level of trainer was main influence
23. Effects of videotaping and audiotaping on rating interpersonal skills (Zolner, 1975)	Videotaped interviews Audiotaped interviews	No significant differences on posttraining ratings; significant differences on pretest ratings ($p < .05$); nonverbal variables appeared to influence ratings
24. Effects of using student workbook in training programs (Hillinger, 1978)	Level of discrimination Level of communication	Significant difference ($p < .05$) No differences
25. Effects of competency-based training compared with conceptual-based training on helpers (Cash & Vellema, 1979)	Level of discrimination Level of communication	Competency-based training significantly higher ($p < .01$) Significantly higher ($p < .01$) Both significantly higher than no training
26. Effects of videotaped and live teacher module presentations on training of attending behaviors (Redgate, 1981)	Level of attending behaviors	Both video and live presentations significantly improved ($p < .05$) over comparison group
27. Effects of counselor level of functioning on client self-exploration (Carkhuff & Alexik, 1967; Holder, Carkhuff, & Berenson, 1967; Piaget, Carkhuff, & Berenson, 1968)	Self-exploration	Client self-exploration was significantly related to counselor level of functioning
28. Effects of helper level of functioning, race, and social class on helpees (Banks, Berenson, & Carkhuff, 1967; Carkhuff & Pierce, 1967)	Self-exploration	Helpee self-exploration was related to helper race and social class

Figure 12-4 *(continued)*

HRD APPLICATIONS: POPULATIONS, OUTCOME MEASURES, AND RESULTS

Helping-Program Study	HRD Outcome Measures	Results
Educational Institutions (teachers, staff, students, and so on)		
29. Effects of helper level of functioning and verbal conditioning on students (Vitalo, 1970)	Student emission of personal pronouns	Both helper level of functioning and verbal conditioning were significant sources of effect ($p < .05$)
30. Effects of helper level of functioning and behavior conditioning on students (Mickelson & Stevic, 1971)	Student vocational-information-seeking behavior	High-level counselors engaged students in significantly more vocational-information seeking ($p < .01$)
31. Effects of teacher level of functioning on students (Aspy, 1969)	Student educational achievement	Significantly more improvement in students of high teachers than students of low teachers on 5 of 6 achievement indexes
32. Effects of teacher level of functioning on students (Aspy & Hadlock, 1967)	Student educational achievement	Significantly greater for students of high teachers than students of low teachers
	Student truancy	Significantly more for students of low teachers than students of high teachers
33. Effects of parent and teacher level of functioning on students (Kratochvil, Carkhuff, & Berenson, 1969)	Student physical functioning Student interpersonal functioning Student intellectual achievement	No differences; physical, interpersonal, and intellectual correlated significantly ($p < .05$)
34. Effects of trainers on trainees (Pierce, Carkhuff, & Berenson, 1967)	Trainee dropout rate and level of interpersonal functioning	Trainees of high trainers stayed and gained significantly ($p < .05$); trainees of low trainers, 55% premature termination and no significant gain
35. Effects of trained teachers on students (Aspy, 1972)	Student educational achievement	Significant improvement ($p < .05$)
	Student IQ	Significant improvement of 9 IQ points ($p < .05$)
	Student self-concept	Significant improvement ($p < .05$)
36. Effects of trained teachers on students (Aspy & Roebuck, 1972)	Student cognitive processes	Significant improvement ($p < .05$)
37. Effects of trained teachers on students (Berenson, 1971, 1972)	Student achievement	Significantly greater achievement for students of trained teachers
38. Effects of trained teachers on students (Mosher & Sprinthall, 1972)	Student interpersonal skills	Significant improvement ($p < .05$)

Figure 12-4 *(continued)*

HRD APPLICATIONS: POPULATIONS, OUTCOME MEASURES, AND RESULTS

Helping-Program Study	HRD Outcome Measures	Results
39. Effects of trained teachers on students (Hefele, 1971)	Student achievement	Teacher level related significantly to group of 10 achievement measures ($p < .0001$)
40. Effects of trained teachers on students (Williams, 1972)	Student knowledge of learning theory	Significantly greater knowledge for students of trained teachers ($p < .05$)
41. Effects of teacher level of functioning on students (Stoffer, 1970)	Student achievement	Student achievement a function of teacher level of functioning ($p < .05$)
42. Effects of trained teachers on students (Henzel, 1974)	Self-concept School attitude	Improved Improved
43. Effects of trained teachers on students (Rockford, 1973)	Math achievement Reading achievement	Significant improvement ($p < .05$) Significant improvement ($p < .05$)
44. Effects of trained teachers on students (Griffin, 1972)	Student interpersonal skills	Significant improvement
45. Effects of in-service training of teachers, counselors, administrators, staff personnel (over 30 studies) (Cash, 1974–1980b)	Level of discrimination Level of communication Trainee self-reports	Significantly improved ($p < .01$) Significantly improved ($p < .01$) 99% positive
46. Effects of staff development programs for college and university faculty, counselors, counselor educators, and staff (8 studies) (Cash, 1974–1980a)	Level of discrimination Level of communication Trainee self-reports	Significantly improved ($p < .01$) Significantly improved ($p < .01$) 95% positive

Health Care Services

47. Effects of trained hospital attendants on psychiatric-hospital patients (Carkhuff & Truax, 1965a, 1965b)	Gross ratings of patient behavior by ward personnel: overall improvement Discharge from hospital	Treatment group: 53% improved, 1% deteriorated Control group: 27% improved, 17% deteriorated Treatment group: 16% discharged Control group: 9% discharged
48. Effects of interpersonal skills training on psychiatric-hospital patients (Pierce & Drasgow, 1969)	Patient level of interpersonal functioning	Improved significantly ($p < .02$) HRD training treatment significantly improved over other treatment control conditions ($p < .001$)
49. Effects of interpersonal skills training on psychiatric-hospital patients (Vitalo, 1971)	Patient level of interpersonal functioning Taped patient statements	Significantly improved over 2 treatment control conditions ($p < .001$)

Figure 12-4 *(continued)*

HRD APPLICATIONS: POPULATIONS, OUTCOME MEASURES, AND RESULTS

Helping-Program Study	HRD Outcome Measures	Results
	Live interaction	Significantly improved over treatment control conditions ($p < .001$)
	Patient ward behavior	Significantly improved over 2 treatment control conditions ($p < .01$)
	Patient clinical pathology	Significantly improved over group-therapy control ($p < .001$)
	Patient anxiety level	Significantly improved over group-therapy control ($p < .025$)
	Patient work level	No differences
50. Effects of training on dental students (Deneen, 1973)	Level of interpersonal skills	Significant improvement
51. Effects of training on nursing personnel (Deneen, King, & Deneen, 1973)	Nurse interpersonal skills	Significant improvement
52. Effects of empathy training on nursing students (Kalish, 1971)	Nurse level of communication	Significant improvement
53. Effects of training on morale and communication skills of medical staff (Seidenschnur, 1973)	Staff morale Staff communication skills	Significant improvement Significant improvement
54. Effects of interpersonal skills training on department of nursing faculty (Cash, 1980)	Level of discrimination	Significantly improved ($p < .01$)
	Level of communication	Significantly improved ($p < .01$)
	Self-reports	100% positive
Parents		
55. Effects of interpersonal skills training on parents (Carkhuff & Bierman, 1970)	Parent level of discrimination	Significantly improved ($p < .01$)
	Parent level of communication	Significantly improved ($p < .01$) Significantly improved over 3 of 4 treatment control conditions ($p < .05$)
	Parent relationship to children inventory	No differences except vs. control proper ($p < .05$)
56. Effect of trained parents on training parents (Huntley, 1973)	Parent level of discrimination	Significantly improved ($p < .01$)
	Parent level of communication	Significantly improved ($p < .01$) Gains similar to parents trained by trained counselors
57. Effects of trained helpers and interpersonal and program development skills training on parents and children (Carkhuff & Pierce, 1974)	Parent interpersonal skills Parent constructive change Child interpersonal skills Child adjustment changes	Significant improvement Significant improvement Significant improvement Significant improvement

Figure 12-4 *(continued)*

HRD APPLICATIONS: POPULATIONS, OUTCOME MEASURES, AND RESULTS

Helping-Program Study	HRD Outcome Measures	Results
58. Effects of interpersonal skills training on parents (Cash, 1972)	Parent level of discrimination	Significantly improved ($p < .01$)
	Parent level of communication	Significantly improved ($p < .01$)
Correctional Institutions		
59. Effects of trained correctional officers on inmates (Carkhuff, Banks, Berenson, Griffin, Hall, Montgomery, & Skinner, 1972)	Inmate interpersonal functioning	Significantly improved ($p < .05$)
60. Effects of trained institutional personnel on delinquents (Carkhuff, Berenson, Griffin, Devine, Angelone, Clinton, Keeling, Muth, Patch, & Steinberg, 1972)	Student physical functioning	Improved 50%
	Student interpersonal functioning	Improved 100%
	Student intellectual functioning	Improved 157%
	Student self-reports	83% positive
	Staff reports of students	84% positive
	Student runaway rate	Reduced 57%
	Student recidivism rate	Reduced 34%
	Student crime rate	Reduced 34% (in communities from which population was drawn)
61. Effects of trained helpers and interpersonal skills training on inmates (Devine & Steinberg, 1974)	Recidivism	Reduced recidivism rate
62. Effects of trained officers on inmates (Hall, 1970)	Self-reports	80–90% positive

Adapted in part from "What's It All About, Anyway?" by R. R. Carkhuff. *The Counseling Psychologist,* 1972, *3*(3), 84–85. Reprinted with permission.

REFERENCES

Anthony, W. Human relations skills and training: Implications for rehabilitation counseling. *Rehabilitation Counseling Bulletin* (Boston University), 1973, *16*, 180–188.

Aspy, D. N. The effect of teacher-offered conditions of empathy, congruence, and positive regard upon student achievement. *Florida Journal of Educational Research,* 1969, *11*, 39–48.

Aspy, D. N. The effects of interpersonal skills training upon student I.Q., achievement, and self-concept of ghetto school children. Mimeographed manuscript, Northeast Louisiana University, 1972.

Aspy, D. N., & Hadlock, W. The effects of high and low functioning teachers upon student performance. In R. R. Carkhuff (Ed.), *Beyond counseling and therapy,* New York: Holt, Rinehart & Winston, 1967.

Aspy, D. N., & Roebuck, F. N. An investigation of the relationship between levels of cognitive functioning and the teacher's classroom behavior. *Journal of Educational Research,* 1972, *65*, 365–368.

Aspy, D. N., & Roebuck, F. N. From humane ideas to human technology. *Journal of Education,* 1974, *95*, 163–171.

Aspy, D. N., & Roebuck, F. N. *Kids don't learn from teachers they "don't like."* Amherst, Mass.: Human Resources Development Press, 1977.

Baker, E., & Popham, W. *Expanding dimensions of instructional objectives.* Englewood Cliffs, N.J.: Prentice-Hall, 1973.

Banks, G. P., & Anthony, W. A. The helping profession's response to Carkhuff: A choice for adolescence or adulthood. *Counseling Psychologist,* 1973, *4*(1), 102–107.

Banks, G. P., Berenson, B. G., & Carkhuff, R. R. The effects of counselor race and training upon counseling process with Negro clients in initial interviews. *Journal of Clinical Psychology,* 1967, *23,* 70–72.

Becker, W. C., Engelmann, S., & Thomas, D. R. *Teaching: A course in applied psychology.* Chicago: Science Research Associates, 1971.

Berenson, D. H. The effects of systematic human relations training upon the classroom performance of elementary school teachers. *Journal of Research and Development in Education,* 1971, *4,* 70–85.

Berenson, D. H. A follow-up study of the effects of interpersonal training upon student achievement. Mimeographed manuscript, Western Connecticut University, 1972.

Bozarth, J. D., Rubin, S. E., Krauft, C. C., Richardson, B. K., & Bolton, B. Client-counselor interaction, patterns of service, and client outcome. Monograph No. 19, Arkansas Rehabilitation Research and Training Center, University of Arkansas, 1974.

Butler, E. R., & Hansen, J. C. Facilitative training: Acquisition, retention, and modes of assessment. *Journal of Counseling Psychology,* 1973, *20*(1), 60–65.

Carkhuff, R. R. *Helping and human relations.* Vol. 1: *Selection and training.* New York: Holt, Rinehart & Winston, 1969. (a)

Carkhuff, R. R. *Helping and human relations.* Vol. 2: *Research and practice.* New York: Holt, Rinehart & Winston, 1969. (b)

Carkhuff, R. R. The development of effective courses of action for ghetto school children. *Psychology in the Schools,* 1970, *7,* 272–274.

Carkhuff, R. R. *The development of human resources.* New York: Holt, Rinehart & Winston, 1971.

Carkhuff, R. R. Major contributions to the development of systematic Human Resource Development models. *Counseling Psychologist,* 1972, *3*(3), 4–11. (a)

Carkhuff, R. R. New directions in training for the helping professions: Toward a technology for human and community resource development. *Counseling Psychologist,* 1972, *3*(3), 12–30. (b)

Carkhuff, R. R. What's it all about, anyway? Some reflections on helping and Human Resources Development models. *Counseling Psychologist,* 1972, *3*(3), 79–82. (c)

Carkhuff, R. R. *The art of helping.* Amherst: Human Resource Development Press, 1973. (a)

Carkhuff, R.R. *The art of problem-solving.* Amherst: Human Resource Development Press, 1973. (b)

Carkhuff, R. R., & Alexik, M. The effects of the manipulation of client depth of self-exploration upon high and low functioning counselors. *Journal of Clinical Psychology,* 1967, *23,* 210–212.

Carkhuff, R. R., & Anthony, W. A. *The skills of helping: An introduction to counseling skills.* Amherst, Mass.: Human Resource Development Press, 1979.

Carkhuff, R. R., Banks, G., Berenson, B. G., Griffin, A. H., Hall, R., Montgomery, C., & Skinner, J. The effects of interpersonal skills training on inmate interpersonal functioning. Mimeographed manuscript, American International College, 1972.

Carkhuff, R. R., & Berenson, B. G. *Teaching as treatment.* Amherst, Mass.: Human Resource Development Press, 1976.

Carkhuff, R. R., Berenson, B. G., Griffin, A. H., Devine, J., Angelone, R., Clinton, L., Keeling, T., Muth, E., Patch, W., & Steinberg, H. The effects of trained institutional personnel upon delinquent physical, emotional and intellectual functioning. Mimeographed manuscript, American International College, 1972.

Carkhuff, R. R., & Bierman, R. Training as a preferred mode of treatment of parents of emotionally disturbed children. *Journal of Counseling Psychology,* 1970, *17,* 157–161.

Carkhuff, R. R., Devine, J., Berenson, B. G., Griffin, A. H., Angelone, R., Keeling, T., Patch, W., & Steinberg, H. *Cry twice.* Amherst, Mass.: Human Resource Development Press, 1974.

Carkhuff, R. R., Friel, T., Berenson, B. G., Bebermeyer, J., Mahrt, J., & Forrest, D. The differential effects of systematic computer and human relations training. In R. R. Carkhuff (Ed.), *People, programs and organizations.* Amherst, Mass.: Human Resource Development Press, 1972.

Carkhuff, R. R., & Griffin, A. H. The selection and training of human relations specialists. *Journal of Counseling Psychology,* 1970, *17,* 443–450.

Carkhuff, R. R., & Griffin, A. H. The selection and training of functional professionals for Concentrated Employment Programs. *Journal of Clinical Psychology,* 1971, *27,* 163–165.

Carkhuff, R. R., & Pierce, R. Differential effects of therapist race and social class upon patient depth of self-exploration in the initial client interview. *Journal of Counseling Psychology,* 1967, *31,* 632–634.

Carkhuff, R. R., & Pierce, R. Training teachers and parents to support student learning. Progress report, Springfield, Mass., 1974.

Carkhuff, R. R., & Truax, C. B. Training in counseling and psychotherapy: An evaluation of an integrated didactic and experiential approach. *Journal of Consulting Psychology,* 1965, *29,* 333–336. (a)

Carkhuff, R. R., & Truax, C. B. Lay mental health counseling: The effectiveness of lay group counseling. *Journal of Consulting Psychology,* 1965, *29,* 426–531. (b)

Cash, R. W. Parent training program in communication skills: Final report. Unpublished manuscript, Long Beach Mental Health Association, Long Beach, Calif., 1972.

Cash, R. W. College and university staff development program: Final reports. Unpublished report, Long Beach, Calif., 1974–1980. (a)

Cash, R. W. School district staff development program: Final reports. Unpublished report, Long Beach, Calif., 1974–1980. (b)

Cash, R. W. Human Resource Development program, State Department of Education drug abuse training project: Final report. Unpublished report, Sacramento, Calif., 1978.

Cash, R. W. Harbor College nursing department faculty staff development program: Final report. Unpublished report, Los Angeles, 1980.

Cash, R. W. Human Resources Development program training delivery kit. Long Beach: California State University, 1981. (a)

Cash, R. W. *Human Resources Development: Trainee's workbook.* Long Beach, Calif: Fortyniner Bookstore, 1981. (b)

Cash, R. W., Scherba, D. S., & Mills, S. S. *Human Resources Development: A competency based training program. Trainer's manual.* Pasadena: Associates in Human Communication, 1975.

Cash, R. W., & Stevens, T. Developing criterion referenced instruction in counselor education programs. Paper presented at meeting of the American Personnel and Guidance Association, Las Vegas, 1980.

Cash, R. W., & Vellema, C. K. Conceptual versus competency approach in human relations training programs. *Personnel and Guidance Journal,* 1979, *58*(2), 91–94.

Cassatta, M. A study of the effect that physical functioning has upon gain in interpersonal skills from a HRD training program. Unpublished master's thesis, California State University, Long Beach, 1974.

Collingwood, T. R. The effects of large group training on facilitative interpersonal communication. *Journal of Clinical Psychology,* 1969, *25,* 461–462.

Cormier, W. H., Cormier, L. S., Zerega, W. D., & Wagaman, G. L. Effects of learning modules on the acquisitions of counseling strategies. *Journal of Counseling Psychology,* 1976, *23,* 136–141.

Deneen, L. The effects of systematic human relations training on the interpersonal functioning of dental students and the characteristics of high and low functioning students. Unpublished doctoral dissertation, University of Georgia, 1973.

Devine, J. P., & Steinberg, H. Kalamazoo county jail rehabilitation program, Progress report. Unpublished report, Kalamazoo, Mich., 1974.

Egan, G. *The skilled helper.* Monterey, Calif.: Brooks/Cole, 1975.

Eysenck, H. J. The effects of psychotherapy. *International Journal of Psychiatry,* 1965, *1,* 99–178.

Ford, J. D. Research on training counselors and clinicians. *Review of Educational Research,* 1979, *7,* 87–130.

Gazda, G. M., Asbury, F. R., Balzer, F. J., Childers, W. C., Desselle, R. E., & Walters, R. P. *Human relations development: A manual for educators.* Boston: Allyn & Bacon, 1977. (First edition, 1973.)

Gazda, G. M., Walters, R. P., & Childers, W. C. *Human relations development: A manual for health sciences.* Boston: Allyn & Bacon, 1975.

Griffin, A. Teaching counselor education to black teenagers. Unpublished doctoral dissertation, Graduate School of Education, Harvard University, 1972.

Gronlund, N. E. *Preparing criterion referenced tests for classroom instruction.* New York: Macmillan, 1973.

Hall, R. *Atlanta correctional and industrial counseling: First annual report.* Washington, D.C.: Federal Bureau of Prisons, 1970.

Hatcher, C., Brooks, B. S., & Associates. *Innovations in counseling psychology: Developing new roles, settings, techniques.* San Francisco: Jossey-Bass, 1977.

Hawley, W. The effect of using rated videotaped interviews vs. written instruments to assess interpersonal communication skill levels. Unpublished master's thesis, California State University, Long Beach, 1978.

Hefele, T. J. The effects of systematic human relations training upon student achievement. *Journal of Research and Development in Education,* 1971, *4,* 52–69.

Henzel, S. A study of HRD trained teachers upon selected student outcome criteria. Unpublished master's thesis, California State University, Long Beach, 1974.

Hillinger, A. The effect of using a student workbook on HRD training outcomes. Unpublished master's thesis, California State University, Long Beach, 1978.

Holder, T. Retention as a function of length of training in interpersonal skills. Unpublished doctoral dissertation, University of New York at Buffalo, 1969.

Holder, T., Carkhuff, R. R., & Berenson, B. G. The differential effects of the manipulation of therapeutic conditions upon high and low functioning clients. *Journal of Counseling Psychology,* 1967, *14,* 63–66.

Horan, J. J. *Counseling for effective decision making.* North Scituate, Mass.: Duxbury Press, 1979.

Huntley, P. Training parents in human relations communication skills. Unpublished master's thesis, California State University, Long Beach, 1973.

Jakubowski-Spector, P., Dustin, R., & George, R. S. Toward developing a behavioral counselor education model. *Counselor Education and Supervision,* 1971, *10,* 242–250.

Kalish, B. J. An experiment in the development of empathy in nursing students. *Nursing Research,* 1971, *20,* 202–211.

Kelly, E. W. Increasing communication skills in traditional master's degree counseling programs. Unpublished document, San Mateo County Educational Resources Center, San Mateo, 1972.

Kratochvil, D., Carkhuff, R. R., & Berenson, B. G. The cumulative effects of parent and teacher-offered levels of facilitative conditions upon indexes of student physical, emotional and intellectual functioning. *Journal of Educational Research,* 1969, *63,* 161–164.

Levitt, E. E. Psychotherapy with children: A further evaluation. *Behavior Research and Therapy,* 1963, *1,* 45–51.

Lewis, W. W. Continuity and intervention in emotional disturbance: A review. *Exceptional Children,* 1965, *31,* 465–475.

Louscher, K. Survey of facilitative communication skills of pre-graduates and graduates of a counselor education program. Unpublished master's thesis, California State University, Long Beach, 1972.

Mager, R. F. *Goal analysis.* Belmont, Calif.: Fearon, 1972.

Mickelson, D. J., & Stevic, R. R. Differential effects of facilitative and non-facilitative behavioral counselors. *Journal of Counseling Psychology,* 1971, *18,* 314–319.

Mitchell, M. Examination of trainer training effect upon interpersonal communication functioning levels. Unpublished master's thesis, California State University, Long Beach, 1974.

Mosher, R. L., & Sprinthall, N. A. Deliberate psychological education. *Counseling Psychologist,* 1972, *2*(4), 3–82.

Pagell, W., Carkhuff, R. R., & Berenson, B. G. The predicted differential effects of the level of counselor functioning upon the level of functioning of outpatients. *Journal of Clinical Psychology,* 1967, *23,* 510–512.

Pasley, D. Subject differentiation by sex and prior group experience on measured gain in Carkhuff's human relations training. Master's thesis, California State University, Long Beach, 1973.

Piaget, G., Carkhuff, R. R., & Berenson, B. G. The development of skills in interpersonal functioning. *Counselor Education and Supervision,* 1968, *2,* 102–106.

Pierce, R. M., Carkhuff, R. R., & Berenson, B. G. The differential effects of high- and low-functioning counselors upon counselors-in-training. *Journal of Clinical Psychology,* 1967, *23,* 212–215.

Pierce, R. M., & Drasgow, J. Teaching facilitative interpersonal functioning to psychiatric inpatients. *Journal of Counseling Psychology,* 1969, *16,* 295–298.

Pierce, R. M., & Schauble, P. Graduate training of facilitative counselors: The effects of individual supervision. *Journal of Counseling Psychology,* 1970, *17,* 210–215.

Pierce, R. M., & Schauble, P. Study on the effects of individual supervision in graduate school training. *Journal of Counseling Psychology,* 1971, *18,* 186–187.

Pipe, P. *Objectives—tool for change.* Belmont, Calif.: Fearon, 1975.

Plummer, M. Relationship of selected personality characteristics to interpersonal communication functioning levels. Unpublished master's thesis, California State University, Long Beach, 1973.

Popham, W. J. *Criterion-referenced instruction.* Belmont, Calif.: Fearon, 1973.

Popham, W. J., & Baker, E. L. *Establishing instructional goals.* Englewood Cliffs, N.J.: Prentice-Hall, 1970. (a)

Popham, W. J., & Baker, E. L. *Planning an instructional sequence.* Englewood Cliffs, N.J.: Prentice-Hall, 1970. (b)

Redgate, C. The effects of training on acquisition of non-verbal counseling skills. Unpublished master's thesis, California State University, 1981.

Renz, L. Pretraining and within training discriminative indices of retention of facilitative conditions. Unpublished doctoral dissertation, University of New York at Buffalo, 1970.

Resnikoff, A. Critiques of the Human Resources Development model from the viewpoint of rigor. *Counseling Psychologist,* 1972, *3*(3), 46–55.

Reynolds, G. S. *A primer of operant conditioning.* Glenview, Ill.: Scott, Foresman, 1968.

Richards, B. Relationships of social intelligence and interpersonal communication skills. Unpublished master's thesis, California State University, Long Beach, 1973.

Rockford, R. Effect of human relations training on student achievement in math and reading. Unpublished master's thesis, California State University, Long Beach, 1973.

Rogers, C. R. The necessary and sufficient conditions of therapeutic personality change. *Journal of Consulting Psychology,* 1957, *21,* 95–103.

Rogers, C. R., Gendlin, E. T., Kiesler, D., & Truax, C. B. *The therapeutic relationship and its impact.* Madison: University of Wisconsin Press, 1967.

Russell, J. D., & Johanningsmeier, K. A. *Improving competence through modular instruction.* Dubuque, Iowa, 1981.

Salcido, F. Retention of communication skills. Unpublished master's thesis, California State University, Long Beach, 1975.

Sawyer, T. The effects of differential sequencing of training in training paraprofessional counselors. Unpublished master's thesis, California State University, Long Beach, 1977.

Scherba, D. S. A survey of facilitative communication skills of beginning and advanced graduate students in a counselor education program. Unpublished master's thesis, California State University, Long Beach, 1973.

Seaman, A. The effect of problem and affect area on Carkhuff's systematic human relations training model. Unpublished master's thesis, California State University, Long Beach, 1972.

Seidenschnur, P. Effects of human relations training upon the morale and communication skills of a medical staff. Unpublished doctoral dissertation, University of Georgia, 1973.

Selfridge, F. F., Weitz, L. J., Calabria, F. M., Steger, J. A., Abramotwitz, C. V., & Abramotwitz, S. I. Sensitivity-oriented versus didactically oriented in-service counselor training. *Journal of Counseling Psychology,* 1975, *22*(2), 156–159.

Stoffer, D. L. Investigation of positive behavioral change as a function of genuineness, non-possessive warmth, and empathic understanding. *Journal of Educational Research,* 1970, *63,* 225–228.

Toukmanian, S. G., & Rennie, D. L. Microcounseling versus human relations training: Relative effectiveness with undergraduate trainees. *Journal of Counseling Psychology,* 1975, *22,* 345–352.

Truax, C. B., & Carkhuff, R. R. *Towards effective counseling and psychotherapy: Training and practice.* Chicago: Aldine, 1967.

Truax, C. B., & Lister, J. L. Effects of short-term training upon accurate empathy and non-possessive warmth. *Counselor Education and Supervision,* 1971, *10,* 120–125.

Vitalo, R. The effects of facilitative interpersonal functioning in a conditioning paradigm. *Journal of Counseling Psychology,* 1970, *17,* 141–144.

Vitalo, R. Teaching improved interpersonal functioning as a preferred mode of treatment. *Journal of Clinical Psychology,* 1971, *27,* 166–171.

Westwood, M. An examination of social worker–client relationship effectiveness. Unpublished doctoral dissertation, University of Alberta, 1972.

Williams, H. E. The effects of teacher interpersonal skills on student knowledge of learning theory. Mimeographed manuscript, Northeast Louisiana University, 1972.

Zolner, P. Effect of using written instruments versus audiotaped interviews to assess interpersonal communication skill levels. Unpublished master's thesis, California State University, Long Beach, 1975.

CHAPTER THIRTEEN

SASHAtapes:
Expanding Options for
Help-Intended Communication

Gerald Goodman

Gerald Goodman is associate professor of psychology at the University of California, Los Angeles. A University of Chicago Ph.D., he specializes in the area of interpersonal communication and self-help training programs. His SASHAtape program is used in over 300 universities and colleges and received a UCLA "Innovations in University Instruction Award."

Previously, Goodman was at the University of California, Berkeley, as a research fellow. He is currently an editorial consultant for the *Psychological Bulletin,* the *Journal of Abnormal Psychology,* the *Journal of Humanistic Psychology,* and the *American Journal of Community Psychology.* He is the author of *Companionship Therapy: Studies in Structured Intimacy* and has written chapters in *A Handbook of Community Psychology and Mental Health* and *New Directions in Client-Centered Psychotherapy.* At the moment, he is writing a book on the repair and maintenance of everyday conversation.

Like so many leading figures in the skills training field, Gerald Goodman has evolved professionally from clinician and psychotherapy researcher to community-oriented psychologist to communication skills theorist to skills trainer. The beginnings of the SASHAtapes program can be found in a community experiment using structured companionship as therapy for fifth- and sixth-grade boys and in Goodman's research on help-intended communication. SASHAtapes are an inexpensive, portable, and programmatic skills training package aimed primarily at self-help groups, paraprofessionals, and students in the human services. The SASHAtapes program has become one of my favorite "teaching assistants" in my own counseling skills courses. Goodman's synthesis of talking tools is ideally suited for giving away the trade secrets of therapists and communication specialists.

SEARCHING FOR A SIMPLE SET OF COMMUNICATION TOOLS

SASHAtapes were born in a shopping bag filled with hundreds of peculiar audio cassettes—peculiar because they contained 1000 recordings of strangers trying to help each other. Part of a companionship-therapy study (Goodman, 1972), the strangers were college students involved in a small-group assessment procedure aimed at measuring natural helping skills. Analyzing the students' efforts made me aware that existing systems of therapy-process analysis were too specialized for the organization of common helping behavior. Eventually, that discovery led to a formal framework for organizing therapy language and untutored language into a basic set of help-intended communications. And that formal framework ultimately became a packaged training program designed to expand options for giving help.

My Interpersonal Process Research Group at UCLA spent several years and several dissertations trying to simplify and integrate the speech acts of professional and nonprofessional helpers. We immersed ourselves in tape recordings. We reviewed the literature for commonalities. What emerged was six basic units, or basic families, of helping behavior. This framework bridged "natural" and technical helping talk and could serve the needs of both research and training. Until that time training and research had not shared a common process framework. Our work produced a rudimentary system for help-intended communication—a standard table of elements.

In order to bridge the gap between therapy-process research and public skill training, we modified guidelines used by therapy-process researchers. That created the following criteria:

1. The categories should be applicable to both training and measurement, as well as be easily identifiable to a lay public.
2. They must have the capacity to organize communication behavior into small, reliably observable units.
3. The framework should include the most important categories employed by theories, primarily psychotherapy theories; it should be pantheoretical.
4. The *process* or style of communication should be emphasized rather than content or topic, to allow for maximum generalization.
5. The accompanying training material should have multisetting applicability (for example, laboratory, community support group, classroom) and be portable, inexpensive, and appealing to untrained populations.

We decided to use linguistic forms instead of helping intentions as category markers because they allow greater reliability in rating tasks, produce fewer categories, and increase facility for studying the more elusive elements.

My first attempt to organize helping behavior into discrete units used the spoken-sentence level. Unfortunately, the attempt to simplify failed owing to clutter: about 50 help-intended response categories with marginal reliability emerged. After some factoring, the 50 responses were condensed to about 20 with adequate reliability. The application of conceptual homogeneity rules to the 20 responses allowed the collapse of overlapping speech acts into six basic response families that divide a continuous band of communication behaviors. The term *response mode* was used to connote that each family clustered around a basic communication modality.

Each of the six response modes appears sufficiently important across applications to be regarded as essential in any comprehensive system. Special settings, populations, and individual research interests may require the emphasis, alteration, or deemphasis of a mode. That is, the essential framework has proved convertible across research and training needs. Refinements and additional categories have been proposed by my former students (Elliot, Stiles, Barker, Burstein, & Goodman, 1982), but the six basic response modes have served as the foundation.

Each response-mode family is identified by a single communication behavior.

The behavior serves as a marker for each class because it is an easily recognizable speech act. These behaviors are—

1. Question
2. Advisement
3. Silence
4. Interpretation
5. Reflection
6. Disclosure

A response-mode family can be broken down into more discrete speech acts that fit its parameters—for example, open and closed or multiple-choice questions within the question family; general, third-party, or personal interpretations within the interpretation family. The size of response families ranges from three to seven members, depending on usage within a research sample or needs of a training population. This convertibility allows maintenance of a simple master framework across applications. The open system reduces the proliferation of "splinter frameworks," which impede progress in the communication skills area.

Development of a communication system convertible across technical and public language and across research and training functions is without precedent. Current systems used for training programs approach communication skills by mixing attitudes, discrete communication acts, and intended impact, which renders them impractical for research.

The response-mode framework and its training programs are aimed at more than a convergence between research and training in the helping professions and para-professional area; we are tooling up for the fourth mental health revolution. We aim at a bridge between researchers and those 15 million Americans in self-help mutual-support groups. Several mental health futurists predict the growth of support groups during the 1980s will outstrip all forms and schools of traditional therapy (Kiesler, 1980). The forecast suggests an increasing need for communication training by a public moving toward mental health self-care.

Mutual-support and group therapy is starting to receive serious attention from serious therapy researchers (Lieberman et al., 1973). Some mental health policy scholars and administrators describe self-help mutual support as the primary mental health method already used by Americans for prevention, repair, coping, maintenance, and advocacy. Their estimate translates into a dramatic ratio: support-group members outnumber therapy outpatients about 4 to 1 (Kiesler, 1980). The general picture of support-group functioning suggests that such groups need some technical and professional assistance for small-group communication and management. Their growing attitude is "Give us the tools and let us do it ourselves." That means the program developer and therapy researcher have a massive new population to serve and a serious old problem to solve: the lack of collaboration between those who develop communication training programs and those who investigate face-to-face communication.

Paraprofessional and nonprofessional training needs have also shaped the SASHAtape format. The great variation among paraprofessional leaders can be simplified by considering three common characteristics:

1. They are involved in face-to-face, help-intended communication with clients

or peers, which parallels a major function of their professional counterparts.
2. Their training is typically brief and very task-specific, with little or no focus on research or theory issues.
3. Their diverse job-specific training formats contain one common essential component—the enhancement of basic interpersonal communication skills.

Although this training is one of the hallmarks of paraprofessional leaders, it tends to be haphazard, lacking in systematic knowledge, and filled with untested innovations. The SASHAtape program standardizes paraprofessional training by giving the basic interpersonal communication skills used by all psychological schools.

The SASHAtape format enables wide-scale, inexpensive dissemination of material. Audio-cassette players are commonly used in this country, even among lower-income populations. At a time when many traditional therapies face budget problems, cost-effectiveness is a serious consideration in reaching the large population that needs mental health care. Almost every scholar in the mental health policy field regards the mutual-support group as a logical method for solving the problem of expense. Tapes can reach a large audience, and audiotapes are less expensive and more portable than video. One 90-minute audio tape can equal 40 pages of print and costs under $2 to reproduce.

Considering paraprofessionals, self-help support groups, and students in human service programs as target populations, I constructed eight criteria for guiding the development of an automated program:

1. Use of two media channels, audio cassette and print.
   Rationale: Increases retention over one-channel learning, inexpensive, tape players in wide use, allows strategic presentation of material, organizes timed group events, combines informal spoken instruction with more formal print communication.
2. Format should operate with or without a professional in attendance. Three formats are possible: full professional participation, partial participation, and self-contained group.
   Rationale: Fits the dependence/independence needs of varied populations, meets requirements of self-help mutual-support groups; allows a practice arena with varying degrees of professional scrutiny, accepts technical input for special populations from professionals outside the group-process area.
3. Instructional style should be nonprescriptive, noninsistent about the precise set of communication tools for effecting change.
   Rationale: An indefinite set of rules is less appealing at first but induces participants to depend more on their own resources, prepares learners for more independent decision making, eventually allows more flexibility for applying skills across settings, attenuates simplistic thinking about communication, forces a broader look at choices.
4. The program should attend to the way anxiety shapes communication and the ways anxiety enters the program.
   Rationale: Performance anxiety is inherent in communication training and is easier to cope with after discussion. Coping suggestions usually reduce confusion, complaint, and pretense. Addressing anxiety issues in the training process adds vividness to learning the topic of anxiety as an element of interpersonal communication.

5. Program should be designed to adjust the ratio of participation opportunity to session length, group size, and exercise format.

    Rationale: Expediency usually dictates group size and lesson length in skills training programs, often resulting in haphazard partitioning of individual group members. Programs need a variety of contingency rules and options, along with participation time ratios determined by group size, to facilitate a balanced group participation.

6. Program teaches only one basic, cohesive communication dimension during each session by blending experiential and cognitive formats.

    Rationale: Helps participants "own" cognitive learning and incorporate it into their personal style of behavior.

7. Program offers metainstruction that interprets the rationales for each teaching episode before it begins.

    Rationale: Changing communication skills means changing high-frequency basic behaviors. Trust can be enhanced by disclosing teaching agendas, especially those with interpersonal risks. Frequent disclosures about the instructional process will bore some secure participants, but the remainder will lower their resistance to practicing awkward new skills.

8. Instructional content will not serve any single theory or doctrine of change. It will be pantheoretical and describe a broad range of intents, communication tools, and impacts used in client-centered, psychodynamic, behavioral, and cognitive interventions.

Using these criteria, we produced an automated program for modifying interpersonal communication during seven years of pilot testing in classrooms, clinics, community projects, and a variety of self-help mutual-support groups. Formal research was funded by NIMH and UCLA grants. The resulting six-part series, called the Self-led Automated Series in Helping Alternatives (SASHA), was launched. Our final research population included 14 cross-section groups (200 participants). The findings were used to revise prototype versions for public distribution at low cost.

SASHAtapes have been distributed by UCLA Extension for use in thousands of settings: community projects, self-help groups, hospitals, corporations, military programs, medical schools, and 260 universities and colleges. (Inside sources reveal that even the CIA has a copy!)

Each two-hour SASHAtape session consists of listening and interaction time, with a ratio of one minute of tape listening to two minutes of group interaction. A combination of short lectures, exercises, examples, group discussions, and individualized practice assignments allows participants to deal with feelings and personal matters as material for learning about giving and receiving help.

Typically, the sessions begin with a short lecture that introduces the skill and provides cognitive information such as a definition and appropriate use. Then an exercise allows some practice in using the skill, followed by another lecture, which builds on the exercise experience. Metacommunications guide the session to be sure participants are gentle and considerate of each other's feelings.

"Unfinished business" periods at the beginning and end of each session are meant for discussing any unsettled feelings. Members can also use the time to plan agendas for the sessions and complete any interactions that have been cut short by time constraints.

SASHAtapes are not a "leaderless" program. The tapes do not displace live leaders. Instead, leaders are drawn from the group itself and trained with a printed manual. A rotating system allows everyone to have a turn. This format makes leadership training part of the skill-building process. The program allows for any amount of professional leadership but can be conducted without it.

HIGHLIGHTS FROM THE SASHATAPE SERIES

Questions

Paradoxically, the question appears to be the most frequently used response by most professional therapists, and yet it has received the least attention from therapy theorists (Strupp & Wallach, 1965; Wile, Bron, & Pollack, 1970). Cartwright (1966) found that both Rogerian and psychoanalytic therapists asked about twice as many questions as did their clients. Inexperienced therapists and naive subjects appear to use the question even more than professionals (Ornston, Cicchetti, Levine, & Fierman, 1968; Phillips & Agnew, 1953).

One of the clearest uses of the question form is to gather information. But questions also carry non-information-gathering intents. Sometimes questions give advice or interpret (Dooley, 1973; Snyder, 1945; Wile et al., 1970). An example of such a hybrid response, an "advising question," is "Do you think it wise to eat between meals if you want to control your weight?" Non-information-gathering questions such as this one may be used to soften the real intent.

The first SASHAtape in the series illustrates the most basic helping skill, the art of asking questions. Dyads are instructed to begin by having one member, the "discloser," state a personal concern about how he or she might improve their communication. The "helper" is instructed to clarify the disclosure. Helpers are cautioned to try to understand their partner's situation and to avoid trying to solve personal problems in the few minutes allowed. But the caution does not extinguish the typical participant's habit of asking questions and giving advice in help-intended conversations. After the exercise a lecture on the nature of questions points out that evidence shows inexperienced helpers tend to ask many questions and give advice, though often the questions also give advice.

Participants are introduced to the two subfamilies of questions: the telling question and the gathering question. Three types of telling questions are introduced:

1. Advising
2. Interpretive
3. Disclosing

The advising question thinly disguises advice—for example, "Don't you think you should put on a sweater?" The interpretive question classifies or labels: "Wouldn't that make you an irresponsible parent?" And the disclosing question tells something not readily apparent, such as "Aren't you going to pay a little attention to me?" Telling questions are unwittingly overused by inexperienced helpers. As responses, they can make messages less presumptuous, more tactful, perhaps kinder, but they can also make messages confusing, weak, and insincere.

Gathering questions differ dramatically from telling questions in their intent and impact and in the responses they get. They are more appropriate in a helping situation because they elicit information from the discloser and may help in a process of self-revelation. Most naive helpers don't realize the importance of such a process but instead feel that the burden for "solving" difficulties lies with the helper rather than within the helpseeker.

The gathering questions also have a spectrum:

1. Open-ended
2. Closed
3. Multiple choice

An open-ended question says "Tell me all about it." The closed question asks only for a yes, no, or maybe, as in "Are you hot?" The multiple-choice question asks, for example, "Do you feel good, bad, or indifferent about this chapter?" The three types of question allow varying degrees of freedom for the respondent. Our program suggests a range of activities across various situations for all three types of gathering questions. No one way of questioning is offered as best. Examples of how the unwitting use of many questions can have an undesired impact are presented. A discussion details how barrages of questions produce unnecessary answers and distract the discloser from true examination of the problem. A helper addicted to questions is communicating with a handicap that can restrict social relations and obstruct help-intended behavior.

In their first helping attempts before hearing a lecture on question overuse, participants tend to ask many questions. The truth of this behavior is made clear as participants listen to tape recordings of themselves as they do the exercises. The strategically spaced sequence of exercises and lectures gives participants clear guidance on how to sharpen their questioning skills.

One participant-observer reviewed the following exchange:

Helper: Was your mother's remarriage painful to you in some way?

Discloser: I was very angry.

Helper: You were?

Discloser: Yeah.

Helper: Tell me about it. What did it mean to you?

The participant identified the first and last questions as gathering questions and focused on the last open-ended question as most helpful. In a journal for recording subjective responses the participant wrote:

> The helper finally asked a meaningful question. Up to this point the discloser had been answering questions according to a tone set by the helper. Questions were asked in clinical terms, suggesting answers of a specific type, length and depth. The helper never seemed to find out what was actually going on inside the discloser or how he felt. Until the last, open-ended questions.

Even in our everyday conversations, questions can set the tone for a discussion and sometimes leave us with the feeling that although we have discussed a lot, nothing has really been understood.

Advisement

SASHAtapes break down advisement into suggestions, demonstrations, explanations, and commands. The intent to advise or guide may be softened by transmitting it indirectly through another mode, such as disclosures or questions—for instance, "I had the same problem and solved it by . . ." or "Do you think it would be better if you tried . . .?" These attenuating forms allow advisement to fall into a range from suggestion to command, though the underlying message is always one that attempts to modify another's behavior or attitudes.

It is typical of the untrained helper to want to solve problems quickly by simply telling a helpseeker what to do. And that is probably why the advisement responses tend to be overused by beginners. Doing what comes naturally in response to a call for help means giving advice.

In the first exercise, two participants at a time enact the roles of adviser and advisee while the other group members act as observers. In the first pair, the adviser is encouraged to give plenty of advice. The advisee reacts to the advisement, and the observers imagine giving advisement. When the dyad finishes, each silent observer condenses his or her advice into a single sentence and relates it to the advisee. The effect of this contrast in helping style is summed up by one participant who described an exercise in which the adviser is told that he is to act as though instruction were a rare and wonderful thing he had to offer and that he should advise constantly:

> The advisee stated that her habit of procrastination created a very real problem at work. She had enough trouble with the material, and this bad habit only exacerbated the dilemma. I jumped back with "Why don't you just do each job when it's assigned?" A particularly unempathic retort, certainly not the type which could help localize and perhaps alleviate the problem. I went on to explain how to deal with the issue, but the stage was set. There was a growing chasm between us from that first exchange.

The lecture material details some general attitudes about advisement. Many of us are only too familiar with the experience of advisement being used to draw respect or display knowledge or enhance the self-esteem of the adviser. It can also be used to dismiss someone revealing real distress or making a complaint. Quick advisements can rid a helper of feelings of fear, annoyance, or boredom aroused by another's problems.

After another exercise and some open discussion, another lecture illustrates critical elements that predict the acceptance or rejection of advisement. When the need is strong, chances are the advice will be taken. But even so, the helper must demonstrate some competence. Participants are made aware of some of the elements that make the acceptance of advisement more probable: empathy, evidence gathering, and a display of competence. If one or two of these elements are missing or weak, advisement will most likely be rejected, or the helpseeker may take the more polite course of "mock acceptance" to deflect the helping intent.

Silence

Research in laboratory settings has found typical pauses (reaction latencies) in helping situations to be about one to two seconds (Matarazzo, Wiens, Matarazzo, & Saslow, 1968), with very few pauses lasting five seconds or longer (Dooley, 1973). Psychotherapists use noticeably longer reaction latencies of about five seconds (Hargrove, 1974). The effect of the therapist's pauses on the helping process is unclear. However, significant changes do result in the helping relationship from increasing the length of silences between utterances, even by a fraction of a second. The major effect we found in our research was one of feeling less crowded or being allowed to speak freely.

This session teaches the functions of silence and interruption in the management of interpersonal attention. The prominent exercise allows participants to play at being in a world where giving and getting information in brief periods of time is considered most valuable. Then they are told to create a world in which quiet is valued. To do this they must give the other person extra time to talk, to finish what he or she has to say, and to feel that whatever the listener has to say in response can wait or even be left out. Through this acting and reacting, participants can see how intentional disruption of another person's spoken message can create "overtalk," a situation that can lead to serious problems in a relationship. They are told that interresponse times of five seconds or longer are often helpful in help-intended communication involving deeply personal problems. That is because crowding with short interresponse times, interruption, and overtalk tends to reduce the disclosure of personal feelings. When the time between responses is expanded, the discloser naturally feels invited to take time to reply, to delve more deeply into what he or she feels, and to try to express it to an uncrowding listener.

A participant described the different effects of silence and crowding as startling:

> The initial exercise on crowding encouraged group members to talk to anyone at any time about anything, regardless of what currently was being discussed. The result was that everybody ended up cutting off everyone else, voices became raised, speech became more rapid, and group members had difficulty remembering topics brought up. Furthermore, a number of members ended up remaining quiet throughout the exercise, apparently feeling uncomfortable both interrupting others as well as being interrupted themselves. In addition, for several minutes after the exercise was over, group members continued to speak loudly and interrupt each other, making discussion of the exercise difficult.
>
> After a brief discussion of the crowding exercise, the group engaged in the exercise on silence. Once again, members were asked to talk about anything they wanted. However, a minimum of five seconds was to elapse between comments, and careful attention was to be paid to each speaker. The results were quite dramatic. In part attributable to the earlier crowding exercise, even a five-second interresponse time felt like a long time. In contrast to the earlier exercise, voices almost immediately became softer, speech slowed down, and speakers felt much more validated and better understood. Furthermore, a greater number of group members contributed during this exercise than any past exercises. Finally, the more relaxed atmosphere that developed during the exercise was maintained for the duration of the session.

Interpretation

In our system *interpretation* is defined as a message intended to create meaning. The speech act involves classifying another person, explaining cause and effect, or making an assumption of a preexisting condition. That assumption may carry an indirect diagnosis, a statement of a problem. The interpretation message offers an explicit description of a condition. It explains the classification of another person directly. In addition to their function of direct classification, interpretations also spell out the cause for an effect. Interpretations exist to explain people to themselves, or explain people to others, or explain cultural or small-group behavior. Giving someone an interpretation is usually like giving the person news about himself or herself.

Interpretation responses tend to evoke strong reactions. SASHAtapes advise that telling people what they are or what they are doing or feeling requires caution. The interpretation response can shock or bring serenity or create disbelief. A typical example of how strongly this response mode works was described by a peer leader of a self-help mutual-support group who transcribed her tape recording of a session.

Me: You seem to be proud that you were getting better and not thinking about what was bothering you. Is . . .

Group member: Well, [raising voice] it's, it's, uh, it's . . . I don't know. [Silence for five seconds. Then he mumbles.]

Me: What did you say?

Group member: I said I shouldn't interrupt you.

Me: Uh-huh.

Group member: When you say something that I feel guilty about, then I interrupt you so you won't be able to say it. I'm trying to figure out why I do it.

Me: So, if I say something that's triggering something in you, you want to stop me in the middle of it.

Group member: Yeah, or else rephrase it fast, so that it doesn't seem as though I did something awful, that I was being lazy. "You were proud of blocking things out" makes it seem like that.

Me: Let's go over that again. When I said you were proud of blocking things out, what happened to you? How did that make you feel?

Group member: I felt instantly guilty and false. It was humiliating. Not humiliating. I would be really not good to be proud of blocking things out. I would do it because I was so nobly ill and hurt inside and not because . . . [silence, then in a soft voice] . . . I was so weak.

The group leader commented in her journal:

> It was clear to me that this interpretation caused the person pain. I have listened to that segment over and over and have thought about whether I did the right thing. I'd like to put aside the value judgment for now and self-disclose a little. I remember picking up the message. He had been talking about not thinking about what was bothering him almost as if it was an achievement. I remember taking a deep breath and letting go with my comment. My voice sounded tentative and I spoke softly. I also remember bracing myself for his response. It wasn't easy for me. I believe it has been difficult in general for me to give interpretations that I suspect the client does not want to hear. It's because I know the interpretation will have impact. I guess my point is that when you speak of the joys and sorrows of interpretation for the client, I believe the same process is true for the therapist. At least for beginning therapists. I'm hoping it will become easier as I have a better sense of the impact of statements and as I learn to trust myself more.

The majority of participants react to interpretation with discomfort, whether they are in the helper or discloser role. The exercise seems to highlight a power differentiation, and the helper experiences a presumptuousness and danger in taking such authority, while the discloser feels resistance to being the target of what can appear to be a pontifical attitude.

Reflection

We have found it useful to teach reflection along dimensions of amplitude, focus, and accuracy. Reflection shows that attention is being paid. At best, reflection discloses empathy. Ivey (1971) described another important function of reflection—as a means of rewarding the speaker for self-exploration.

Some helpers just can't believe that re-presenting the heart of a message can be helpful. Their attitude creates a problem because it reduces the opportunity to demonstrate understanding of feelings before providing guidance. People repeat their own messages under three conditions: when the message is not acknowledged by another person, when the message is misunderstood, and when the message does not do a fair job of communicating the speaker's feelings or intention. Reflection can be used by a professional to give the client an experience of being known. This method became familiar to counselors through the popularization of client-centered therapy and is used by Rogerian therapists about 75% of the time (Strupp, 1955). It is a relatively nonarousing way of confirming the advisee's expressed thoughts and feelings.

The reflection session guides participants through lectures and exercises on reflection as a way to get to the essence of the discloser's message. They are asked to practice reflection without adding anything new or diagnosing or giving meaning. Their instruction is to bring the important aspects of the message to the foreground. Participants are urged to take their time and listen carefully so they will not distort messages by exaggeration, softening, or adding or omitting important content.

Typically, some group members feel frustrated at first by the difficulty of using this response with skill. Others feel relief in their experience of having their feelings heard.

Disclosure

The disclosure response is often used at significant moments by naive and untrained people in helping roles, but it is used infrequently (Dooley, 1973). It is rarely used as a major response in most current psychotherapies, but it appears to be attracting interest in existential approaches. It is used quite frequently by client-centered therapists but appears overshadowed by the prominence of reflection usage. Perhaps because of its infrequency, the disclosure has been bypassed in comprehensive therapy-analysis systems. It is given its own session in the SASHA program not only for conceptual coherence but because disclosures are recognized by beginners as helping tools used in their personal conversations.

In a trivial sense all utterances may be said to disclose something about the speaker. Some investigators have classified all responses initiated with the pronoun *I* as self-disclosures (Hekmat & Theiss, 1971). In our system *I*-initiated responses are often advisements or interpretations. For our purposes, therefore, disclosures are utterances in which the speaker reveals a nonobvious aspect of his or her condition (feelings, thoughts, or experiences) through a distinct self-reference.

To facilitate learning in this session, participants take part in a "secret pooling." This two-part exercise has everyone write a plain, sincere inner secret, which will remain anonymous. Care is taken to have all participants write with similar pens and so on to make the scraps of paper unidentifiable. After everyone has written a secret, the papers are mixed together. Each member then removes a message and reads it out loud to the group, pretending it is his or her own. That member tells the group how he or she might feel if the secret were personal. Members are warned not to poke fun, even if the disclosure sounds light, silly, or simplistic. For example, "Nobody loves me" can be said teasingly or with deep significance.

The other group members act as helpers and explore what the secret means to the person. Each group member may use any response that allows the secret to be more fully explored, with emphasis on "me too" disclosures.

Me-too disclosures are the easiest type to use, though they can wear thin if overused in actual helping situations. They must be sincere to be appreciated. Me-too disclosure helps reveal feelings or thoughts that are important to the helpseeker. The various forms of this unusual helping response appear to create a range of impacts, such as providing a less authoritarian situation, reducing the helpseeker's loneliness, removing artificialities, stimulating new views of personal experience, and building trust. The only drawback is that the disclosure response requires much practice before it can be used effectively.

The secret-pooling exercise is designed to produce unusual communication in which both helpseeker and helper emphasize disclosures. It is also designed to get the group in touch with some of its members' deeper concerns. The depth of disclosure generally characterizes the group's trust or willingness to explore.

Sometimes a few participants in a secret pooling experience a deep sense of helplessness. Some have been unable to respond because the secret felt overwhelming, or painful, or insoluble. Beginners want to solve the problem and aren't satisfied unless they have some direct impact on the helpseeker. Typically, the first reaction from those listening to their secret being read is surprise at hearing how well the essence of their secret was understood by others. Next comes a little frustration because some of the details aren't discussed accurately. Another surprise comes as other group members are able to relate the secret to their own lives.

RESEARCH ON APPLICATIONS

Programmed instruction is not new in education and psychology. Burgeoning in the late 1950s and becoming "new wave" in the 1960s, programmed instruction is an application of certain aspects of operant conditioning. The theoretical formulations behind programmed instruction represent the development of learning theory over the past 75 years.

In the early 1960s Berzon and her colleagues pioneered the development and research of audiotape programs for self-directed groups. Several studies examined their efficacy. Pre- and posttests included measurement of self-concept, self-disclosure, and self- and peer ratings of understanding. Her findings indicate that the professionally directed and self-directed groups were "sufficiently alike" in the positive change accruing in group participants (Berzon, Solomon, & Reisel, 1972). A later study compared a self-led group with a nontreatment control and found subjects in the experimental condition to be more open, sensitive to others, self-disclosing, self-accepting, and self-motivating (Solomon, Berzon, & Davis, 1970). In a critique of the research on the work of Berzon et al., Taylor (1976) mentions the lack of a nonspecific control group to distinguish the effects of the tape experience from the "personal interactive nature of the experience" (p. 402). Although this is a valid criticism in general, the lack of a nonspecific control group in the live-leader condition versus the tape-led condition does not strongly detract from the conclusion that audio programs have at least as good a chance of producing nonspecifically positive effects as live leaders.

In a pilot study, Dooley (1971) administered an experimental version of audiotaped experioconceptual lessons on the six response modes to a group of undergraduates. Compared with a control group that took the pre- and postassessments but did not participate in the training, the members of the experimental group significantly altered their helping-response style. Dooley concluded that the method of teaching response modes by audiotape was operationally feasible. The prototype training tapes, though rough first drafts and even inaudible in parts, were effective in directing the small-group experiences of these undergraduates. The trained group used more reflections, silences, and disclosures than the untrained group.

In a further investigation of audiotaped instructional methods, Dooley (1973, 1975) used brief automated instruction to successfully train a group of adult candidates for a paraprofessional training program in one response mode, the reflection. In this study, the audiotape-trained applicants used significantly more reflection than the controls in naturalistic settings.

Two later studies from our research group used populations of undergraduates in an attempt to refine format elements of audiotape training as well as solve theoretical problems regarding learning. Burstein (1982) demonstrated in a population of 163 adults randomly assigned to three groups (tape-led, live leader, and waiting-list control) that a tape-led group were as effective and sometimes more effective than live leader groups in successfully teaching communication skills. Hanson (1979) compared tape-led groups with groups run by live leaders. The study was designed to evaluate a procedure for measuring helper empathy and found no significant differences in outcome empathy scores between groups who participated in tape-led and in live-leader training. Both groups gained equally and significantly in contrast to the wait-list controls.

PROSPECTS FOR SASHATAPES AND THEIR KIND

The initial investigations just summarized demonstrate the potential of audiotape-based programs for successfully guiding groups through complex learning procedures. All 15 tape-assisted and live-leader groups in the Burstein study generated gains in communication skills on naturalistic performance measures, on the quality of their responses to video problem vignettes, and on assessments of their written responses to standard problem descriptions. The gains confirmed hypotheses about the capacity of the response-mode framework to alter basic communication behavior. But the surprise came when the SASHAtape-led groups showed greater gains in some areas than the live-leader groups. The research was asking whether tape-group gains would "fall in the same ballpark" as live-leader-group gains. A set of significant findings demonstrated that tape-led groups used more me-too disclosures (an advanced skill), spent less time talking (less attention seeking and more listening), used fewer closed questions (the most limiting type of query), and did less verbal crowding (less interrupting, less simultaneous talking, and fewer rushed responses). Almost all the findings were contrary to expectations. Few investigators would predict that a packaged program could outperform experienced leaders on *any* aspect of skill training. I believe that most clinicians and teachers of psychological skills would doubt research suggesting that a tape-and-print program might rival the effectiveness of their direct presence in a personal change group. They might ask how an automated audio-and-print package could handle a group's need for immediate, authoritative responsiveness. I must admit my own early doubts (as someone shaped by classical clinical psychology) about the capacity of any small-group media intervention for addressing individual differences. I believed a personal change group was in danger without the direct presence of a trained professional. My perspective changed after observing the first dozen tape-assisted groups. They worked—repeatedly. The evidence brought visions of a new format for delivering some mental health services in the near future. That meant building pilot programs that could serve as standardized stimuli for serious research. It also meant organizing theoretical issues for guiding thought on the dynamics of tape-assisted or self-contained groups. Here are some starter hypotheses toward explaining their viability.

Tape-assisted groups that rotate leadership among participants suffer less from passivity and from tension between outgoing and reserved participants. Rotation of leadership is a strong equalizer of group power, participation privileges, and responsibility for maintaining group processes and achieving group goals. The common bond of leadership training and responsibility seems to foster cohesion. Fears of bungling the leadership task melt quickly because the program materials guide every small step.

Practicing interpersonal performance skills in a small, media-assisted group free from the direct scrutiny of an authority allows quicker skill acquisition. Our research indicates that participants feel pride in mastering the material without professional supervision. They claim greater efficiency in practicing weak skills and more safety in trial-and-error routines with advanced skills because experts were not watching. Detecting weak skills and errors through collaborative group use of programmed diagnostic procedures was done easily.

Despite its apparently inert form, the audio cassette can create aspects of group climate usually associated with the skilled presence of a live leader. Participants rated audio cassettes as "very" to "extremely" warm, kind, understanding, and empathic! The tape script language never had the narrator pretending to be in the room with the group. Even subtle assumptions of presence such as "Let me tell you . . ." or "You're probably tired after that exercise . . ." were usually avoided. Meta-communications about the narration were common, and predictions about highly probable aspects of group process (gleaned from earlier research groups) were offered to gain credibility. Such procedures for confronting the mechanical aspects of the program may paradoxically allow a stronger sense of the narrator's presence by eliminating the distractions of pretending to "be there" and to provide the empathy, responsiveness, and charisma of a skilled leader.

Watching SASHAtapes work as a training device for therapy groups and other populations in predicament has encouraged our UCLA research and development team to make and study specialized versions for assisting support groups. Using SASHAtape procedures such as rotating leadership, faith in "expert-free" practice arenas, and writing narration that avoids the presumption of being present and emphasizes metacommunication, we are building programs that guide groups of strangers with common concerns into becoming fully functioning, self-help, mutual-support groups. These packaged programs will be aimed at recent widows, couples coping with infertility, cancer patients, parents of developmentally handicapped children, women coping with long-term effects of incest, hospice patients and their helpers, parents of children killed by accidents, parents of physically handicapped children, single Black mothers, families of victims of Alzheimer's disease, and people in other personal predicaments that can be addressed in support groups. At first the programs will be disseminated around California by the Department of Mental Health; we expect nationwide use later on. The starting point for this large-scale mental health effort was the SASHAtape program. California's lead could demonstrate that teaching psychological skills with packaged programs is a serious option for prevention, repair, and maintenance in mental health efforts. I expect that giving away psychological skills in inexpensive packages will be a mainstream intervention method for psychologists, educators, social workers, and even psychiatrists during the 1990s. That should be enough time for my dubious colleagues to reshape their professional specialties into programs fit for public consumption. Studying packaged programs like SASHAtapes as standardized stimuli can create new research paradigms in mental health and skills training. It all boils down to getting serious about *learning how* to teach people to help themselves.

REFERENCES

Berzon, B., Solomon, L. N., & Reisel, J. Audiotaped programs for self-directed groups. In L. N. Solomon & B. Berzon (Eds.), *New perspectives on encounter groups.* San Francisco: Jossey-Bass, 1972.

Burstein, B. The structure of helping language as an outcome of two communication skills training programs: Live versus automated. Unpublished doctoral dissertation, University of California, Los Angeles, 1982.

Cartwright, R. D. A comparison of the response to psychoanalytic and client-centered psychotherapy. In L. A. Gottschalk & A. H. Auerbach (Eds.), *Methods of research in psychotherapy.* New York: Appleton-Century-Crofts, 1966.

Dooley, C. D. Preliminary report on pilot study of interpersonal process instructional tapes: An experimental teaching method. Unpublished paper, University of California, Los Angeles, 1971.

Dooley, C. D. Effects of response interaction training on the group assessment of interpersonal traits. Unpublished doctoral dissertation, University of California, Los Angeles, 1973.

Dooley, C. D. Effect of automated reflection response training on the group assessment of interpersonal traits. *Journal of Counseling Psychology,* 1975, *22*(6), 535–541.

Elliot, R., Stiles, W. B., Barker, C., Burstein, B., & Goodman, G. Response modes in help-intended communication: Framework and recent research. In T. A. Wills (Ed.), *Basic processes in helping relationships.* New York: Academic Press, 1982.

Goodman, G. *Companionship therapy: Studies in structured intimacy.* San Francisco: Jossey-Bass, 1972.

Hanson, C. E. Measuring empathy as an outcome of training in help-intended communication. Unpublished doctoral dissertation, University of California, Los Angeles, 1979.

Hargrove, D. S. Verbal interaction analysis of empathic and nonempathic responses of therapists. *Journal of Consulting and Clinical Psychology,* 1974, *42,* 305.

Hekmat, H., & Theiss, M. Self-actualization and modification of affective self-disclosure during a social conditioning interview. *Journal of Counseling Psychology,* 1971, *18,* 101–105.

Ivey, A. E. *Microcounseling: Innovations in interviewing training.* Springfield, Ill.: Charles C Thomas, 1971.

Kiesler, C. A. Mental health policy as a field of inquiry for psychology. *American Psychologist,* 1980, *35*(12), 1066–1080.

Lieberman, M. A., Yalom, I. D., & Miles, M. B. *Encounter groups: First facts.* New York: Basic Books, 1973.

Matarazzo, J. D., Wiens, A. N., Matarazzo, R. G., & Saslow, G. Speech and silence behavior in clinical psychotherapy and its laboratory correlates. In J. M. Shlien (Ed.), *Research in psychotherapy* (Vol. 3). Washington, D.C.: American Psychological Association, 1968.

Moreland, J. R., Ivey, A. E., & Phillips, J. An evaluation of micro-counseling as an interview training tool. *Journal of Consulting and Clinical Psychology,* 1973, *41,* 294–300.

Ornston, P. S., Cicchetti, D. V., Levine, J., & Fierman, L. D. Some parameters of verbal behavior that reliably differentiate novice from experienced therapists. *Journal of Abnormal Psychology,* 1968, *73,* 240–244.

Perls, F. S. *Gestalt therapy verbatim.* Lafayette, Calif.: Real People Press, 1969.

Phillips, E. L., & Agnew, J. W., Jr. A study of Rogers' "reflection hypothesis." *Journal of Clinical Psychology,* 1953, *9,* 281–284.

Solomon, L. N., Berzon, B., & Davis, D. A personal growth program for self-directed groups. *Journal of Applied Behavioral Science,* 1970, *6,* 427–451.

Snyder, W. U. An investigation of the nature of nondirective psychotherapy. *Journal of General Psychology,* 1945, *33,* 193–223.

Strupp, H. H. An objective comparison of Rogerian and psychoanalytic techniques. *Journal of Consulting Psychology,* 1955, *19,* 1–7.

Strupp, H. H., & Wallach, M. S. A further study of psychiatrists' responses in quasi-therapy situations. *Behavioral Science,* 1965, *10,* 113–134.

Taylor, M. H. Encounter tapes for personal growth groups, how useful? *Small Group Behavior,* 1976, *7*(4), 397–406.

Wile, D. B., Bron, G. D., & Pollack, H. B. Preliminary validational evidence for the group therapy questionnaire. *Journal of Consulting and Clinical Psychology,* 1970, *34,* 367–374.

CHAPTER FOURTEEN

The Politics of Giving Therapy Away: Listening and Focusing

Eugene T. Gendlin

Eugene T. Gendlin, author of the book *Focusing*, is a professor in the Department of Behavioral Sciences at the University of Chicago. He is the founder, and was for many years the editor, of *Psychotherapy: Theory, Research, and Practice*, the quarterly journal of the American Psychological Association. In 1970 he was chosen by the Psychotherapy Division of the American Psychological Association for its Distinguished Professional Psychologist of the Year award. Gendlin has written extensively in psychology and philosophy. He is now working with many others to extend the application of focusing to diverse fields and to publish the *Focusing Folio*.

The focusing method is perhaps the purest statement of the theme of this book, for it seeks to give away the very process of therapeutic change as a teachable skill. Gendlin, a former student and later a colleague of Carl Rogers, defines focusing as a technique for "attending to the physically sensed border zone between the conscious and unconscious." Once people have learned to sense concrete change events in their bodies, they can recognize when they are changing and can better facilitate this process. In this essay Gendlin presents the focusing technique and discusses some political issues in the giving away of psychotherapy—such as the fear among professionals that their clients will no longer need them. Gendlin assures us, however, that the more we teach skills directly, the more in demand we will become. Gendlin also introduces the Changes program (described in greater detail by Boukydis in the following chapter) and makes the point that this peer-counseling group, which actively teaches the skills of listening and focusing, offers free assistance to all its members—and thus "gives away" psychotherapy in another important sense.

Socrates once said: "The Athenians, it seems to me, are not very much disturbed if they think someone is clever. . . . But the moment they suspect that he is giving his ability to others, they get angry" (*Euthyphro* 3c). Many professionals fear the day (which is surely coming) when people will learn the skills of psychotherapy routinely in public school and practice them with each other. Actually they need not fear. The more people engage in processes of this sort, the more experts will be wanted and needed. It is true, however, that such experts will have to be more able than the general population. Currently this is often not the case; some of the self-help training is better than the so-called professional training. Many professionals know a large vocabulary of general terms but no specific practical skills. In the future most people will have been trained in *specific* skills. They will also know what helpful change feels like within themselves. They will be able to recognize when an "expert" can do more than they can do alone or with a partner.

In this chapter I will first discuss the two therapeutic skills we are giving away. I will then discuss some political principles that I think apply to all *genuine* forms of giving therapy away. These principles have implications both for the politics of therapy and for politics in general. Finally I will present our own organizational model.

LISTENING AND FOCUSING

Listening

In our organization we welcome anyone to teach *any* skill to those of us who want to learn it. We do not make a sect out of our group. The two skills we give away are listening and focusing.

Listening comes from client-centered therapy. (See also Thomas Gordon's chapter in this book.) We have specified listening in our particular way. There is a "Listening Manual" (included in Gendlin, 1981), which has been widely used in many public agencies. We concentrate on specificity—exactly what to do when and also exactly what signs show that listening is being done well and exactly what happens when it is not.

We find that the learning of listening makes our whole organization a good place to be.

What is listening? It is receiving what someone wishes to convey and saying it back to the person exactly as it was meant. One usually fails in one's first attempt to say a message back. The speaker corrects it: "No, that's not what I meant, it's . . ." The listener says "Oh, I see, you meant . . ." Even at the second try, the speaker typically says "Yes, that's right, but not exactly—I mean it just this way . . ." The listener grasps that too: "It's exactly this . . ." There is then usually a visible relief in the speaker. What needed to be heard has actually got heard. It was received. There is no need to say it over and over. Now there is a little silence usually. The person feels inwardly freed from what needed to be said, because it was said and heard. There is a freed space inside. Something new can now come up from deeper within the person. Usually it is a further bit of whatever the speaker is working on. If this new bit is again received by the listener, there is again a freed space inside. More and more further steps arise within the speaker. Aspects of the problem develop that are new to the speaker. A change process is inwardly experienced, step by step.

People begin this process by trying to convey what they know and feel. But very soon much more arises than that. There is a bit of inward movement with each such step.

Fifteen minutes of being listened to is worth coming all the way across the city to a meeting. People take turns listening to each other, sometimes for half an hour or an hour each.

Even apart from therapy, *any* discussion is vastly better if people listen. The nature of group process changes. No longer does one have to fight for the chance to make one fast statement. A listening response invites the speakers to go more deeply into what motivates them to make the point. Once that underlying good sense has been heard, people don't need to say their point over and over every time they speak in the meeting.

Most people have no one who will hear and receive their own inward experience *just as it is.* No one wants to know exactly how *you* experience your personal struggle. Everyone wants to edit it, change it, improve it, put his or her meaning onto it. Another person is a very powerful aid in letting one's feelings and meanings open up and develop through steps, but only if that other person can listen. To our organization that means putting nothing extraneous in and receiving each bit of experience just as the speaker means to convey it.

When people experience listening and being listened to, it soon seems like an inalienable right that goes with being human. Then, when people don't listen, it seems a shocking disrespect. How can they not respect the good sense that my inwardly arising experience makes when it is allowed to emerge in its own meanings?

We teach listening to everyone. The first evening people come, they learn it in the "New People's Group." It lets each newcomer discover our climate and become comfortable. We teach it in a round. The person on one's left says something, and one repeats it back. When that has been done successfully, one is listened to by the person on one's right. The leaders first model listening with each other and then help each person say back what the person on his or her left said.

At first we teach listening as repeating. Oddly, we find that only this "parroting" teaches people to pay attention to what someone says. New people are always surprised to discover that they did not hear what the person said and that others do not hear them. Only the "saying back" reveals this! (If you have not made this discovery, and you think you hear all right—just try saying back! You will be corrected and will discover how you don't usually hear.)

After someone has learned to hear what is being said so that it can be repeated (some weeks), then it is time to learn how to say back only what matters—the personal feelings, meanings, and "edges."

I think listening is a crucial new factor in developing free people. A mere ideology of freedom is only an abstraction. Until people experience their own, *inwardly arising* steps of making sense, they will accept ideas imposed on them by others.

Once people are used to being listened to, they are "spoiled" for any organization that violates their own inner source of good sense. They do not accept being told about themselves by someone who has not first heard *them.* Anyone who does not even know that this needs to be done will not be taken as an authority in personal matters. People who are used to being listened to will receive psychological direction tentatively, pending their own inwardly arising process.

Without the individual's *experience* of that inward source of good sense and personal truth, all varieties of political programs add up to the same thing: externally imposed straitjackets, whatever the ideology.

Focusing

The steps of focusing are presented in a paperback (Gendlin, 1981) that includes highly specific instructions for many typical difficulties in learning focusing. It is a simply written book, an example of giving therapy away.

Here I cannot repeat all those specifics. Consequently, you won't know exactly what focusing is. It involves an odd kind of bodily attention that cannot usually be found without a little practice. Most people have one or another typical difficulty learning it.

Let me return to listening for a moment. Listening is taught to the listener. Certain "inwardly arising steps of change" are supposed to happen in the person being listened to. But sometimes nothing like that happens. The person only talks and expresses the same feelings over and over. There has been no way, until recently, to show such a person that it is possible to attend, inwardly, to something sensed very directly but unclearly. It is from that sort of inward sensing that change steps arise. From my description of listening you may not have understood what these "steps" are like. To explain focusing, I shall discuss these "steps" and how they can be helped to come.

Repetitiousness, lack of therapeutic movement, is a problem in every kind of therapy. In a series of research studies over many years we found that those patients who changed did not work only with "feelings" and emotions they recognized. They spent time during interviews directly sensing something unclear, yet physically experienced.

The difference is hard to grasp: emotions such as anger, fear, sadness, disappointment are recognizable. We know what these are. In contrast, there can also be a deeper "sense of something" that is "right there" but unclear as yet.

If people stay entirely with what they clearly feel, then this bodily sense of the problem does not even come. Some learning is needed to know how to let an unclear bodily sense of a problem arise in one's body. Then there are specific ways of keeping one's attention on it so that it shifts in the body, opens, "comes into focus."

Focusing has its beginnings in therapy, although now it is quite independent of therapy. Focusing has been taught to many people not in therapy—for example, people in business, spiritual groups, children, hospitalized patients, and bright college students. It is used in healing, in stress reduction, and in creative writing. It has been found that if a person wants to write, it is better to begin focusing on the directly felt body sense of what is to be written rather than words and ideas. As one attends to what shifts and opens, one is then more able to write as one would wish.

In any therapy or growth process something new must open within the person. Sometimes this happens and one doesn't know how. But one great aid is to pay direct attention to the border zone (you might say) between conscious and unconscious. What has been called "unconscious" is not completely unknown but has an entry into consciousness that is quite aware: it is a fuzzy, vague, unclear sense one has *in one's body.* Such a "felt sense" can form in regard to any topic of concern.

To pay this kind of attention is odd. Most people don't know about this implicitly complex, vague body sense. Instead, they spend most of their time with *recognizable* thoughts and feelings. The felt sense in focusing is different.

To let a "felt sense" form requires much more specific steps than I can give here. But I can give you some initial experiential description of it.

If you were now to turn your attention inward to a problem of yours, you would find certain familiar feelings. How would you bypass these so that an *un*clear bodily sense of the problem can come?

First we would have to show you a preliminary step: how not to go inside a problem to those familiar feelings. There is another "place" in an odd "space." It is a "third" place, neither away from the problem nor inside it. We have specific ways to help people find this "third" place.

When you have found that "place," you can refuse to go inside the problem to the usual feelings. Now you can wait for the bodily sense of the whole problem to come.

At first this is rather like attending very carefully to something that is not there yet. You would attend in the middle of your body and wait.

We would show you a number of ways to let that unclear sense form. One of them would eventually work for you. Just as an example, here is one way:

You know the problem is not solved, but you can say to yourself "This problem is really all solved, all OK; I can feel fine about it—*in my body.*" As you say this, you attend to the middle of your body. Very quickly a bodily sense of discomfort with this problem comes. It is a queasy, fuzzy, murky, indefinable sense, but you know it is the unique bodily quality that *this* problem makes in your body.

The body talks back! We ask you to say "The problem is all right" so that the body can respond with a physical contradiction to that statement.

If you are not experienced with focusing, you might not think highly of this bodily sense. You might say "That's too vague. It's just murky. I know a lot about my problem already. I can't expect anything to come from this confused 'edge' here. *This* can't be what they're telling me to stay with."

And yet, this murky bodily discomfort *comes* when you attend in this way to this problem. It is *the bodily version of this problem.*

A "felt sense" (as we call it) is very different from the usual emotions, however bodily these are "in the gut." Emotions are recognizable: we know when we are angry, afraid, or sad. Emotions are only *parts* of life situations; they are *inside* a problem. The *whole* of a problem feels different. It makes a unique, indefinable bodily sense.

When this sense shifts and changes, all the parts inside the problem change. Later new emotions may arise. These may be quite strong, but at first the bodily sense of the whole problem is usually not intense. In fact, it is slight and fleeting and can easily be lost hold of.

We have specific ways of helping people to stay with such an unclear felt sense. It helps to attend to the "quality" of it. Is it heavy, or jumpy, or how? A word, phrase, or image might fit this unique quality. Finding such a "handle" helps one to stay with the felt sense and to attend to its bodily quality. When words or an image "resonate" with a felt sense, there is a physical loosening, a bodily signal, breath, or energy flow.

Only now, having worked for a while with the bodily sense itself, you ask: What is it about the problem that makes *this* bodily sense?

I have to make all this sound very simple and easy in order to explain it here. Actually, there are again specific ways for letting that question reach down into the body. Otherwise the question rouses only the old answers, the explanations ready in your mind. When the asking reaches down to the felt sense, there is soon (30 seconds or so—a long time to stay quiet) a *physical* shift. A further bit of the problem or a step toward solving it comes.

Any ideas that come without a physically felt easing are simply allowed to fly by. One waits for anything about the problem, any thought, feeling, bit of detail, or direction of solution that is accompanied by a physical release in the felt sense.

There are specific ways to help a "felt shift" to happen if this simple asking didn't bring it on.

It takes some learning to recognize a felt shift. Sometimes it is huge and unmistakable, but there are often small shifts, little "steps." Most people's tension level is chronically at a maximum, so that they don't recognize small changes. Or they may have learned meditation or hypnosis, a relaxation so deep that the body no longer "talks back" at all. Such relaxed states are valuable, but focusing requires a middle level of relaxation, so that slight bodily changes can be sensed. Only in that way can one work directly with the bodily version of a particular problem.

Today many people are "in touch" with their feelings. They think various thoughts that have "gut-felt" results. This can be very intense and is usually quite painful. It is a kind of "vivisection."

It is very different to let the bodily sense of the *whole problem* form (if it isn't already there). Touching *that* is not painful. Usually there is already a little relief when the felt sense first comes. Then, the "felt shift" always involves a physical relief (even if one doesn't like what emerges).

The main purpose of focusing is the bodily change of the problem *as a whole*. At each "step" the whole changes, and therefore also every part. Therefore one may not immediately find words for what comes at such a step.

The purpose is not the information one may discover. Further steps will change this information anyway. A major problem will require many steps.

"Getting information" is based on the false assumption that a problem is something fixed. Most theories assume that whatever is wrong happened long ago and that we can only find out, relive, repeat. Such theories do not explain change and growth. They assume that we can "throw out the garbage" by reliving it. In fact, the relived experience needs to be different from the original experience. Sensing a problem as a bodily whole in the present is a new living and changes that whole. The problem is then found to be quite different. Further steps let it become still more different.

So much of psychotherapy is just the usual feelings over and over. Emotional discharges can be very intense but soon become repetitive. I don't mean to denigrate catharsis; it is precious and often needed. But reliving old emotions does not alone bring steps of change in the whole way someone is.

Only rarely do people in therapy sense a problem *as a whole* rather than only this or that emotion, which is only part of the problem. A whole problem can be sensed in the body only as a holistic sense. *New* steps and a bit of change come from such a sense, which must form and come in the body.

Focusing lifts out of therapy the essential moments in which the body forms the whole of something, and new steps of change arise. It specifies how this kind of inward attention is found. One can then do that alone, although it helps to have another person's attention and company silently, sometimes interspersed with listening.

Every person is unique. All instructions must therefore be taken in two ways: one should try them out exactly as given. But stop the moment you do violence inside. If that happens, don't quit completely; just stop and sense what went wrong. The steps of focusing feel natural; they feel like physical relief.

The preliminary movement.   In a three-day workshop we spend one day on just this movement. It greatly helps the rest of focusing. Please notice the specifics.

Check first whether you can put your attention in the middle of your body. Some people sense only the periphery of their bodies, shoulders, arms, and back. They cannot bring their attention into the middle. It may take you some time to attend there. If you are not used to that, you might begin by sensing your toes and then your knee. Can you find your knee without moving it first? Then bring your attention up into your stomach and chest. (If that fails, we know other ways.)

Now see how life is going for you, just now. But do it in this specific way: instead of reciting all your problems and situations, ask *only* about what your body is just now carrying. What is now in the way of feeling very good inside your body? You are probably sure you already know. Instead of what you know, here is how you would do this preliminary step:

Put your attention in the middle of your body, and say to it: "Everything is fine. I can feel fine now. Life is going very well." Wave aside your thoughts about this, and wait for your body to answer. Very soon it answers: a not-fine body sense arises to let you know things are not all fine. Your body is not now able to feel all good about life.

As you attend to this not-fine feeling, you can sense that it is a mix of a number of things. If you try to push the whole mix away at once, you will feel only very slightly better. Instead, you let it sort itself out. Very quickly one problem arises out of this mix.

"Oh . . . yes. That's one of them all right . . . ," you say, with a sigh. "Sure, that's there. Yes." You don't go inside it. Instead, you "place" it at some little distance before you. It is *there*. You don't deny it or avoid it. But you also don't fall into it. You keep your fingers on it, so to speak. You shelve it or park it where you can find it again easily. From here you can relate to that problem as a whole. You may come back to it later. You can sense whether you feel ready to go into it today or not.

But this is only the preliminary to focusing. Right now you don't work on that problem, even if you are ready to do so. Instead, you put your attention in the middle of your body, and you say "*Except* for that problem (if that were somehow well solved), would I feel fine in here?"

Typically, now, one's mind answers: "Sure, I'd be great, all free and easy." But that is not yet the bodily response! One must wait, keeping one's attention in the middle of the body, and *there* ask "Except for this thing, if it were OK, what would come in my body here?"

There is then, after a few seconds, an easing, a release, a flow of new energy, sometimes some specific effect one had not suspected. At any rate the change is concrete, bodily, not just an idea or a visual picture.

"Now, except for that, is life going all fine?" Again the attention is in the middle of the body. "Hmm . . . well, much better but still something uneasy, funny, a little tight, there . . . wonder what *that* is about." Again after a little while one knows. It is that other problem. Again one puts it in a safe place, slightly aside (not away). "Now, if that were all OK, how would it feel in my body?"

At any given time four or five such concerns are being carried by your body. Some big problems you know of are not here now. Some trivial things are, even though they're the sort you won't even recall next week. What the body now carries is not the same as your mental list of main concerns. It is *this* uneasy mix, now.

For example, you might find that one thing is your main life relationship. "Yes, sure, that's there . . . our fight last night, my doubts about the relationship, what to do . . . that whole thing." When you "place" that before you and return into your body, asking what would come if that whole problem were solved, you feel some new way, physically. Then, sensing whether you feel *all* OK, you don't. Soon another thing emerges: that silly remark you made this morning. You know this isn't important, but you don't argue with it. There it is. You feel uneasy about that stupid remark. A breath comes. "Yes, that's still there . . ." You might have to look into it further, but if so, you will do that later. Except for that, are you *all* fine? In this way your body might give you a few more concerns as the "mix" sorts itself out.

When one puts one of these concerns aside, and then the body is no different (only a visual picture of putting it aside comes), then we say that it hasn't really been put aside. Other ways of doing that are used, until it does let itself be placed aside, with a bodily release.

Usually, after a few minutes one reaches the end of the present list (what is *now* bodily carried), and still one isn't totally fine. There is usually a "background feeling," one that is always there for the person, always tense, always trying hard, always a little cautious, always a little sad—whatever. Taking this background feeling too as "something" to "put aside a little," one says "I may work on this later. For now . . . what would come in my body if this background feeling were not there, if it were made OK somehow?" After some moments, what comes in the body at this point is usually quite a large free space.

This procedure is very different from turning *away* from everything the body carries and merely stopping thinking and attending to problems *all at once.* That leaves them all in a bunch, in a bodily-carried way, even if one relaxes, meditates, or otherwise spends time in a restful way. The *specific* way each concern cramps the body is not thereby released. The vast open space isn't found that way.

The "movements" of focusing.

All this is only the preparatory movement *before* focusing. At this point one begins to focus on one problem, one concern. (It could be something positive, of course—something one wants to write, perhaps, or develop further. It need not be a problem.)

Now pick *one* of these "things" you have placed.

Suppose you pick that big relationship problem to work on. Now you could quickly make yourself feel very bad. You might then feel bad the rest of the day. We all know how to do that. Unfortunately, this self-hurting way is called laudable names: facing things, having "gut feelings," "intense experiencing." But I assume these bad feelings are familiar enough. One more time will not bring anything new. Instead, in focusing you would *stay outside the problem,* and sense it *as a whole.* That will bring a new "step."

Let us say you sense that the familiar bad feelings are very close. You decide to keep that problem at a good distance. You don't think about any of it. You refer to the problem as "all that."

Putting your attention in the middle of your body you say "*All that* is all fine, all solved, isn't it?" Instantly a jangly, uneasy body sense comes.

"OK, let's stay with *that*," you say.

That is a felt sense. It is at first *un*clear. You know much about your problem, but you do *not* know what that felt sense is.

"What is the quality of fear?" you ask. In order to stay with the felt sense, you try to name its bodily quality more exactly: "Jangly . . . ?" That seems right, but not quite. "Nervous . . . ?" That is also right, but not quite. Then "Touchy!" comes and is *exactly* right. "Yes! It's just like a spot that cannot stand to be touched. Yes! Whew (breath)."

Now you spend a minute or so *"resonating"* the word with the felt sense: every time you think "touchy," there is that flow of bodily agreement and a little breath. There is a tiny bit of loosening in your body.

At this point you would not take five dollars for the word *touchy*. You would not agree to use *nervous* instead, because that word does not have the physical resonance and slight but very grateful easing that *touchy* makes.

When that effect is no longer so fresh and powerful (a minute or less later), you go on to the next focusing movement. You ask *"What is that?"* You mean, of course, *"What is it about that whole problem that is now making this sense here?"*

For a while nothing stirs in your body. Various thoughts interrupt you, and you return each time. "Where was I? Oh . . . yes . . . touchy . . . ah, there it is again!"

Then it opens and shifts, suddenly. "Oh . . . yes . . . touchy . . . ah, there it is again!" That's too touchy to touch right now. I've got to stay away from the deciding pressure. That's the touchy spot!"

A felt shift comes with an easing. You feel physically better. But you are quickly interrupted by familiar thoughts: "You have to decide, it won't do to avoid that. Not deciding is also deciding." And so on. You push these aside with an "I know." You protect this little step: "I must not touch deciding . . . whew (breath), that's what's so 'touchy.'"

You have now gone through the six "movements" of focusing: (1) the preliminary space-making, (2) the felt sense coming, (3) the quality "handle"—the word *touchy*, (4) the resonating, (5) the asking, and, after the felt shift, (6) protecting the little step that came.

"Is that it for now?," you ask, sensing your body. You get a sense that your body wants to stop. You do. Or a nervous sense tells you that if you stop now, it's no good. So you continue, doing the same steps again, from here.

Of course, for the moment you obey the little step that just came. You do *not* now attempt to decide whether you want to stay in your relationship.

As with anything that might be called "resistance," anything that comes in the way of working on a problem, you neither run away nor push in. You focus on what is in the way. Instead of trying to decide, you focus on what this "don't touch it" feeling is.

You might take a short break, a few seconds. Stretch. Ease your body. Be in relation to this "touchy" without being too much in it (first movement: making a space).

Now (second movement: felt sense) what's *the whole felt sense that can come along with this* "touchy"? Is it still there? You say "touchy . . . ," and with your attention in your body, you wait: "Ah . . . there it is again. Now, let it be here. Let it widen, sense more coming with it, as one global *un*clear body sense." *What is its quality?* (third movement: handle for the quality). "Hurt? . . . No." "Hurting itself" comes. "That feels right! (fourth movement: resonating). Trying to make the decision somehow hurt itself . . . it's as if that spot hurts *itself.* What *is* that?"

Upstairs, your mind suddenly has a lot to say: "Of course, that's the conflict. You know very well that you are hurt, and that is the side that wants to leave. The good things want you to stay. You have to choose one way or the other." This makes perfect sense, of course, but it is your *old information.* That's what you have been thinking all along: Two sides to this, fighting each other. The good and the bad. As you think these old thoughts, it hurts in your stomach. You are having "gut feelings," all right, but they are being made from your head, downward. Your head has a map and cuts your stomach to fit it. It hurts. We call it "vivisection."

You push all that away, quickly. "Right now we're *not* deciding. What was I doing? Oh . . . yes . . . 'touchy' . . . and . . . Oh . . . yes . . . 'hurting itself' . . . yes, whew (breath), that's sure right there. It feels like deciding hurts *itself.* Yeah . . . that's right."

Now you ask "What is this hurting-itself-thing?" (fifth movement: asking). Slowly, almost with a physical creaking, it loosens and opens a little, and there is some relief. Along with that, you suddenly find an intricacy, all different from what you thought. This intricacy has no ready words. The "territory" as it is in your body sense differs completely from the map in your mind and the words you know to use. But there it is, "Whew (breath). . . ." After a few seconds you can try to think what you found: "Oh . . . it's just *one* thing, not two that fight. The hurt and anger do *not* push me to leave. It threatens and hurts and argues to leave, but it is really a way of staying! It's trying to hold onto the relationship *by* being angry and hurt." It makes no logical sense, but your body eases. A few more seconds, and it makes more logical sense: "Oh . . . if I *stay,* I have to be hurt and think about leaving. It wants to stay and hurt itself, rather than let go! Whew (breath again) . . . ."

Very often what emerges in focusing is utterly different from the obvious old information. Often the whole problem is not cut into those pieces and concepts one had. The way it actually exists in the body has very much its own intricacy.

But finding this out is not the main effect. Rather, this kind of "finding out" comes with a physical change, a shift in the body. In the very moments when you come to "know" how the problem has actually been, that problem physically changes. It is no longer the way you just found.

You can sense that your body does not wish to go on, further, just now. "We just got to this!" it says. So you repeat that last effective phrase a few times, to be sure you won't easily lose it (sixth movement: receiving/protecting). "Yes . . . *by* hurting it is holding on." It seems very important to stress the "by"; that is how the body demands just the right words. "Whew (breath) . . . yes, I won't lose that."

You feel vastly better, and it is only ten minutes later! It also seems to you that this self-hurting spot doesn't need to hurt itself if you keep this phrase. But when you try to think why that might be, your stomach or chest clouds up again. So you accept it as "a step." You know that tomorrow and the next day there will be other steps. You protect *this* step from your tendency to want to go on and "face" everything immediately. You can sense that your body wants to keep and digest *this* step for a while.

In this example I have followed the usual six movements of focusing. Nothing human is that regular or predictable. A felt shift may come anywhere along the line or may not come. Some of these "movements" may not fit at times or may not happen. But the six movements help in teaching focusing and are often just right.

POLITICAL PRINCIPLES OF GIVING THERAPY AWAY

Carl Rogers first opened psychotherapy to the possibility of self-help. He was constantly attacked for "splitting psychoanalysis," for "practicing without a license," for opening psychotherapy to nonmedical people, and above all, I think, for demystifying it and dethroning the medical model. By *demystifying* I don't mean that the process of human growth stops being mysterious. It becomes always more obviously sacred as we learn more about it. But Rogers *specified* what the therapist does. Other approaches can be specified, too.

Specifying makes training systematic, and it makes research possible. Yes, the very same specificity that lets something be taught also enables it to be observed. It lets one decide with sureness whether a particular procedure is or is not being done just then by a given therapist on a given tape recording. Applying that to a large number of cases, one can observe what results occur.

With Rogers it also became obvious that current doctoral training is mostly irrelevant to psychotherapy. Whatever would prevent someone from learning to do it well, it isn't a lack of intellectual knowledge.

In addition to specificity, Rogers's method brought it home that the decisions a person must make are inherently that person's own. No book knowledge enables another person to decide for anyone. That goes for life decisions and life-style as well as, moment by moment, what to talk about, feel into, struggle with. Another person might make a guess, but ultimately personal growth is from the inside outward. A process of change begins inside and moves in ways even the person's own mind cannot direct, let alone another person's mind.

These developments made it possible to think that psychotherapy might be given away.

Tom Gordon has been the one who made all this fruitful with his P.E.T. organization, now imitated by a host of others. Half a million people have been taught Rogerian listening in his network alone, and it is now taught by many others as well.

As self-help skill training spreads and becomes varied, it is necessary to spell out some principles. As I see it, these principles are already being violated—or, at least, forgotten, so that they soon will be violated. Even if not everyone agrees, I believe a discussion of these points will be valuable.

Specificity enables skill training. It is training that we are giving away! What differentiates the credentialed professional from anyone else? It is the pretension—or reality—of training.

1. *If we don't give the training away, then we are not giving therapy away.* In many networks today large numbers of people are given growth-producing experiences, but they aren't taught how it was done. It may be called "training," but what the trainer knows is not available. Then people cannot continue the process in themselves or with others. All they can do is urge others to attend the same

organization. Therapy has not been given them as a process they can continue in themselves and with others. Someone has kept it for his or her organization, for his or her power, and is not empowering the people coming through. In some networks people are even made to promise that they will not spread what they have learned, that they will not even describe it, so that the mystification of the public will continue and so that people must come to the horse's mouth itself, whoever the horse is.

We want to give people the process, not one experience. We don't want to give them a fish; we want to teach them how to fish.

If this intention is clear, then the skill has to be defined specifically. Giving away and specificity are inherently related because skills that cannot be specified cannot be taught to others.

2. *Skills can be formulated so that they are done by individuals from within and help them to find, rather than block them from finding, their own inward source.* To do this we may have to specify what it feels like from inside when one does the skill effectively, and we may need to define it from a new vantage point. In that form it can be given away.

Each person must find the inner source of growth, change, and life direction. This cannot be done by running people through arranged experiences that have an impact on them that they cannot fathom. Whatever we do, let us rework it until people can do it from inside themselves.

For example, Skinnerian operant conditioning is done *to* people. An institution arranges with a psychologist to reward certain behaviors in some population, perhaps jail inmates or schoolchildren. But the same skill can be taught so that each individual can use it. It then becomes an extension of the individual's own power and self-control over life. In that form it can be given away. People can define for themselves what behavior they would like to eliminate or increase. They can keep a chart of when and how it happens, and they can reward themselves by celebrating or by giving themselves something they like. They can change the "target behavior" when they wish and as they themselves change.

As we become more and more able to enter into the fascinating territory of personal development, we meet the problems that have always come along with this dimension throughout history. One such problem is the rigidity of doctrines and churches. Today both psychological and spiritual offerings show this same tendency. Every network demands that we engage in just some one practice and tells us that all others are bad or useless. The guru says we must find our inner source, but in practice he may demand that we silence it. In our own development—just where we most need to be free—we are also most willing to make sacrifices. Those who want power can use our willingness to control us.

An individual is not an appendage of anyone. Each person is a unique being and has an open life to direct and an individuality to develop. We may make bad messes. But self-direction from inside is the essence of the human kind of being we are. Would we trade that in for some set of "good" results if we could be a different kind of being, one that *can* be managed from outside?

3. *When we teach specifics, we can research and count whether these specifics are indeed being practiced and just what happens when they are.* Research publicly defines what we teach and makes it available, rather than its being the property of some mystifying leader or special group.

4. *In giving therapy away we can come to a kind of knowledge, a way of using concepts, so that each assertion is tied to an aspect of experience.* Mystification is saying truths in such a way that an individual cannot find those truths directly. The

statements have to be kept and transmitted, because there is no direct access to what the statement is about. One example is the therapeutic interpretation that does not, just now, corroborate itself within the individual. It has to be believed on the authority of the doctor. Some other time the statement may help bring up something in the individual that is internally valid as soon as it arises. But if this does not happen now, the interpretation must be discarded for now. Therefore it should be given tentatively, as an invitation to sense directly, not as a fact.

Indeed, theoretical concepts in general also need to be like that. They need to point directly to an aspect of experience anyone can find. When psychological knowledge is translated into such an "experience-pointing" form, it can be taught to anyone.

Knowledge needs to be reunderstood not as expert property but as directly relating to and articulating someone's experience. Physical technology creates experts who alone know the science. These experts work for politicians who control what the science is used for. The politicians, in turn, take their orders from the powers that be. This social structure is a problem. A human science that is desirable is not like that.

For example, it may help to know that generally a depressed person *may* discover a lot of anger later on, with experiential exploring. Or it might help to know that people who have been violent against others *could* turn the violence against themselves. Such knowing can enable a helping person to be more sensitive. But knowledge helps only if we change how knowledge is usually used. The human process is inherently unique and implicitly complex in everyone. No set of abstractions can equal or undercut what concretely arises. Knowledge of general patterns can only help one to be sensitive to what may emerge. The general expectation cannot substitute for what actually emerges and must be worked with.

What arises directly in the individual must have priority over any concept. A concept may help one lift out some aspect of experience. Even so, at the next moment further steps can move quite differently than that very concept would have led one to expect.

Until now "knowledge" was said to be too complex and too good to give away. I think it has been too poor. If we make "giving away" the model for knowledge, we move toward the kind of human science we want: concepts that refer specifically to what can be experienced and a use of concepts that modifies them by what is newly experienced in a free individual.

5. *People can learn to recognize whether they are helped or not; they can sense concrete change events in their bodies and in their lives.* In medicine the doctor determines whether there is improvement or not. The doctor tells us whether we have to keep going to the doctor.

People go to traditional psychotherapy for years and believe that they must be changing. To say "must be" shows that it is an inference, rather than a direct sense of change from within. People infer that they must be getting something, since the doctor keeps working. After five years or nine years patients/clients may begin to doubt this. The public has not yet grasped that psychological "doctors" cannot know that something is helping when the person does not know it. Self-help networks that involve trained teachers pose a similar problem. The "accredited" teachers are assumed to be effective. A person who went to someone "accredited" is made to believe that whatever went on "must be" how the offered process is intended to work. I do not deny the need for training. We may keep a list of those we trust to teach it well. We may institute various checks, and we should. But we need to tell the public *not* to trust an accredited person. Rather, let us tell people that they must inwardly check and sense, in a bodily way, whether a good change is happening. If not, they should work with a different person. When the public grasps this, it will be the best quality control.

Focusing enables a person to experience this inward bodily sensing of bits of concrete change. Having once experienced that, people can recognize when they are changing.

Some important by-products of focusing: One comes to know how to find one's own inner source, in regard to almost any situation or concern. It puts one beyond depending on a therapist or a guru for how to live. One also discovers, "Oh . . . I *am* not these problems. I am here, and they are over there . . . I have them, I am not them." One discovers a "me" that is not anything one could name.

HOW FOCUSING WAS DEVELOPED FROM RESEARCH

A series of earlier research studies (Gendlin, Beebe, Cassens, Klein, & Oberlander, 1967) showed that successful clients in psychotherapy could be picked out from their tape-recorded therapy interviews. The successful clients were less than half in most groups studied; sometimes they were few. Various outcome measures and the judgments of therapist and client separately did agree in most cases, with small variations.

The successful clients did something in their therapy interviews that at that time had no name or familiar description. While all clients sometimes intellectualize, sometimes report events, sometimes manifest very strong emotions, the successful ones did something else in addition: At most times they checked themselves. Against what? They can be heard on the tape recording, in a characteristic form of language, such as : "I feel so and so . . . is that right?" Silence. Then "No, that's not right. I don't know what *that* is, but it's not what I said." Silence again. Then "Oh . . . yes . . . uh . . . this just came, so and so . . . " Then "Is that right?" Silence. "Yes . . . whew (breath), . . . that's right, yes, that's *so* right, that's what it is . . ."

In this form of language one can observe the person checking what is spoken clearly against something else that is also right there. The person has not only what is clearly thought and felt but also something that cannot yet be described—and nevertheless it is totally certain that whatever that something is, it is *not* what was just said, tried out, which seemed for a moment to be right.

But now I must tell you the negative, puzzling, disappointing side of our research findings—at least they were disappointing when we first found them. If left to themselves, people usually do not know how to engage in therapy in this way, and more often than not, they find no powerful process arising.

In our research studies, replicated several times, the successful clients, those who showed much positive change, were those who somehow approached themselves inwardly in this way. But we found that they did so from the beginning! And those who didn't never seemed to develop this mode and failed, often after a number of years. It was because of this finding, and only because of it, that we moved into teaching this mode of inward approach. This teaching is now called "focusing," and we are finding that anyone can learn it.

It is so difficult for human beings to overcome their own training and tradition! While one is tradition-bound in a given way, one hardly knows it. To teach people exactly how to engage in therapy? It was against everything we had been trained to think. In my case this was not because I thought only professionals should do psychotherapy. I was trained by Carl Rogers, who never believed that and who wrote about training nonprofessionals back in the 1950s.

But psychotherapy, isn't it an art? Isn't it foolish to want to *tell* the patient how to do it? Besides, if people can't sense this bodily edge, isn't that due to their defenses? Must it not be innocent and futile to try to teach people to overcome defenses? Shouldn't this happen gradually in therapy, anyway?

But the research had shown that this mode of bodily experience is not acquired through therapy if someone doesn't have it already. Research really can put one up against something one did not know!

All these doubts slowed us down considerably. Nevertheless, after some years we now have, through many series of applications and modifications, a group of highly specified instructions that teach this skill, and many studies that show it can be taught. Populations to whom it has been taught include hospitalized "psychotics," "borderline" patients, very bright college students, ghetto kids, and many others.

Among more recent research findings, the "shift" in the felt sense was found to have EEG correlates (Don, 1977). Focusing has been used in biofeedback (Briscoe, 1980), with cancer patients (Grindler, 1982; Olsen, 1981), in dance therapy (Alperson, 1974; Noel & Noel, 1981), with schoolchildren concerning their most difficult subject (Murray, 1978), and in relation to images (Olsen, 1975), dreams (Hendricks & Cartwright, 1978), and meditation (Weiss, 1978; Amodeo, 1981). A longer list is available (Gendlin, 1981), and the most recent work is obtainable from the author at the University of Chicago.

ORGANIZATIONAL MODEL

The next chapter presents a description of our organization. Here I would like only to present a few innovations that seem valuable.

"Changes" is our self-help network. We also have focusing teachers all over the country who charge a fee. Changes is free, of course, and if you get focusing there, you are in a good position to know whether you get anything more or better for pay.

We began as a hotline for troubled people but soon found that the best way to work with "them" was to invite anyone calling into "us." We work with each other, and we don't ask or know whether someone is most interested in getting or giving help. We have no leaders who only give. It is always good to do both. *No one should go home without having got something. Everyone is listened to for ten minutes or so in a small group, unless someone doesn't wish to be.* This eliminates the service role. One goes home sustained, rather than tired. It is a very important innovation. Many organizations offer those who come only sitting and being passive attendants to "programs" for the evening. People go home as they came, only tired.

Before listening begins, we give focusing instructions to help everyone to come to a deep level where something opens. This can be done with the whole group or in a little group. *Focusing instructions teach focusing, but they also enable people to go deeply to their own edge so that then whatever happens in the group comes from that deep opening.*

There are special subgroups later in the evening that teach focusing and listening, as well as other groups. Some go for many weeks, others just that evening. *Anyone can announce that a group for any purpose will form if others want to join it.* That brings us many viewpoints and skills and takes the leadership away from the usual few who do everything.

From the political point of view, the two most important innovations are the next two.

The group as a whole never does any "business" or makes any decisions. Such business as we have is done by a small group at a different time, usually before or after a big meeting. *The time and place are known, and anyone can come and be a part of the directing group.*

Group decisions bind! Once a decision is made, I must abide or leave. If there are decision meetings, I must convince the group. If you disagree with me, I cannot listen and cannot help you make sense, because the decision will go against me and I'll be bound by it. Instead of helping you show the good sense of your point, I may have to hope that you fail to convey it to the others, even if I know what you mean.

At the National Training Laboratory, years ago, certain laws of groups were formulated. We have discovered that these laws don't hold when a group is free in this way. The laws hold only on the constraining assumption that all must agree and that all must remain in the group unless the group decides to break into smaller units. And, believe me, we are very well off without what some of those laws state, which is regularly found in most groups!

In most groups a person cannot go *in steps* into whatever is discussed or done. Each person gets one try and must then wait until a turn comes again. On one try one cannot express the deeper layers of what one means. So on one's next turn one can only say the same thing again, the same opener. The pace is frenetic; few listen. To be sure, if the group knows listening, then it is not like that. People invite each other to go more deeply into what they mean, and it is much better. But we must go further to change what *group* has meant.

Although we didn't notice it and didn't think of it that way, what we have meant by *group* and by *democratic decisions* is really a binding structure. We are told that since we attended, the decision is "ours." Usually it isn't. Those few who function know the facts and know how the decision has to come out. If we decide otherwise, there will only be another meeting to set it right.

In our way everyone is a member by being there, and no decisions are made that can bind anyone. This means that those who want to do something do it, without requiring that everyone do it or agree to it. One stands up and says "I (or some of us) will do such-and-so now (or at a given time). All those who would like to do it also, meet in this part of the room during the break (or at a given time and place)." No one's approval is necessary in advance of doing this. It is never assumed that all will do anything. During almost any meeting some people are in the hall talking, socializing. When one wishes, one goes out to join them. Those who are in the room are there because they want to be.

This innovation has many powerful effects: First, it frees the main space for interpersonal processes or whatever the people need. Most organizations spend most of their time and effort on business to hold the organization together and relatively little on what the organization is supposedly for. To prevent this, we split business and substance. Business is best handled by those who want to. They are usually few, but since everyone *can* come and is then equal, no one feels helpless. People come either when something they care about isn't happening as they wish or if they happen to like, and be good at, administrative work. That little group is therefore usually surprisingly trouble-free.

Mixing business and interpersonal process is very hurtful and ineffective. We are all told by "participatory democracy" that all should make every decision. Usually that means even a window can't be easily opened or closed. Bright people can be reduced to a state in which they cannot even leave the room because they cannot decide what activity to do next or whether to break up into small groups. Most of us have been in such sessions, and we know from experience that they have not helped us grow—although we were told that all this wrangling and hurting each other was great training for life.

When business and interpersonal process are mixed, neither can happen. People who care about the issue have little patience to listen to another person who seems in the way of getting things done. Conversely, many people take part in business when they really don't care about the issue and want to engage each other. What two people could do easily, twenty cannot do at all. People hurt each other, express "feelings," attack each other, then pretend to make up, hug each other—and never forget the hurt they felt from the other person, even years later.

When business is dealt with separately, *the main space is open for interpersonal process as such.* The air is free and there is a sense of depth. It is all about me, not bootlegged, not hurried, no fight for air time, nothing indirect. You listen to me and help me discover that my feelings make sense—not about how we should pay for coffee, but about me and my life.

Closely related is our way of not having any policy and of making no decisions. We think we are a whole step past "participatory democracy."

Decision making in large groups is a pretense. Only from functioning can one know what one needs to know to decide. There is always a little group of people who function administratively, and they know everything and run everything. To make things democratic means to open that little group to those who wish to participate in it. Few do, but everyone wants that right.

Now about policies: in Changes anyone can put a statement on the wall and can argue or state any policy. But there is no way "we" can adopt it so that it binds everyone. This is very frustrating to outside agencies, but it has also at times saved the group from them and their pressures and even from being closed down. We do not need *a* policy! Those who want to follow a particular way will do that. Why do we need to bind the others?

The individuals who begin a Changes sometimes don't grasp this principle. We are all still in the orbit of participatory democracy. The leaders assume they shouldn't be seen as leaders. Instead of arranging training and some structure, they ask the group to decide. Those asked don't know anything about it, but the question becomes the occasion for the usual half-personal, half-business wrangling. People believe that wrangling is "the group process" and that it must be valuable. But soon they don't come back, and others come and have the same experience.

Instead, our way is for the small group to set up whatever way seems best (and to hear from people who didn't like it or have a different idea later on). Kristin Glaser, who is the actual originator of Changes (together with four other women and some ideas from my class, but without me), began this new way one day. Wrangling had pretty well been all Changes had done for some time. She proposed that we train everyone in listening and that we not even ask the group about it. We few who met between times to arrange Changes were stunned. How could we foist this on everyone? We knew, as with anything else, that some people wouldn't like whatever was proposed. Of course, those who didn't want the training could do something else (and did). But at that time we had not yet had the insight to open our little conspiratorial leading group to everyone—because we were not yet able to avow it and admit we were leading the group. But leading is fine if everyone can be in the leader group and if no one must follow. Later we could invite anyone into this group. I say "we," but I soon stopped being in it.

Now, wasn't that a policy? Yes and no. Nothing is binding on everyone. But this fact, that nothing is binding, isn't *that* a policy? It is a sort of metapolicy. Those who want a policy can have it but only for themselves and those that agree with them, not as defining what others must do.

POLITICS

Current political organizations don't include interpersonal processes, and political people are typically not interested in them. Indeed, if done without training, personal self-expression tends to be sticky and hurtful in groups, as just described. Some politically interested people have had that bad experience and want no more of it.

Politics is about people organized together. Any organized group, even a small organization, is a miniature society. The vital question of politics is not this or that program. The vital question is how people might better organize so as to be together in a more livable way and one that enables them to act.

Gandhi said long ago that if an organization oppresses its members, then the society that that organization will bring will be oppressive. It is the main blind spot of Marx to have missed that.

Ideas are important for social action. Many people are interested in ideas (I am one of them), but people get worn out just thinking and talking or doing small actions. And then, too, many more people cannot afford to spend time and effort getting dressed and coming if they are only going to listen to abstractions and perhaps now and then say a sentence or two. For them nothing is offered and they go home untouched.

How different would it be if politics were about human organizing! We would attend to how we are together with one another. We would make our organization a space in which each person is inwardly aided and strengthened and finds an inward source of good sense and energy. Each person would go home stronger, having got something of importance from every meeting.

The basic principles would be lived, concerning the freedom and inward source of each person. Each would find that source. Acting together does not mean concentrating only on externals and leaving one another to inward aloneness and starvation for contact and new energy. There is no inherent conflict between the political and the interpersonal if they have the same spirit. Above all, we do not need to bind one another. We don't need to eject people who happen not to want to do something with us, and they need not stop those who do want to do it. We can form subgroups, announced or otherwise, for anything we need, without losing the larger free space.

People can be equals if all are free to join whatever directing group or groups there are. That way the fiction of leaderlessness is not a cover for a few to control others (or carry all the weight of responsibility even when they are tired of it and don't want to).

Under such conditions individuals grow stronger and more able to act; they don't (as some fear) become interested only in themselves. But those who genuinely want to take action are better able to do it when those who don't aren't in the way.

Of course, this is not the whole answer. It is only one piece of the larger political problem. But these developments do move slowly toward a new meaning of politics.

REFERENCES

Alperson, E. D. Carrying experiencing forward through authentic body movement. *Psychotherapy: Theory, Research, and Practice,* 1974, *11*(3), 211–214.

Amodeo, J. The complementary effects of meditation and focusing. Unpublished doctoral dissertation, California Institute of Transpersonal Psychology (Menlo Park, Calif.), 1981.

Briscoe, M. Quantification of the concept of congruence between interoceptive awareness and autonomic change. Unpublished master's thesis, California State University, Los Angeles, 1980.

Don, N. S. The transformation of conscious experience and its EEG correlates. *Journal of Altered States of Consciousness,* 1977–78, *3*(2), 147–168. Also in *Brain Mind Bulletin,* May 16, 1977, *2*(13).

Gendlin, E. T. *Focusing.* New York: Bantam Books, 1981.

Gendlin, E. T., Beebe, J., Cassens, J., Klein, M., & Oberlander, M. Focusing ability in psychotherapy, personality, and creativity. In J. M. Shlien (Ed.), *Research in psychotherapy* (Vol. 3). Washington, D.C.: American Psychological Association, 1967.

Grindler, D. "Clearing a space" with someone who has cancer. *Focusing Folio,* 1982, *2*(1), 11–23.

Hendricks, M., & Cartwright, R. Experiencing level in dreams: An individual difference variable. *Psychotherapy: Theory, Research, and Practice,* 1978, *15*(3), 292–298.

Murray, V. Experiential focusing and classroom verbal behavior. Unpublished doctoral dissertation, Rutgers University, 1978.

Noel, P. J., & Noel, J. The use of experiential focusing in movement therapy. *Focusing Folio,* 1981, *1*(2), 31–34.

Olsen, L. E. The use of visual imagery and experiential focusing in psychotherapy. Unpublished doctoral dissertation, University of Chicago, 1975.

Olsen, L. E. Focusing and healing. *Focusing Folio,* 1981, *1*(1), 17–21.

Weiss, J. The effects of meditation on experiential focusing. Unpublished doctoral dissertation, Northwestern University, 1978.

CHAPTER FIFTEEN

Changes: Peer-Counseling Supportive Communities as a Model for Community Mental Health

Kathleen McGuire Boukydis

Kathleen McGuire Boukydis is codirector of the Center for Client-Centered Therapy, Cambridge, Massachusetts. She received her Ph.D. in clinical psychology under Dr. Eugene T. Gendlin at the University of Chicago in 1975. She is a member of the Society for Psychotherapy Research, Division 35 (Psychology of Women) of APA and the Association for Women in Psychology. Her primary interests are in psychotherapy research, existential and phenomeno-logical theories and methodologies as they relate to the experience of women, and peer self-help. Along with Gendlin and others at the University of Chicago, Boukydis was a founder of the first Changes listening community in 1970. Since then, she has devoted the majority of her professional efforts to starting listening/focusing communities in a variety of settings and attempting to refine a model for starting such self-help communities. She is a practicing psychotherapist and is the author of *Building Supportive Community: Mutual Self-Help through Peer Counseling,* a self-help manual.

The Changes program, presented by Boukydis, is the vehicle for giving the skills of focusing and listening away to members of a supportive peer-counseling community. Boukydis shows how mutual-support groups can be developed and sustained with little financing and administration and how specific psychological skills can help such a group develop into a supportive and healing milieu. Most important, the peer-counseling, mutual-help model breaks down the distinction between helpers and helpees and gives individuals the responsibility and skills not only for coping with their own lives but for helping others as well.

The Changes South community in Chicago has been in existence since 1970. At its peak, between 1971 and 1974, it had a standing membership of between 30 and 60 people. Through the years, hundreds of persons have been helped in a short-term, crisis-intervention way. Perhaps another hundred have had the experience of supportive community for one to six years. Since 1974, when some Changes Chicago people began moving to other parts of the country. Changes-like communities have been started in a number of other places. This chapter presents Changes as a model that can be looked at as one approach to community mental health, either as an adjunct to existing programs or as a program standing on its own.

Please address correspondence to the Center for Supportive Community, 186 Hampshire St., Cambridge, Mass. 02139.

The Changes model is different from most programs for "giving therapy away" in that it is based on the concept of peer counseling: I listen to you for an hour on some concern of yours; then you listen to me for an hour on some concern of mine. Rather than creating another level of paraprofessionals in the therapy hierarchy, the Changes model allows participants to practice self-help skills in a nonhierarchical structure. Each person is equal in help given and received.

One root of the idea of a peer-counseling supportive community is Gendlin's (1962) theory of "experiencing." Gendlin, Beebe, Cassens, Klein, and Oberlander (1967) found that it was the client's manner of relating words to inner experiencing that determined whether psychotherapy would be successful. Experiential psychotherapy (Gendlin, 1973) was then developed as a method for raising the experiencing level of individuals so that they might engage in therapy in a meaningful way and for doing a kind of therapy that is change-producing because of its direct relation to the client's ongoing experiencing. When translated from the therapist's office into the community, experiential psychotherapy becomes the concrete skills of listening and focusing (Gendlin, 1974), which can be taught to anybody (see Chapter 14 in the present volume for a description of listening and focusing skills).

Most basically, a Changes is a group of people who exchange listening turns—a peer-counseling community. Everyone learns how to listen and how to be listened to, and community members meet in pairs, triads, and small groups for the exchange of listening turns. "Listening" is a way of being with another person that can help that person to go more deeply into exploring a feeling. It involves setting aside assumptions and attending to the fresh personal feeling matter in what a person is sharing. "Focusing" is a way of going inside, either alone or while being listened to, which makes it more likely that a person will be able to get in touch with his or her own feelings. The minimum structure of a Changes is a two- or three-hour meeting once a week where people learn listening and focusing skills and, as they become able, pair off for the exchange of listening turns. As a next step, some people may decide to meet at other times during the week for the exchange of additional listening turns.

For some people, the deep level of personal sharing that occurs during listening turns leads to the development of caring friendships, and for these people the Changes, or some subgroup within it, begins to function as a supportive community. People feel free to call on Changes friends not only for structured listening turns but at any time during the week that they need to be listened to and for as many hours of listening as they need to make it through a crisis time. They also look to Changes friends for other kinds of support—help in finding a job or moving into a new apartment, a ride to the hospital, a babysitter, people to go to the movies with or have a party with, a group to study family therapy with, and so on.

The Changes model has grown up as an attempt to respond to mental health problems as seen from an interactional theory. The human person is seen as, by his or her nature, a "being-in-the-world," in a mutually influencing relationship with an environment. Mental illness is then a problem of relatedness, not a solely intrapsychic phenomenon (Gendlin, 1970). It is a natural next step for therapists with this orientation to move toward an interactional, interrelational supportive community as a way both of preventing and of responding to individual crisis.

The first Changes actually began as a hotline, and phone volunteers were taught empathic listening as an aid in crisis intervention. In addition, people who called on the hotline were invited to become part of the Changes weekly meeting. As people trained in listening began to interact with one another around hotline and community issues, they began to demand that listening be carried over into these interactions. So, at a decision-making meeting, if someone felt unheard, she might proclaim "Wait. I need to be listened to" or "I need someone to say that back so I'm sure I was understood." Listening developed into a way of relating, not just a way of being during structured peer-counseling hours. Changes communities came to be distinguished from other gatherings of people by the fact that they have as their basis "listening norms." Everyone in the community learns how to listen (how to make space for another person's experiencing) and how to focus (how to attend to one's own inner experience in a change-producing way). These skills are then carried over into all forms of interaction—not just counseling hours but interpersonal relationships, group decision making, and the sharing of ideas.

A basic premise of any Changes community is the idea of "peerness" or egalitarianism. No distinction is made between "helpers" and "helpees," people who come to help and people who come for help. Traditional therapist/client roles are seen as reinforcing the "client's" already strong feelings of inadequacy and "sick" role and leading "therapists" to lose touch with their own needs to be listened to or attracting to the therapist role persons who feed on the position of superiority rather than human relatedness. Hinterkopf and Brunswick (1975), two Changes persons who have taught listening and focusing skills to chronic schizophrenics in a peer-counseling situation, found that the patients gained as much from the helper role as from being the helpee, especially if they exchanged listening turns with the group trainer as well as with the other patients. Treating everyone as an equal at Changes is also not simply a strategy used by the "real" helpers to make the defined "helpees" feel that they are equal. Experience at Changes has shown that there is no such thing as a helper/helpee distinction when that set of roles has not been structured in, that everybody is in each role at some time or the other (Glaser & Gendlin, 1973), that "helpers" may suddenly be in the role of "helpee" (needing a team for support, confronting psychotic experiences, facing a life crisis) and "helpees" in the role of "helpers" (knowing better how to relate to people going through psychotic experiences, moving through their own crises and becoming excellent listeners, and so on).

The lack of a distinction between "helpers" and "helpees" at community meetings is not meant to imply that, in a Changes community, there is never a point at which "expert" mental health advice or collaboration is sought. Changes groups are often started with the active participation of a mental health professional, and where this is not the case, in any group larger than three or four friends, linkage with mental health professionals and agencies in the surrounding area is sought. The salient point is that when a mental health professional *participates* in a Changes meeting, he or she enters into listening turns, expecting to receive as well as to give help.

DESCRIPTION OF THE MODEL

Changes communities cannot be described as a given structure with particular contents. What a particular group becomes, the kind of programs it will have, grows out of the needs of the particular persons who are involved in it. Changes communities are better described as a set of norms for being with other people. The following are some of the basic attitudes that make up the listening philosophy and are reflected in the behavioral norms of a Changes community:

1. Inner experiences are to be treasured. Hearing how something is for somebody else inside is the most profound kind of sharing that one person can have with another. Experiencing one's own inner meanings is profoundly healthy—the things inside are not "bad" or "crazy." "Craziness" is more the result of a loss of relationship to one's own inner meanings—people get "crazy" because they are not in interaction with the world (Gendlin, 1970; Prouty, 1977). Putting someone in a mental hospital when she is being crazy can often put her even further into isolation and away from the people who are most likely to keep trying to establish a relationship with her. An alternative is a supportive community—a group of people who can take turns staying with the person through the craziness and constantly insisting on relationship with her.

2. Feelings and perceptions change. If a person gets listened to on some way that he is feeling, his experience will be carried forward, and his feeling and interaction with the world will be changed. If he gets listened to on some way that another person bothers him, he may get in touch with something new in him that will change what he feels about the other or how he perceives her. These changes in behavior can lead to changes in experiencing. The person is process, not content, in ever-changing relationship with the world.

3. Everybody is right or rational in what he is doing, on some level. If a person gets listened to long enough on why he is the way he is, something will be heard that suddenly makes sense out of the way he is being and helps others to understand the meaning of his behavior for him and to empathize with him. This doesn't mean that they still may not wish he would change or that it might not be the best thing for him, in the long run, to change—it simply means that they can come to see him and to care about him in the middle of the way he is right now. It's also possible that as he gets in touch with the meanings involved in being the way he is, this may already bring about some change in that way that he is, as in item number 2 above.

4. Interpersonal conflicts are an interaction (Glaser & Gendlin, 1973). The reason a person becomes so emotionally upset because of what someone else is doing has to do with the way he is as much as it has to do with the way the other person is being. So, in any confrontation, a person stands to learn something new about himself as well as to communicate to the other something he feels about her.

5. Verbal expressions are considered symbolizations of inner experiencing and cannot be assessed solely in terms of objective right- and wrongness. If a person disagrees with what another is saying, he needs to ask to hear more about why she sees the world that way, until he can understand her statement as a meaningful verbalization in terms of her own inner meanings. He can still have a difference of opinion and state his reasons, from his particular set of inner meanings, and she may in fact decide to change her opinion, having got a new perspective on the matter from what he has shared, but that does not make her initial position objectively wrong; her position merely comes out of a different set of subjective inner meanings.

6. Conflict resolution and problem solving are also not purely objective weighings of possible solutions but involve understanding of emotional investment. Resolution comes from dealing with the subjective feelings or needs conveyed in the verbal expressions (K. M. Boukydis, 1975, 1977; Henderson, 1974).

These basic attitudes find expression in the following specific behavioral norms or structures for relating at a Changes:

1. No one is excluded from a Changes. Every person has an equal right to be

there. If there are tensions, conflict resolution begins from the assumption that all belong (Gendlin & Beebe, 1968).

2. When someone is having trouble with the way someone else is being, he goes to that person directly, and they arrange to work on the interaction in a listening way, often with the help of a third person, who serves as a listening facilitator. Each person says back what the other has said until the speaker feels understood before saying his or her own side. Each person focuses inward, looking for the "meaning" of this trouble for her and trying to get in touch with her feelings in a way that may mean finding out something new about the way she is in this interaction and thereby changing the way she is in it.

3. There is little making of rules excluding all sorts of behavior and participation. Anybody can do almost anything she wants to do. If another Changes person doesn't like what someone is doing and thinks it is hurting someone, she goes to the other, and they work the trouble through in a listening way. If she doesn't like the activity but sees no harm in it, she can just decide not to participate.

4. Decision making is open to anyone who is interested and proceeds in a listening way until a solution arises that meets everyone's needs. Listening norms are carried over: people try not to interrupt, ask to hear more about feelings expressed, and say back what the other is trying to say before saying their own opinion.

5. If someone is having a lot of feelings, a way is found to deal with those feelings directly. Feelings are a priority, not to be shoved aside to get other things done. Working through the feelings may involve listening to the person right in the situation or arranging to have someone go with the person to a separate room. For example, if a very "crazy-acting" person starts interrupting at a group meeting, the chairperson will respond to that person in a listening way or will stop the meeting long enough to arrange that someone else listen to him.

6. Nobody does anything she doesn't want to do. People learn to say no in a nonblaming way and often work to provide teams for very needy people, so that someone else can be found to take over when a particular team member is exhausted.

7. Whatever else a Changes becomes develops out of the needs of the particular group. There are no rules like "There must be a hotline," "Ideas must be cleared with the parent organization," or "You must (or must not) involve any money."

The attitudes and norms of a Changes are learned in part by reading the writings of Gendlin and others, in part through the experience of exchanging listening and focusing turns in a peer-counseling situation, in part by being around a Changes community where the norms are in force. However, they seem to be teachable as four specific skills, which are presently being formulated in writings as well as in specific workshop techniques:

1. *Focusing:* how to get in touch with, and to move through steps in, one's inner experience. The ability to focus is needed, not only as a way of maximizing personal growth during listening hours but also in working through interpersonal conflicts and in participating in group decision making (see Gendlin, 1969, 1981; Gendlin & Olsen, 1970; Brunswick, Hinterkopf, & Burbridge, 1975; C. F. Z. Boukydis, 1979; K. M. Boukydis, 1981; Hendricks, 1978).

2. *Listening:* how to set aside one's own assumptions and to hear and reflect another person's experiencing in a way that helps her to go through steps of change in it (Gendlin, 1974, 1981; Gendlin & Hendricks, 1972; Prouty, 1977; C. F. Z. Boukydis, 1977; K. M. Boukydis, 1981).

3. *Interpersonal processing:* how to use a third person as a listening facilitator in an interpersonal-conflict situation so that each person has a turn to get listened to and heard on his or her side of a conflict and to go through steps of change in these feelings (van der Veen, 1977; K. M. Boukydis, 1981).

4. *Listening in groups:* how to structure a group situation so that listening norms can be maintained (Gendlin & Beebe, 1968; Barrett-Lennard, 1974; Massad, 1973; Henderson, 1974; K. M. Boukydis, 1975, 1977, 1981).

The structure of Changes South in Chicago follows as an example of one way in which these basic attitudes and norms took form for a particular group of people. However, as Changes communities are started in other places, each structures itself to meet the needs of that group of people. It is too early to say that the following will arise as some kind of prototypical structure for the Changes model.

Changes South consists of two basic parts. First, there is a weekly gathering open to anyone on Sunday evenings. Second, throughout the week, various subgroups of Changes people meet for specific activities, ranging from the exchange of listening turns to going to the movies.

The Sunday night meetings have something like the following structure:

Whenever called for by someone, there is a planning meeting for an hour before the general meeting, in which people can bring up their concerns about how things are being done, their ideas for new things to do, and so on. Separate planning meetings arose as a way of ensuring that the time for the general meeting was not usurped by decision making. Planning is left to those persons who are interested in participating in it, and the emphasis on growth-related activities at the general meeting is protected (Glaser & Gendlin, 1973).

The general meeting starts with a short introduction of what Changes is, followed by an hour for presentations. Traditionally, presentations at Changes have provided a place for Changes people and invited others to present new ideas, different kinds of therapies—really, anything that anybody wants to talk about. Because almost everybody in the "audience" knows listening and focusing, the presentations time provides a place for people to try out their ideas in a supportive atmosphere— with no punishment and with a respect for the tentativeness that accompanies new thinking. Presentations are arranged by those at the planning meetings. The philosophy is generally that anyone can make a presentation on anything he wants, or invite someone to do so, and individual Changes members can decide whether they want to attend. Examples of past presentations include Gestalt therapy, African art, square dancing, meditation, and food co-ops.

After the presentation there is a short period for announcements. The announcements time is one of the ways that the Changes can be a supportive network for all aspects of people's living. A person can announce anything—that she is looking for a job or an apartment, that she is happy because she has found a job, that she is inviting everybody to a party, that she has kittens to give away, that she needs to borrow a car or find a ride somewhere. After announcements, there is a short period for socializing—mainly, connecting up with people who have made announcements.

After socializing people break up into small groups for about two hours. There are a new people's group and several types of listening and focusing training groups. The new people's group gives people there for the first time a chance to ask questions and to hear more about what Changes is and to try out listening to see what it's like. The training groups provide ways for people to practice listening and focusing in an ongoing way and to set up listening hours at other times during the week.

Some examples of the during-the-week activities that have been part of Changes South are a phone hotline, potluck dinners, teams for people in crisis, women's groups, men's groups, a Ph.D. candidates' support group, discussion groups on a variety of issues, skills- and resource-sharing groups, an art class, food co-ops, photography workshops, going-to-the-movies groups, dream workshops, volleyball teams, and communal-living groups.

VIABILITY OF THE MODEL

In considering whether the Changes model has something to add to traditional approaches to community mental health, it is necessary to come to some assessment of the kinds of people in a given larger community that a Changes serves. It is difficult, however, to come up with lists of clients served versus staff utilized, because this distinction does not exist at Changes. However, a listing of 60 persons who were involved in Changes South in Chicago for one year or more within the author's own experience (1970–1974) indicates that about one half of these persons were otherwise engaged in the helping professions (including graduate students as well as professionals). The other half were involved in every kind of occupation or were jobless. Of these 60 long-term members (many of whom have actually been involved continuously for four to six years), a large majority are now skilled enough in listening and focusing that they can go and teach these skills to other groups and could start a Changes on their own if they wanted to—so, Changes not only serves people in crisis but at the same time produces large numbers of highly trained "helping" persons. At least 10 of these long-term people had come to Changes just after being in a mental hospital or acting or feeling in a way that would ordinarily lead into one. At any point in its history, the Changes has had about 30 people involved in this "long-term" way in supportive community. There have also been hundreds of other people who have found the Changes a place to go for at least one Sunday night or who have received some kind of crisis intervention (a place to sleep overnight, a drug talk-down, help getting on welfare, referral to another agency, emergency childcare, a session of listening, and so on).

More qualitatively, a Changes seems to provide a place for persons in the following sorts of situations. It is not possible to label any person as being in any category—the same person may be in any number of these situations at one time or another or even simultaneously:

1. Some people come to Changes needing short-term crisis intervention. Such persons are always invited to join the community at its general meetings. Some become long-term members; some leave after their crisis need is met.

2. Some people come looking for friends or for support for their own personal growth or for "community." These people, though not acutely headed for crisis, are suffering just the same from the chronic loneliness, alienation, and lack of intimacy of much of our culture.

3. Some people come wanting to learn more about helping other people.

Although these people may initially present themselves as more interested in helping others than in getting help themselves, many take part in all of the possibilities of supportive community.

4. Some persons come to Changes in a highly anxious, "crazy-feeling" state which traditionally might lead to hospitalization but which seems to dissolve relatively quickly (after several listening hours), leaving a healthy-looking, creative, self-actualizing, and productive person. For these persons, "craziness" seems to have come from being in touch with inner experiencing but constantly having this experiencing disconfirmed, rather than validated, in a nonlistening work or family situation. For example, although what a person is doing at work may be highly creative, the person may be being scapegoated by other workers who are threatened by innovation. For persons in this situation, just getting listened to and validated for one's inner experiencing seems to relieve the crushing anxiety and to bring forward a huge potential for growth. For example, persons who have come to Changes in this way have gone on to complete Ph.D.-level work in a variety of fields.

5. Some people have come to Changes being highly symptomatic in traditional ways and perhaps caught in a psychotic process at times. Some of these people have remained highly symptomatic throughout their stay at Changes or have changed radically only through a long-term listening relationship with a highly skilled listener or therapist. A major difficulty for Changes with persons in this situation has been an inability to provide them with a long-term living situation, so that some people have drifted away or have been hospitalized. However, in many other situations, Changes has been able to work as an adjunct to other therapeutic relationships in at least four ways:

• The acceptance by Changes participants of the reality of inner troubles has made it possible for people whose own relationship with reality is very different to be fully accepted into the Changes community—to be invited along to the movies or an apartment-painting party, to be related to and cared about over long periods of time. For example, a person may come to a Changes meeting and sit in total silence or whispering to herself and be accepted (she may even be joined gently by another person who feels sort of the same way, wanting to be around other people but not able, or wanting, right then, to interact). If the person returns again, she will be remembered and given recognition for her past being-there and related to in a caring way. One person has related to the larger group in this way for the past four or five years, sometimes disappearing for several months, then reappearing.

• Changes members can form a 24-hour-a-day team for a person going through a crisis that demands constant attention. Traditionally, because a therapist cannot provide this kind of intensive relationship, a person in this kind of crisis has had to be hospitalized. Instead, Changes members are able to work with the primary therapist, helping to keep the person out of the hospital.

• Changes has offered support to the family or roommates of persons going through crisis, helping these related others to work through their own feelings about the way the person is acting so that the person can continue to stay in a context of meaningful relationships, rather than being hospitalized. For example, listening to family members on their fear of violence and loss of control may enable them to get "unhooked" and to realize that the crazy-acting person probably will not do the terrible things that they fear.

• When a person has been hospitalized for a period of time, Changes friends have been able to maintain relationship by visiting the person in the hospital and keeping avenues open for return to the community.

A plus of the Changes model is that it need not involve the expenditure of any money. Although it might be helpful to have money to pay some initial trainers or to mimeograph materials or to set up a phone line, a Changes in its essence is a peer-based community where people get help as well as give help and where the people are there because they are getting their own needs for supportive community met. It is perhaps only this turning toward "peer self-help" that can break the pattern of having to pay some people for helping others. The importation of money, especially if it leads to some persons' being paid while others are not, can invite the kind of breakup into hierarchies that a Changes seeks to avoid (although a particular Changes group might decide to have money and then process whatever issues come up). Changes South has operated for 13 years with one small grant covering a hotline phone bill, one small grant to pay some coordinators (rapidly phased out because of the problems of "hierarchy" that arose), and occasional passings of the hat to cover emergency expenses (mimeographing, mailings, parties, and the like). Space has been provided for minimal rent by a neighborhood church. During this time, Changes has had the free services of highly skilled people from every kind of occupation who came there to learn listening and focusing, to get help, and to share their skills with a community of friends.

DISSEMINATION OF THE MODEL

Changes-like groups have been started in a variety of settings. Hinterkopf and Brunswick (1975) established a listening community among chronic schizophrenics. Egendorf (1978) received an NIMH grant to research the use of listening communities as a treatment modality for Vietnam veterans. Changes-like groups have been started in small towns, metropolitan areas, student mental health centers, continuing education classes, senior citizen centers, parent support groups. The author has used a listening community as an adjunct to a private practice in individual and couples therapy. The peer-counseling model has also been used among the staff of several service-oriented agencies. In such a setting, the listening exchange among staff minimizes burnout and facilitates a supportive, nonhierarchical work environment. Changes groups have been as small as three friends who exchange listening turns and as large as the open community in Chicago, with 30 to 60 members. They have been started by ministers, teachers, psychologists, nurses, and persons outside the helping professions. They usually last at least three years and have been able to continue operating after the departure of the initial teachers. Most groups tend to be smaller than the original Changes and seem to grow as one member brings a friend rather than by advertising and hotline referral. In other respects, they seem to reflect the basic elements of a Changes in that anyone in the community is welcome, listening and focusing training are provided to everyone who comes, listening norms seem to carry over from peer-counseling hours into the processing of interpersonal tensions and group decision making, and Changes members see themselves as offering support to friends in crisis as much as possible.

Many methods of starting a Changes are arising, each meeting the needs of the persons involved in the starting, as in the case when the "listening" method of decision making is used. The following are some general principles about starting a Changes:

1. Once a person has had the experience of participation in a Changes group, it is easy for that person to start a new group by going to various helping agencies and growth or community-oriented groups and presenting a short workshop where people can experience listening and focusing. Interested persons can then be invited to a Changes meeting.

2. Once a core group of six to ten persons has been gathered, it is a good idea to work with this group for several months until the listening/focusing norms and commitment are well established. Then, if the group is opened to the larger community through advertising, new people will be coming into a group with established norms, and endless power struggles and wrangling about what the group is for can be avoided (for example, "We should be leftist radicals and go picketing"; "I'd rather do confrontation than listening").

3. A Changes group can remain open by invitation only, with new members brought in as existing members want to share their experience with friends, family, and acquaintances. This is often the form chosen when there is no one in the group who feels capable of or interested in providing the kind of team support that is needed in working with the very "heavy" and needy people who may walk in off the street (Glaser, 1972).

4. Sometimes interest in a Changes group fades after several years of weekly meetings. However, the demise of the formal meeting simply means that the listening functions have been integrated into the daily lives of former participants. A close look at the lives of such people shows that they continue to call selected others for listening turns in crisis, that they are called on by others in their friendship network to function as listening facilitators during interpersonal conflict, that they teach listening and focusing to their friends and family, and that they carry the listening philosophy into their work environments as much as possible. Many people have continued to use the supportive community skills in these ways for ten or more years.

5. A listening group can be offered for a nominal fee, although a special effort must then be made by the paid trainer to teach the participants how to become teachers and to take over the running of the group as soon as possible.

6. The core of any Changes meeting is the exchange of listening turns. As long as participants exchange listening turns, they will become bonded together in empathy and mutual concern, and the other aspects of supportive community will arise naturally.

There has been some hesitancy to crystallize a model for the dissemination of the Changes idea. Dissemination through traditional "service delivery" or "case handling" approaches has been avoided. In the language of Martin Buber (1958), there is the danger that this sort of approach may already define the recipients of services as objects to be manipulated, rather than as equal human beings to be encountered in relationship. Such an orientation can lend itself to the reinforcement of the "helper/helpee," "one-up, one-down" system of roles that a Changes seeks to dispel. It seems unlikely that the administration of a mental health clinic can decide to set up a Changes solely for the "good" of its clients or as an economy measure. In such a situation, a facilitator must be found who is willing to participate in the group as an equal member, or volunteer facilitators can be found in the community to be served. A Changes must have somewhere at its core a group of people who have become deeply convinced that listening norms are what they want as their way of life and who are there so that they can get *their* needs for this kind of relating met.

Until recently, Changes groups have been started mainly by someone who has previously belonged to a Changes. However, with the publication of Gendlin's *Focusing* (1981), there has been a demand for information on how to start a Changes. A manual by Boukydis (1981) provides instruction in the four skills needed for starting a listening community: listening, focusing, the use of listening and focusing to process interpersonal conflicts, and the listening/focusing method of cooperative, consensual decision making. The Center for Supportive Community also offers a facilitators' training program, which includes ten weeks of participation in a Changes group, ten weeks of supervision on teaching listening and focusing and leading a Changes meeting, and an ongoing seminar for support and theoretical reading while pairs of facilitator trainees go out into the larger community and try to start Changes groups in various settings. The center also offers a two-week intensive Changes Institute during the summer, where interested persons can have the experience of participating in a Changes community.

In terms of self-help, egalitarianism, and "giving therapy away," it seems ideal that Changes groups be started when one person reads a listening manual (Boukydis, 1981) and invites one or more close friends to try out the listening/focusing exchange as described. Since there will then be no one who is more skilled, shared leadership should arise naturally. However, as Carl Rogers discovered in his early years of nondirective teaching, it is not always easy to give power away. Many clients in therapy prefer expensive individual sessions even when the option of a self-help group is made readily available. Although a Changes can be started by anyone, those who come forward to learn to be facilitators are often already involved in the helping professions. Publishers approached with a manual for starting supportive communities addressed to laypeople have said "This is not appropriate for the general trade audience. Why don't you address it to those in the helping professions?" Gendlin's *Focusing* book (1981) and those of others that give skills directly to laypeople can begin to change the attitude among professionals and laypersons alike about self-help. However, those who are deeply committed to "giving therapy away" will have to consistently address issues of power and powerlessness implicit in the helping relationship and will have to make a conscious effort to divest themselves of power when it is given to them. Only then can we empower others.

REFERENCES

Barrett-Lennard, G. T. Experiential learning groups. *Psychotherapy: Theory, Research, and Practice,* 1974, *11,* 71–75.

Boukydis, C. F. Z. Some suggestions on ways to relate to people's feelings. Changes Discussion Paper,* *1*(4), 1977.

Boukydis, C. F. Z. Creative applications of Gendlin's focusing process. Client-Centered/Experiential Discussion Papers,* 1979.

Boukydis, K. M. Expression of negative feelings and explication of meaning as a function of

*Available from the Center for Supportive Community, 186 Hampshire St., Cambridge, Mass. 02139.

contingent interruptions and contingent listening responses in task-oriented groups. Unpublished doctoral dissertation, University of Chicago, 1975.

Boukydis, K. M. Listening in groups. In K. Glaser (Ed.), *Interchanges,* unpublished newsletter,* 1977.

Boukydis, K. M. *Building supportive community: Mutual self-help through peer counseling,** 1981.

Brunswick, L. K., Hinterkopf, E., & Burbridge, R. Cultivating positive empathic self-responding. *Voices,* Spring 1975, pp. 62–65.

Buber, M. *I and thou.* New York: Scribner's, 1958.

Egendorf, A. Suggestions for psychotherapy with Vietnam veterans. In C. R. Figley, *Stress disorders among Vietnam veterans: Theory, research, and treatment implications.* New York: Brunner/Mazel, 1978.

Gendlin, E. T. *Experiencing and the creation of meaning.* New York: Free Press, 1962.

Gendlin, E. T. Focusing. *Psychotherapy: Theory, Research, and Practice,* 1969, *6,* 4–15.

Gendlin, E. T. Existentialism and experiential psychotherapy. In J. T. Hart & T. M. Tomlinson (Eds.), *New directions in client-centered therapy.* Boston: Houghton Mifflin, 1970.

Gendlin, E. T. Experiential psychotherapy. In R. Corsini (Ed.), *Current psychotherapies.* Itasca, Ill.: Peacock, 1973.

Gendlin, E. T. Client-centered and experiential psychotherapy. In D. A. Wexler & L. N. Rice (Eds.), *Innovations in client-centered therapy.* New York: Wiley, 1974.

Gendlin, E. T. *Focusing.* New York: Bantam Books, 1981.

Gendlin, E. T., & Beebe, J. Experiential groups: Instructions for groups. In G. M. Gazda (Ed.), *Innovations to group psychotherapy.* Bloomington, Ill.: Charles C Thomas, 1968.

Gendlin, E. T., Beebe, J., Cassens, J., Klein, M., & Oberlander, M. Focusing ability in psychotherapy, personality, and creativity. In J. M. Shlien (Ed.), *Research in psychotherapy* (Vol. 3). Washington, D.C.: American Psychological Association, 1967.

Gendlin, E. T., & Hendricks, M. Rap Manual. Unpublished mimeograph,* 1972.

Gendlin, E. T., & Olsen, L. The use of imagery in experiential focusing. *Psychotherapy: Theory, Research, and Practice,* 1970, *7,* 221–223.

Glaser, K. Suggestions for working with heavy strangers and friends. *Rough Times,** July 1972.

Glaser, K., & Gendlin, E. T. Main themes in *Changes,* a therapeutic community. *Rough Times,** June/July 1973, pp. 2–4.

Henderson, J. The politics of group process. *Rough Times,** Jan./Feb. 1974.

Hendricks, M. A focusing group. Changes Discussion Paper,* *2*(5), 1978.

Hinterkopf, E., & Brunswick, L. Teaching therapeutic skills to mental patients. *Psychotherapy: Theory, Research, and Practice,* 1975, *12*(1), 8–12.

Massad, D. About the Thursday night listening-focusing group. *Rough Times,** Sept./Oct. 1973.

Prouty, G. Protosymbolic method: A phenomenological treatment of schizophrenic hallucinations. *Journal of Mental Imagery,* 1977, *1*(2), 339–342.

van der Veen, F. Dialoguing: A way of learning to relate constructively in close relationships. In K. Glaser (Ed.), *Interchanges,* unpublished newsletter,* 1977.

*Available from the Center for Supportive Community, 186 Hampshire St., Cambridge, Mass. 02139.

EPILOGUE

The skills training field is still in its infancy and faces a great many developmental challenges. In this epilogue I will attempt to bring into clearer focus some of the challenges in three broad areas: research, theory, and professional responsibility.

RESEARCH

As Goldstein (1981) notes, a substantial research base is "clearly one of the strongest qualities of the psychological skills training movement" (p. 11). One reason such an impressive research base has developed is, as the work reported in the current volume suggests, that the skills training model readily lends itself to empirical study owing to its replicability and goal specificity. Indeed, the emergence of skills training approaches can be a boon to psychotherapy research in general. In his recommendations for the entire psychotherapy field, Bergin (1971) called for exactly the kind of work that skills trainers now do: "It is essential that the entire therapeutic enterprise be broken down into specific sets of measures and operations, or in other words, be dimensionalized. Otherwise, there will continue to be little progress" (p. 253). Paul's (1967) oft-quoted question—"*What* treatment, by *whom,* is most effective for *this* individual with *that* specific problem and under *which* set of circumstances" (p. 111)—may find an answer in skills training research.

Major reviewers of skills training approaches to helping (for example, Authier, Gustafson, Guerney, & Kasdorf, 1975) and helper training (for example, Burstein, 1980; Ford, 1979), as well as the authors in this volume, suggest several directions for future research. First, a continuing effort must be directed toward evaluating the efficacy of skills training programs and their potential for prevention. Second, skills approaches must be more rigorously and systematically compared with traditional therapies and training methods. Third, the relations among trainee personality characteristics, target skills, and teaching methods need to be assessed further. Fourth, the most effective sequencing and combinations of skills training interventions should be determined. Fifth, more investigations should be undertaken to find state, trait, cognitive, demographic, and sociometric predictors of high levels of skill acquisition. Finally, what is perhaps most urgently needed is research into skill transfer—that is, the transfer of skills learned in the training context to the real world—and the development of transfer-enhancing techniques.

THEORY

To strengthen its identity and impact, the skills training field must address the critical need for an expanded psychology of human skills. Such a psychology can draw from many traditional areas of psychological inquiry, including the personality, social, and developmental psychological fields.

A more developed psychology of human skills could, for example, begin to clarify the relations between skills and attitudes, intentions, beliefs, emotions, and other personality dimensions. The failure to do this has resulted in what I believe is a false distinction between skills (equated with observable behaviors) and internal traits and states. This distinction has been the take-off point for a number of critics of skills-oriented approaches to helper training. These critics (for example, Mahon & Altmann, 1977; Calia, 1974) invoke the specter of "skilled" yet ineffective or even destructive helpers whose technique-oriented behaviors are not congruent with their inner attitudes, beliefs, and perceptions. These people, obsessive imitations of the effective helper, make technically sound responses and apply verbal formulas cookbook-style.

Are the behaviors taught by skills trainers, such as "empathy," unrelated to the inner perceptions and attitudes of the helper? Certainly, in a few instances this could be the case, but skills trainers argue, in their own defense, that skills and attitudes are most often interdependent. For example, Gordon (1976) writes: "When parents learn the technique and use it continually, they begin to experience the requisite attitudes and feelings. The use of Active Listening, at first a mere mechanism, will in time make parents more genuinely accepting and caring of their children" (p. 58). Ivey and Authier (1978) report that their trainees often begin "attending" (a Microcounseling skill) in an artificial manner and soon find themselves lost in the other person, who has become more animated in response to their attending. Thus, what begins as a technique rapidly becomes a skillful and natural performance. William James wrote "To feel brave, act as if you were brave, and a courage fit will very likely replace the fit of fear." In my experience training therapists and health care workers, I have seen countless "fits" of caring replace "fits" of despair once students were given effective interpersonal helping skills.

The psychology of human skills, as it develops, will also have to address some more basic aspects of skills and skill acquisition. For example, Ivey and Authier (1978) suggest that skills trainers take into account the theory of "tacit knowing" advanced by the philosopher Michael Polanyi in explaining how subskills are unconsciously integrated into larger gestalts, or behavior patterns. Following is Polanyi's (1958) discussion of the skillful performance we know as swimming:

> The aim of a skillful performance is achieved by the observance of a set of rules which are not known as such to the person following them. For example, the decisive factor by which the swimmer keeps himself afloat is the manner by which he regulates his respiration; he keeps his buoyancy at an increased level by refraining from emptying his lungs when breathing out and by inflating them more than usual when breathing in; yet this is not generally known to swimmers. A well-known scientist, who in his youth had to support himself by giving swimming lessons, told me how puzzled he was when he tried to discover what made him swim; whatever he tried to do in the water, he always kept afloat [p. 49].

Polanyi's account points to just one of the complexities that would need to be included in a complete theory of skills acquisition. Clearly, further systematic research and theoretical exploration are needed to advance our understanding of what skills are and how we learn them.

PROFESSIONAL RESPONSIBILITY

Converting psychological principles and knowledge into teachable skills is meeting the demand for more effective responses to problems in living and helping. As the avenues for dissemination continue to expand, psychological skills training will reach widening segments of our society. These efforts to give psychology away hold great promise, but with this promise comes responsibility. Issues of accountability and quality control, and important decisions about the applications of skills training models, will require careful attention. Ideally, new programs would be like those described in this book—empirically based and conscientiously delivered. The teaching of psychological skills, like any development of consequence, contains pitfalls as well as potential. Our task is to guide the work in this growing field so that it may remain a responsible sharing of our most helpful psychological knowledge.

REFERENCES

Authier, J., Gustafson, K., Guerney, B., Jr., & Kasdorf, J. The psychological practitioner as a teacher: A theoretical-historical and practical review. *Counseling Psychologist,* 1975, *5,* 31–50.

Bergin, A. E. The evaluation of therapeutic outcomes. In A. E. Bergin & S. L. Garfield (Eds.), *Handbook of psychotherapy and behavior change: An empirical evaluation.* New York: Wiley, 1971.

Burstein, B. *Basic tools for more effective service delivery: Self-contained instructional programs for training paraprofessionals in interviewing skills and face-to-face helping competencies—A review.* San Rafael, Calif.: Social Action Research Center, 1980.

Calia, V. F. Systematic human relations training: Appraisal and status. *Counselor Education and Supervision,* 1974, *14*(2), 85–94.

Ford, J. D. Research on training counselors and clinicians. *Review of Educational Research,* 1979, *49,* 87–130.

Goldstein, A. P. *Psychological skill training: The structured learning technique.* New York: Pergamon Press, 1981.

Gordon, T. *P.E.T. in action.* New York: Bantam, 1976.

Ivey, A. E., & Authier, J. *Microcounseling: Innovations in interviewing, counseling, psychotherapy, and psychoeducation* (2nd ed.). Springfield, Ill.: Charles C Thomas, 1978.

Mahon, B. R., & Altmann, H. A. Skill training: Cautions and recommendations. *Counselor Education and Supervision,* 1977, *17,* 42–50.

Paul, G. Strategy of outcome research in psychotherapy. *Journal of Consulting Psychology,* 1967, *31,* 109–118.

Polanyi, M. *Personal knowledge: Towards a post-critical philosophy.* Chicago: University of Chicago Press, 1958.

NAME INDEX

SUBJECT INDEX